Critical Feminist Approache Dis/Orders

Over the past decade there have been significant shifts both in feminist approaches to the field of eating disorders and in the ways in which gender, bodies, body weight, body management and food are understood, represented and regulated within the dominant cultural milieus of the early twenty-first century.

Critical Feminist Approaches to Eating Dis/Orders addresses these developments, exploring how eating disordered subjectivities, experiences and body management practices are theorised and researched within postmodern and post-structuralist feminist frameworks.

Bringing together an international range of cutting-edge, contemporary feminist research and theory on eating disorders, this book explores how anorexia nervosa, bulimia nervosa and obesity cannot be adequately understood in terms of individual mental illness and deviation from the norm but are instead continuous with the dominant ideas and values of contemporary cultures.

This book will be essential reading for academic, graduate and post-graduate researchers with an interest in eating disorders and critical feminist scholarship, across a range of disciplines including psychology, sociology, cultural studies and gender studies, as well as clinicians interested in exploring innovative theory and practice in this field.

Helen Malson is a Reader in Social Psychology at the Centre for Appearance Research, University of the West of England, Bristol.

Maree Burns is the co-ordinator of the Eating Difficulties Education Network in New Zealand.

Critical Feminist Approaches to Eating Dis/Orders

Edited by Helen Malson and Maree Burns

Routledge
Taylor & Francis Group

LONDON AND NEW YORK

First published 2009
by Routledge
27 Church Road, Hove, East Sussex BN3 2FA

Simultaneously published in the USA and Canada
by Routledge
270 Madison Avenue, New York, NY 10016

*Routledge is an imprint of the Taylor & Francis Group, an Informa
business*

Typeset in Times by Garfield Morgan, Swansea, West Glamorgan
Printed and bound in Great Britain by TJ International Ltd, Padstow,
Cornwall
Paperback cover design by Lisa Dynan

This publication has been produced with paper manufactured to strict
environmental standards and with pulp derived from sustainable
forests.

British Library Cataloguing in Publication Data
A catalogue record for this book is available from the British Library

Library of Congress Cataloging-in-Publication Data
Critical feminist approaches to eating dis/orders / edited by Helen
Malson & Maree Burns.
   p. cm.
  Includes bibliographical references.
  ISBN 978-0-415-41811-9 (hardback) – ISBN 978-0-415-41810-2
(pbk.) 1. Eating disorders in women—Social aspects. 2. Feminist
psychology. I. Malson, Helen, 1965– II. Burns, Maree, 1970–
  RC552.E18C756 2009
  362.196'85260082–dc22

2008051476

ISBN: 978-0-415-41811-9 (hbk)
ISBN: 978-0-415-41810-2 (pbk)

Dedications

To my daughter, Lauren, whose invention of the role of 'blood sucking alien baby rabbit princess pirate' so brilliantly subverts the parameters of gendered embodiment. In the hope that she always knows how beautiful she is and how much this is the very least of how she is so wonderful. To Nana. And to Maree for her friendship and being such a great woman to work with. *HM*

To my mother, Lyn, who is a remarkable woman. To my colleagues at EDEN for their passion, hard work and commitment to providing a community-based service that is sensitive and responsive to so many of the issues discussed in this volume. To Craig A., who knows that laughter is the best medicine. And to Helen especially for her patience, commitment and friendship. *MB*

There are times in life when the question of knowing if one can think differently than one thinks, and perceive differently than one sees, is absolutely necessary if one is to go on looking and reflecting at all.

(Foucault, *The Uses of Pleasure*, 1992: 8)

If we are to achieve a richer culture, rich in contrasting values, we must recognize the whole gamut of human potentialities, and so weave a less arbitrary social fabric, one in which each diverse gift will find a fitting place.

(Margaret Mead, *Sex and Temperament*, 1963: 322)

To know is nothing at all; to imagine is everything.

(Anatole France)

Contents

List of contributors   xi
Foreword by Melanie A. Katzman   xvii
Acknowledgements   xxi

1   Re-theorising the slash of dis/order: An introduction to
    critical feminist approaches to eating dis/orders   1
    HELEN MALSON AND MAREE BURNS

PART I
Theorising eating dis/orders in a changing world   7

2   Theorising self-starvation: Beyond risk, governmentality
    and the normalizing gaze   9
    LIZ ECKERMANN

3   Feeding the body   22
    JANET SAYERS

4   Understanding obesity by understanding desire   35
    MICHAEL GARD

5   Not just 'a white girl's thing': The changing face of
    food and body image problems   46
    SUSAN BORDO

PART II
Interrogating cultural contexts of dis/ordered eating   61

6   A critical discussion of normativity in discourses on
    eating disorders   63
    PAULA SAUKKO

7 Beyond western dis/orders: Thinness and self-starvation
   of other-ed women   74
   MERVAT NASSER AND HELEN MALSON

8 Anorexia/bulimia as resistance and conformity in
   pro-Ana and pro-Mia virtual conversations   87
   KATY DAY AND TAMMY KEYS

9 How big girls become fat girls: The cultural production
   of problem eating and physical inactivity   97
   CARLA RICE

PART III
In/visible bodies and embodiment   111

10 Fat, feelings, bodies: A critical approach to obesity   113
    ELSPETH PROBYN

11 Bodies as (im)material? Bulimia and body image
    discourse   124
    MAREE BURNS

12 Appearing to disappear: Postmodern femininities and
    self-starved subjectivities   135
    HELEN MALSON

13 Weight management, good health and the will to
    normality   146
    KATHLEEN LEBESCO

PART IV
Critiquing the discourses and discursive practices of treatment   157

14 Food for thought: Embodied slimness and nursing
    within an eating disorders unit   159
    RUTH SURTEES

15 The anorexic as femme fatale: Reproducing gender
    through the father/psychiatrist–daughter/patient
    relationship   172
    NICOLE MOULDING

16 'There's something in my brain that doesn't work
   properly': Weight loss surgery and the medicalisation
   of obesity   185
   KAREN THROSBY

17 Therapeutic discourse and eating disorders in the
   context of power   196
   MICHAEL GUILFOYLE

PART V
Critical interventions   207

18 Anti-anorexia/bulimia: A polemics of life and death   209
   DAVID EPSTON AND RICK MAISEL

19 Feminisms in practice: Challenges and opportunities
   for an eating issues community agency   221
   MAREE BURNS, JANE TYRER AND THE EATING DIFFICULTIES
   EDUCATION NETWORK (EDEN)

20 Rediscovering a daughter   233
   RICHARD TREADGOLD, ANN TREADGOLD AND DIANA TREADGOLD

21 Complexities of power and meaning: A reflection on
   Parts IV and V   245
   HELEN GREMILLION

   Index   253

Contributors

Susan Bordo holds the Otis A. Singletary Endowed Chair in the Humanities and is a Professor of English and Gender Studies at the University of Kentucky, USA. She is the author of *Unbearable Weight: Feminism, Western Culture and the Body* (University of California Press, 1995); *The Male Body: A New Look at Men in Public and in Private* (Farrer, Straus and Giroux, 2000), and other influential books and articles. She is currently writing a novel and 'an unconventional self-help book' about Anne Boleyn.

Maree Burns coordinates the Eating Difficulties Education Network in New Zealand. Her research interests include critical feminist approaches to disordered eating and weight/body management. Maree has published articles examining the construction, experience and practice of 'bulimia' and is co-editor of *Critical Bodies: Representations, Identities and Practices of Weight and Body Management* (Palgrave Macmillan, 2008). Maree is also passionate about working in an agency that provides community-based support for eating difficulties.

Katy Day is a Senior Lecturer in Psychology at Leeds Metropolitan University. She set up the Feminism and Health Research Group in 2006, along with Sally Johnson and Bridgette Rickett, which now has members from a number of academic institutions across Yorkshire. She completed her doctorate research on discourses around women and alcohol at Sheffield Hallam University in 2002. More recently, she has conducted research examining the discourses on pro-eating disorder websites.

Eating Difficulties Education Network is a not-for-profit community agency in Auckland, New Zealand that provides support and information services for people with eating and body image difficulties. EDEN also works in the community providing education and training, advocating for service users and lobbying for social and political change to support the prevention of disordered eating. See www.eden.org.nz.

Liz Eckermann is Associate Professor and Head of the School of History Heritage and Society at Deakin University, Australia. She teaches, supervises and publishes on the sociology of health and illness, sociology of the body, quality of life and public health, and has undertaken over 20 consultancies on gender and health for the World Health Organization in Geneva and the Western Pacific Region. She is currently conducting research on risk and reproductive health in Lao PDR.

David Epston was, along with Michael White, an originator of narrative therapy. He co-authored *Narrative Means to Therapeutic Ends* (Norton, 1990) and *Experience, Contradiction, Narrative and Imagination* (Dulwich Centre Publications, 1992) with Michael. Amongst many other publications, he co-authored *Playful Approaches to Serious Problems: Narrative Therapy with Children and Their Families* (Norton, 1997) and *Biting the Hand that Starves You: Inspiring Resistance to Anorexia/bulimia* (Norton, 2004). He is a Lecturer at the School of Social Practice, UNITEC Institute of Technology in Auckland, New Zealand.

Michael Gard is an Associate Professor of Dance, Physical and Health Education at Charles Sturt University's Bathurst campus, Australia. He teaches and writes about the human body, gender and sexuality, the shortcomings of biological determinism in all its forms, and the use and misuse of dance within physical education. He is the author of two books: *The Obesity Epidemic: Science, Morality and Ideology* (with Jan Wright) (Routledge, 2005) and *Men Who Dance: Aesthetics, Athletics and the Art of Masculinity* (Peter Lang, 2006).

Helen Gremillion is an Associate Professor of Social Practice at UNITEC Institute of Technology, Auckland, New Zealand. Her research and teaching interests include narrative therapy, constructionist theories of the body, gender and science, consumer culture, medical anthropology, and feminist ethnographies. Her book *Feeding Anorexia: Gender and Power at a Treatment Center* was published by Duke University Press (2003). She has also published in *Signs* and the *Journal of Constructivist Psychology*.

Michael Guilfoyle is a Lecturer in Clinical Psychology at Trinity College Dublin, Ireland. He has a PhD from Utrecht University (The Netherlands), and has published numerous papers on power dynamics and therapeutic practice. He is currently trying to use aspects of post-structuralism and discourse theory to think about such issues as hope and hopelessness, suicide, sense of belonging, and the dynamics of the therapeutic relationship.

Melanie A. Katzman is a Clinical Associate Professor at Weill Cornell Medical School in New York. In addition to her writing and work with patients, Melanie remains committed to facilitating conversations cross-culturally and across disciplines. She is a partner in the social enterprise, Leaders' Quest, which brings leaders from around the globe to meet leaders in the emerging world. Melanie's books include *Feminist Perspectives on Eating Disorders* (Guilford Press, 1996) and *Eating Disorders and Cultures in Transition* (Brunner-Routledge, 2001).

Tammy Keys graduated from Leeds Metropolitan University in 2003 with joint honours in Sociology and Psychology. Her interests are in femininity, body image and women's health.

Kathleen LeBesco is Professor and Chair of Communication Arts at Marymount Manhattan College in New York. She is author of *Revolting Bodies? The Struggle to Redefine Fat Identity* (University of Massachusetts Press, 2004), and co-editor of *Bodies Out of Bounds: Fatness and Transgression* (University of California Press, 2001). She has written and lectured extensively on the politics of fatness.

Rick Maisel is an Adjunct Professor at Alliant International University in San Francisco and at the Wright Institute in Berkeley, California. He maintains a private practice in Berkeley. Rick has published and presented extensively on narrative therapy and on anorexia/bulimia. He is the author (along with David Epston and Ali Borden) of *Biting the Hand that Starves You: Inspiring Resistance to Anorexia/Bulimia* (Norton, 2004).

Helen Malson is a Reader in Social Psychology in the Centre for Appearance Research at the University of the West of England, Bristol. Her research focuses around feminist post-structuralist analyses of girls' and women's 'eating disordered' subjectivities and practices and her publications include *The Thin Woman: Feminism, Post-structuralism and the Social Psychology of Anorexia Nervosa* (Routledge, 1998). More recently, she has been exploring service users' and service providers' accounts about the treatment of 'eating disorders'.

Nicole Moulding has a background in the social sciences, where she has developed a strong research interest in gender and mental health. After graduating with a professional social work degree, she worked in women's health as a therapeutic social worker, carrying some of the observations and experiences from this arena into her doctoral studies. She is now based at the School of Psychology, Social Work and Social Policy, at the University of South Australia, lecturing in mental health and continuing to explore the social construction of mental health and illness through research.

Mervat Nasser is a Consultant Psychiatrist and visiting Senior Research Fellow in the Department of Mental Health and Cultural Diversity, Institute of Psychiatry, Kings College, London. She acquired an international reputation through her various publications in the field of eating disorders and culture, as well as women's mental health. Among her publications are *Culture and Weight Consciousness* (Routledge,

1997), *Eating Disorders and Cultures in Transition* (Brunner-Routledge, 2001) and *The Female Body in Mind: The Interface between the Female Body and Mental Health* (Routledge, 2007).

Elspeth Probyn is the Research SA Chair and Professor of Gender and Cultural Studies at the University of South Australia. She has published widely on questions of gender, sexuality, eating, food, bodies and subjectivity. Her books include *Carnal Appetites: FoodSexIdentities* (Routledge, 2007) and *Blush: Faces of Shame* (University of Minnesota Press, 2005). Her forthcoming book, *Taste and Place* (Reaktion), explores local places of taste in the global context.

Carla Rice is Associate Professor in Women's Studies at Trent University in Ontario, Canada, where she lectures in culture, health, and psychology. A leader in the field of body image within Canada, she is founder and former director of innovative initiatives such as the National Eating Disorder Information Centre and the Body Image Project in Toronto. Her award-winning research explores women's diverse narratives of embodiment and their arts-based interventions to create new depictions of difference.

Paula Saukko is a Senior Lecturer in Sociology at the Department of Social Sciences, Loughborough University. Her work focuses on eating disorders, new genetics and qualitative methodology. She is the author of *The Anorexic Self: A Personal, Political Analysis of a Diagnostic Discourse* (State University of New York (SUNY) Press, 2008) and *Doing Research in Cultural Studies* (Sage, 2003) and is co-editor (with L. Reed) of *Governing the Female Body: Gender, Health and Networks of Power* (forthcoming, from SUNY Press).

Janet Sayers is Professor of Psychoanalytic Psychology at the University of Kent in Canterbury, where she also works as an NHS psychotherapist. Her books include *Mothering Psychoanalysis* (Penguin, 1992), *Freudian Tales* (Vintage, 1997), and *Freud's Art* (Routledge, 2007). Her next book is provisionally called *Picasso's Freud*.

Ruth Surtees worked for five years as a staff nurse on the Eating Disorders team in the unit referred to in her chapter, and now works on the Mothers and Babies team in the same unit. She has worked previously as a part-time lecturer in the Departments of Gender Studies and of Sociology and Anthropology at Canterbury University, and in the Schools of Nursing and of Midwifery at Christchurch Polytechnic. Her doctoral work and interest in postmodern ethnographic research have also led to publications concerning midwifery discourses in Aotearoa/ New Zealand.

Karen Throsby is an Associate Professor in the Department of Sociology at the University of Warwick. Her research focuses on issues of gender, technology and the body, and she is the author of *When IVF Fails: Feminism, Infertility and the Negotiation of Normality* (Palgrave, 2004). She is currently researching people's experiences of obesity surgery.

Ann Treadgold and Richard Treadgold were married 36 years ago, when Ann was studying accountancy and Richard was head librarian at the *NZ Herald*. They had five children and studied philosophy for many years. Richard founded a technical writing consultancy. They met David Epston in 1996 when searching for a counsellor to help their daughter, **Diana**, out of anorexia. When Diana refused counselling, they accepted the challenge of themselves learning the narrative therapy she needed.

Jane Tyrer is a founding member of the Eating Difficulties Education Network based in Auckland, New Zealand and has been providing services in the community since 1990. Jane is currently the education worker at this service and completed a graduate diploma in narrative counselling in 2008.

Foreword

How much other is enough? Contemporary narratives assert that many anorexic women are waif warriors writing a social history with their bodies, which are at once an extreme, distorted vision of beauty and a living example of social ills. They are the ultimate insider and outsider all in one. The contributors to the current volume create a prism of perspectives, offering analyses that position our thinking both within and outside of the mainstream and thereby provide a critique of the very field that each of these authors has helped create.

Critical Feminist Approaches to Eating Dis/Orders offers insights across colour and size (Bordo, Rice), East and West (Sayers, Nasser and Malson), and parent, patient and provider of care (Treadgold et al., Surtees, Moulding, Burns et al.). We are challenged to consider the multiple and contradictory influences on individuals and their body projects (Eckermann, Burns, Malson), given a chance to review the impact of the world wide web on patient experience (Day and Keys), prodded to recalibrate what is 'normal' (Saukko, Throsby, LeBesco), and asked to mull over the morality of consumption (Gard, Probyn, Epston and Maisel).

In the nineteenth century, cholera, a *medical* problem, exposed problems with rapid urbanisation such as poor sanitation and limited public health services. The response to the epidemic revealed divisions of class and race, while also acting as a key impetus for greater social responsibility towards the disadvantaged (Evans, 1988). As the contributors to *Critical Feminist Approaches to Eating Dis/Orders* illustrate so well, encapsulated in the 'disease' of eating disorders are the twentieth and early twenty-first century issues of identity, gender politics and the prospect of profits from marketing unobtainable ideals.

Throughout this comprehensive compendium we dip into the details of deconstruction and then step out to reflect on the movement in the field. It is an exhilarating dance step. In the narrative of 'what's next' in the field of eating disorders, the challenge is to adopt a lens of possibility, to not only deconstruct but to rebuild, to recombine concepts across disciplines, and to tap unexpected sources for ideas, influence and funding. This is a time of possibility.

A new generation of business leaders appear to have moral compasses with a gravitational pull towards achieving greater social impact. Corporate social responsibility programs are becoming a part of the business culture – dedicating *intellectual* and *monetary* capital to community development and the alleviation of societal ills. Google has set up a for-profit 'charity' that can both make grants and lobby the government; eBay's founder has invested (US)$90 million in a non-profit organisation to nurture environments that *'unleash people's potential'* and eBay's first president, Jeff Skoll, established a $55 million foundation to support social entrepreneurs (i.e. people who make a difference while making a profit).

How can the interest in social action and contributions emerging from other fields be harnessed to respond to the precipitants of disordered eating? In two different chapters, one by Gard and one by Throsby, the rhetoric of crisis is examined. Today's media presents the war *on terrorism*, the *war for resources* and, of course, the *war on fat*. This very aggressive language marshals attention and demands a response. How do we parlay the attention into positive action? Gard informs us that obesity science is 'an Alice-in-Wonderland place where nothing is as it seems' (p. 36), where the risks of global warming and obesity are equated even in the absence of confirmatory data. Gard suggests that we respond to the *war on obesity* not by reigning in desire, but rather by recognising the need to cultivate new desires.

Cultivating new desires sounds exciting! How does one do that? Perhaps there are creative ways to partner with people beyond our disciplines to explore alternatives that are healthy and, if necessary, profitable too.

With respect to prevention of disordered eating, Bordo posits, 'There is no king to depose, no government to overthrow, no conspiracy to unmask' (p. 57). The feminist, social/cultural analysis has been both inclusive of various disciplines and often the most self-critical, as the authors featured in this volume reveal. Yet, we remain handicapped in our ability to influence finance and politics to a meaningful extent. Much of our scientific research looks at MRIs not ROIs (returns on investment). We talk of power and recognise that it is gendered; but hierarchy is not merely pink or blue. The better able we are to analyse and respond to the economic realities that inform the marketing of mental distress, the better able we will be to craft creative, healthy solutions.

Our challenge as a field is how to communicate outside of academia. What are the words and arguments that will capture the attention of business leaders and social entrepreneurs in addition to our traditional granting agencies and policy makers? Our formulisations and suggestions cannot make sense only to ourselves, and we can surely benefit from the intellectual prowess of other applied fields.

What is the knowledge that is needed to act; how do we create a language of persuasion and change? Probyn writes, 'I realise that this is a big ask, but that is the challenge I see for our discipline.' Being practical may be a challenge but there is no excuse not to be. Do we want to be so specialised in our interventions that we become marginalised? Or do we want to create an 'other' that means another, more novel way of responding to socio-cultural forces?

For many years now, I have split my professional focus between studying the presentation of eating disorders in countries undergoing rapid transition (an area dominated by great ideas and limited influence) and coaching executives leading multinational, multicultural teams (a group of individuals with a great deal of influence but often limited exposure to grass roots concerns). Recently I have worked to bring these two worlds together, and have been excited at the almost audible synaptic firing that happens when experts experiment across disciplines. I have met numerous social entrepreneurs who are creating sustainable, profitable responses to domestic violence, physical disability and impoverished children's health. Many have been doctors, frustrated at 'curing' one patient at a time yet motivated to treat an ill society (for good examples see Bornstein, 2007). Where are the social entrepreneurs in the eating disorders field, and if they don't yet exist or we can't find them yet, how can we begin to cultivate them? How do we shift our training and our discourse?

Previously, we joined forces with professionals from the field of addiction, abuse and depression. Perhaps now the forces we need to join with are those professionals who are tackling over-consumption – of food, retail goods, energy – social diseases or disorders born of a quest for wellbeing and self-definition.

Thomas Friedman, in the *The World is Flat* (2005), argues that historical, regional and geographic divisions are becoming increasingly irrelevant in today's global marketplace. Indeed, eating disorders, once the province of privileged white rich girls in the United States, have proven to be far more democratic. Nasser and Malson carefully elucidate that eating disorders have gone global but that the expressions of distress are local and nuanced, reflecting the world's ever shifting 'traditional' and 'modern' cultures. Their work reminds us that, as a field, we have developed multiple tools to measure impacts on women. We may have some new opportunities to apply our skills.

Bill Gates, the founder of Microsoft, says he is 'reordering his priorities' to work on his $29 billion foundation, focusing primarily on global health. The investment bank Goldman Sachs recently announced that it will invest $100 million over the next five years in providing 10,000 women in developing economies with business and management education – a decision based on their research indicating that investing in women in the developing world is most likely going to yield the greatest social return. Is this not the same group that we would identify as at risk for eating disorders because of the possibility for greatest disparity between what is possible and what is likely? Gremillion urges us to consider alternative ways of being that are crafted in active relationship to the norm rather than from a space 'outside' of the status quo.

In the *war* against eating disorders, as good foremothers and forefathers to the field, it behoves us to introduce new confident, pragmatic conceptualisations and the requisite tools for change. Malson and Burns insert, and assert, a slash between dis and order. That slash between order and chaos stimulated by the chapters that follow should send us dashing to think of ways that we can partner *big*, think broadly, inclusively and less as 'other'.

References

Bornstein, D. (2007) *How to Change the World: Social Entrepreneurs and the Power of New Ideas*, London: Oxford University Press.

Evans, R.J. (1988) Epidemics and revolutions: cholera in nineteenth century Europe, *Past and Present*, 120(1): 123–146.

Freidman, T. (2005) *The World is Flat: A Brief History of the Twenty-first Century*, New York: Farrar, Straus and Giroux.

Melanie A. Katzman

Acknowledgements

We would like to thank, first and foremost, all the contributors to this volume with whom it has been such a privilege to work, for sharing our enthusiasm for this book, for bearing with our somewhat shifting time-tables and, of course, for their hugely inspiring chapters. Thanks also to Laurence Weedy for contributing the design concept in creating the cover of this book. Thanks are also due to Palgrave Publishers for their kind permission to include an abridged version of Janet Sayers' chapter *Feeding The Body* and to ParticipACTION Canada and the late Russ Kisby for permission to reprint the Fit-Fat graphic.

1 Re-theorising the slash of dis/order

An introduction to critical feminist approaches to eating dis/orders

Helen Malson and Maree Burns

The trajectory from our initial thoughts to bring together a collection of critical feminist work on 'eating disorders' to the completion of this edited volume has been an exciting, though also challenging and sometimes bumpy, journey. Navigating our way through our combined surfeit of frequently major life events whilst bringing the book together was, at times, somewhat daunting but stands, we think, as testimony to our enthusiasm – and the enthusiasm of the contributors – for the project that this book represents and to the value of feminist collaboration. Working together as editors and working with all of the contributors to this volume has been such a personally pleasurable as well as intellectually stimulating experience.

Our commitment to producing this book was inspired by several things. Not least among these is the necessity of adding to the already mobilised challenges to the continued dominance across academic, clinical and popular contexts of objectivist, medical and quasi-medical perspectives whereby 'eating disorders' – primarily anorexia and bulimia but also more recently binge eating disorder, EDNOS (eating disorders not otherwise specified) and obesity – are viewed as *individual* (psycho)pathologies originating in the interior, psychologised 'peculiarities' of the individual women diagnosed, viewed as categorically separate and deviant from 'the norm'. And this dominance persists in many quarters – perhaps unsurprisingly and yet at the same time almost incomprehensibly – despite feminist perspectives that have circulated since the 1970s. Susie Orbach's (1979) *Fat Is a Feminist Issue* represented a seminal publication in this development, but many other authors, for example Kim Chernin (1983) and Marilyn Lawrence (1984), also elaborated this development in feminist thinking about 'eating dis orders', arguing in various ways that these distressed experiences and damaging body management practices of girls and women (and much less often boys and men) can only be adequately understood within the context of the oppressive gender ideologies and inequalities in gender power-relations operating in (western/ised) patriarchal cultures.

Within this body of feminist literature, Patricia Fallon, Melanie Katzman and Susan Wooley's (1994) edited collection *Feminist Perspectives on Eating Disorders* marked not only significant developments in thinking about 'eating disorders' but was also clearly groundbreaking in bringing together and establishing feminist perspectives in this field. And, as Fallon et al. (1994) forecast, feminist theorising and research into 'eating disorders' has burgeoned and developed in significant ways since the publication of *Feminist Perspectives* over a decade ago. In particular, postmodern and post-structuralist theory and critical qualitative methodologies have become established across the social sciences and feminist scholars have drawn on and elaborated these in developing new *critical* feminist approaches to understanding 'eating disorders'. From these more recent perspectives, 'eating disorders' are now theorised and researched as discursively consti-tuted and regulated categories of subjectivity, experience and body manage-ment practices: they are fictioned into being within and by a plethora of culturally constituted discourses, values, 'ideals' and concerns (see e.g. Bordo, 1993; Eckermann, 1997; Hepworth, 1999; Malson, 1998; Probyn, 1987; Riley et al., 2008). The seemingly categorical divide between the normal and the pathological is disrupted and shown to be illusory, such that within critical feminist perspectives 'eating disorders' are not so much viewed as individual pathological responses to patriarchal cultures. Rather, eating dis/orders are theorised here as (multiply) constituted within and by the always-gendered discursive contexts in which we live: (individual) 'disorder' is re-theorised as part and parcel of the (culturally normative) order of things.

Critical Feminist Approaches To Eating Dis/Orders was inspired in no small part by the enduring seminal value of Fallon et al.'s (1994) edited volume and by the equally impressive extent to which feminist work in this field has grown and evolved since then across a range of academic disciplines and fields of intervention. Since the publication in the late 1980s of Susan Bordo's (1988) *Anorexia Nervosa: Psychopathology as the Crystal-lization of Culture*, Elspeth Probyn's (1987) *The Anorexic Body* and Joan Brumberg's (1988) *Fasting Girls*, critical feminist literature on eating dis/orders has become a vibrant and well-established body of work, which is at once clearly cohesive and also all the stronger for its transdisciplinarity and diversity. *Critical Feminist Approaches* brings an international collection of this work together, illustrating the strengths and scope of current work that theorises 'eating *disorders*' as constituted and regulated within the norma-tive *orders* of contemporary cultures and which thereby problematises and disrupts the commonplace objectivist dichotomisation of (cultural) order and (individualised) disorder (see especially Chapter 2 for a more detailed discussion of this). *Critical Feminist Approaches* thus comprises chapters which interrogate the ways in which culture is constitutive, in numerous ways, of girls' and women's pathologised bodies, subjectivities, experiences and practices; which analyse these as discursively constituted within nor-mative 'regimes of truth' (see especially Chapters 2–13); and which deploy these critical feminist perspectives both in critiquing existing therapeutic interventions (see especially Chapters 14–17 and 21) and in developing and engaging in different, critically informed modes of analytical, political and therapeutic intervention in this field (see especially Chapters 18–21).

Whilst all working within and amply illustrating the academic, socio-cultural and political significances of this broadly defined critical feminist framework for understanding eating dis/ordered bodies, subjectivities, experiences and practices, the chapters in *Critical Feminist Approaches* also illustrate much of the diversity within this body of critical feminist work. Perhaps, most obviously, this diversity is apparent in the chapters' different objects of analysis, focusing variously on 'eating disorders' as a combined general category; taking 'anorexia' and/or 'bulimia' as their primary focus and/or concentrating on pathologised fatness. The inclusion of 'obesity' in a book on dis/ordered eating no longer appears unusual given that main-stream psychology and medicine now stake this territory as a medical condition indicative of a form of disordered eating alongside the indivi-dual(ised) pathologies of 'anorexia' and 'bulimia'. However, our inclusion of chapters on 'obesity' and fatness in this volume (see Chapters 4, 9, 10, 13 and 16) is informed by a radically different conceptualisation of the issues entailed. Commensurate with critical feminist commitments to theorising the ways in which dis/ordered bodies and pathologised embodiment are constituted within and by socio-cultural discourses, and given the ubiquity of healthism and moral panics about large bodies, we considered it imperative to include chapters examining the discourses, practices and subjectivities of fat embodiment. Indeed, as this newly prominent category of 'disorder' becomes further sedimented within academic, clinical and popular contexts, critical feminist analyses will have a valuable role to play in deconstructing those medicalised and pathologised constructions of fatness as much as thinness.

Whilst the coverage in this volume is broad, there are inevitably some lacunae in the collection that require acknowledgement and which await, perhaps, a further volume! These important areas for critical feminist research include – but are not limited to – the ways in which sexual orientation, masculinities, heteronormativity, different abilities (although see Chapter 9), and socio-economic status (although see Chapter 3) are imbricated in the experiences, practices and constructions of pathologised embodiment and dis/ordered eating. Finally, with regard to coverage, it is interesting to note that this volume was more readily populated with chapters on 'anorexia' or 'eating disorders' than with those dealing speci-fically with 'bulimia'. This is despite the probability that the latter is, statistically, the more common category of pathologised eating.

In addition to the diverse topics of analysis outlined above, the chapters here also differ from each other in their foci variously on theoretical dis-cussion, on analysing data and/or on mobilising critical feminist approaches in critiquing and/or developing interventions. Rather than taking the broader remit of eating and body weight issues, our intention in *Critical Feminist Approaches* is to take a more sharply defined focus, staking the book's parameters as being those delineated by the violences of path-ologisation – a delineation which each chapter then tears down – and to illustrate the sheer range of critical feminist work in this field of pathologised bodies, subjectivities and practices. Alongside deconstructing the binarised assembly of order and disorder this volume also troubles conceptualisations of women's pathologised eating/embodiment as *either* resistance *or* conformity to 'cultural norms', imagining instead that these distressed experiences and practices simultaneously express a multiplicity of potentially contradictory positions and effects. Rather than utilising pathologised eating/embodiment as a synecdoche of women's struggles in oppressive cultures (as either protest or capitulation), many of the chapters in this volume (e.g. Chapters 2, 6, 7, 8, 11, 12 and 14) undermine this distinction and offer analyses that deal with the complex, shifting and varied meanings embedded in these experiences, bodies and practices.

Equally importantly, in terms of diversity, the chapters of *Critical Feminist Approaches* span various disciplines including Cultural Studies, Gender Studies, Sociology, Philosophy, Psychology, Psychiatry, Sports and Education, Social Work and Social Policy, Communication, and Critical Anthropology, as well as including contributions from nurses, counsellors, narrative therapists, community agency workers, parents and a sufferer/survivor. Indeed, one of the ways in which the process of bringing this book together has been so exciting has been in the re-realisation of the political/theoretical congruencies and resonances – as well as the divergences – between work of scholars, activists and practitioners from such a range of otherwise dispersed backgrounds. And inevitably, then, but no doubt only in part because of disciplinary diversity, whilst all taking up a critical feminist perspective in one way or another, these chapters also differ from each other in some important respects: in terms of their engagements with different critical theories, for example, with Foucauldian theory, social constructionism or, less often, psychoanalytic theory, phenomenology and dialogics. They differ in the terminologies (such as 'scare quotes' and slashes) used to denote the problematics of the pathologised categories with which we are concerned. And they differ in the ways in which theory is deployed and made more or less prominent in their discussions, in the more or less prominent place of experiential accounts and reflexivity and inevitably therefore in terms of their authorial voices.

The chapters differ, too, in terms of methodologies used and the kinds of data that are analysed; in terms of the sometimes conflicting, theoretical and political analyses of issues; and, not least, in terms of the numerous socio-cultural contexts analysed; the sheer range of ways in which eating dis/ordered bodies, subjectivities and practices are culturally located and the ways in which they are made intelligible and mobilised by these discursive contexts. From analyses of the historical to the present, the global and the local, western and non-western cultures; from analyses of scientific, social scientific and clinical texts, interview texts, virtual texts and media representations to analyses of personal experience, therapeutic interactions, micro- and macro-political contexts; from explications of the politics of gender, ethnicity and social class, of industrialisation, post/colonialism, transnational consumer capitalism, and globalisation, to the politics of body weight in the context of healthism and the so-called obesity epidemic, as well as analysis of the more familiar plurality of gendered discursive contexts of idealised slenderness/thinness.

And above and beyond the pleasure of working with contributors in bringing together, in one cohesive collection, such a rich diversity of analyses has been the less expected pleasure of being reminded of the extent to which critical feminist work on eating dis/orders continues to evolve. Thus, for example, there is considerable engagement with both historical and contemporary socio-cultural changes, for instance with changes in the availability of and tastes for food across time, country, gender and class (see Chapters 3, 4 and 6); with socio-cultural shifts associated with virtual environments (see Chapters 2 and 8); with globalisation (see Chapters 5, 7 and 10) and the politics of ethnicity (see Chapters 5, 7 and 9), and with the recent hegemonisation of 'healthism' and the intensified pathologisation of fatness (see Chapters 4, 6, 9, 10, 13, 16 and 19).

In addition, the chapters in *Critical Feminist Approaches* can be seen to illustrate a range of very current and on-going debates, issues and developments within critical feminist work in this field concerning, for example, questions about how we theorise context (see especially Chapters 2, 4 and 7). And how, when the body is understood as discursively constituted, do we negotiate the tensions between lived embodiment and a view/analysis of the body as inscribed surface (see especially Chapters 10–13)? How, when we theorise eating dis/orders and subjectivity more generally as discursively produced within normative regimes of truth, do we negotiate issues of resistance and conformity, agency and determinism, the activity and passivity of the always-gendered subject (see especially Chapters 2, 4, 6, 8, 9, 10, 14 and 16–20)? How might we engage in reflexivity and draw on personal experience to enrich our analyses (see especially Chapters 5, 10, 14 and 20) and therapeutic/political practice (see especially Chapters 14 and 18–21)? What relationships pertain between theory, politics, dis/order and intervention (see especially Chapters 4, 6, 13 and 17)? What are the implications of our critical feminist theory and research for political and therapeutic practice (see especially Chapters 5, 6, 10 and 13–17) and how might better praxis be realised (see especially Chapters 18–21). Indeed, how might our daughters fare (see especially Chapter 5)?

References

Bordo, S. (1988) Anorexia nervosa – psychopathology as the crystallization of culture, in I. Diamond and L. Quinby (eds), *Feminism and Foucault: Reflections on Resistance*, Boston, MA: North-eastern University Press.

Bordo, S. (1993) *Unbearable Weight*, Berkeley, CA: University of California Press.

Brumberg, J. (1988) *Fasting Girls*, Cambridge, MA: Harvard University Press.

Chernin, K. (1983) *Womansize: The Tyranny of Slenderness*, London: Women's Press.

Eckermann, L. (1997) Foucault, embodiment and gendered subjectivities: the case of voluntary self-starvation, in A. Petersen and R. Bunton (eds), *Foucault, Health and Medicine*, London: Routledge.

Fallon, P., Katzman, M.A. and Wooley, S.C. (1994) *Feminist Perspectives on Eating Disorders* New York: Guilford Press.

Hepworth, J. (1999) *The Social Construction of Anorexia Nervosa*, London: Sage.

Lawrence, M. (1984) *The Anorexic Experience*, London: Women's Press.

Malson, H. (1998) *The Thin Woman: Feminism, Post-structuralism and the Social Psychology of Anorexia Nervosa*, London: Routledge.

Orbach, S. (1979) *Fat Is a Feminist Issue*, London: Hamlyn.

Probyn, E. (1987) The anorexic body, in A. Kroker and M. Kroker (eds), *Body Invaders: Panic Sex in America*, New York: St Martin's Press.

Riley, S., Burns, M., Frith, H., Wiggins, S. and Markula, P. (2008) *Critical Bodies: Representations, Identities and Practices of Weight and Body Management*, Basingstoke: Palgrave Macmillan.

Part I

Theorising eating dis/orders in a changing world

2 Theorising self-starvation

Beyond risk, governmentality and the normalising gaze

Liz Eckermann

Introduction

Research in the 1990s, using in-depth interviews with young women who self-starved and binge-purged (Eckermann, 1994a) found conflicting imperatives between a search for selfhood (the body as a project of the unique self) and a quest for sainthood (goodness by denying or degrading the body) in constructions of young women's identities. This tension paralleled both contradictory values in discourses on health and wellbeing at the time, and theoretical tensions around explanations for the phenomena in academic, professional, therapeutic and popular literature at the end of the twentieth century. Emanating from the discipline of sociology, the study revealed major shortcomings in the capacity of this single discipline to account for women's embodiment and led me to critical feminist theory.

The research examined the processes whereby cultural representations were reflected in the constitution of the embodied self of women who self-starved and binge-purged and the self in turn reflected back upon cultural constructions. Thus the construction and maintenance of selves, bodies and social relations encapsulated both agency and structure, but language played a key part in their embodied identity. The narratives conveyed by individuals who self-starved and binge-purged represented an amalgam of dominant, remnant and emergent discourses.

Postmodern and post-structuralist feminist theories, by emphasising gender, embodiment, language and the multiply constituted self, opened avenues for explanation not available in the classical and modern sociological traditions. These theorists allowed reconciliation of conflicting interpretations of self-starvation, binge-eating and self-induced vomiting between authors who saw such activities as a search for selfhood and those authors who emphasised the continuity between the historical search for sainthood amongst mediaeval self-starving saints and late twentieth-century self-starvers.

In the light of the social impact of the many facets of globalisation (Siochru, 2004; see also Bordo, Probyn, Nasser and Malson, all this volume) and further developments in communication technology (see also

Day and Keys, this volume) in the past decade, this chapter asks whether critical feminist theories still provide the most appropriate framework for theorising self-starvation in the twenty-first century. It could be argued that globalisation has been so all-pervasive in the 'cultural preparation for consumerism' (Siochru, 2004), and the universalising of communication, that it has reversed the diversification and articulation of interest and identity construction which set the scene for the rise of postmodern and post-structuralist thinking in the late twentieth century. Conversely, the proliferation of niche blogs and sub-cultural knowledge creation spaces on the web may have further postmodernised the discursive and material fields of young people.

Multiple cults of thinness

The late twentieth-century 'cultural fascination with all things "anorexic"' (Malson, 1998: 188) appears to have survived into the twenty-first century. However, the symbolic meanings of thinness have diversified. 'Heroin chic' models are just one manifestation of a plethora of symbolic representations of thinness from 'healthism saints', 'carbon footprint minimisers' and 'gym junkies' to 'emo (emotional) gaunt'. Blogs, in particular, reveal that many young women see fashion shows as rarefied enclaves of activity for older, richer women bearing little resemblance to their own lives. The only young women at most fashion shows are the pubescent models. The symbolic significance of the thinness of 'emo gaunt' young women is totally divorced from the 'body as coat hanger' symbolism of runway models (e.g. www. livejournal.com; www.forfa.com; www.euroresidentes.com/Blogs/2006/ spanish-fashion-show-rejects-thinnest). The term 'multiple cults of thinness' more accurately represents the cultural landscape for young women in the first decade of the twenty-first century than '*The* cult of thinness'.

Do these changes mirror shifts that started over 20 years ago in the academic literature with the introduction of existential, post-structuralist and postmodern analyses of the discursive construction of eating dis/ orders? It could be argued that the greater accessibility of all knowledge online, through search engines such as Google, has democratised the academic literature, but it is more likely that this diversification merely reflects the move from mass media audiences to niche ones, especially on the web.

The amount of time that young people in the western world devote to niche internet communication (generating as well as gathering information) and the proliferation of special interest websites into which they can immerse their lives (embodied and virtual) suggest limited opportunities for standard scripts for living (Rideout et al., 2005). In particular, the 'emo' (emotional), 'pro-ana' (pro-'anorexia') and 'pro-mia' (pro-'bulimia') sites attract niche clients and circulate ideas about the role of self-starvation in the constitution of the self which contrast markedly with the mainstream therapeutic and academic discourses, and with runway models' rationales for starving themselves (see also Day and Keys, this volume). The site www.livejournal.com invites people from a variety of sub-cultures to promote themselves and their groups using *myspace.msm*. These are the spaces where many young people are forming and circulating their opinions, rather than through mainstream media and traditional sources of influence. Thus '*the* normalizing gaze' that Foucault proposes to explain the objectification of women's bodies since the seventeenth century, transmutes into a plethora of often contradictory 'normalising gazes' for young women, in the twenty-first century.

Remnant unitary explanations for self-starvation

Early attempts to contextualise eating dis/orders within cultural, social and political structures and practices tended to use unitary explanatory frameworks and concentrated on the family and/or the media (see also Probyn, this volume) and fashion industries as the key culprits for the 'epidemics' of 'anorexia nervosa' and 'bulimia'. These perspectives assumed standard scripts about thinness which were effective in meeting standard needs among young women.

The concept of self-starvation as a family issue has been promoted by professional psychiatric journals and other psychiatric literature since the 1970s. Minuchin's early work (1975) on 'psychosomatic families', Kalucy et al.'s (1977) definitive study of '56 families with anorexia nervosa' and Palazzoli's work (1985) all emphasised family dynamics as a key to understanding 'eating dis/orders'. Bruch (1974, 1980, 1988) popularised this psychiatric emphasis on dysfunctional families and a range of influencial medical and allied professional journals have maintained a steady stream of articles on familial factors (see Saukko, this volume). An emphasis on the negative role of the media in inciting young women to diet has been evident since Bruch's (1974) seminal work on social aetiology, which promoted the culturally conditioned 'pursuit of thinness' as the key to understanding self-starvation. Discussion of the role of the media in promoting 'a thin standard of bodily attractiveness' started to appear in the psychiatric literature in the 1980s (Silverstein et al., 1986) and continues into the 2000s (e.g. Rosenzweig and Spruill, 1987; Wiseman et al., 1992). The sociological literature is similarly replete with reference to the media as responsible for the 'relentless pursuit of slenderness' in young women (Chernin, 1981, 1988; Lawrence, 1984, 1987; Orbach, 1978, 1982, 1985).

The implication in many of these analyses – that those who self-starve are more susceptible than the rest of the population to media messages – which many self-starvers find offensive (Eckermann, 1994a) – continues to underlie much of the academic literature as well as some popular accounts of self-starvation (see also Part III, this volume). However, by the 1980s new approaches to understanding corporeal experience and representation began to emerge which dramatically challenged traditional socio-cultural explanatory frameworks and examined the role of language, particularly diagnostic categories such as 'anorexia nervosa' and 'bulimia', in constituting eating dis/orders.

Embodying and gendering the self in starvation

In the last two decades of the twentieth century social theorists of the body (Featherstone, 1987; Martin, 1989; Shilling, 1993; Turner, 1984; and others) wrote the body into what had been up until then a disembodied and gender neutral social theoretical tradition. By operating within a Cartesian framework of mind–body dualism, and focusing on the rational reflexive mind as the site of human experience, the classical and modern traditions of social theory were unable to provide any heuristic purchase in understanding corporeal aspects of human experience. Self-starvation was thus beyond the scope of social enquiry until the humanities and social sciences incorporated concepts of embodiment and gender into their repertoires. Key influences on social theorists of the body, and on critical feminist scholarship in general, have been the feminist writers of the mid-twentieth century, who theorised the body as a cultural/political site which is oppressed by patriarchal power and post-structuralist theorists such as Foucault. Both the pre-post-structuralist feminists' and Foucault's contributions to understanding self-starvation are covered elsewhere (Bordo, 1988; Eckermann, 1997; Malson, 1997; Turner, 1992; Weedon, 1987; White and Epston, 1989), so only a very brief overview of Foucault's key influences in the field is provided here.

Foucault's theory about governmentality and regulation of the body (1967, 1970, 1972, 1973, 1979) explains the progressive medicalisation and objectification of bodies since the seventeenth century and provides a backdrop for understanding the normalisation of contemporary bodily self-surveillance practices. His emphasis on the centrality of language in the exercise of power (Foucault, 1977, 1980) furnishes researchers in the field with an invaluable framework for critiquing the medical and psychiatric gaze, in particular the psychiatric diagnostic categories and therapeutic modes imposed on those who self-starve (Eckermann, 1997; Turner, 1992). Weedon (1987) and McNay (1992) suggest that his analysis aided the development of a feminist political practice as well as critical feminist theory (Eckermann, 1997). Weedon (1987: 125) emphasises Foucault's constitutive interpretation of power, which allows for agency, physicality, structure and discursive practices in the construction of selves, and she attributes to Foucault (1981, 1987, 1988) the notion that, '[a]lthough the subject in post-structuralism is socially constructed in discursive practices, she nonetheless exists as a thinking, feeling, subject and social agent capable of resistance and innovations produced out of the clash between contradictory subject positions and practices'. This revolutionises the understanding of self-starvation from both a psychiatric and a sociological stance. It moves self-starvation out of simple unitary categorisation (as 'victim', as 'sick', as 'deviant', as 'naughty', or as 'healthy', as 'good', as 'compliant') to a complex practice of embodied communication and active identity construction.

The project that Foucault generated was taken further in the development and sophistication of theories of embodiment and gendered subjectivities by the post-structuralist and postmodern feminist writers, who allowed social scientists to better 'read the body' of self-starvers (e.g. Cixous, 1981; Grosz, 1994; Irigaray, 1985; Kristeva, 1986; Malson, 1997, 1998; Place, 1989; Probyn, 1988). Foucault saw language as central to the process of individuals' bodies being operated on, excluded and turned into objects and the subsequent self-operation whereby individuals developed self-understanding, insights, guilt and secular confession. The new feminist theorists acknowledged that Foucault offered some solutions to the problems of normalising tendencies in an administered society via the development of de-centred knowledge bases and de-centred and multiple ways of being. Foucault also provided insights on how consumerism promoted the commoditisation of the body (see Spitzack's (1987) use of Foucault) and at least theoretically allowed for language as enabling. Most importantly, for understandings of self-starvation as a practice, postmodern and post-structuralist feminists developed Foucault's work, introducing the concept of the multiple and contradictorily constituted self and 'multiple gazes'.

The traditional feminist works of Lawrence (1987), Chernin (1981), MacLeod (1981) and Orbach (1978) suggested a key role for patriarchy in explanatory frameworks used to explain the emergence of 'eating dis/orders' in the second half of the twentieth century. The new feminist writers from the postmodern tradition in the last decades of the twentieth century carried this project further. Postmodern feminisms drew upon the embodied traditions, phenomenology and post-structuralism 'to formulate an agenda for significant social change' in the service of women (Grosz, 1987). The postmodern psychoanalysis of Lacan (1977) inspired postmodern feminists, especially his emphasis on language as a key explanatory factor in the silencing of women since the Enlightenment (Grosz, 1990). Like Foucault, Lacan stressed the centrality of language in creating human consciousness and constructing the contents of the unconscious (see also Sayers, this volume). But, what both Foucault and Lacan failed to recognise (and Mary Daly (1984) emphasised) was that masculine discourse *cannot name for a woman* and that a feminist discourse needed to be developed if women were to become visible and heard (Grosz, 1986). This is where new feminists diverge from orthodox or traditional feminism. Daly (1984) in particular emphasised that language, the very vehicle for constructing and communicating self-identity, needed to be invented to reflect feminine thought.

New feminism developed largely in North America (mainly Canada) and France from the early 1970s. One of the key agendas of the new feminist movement was to resubjectivise bodies in a world which had become disenchanted with the Enlightenment project's hegemony of scientific, instrumentally rational discourse. Theorists suggested ways in which a world could be created where women were proud to have hips, breasts and desires, and where a multiplicity of epistemological bases were acceptable as foundations of knowledge. Celermajer (1987) suggested that 'anorexia nervosa' may represent an attempt to develop a liberating feminist discourse of the body, which is required to conceptualise women's corporeality in a positive way. 'Anorexia', she argued, is one of the avenues women use to seek self-expression to overcome the experience of their bodies as limited by the discourses of patriarchy. The self-starving individual feels silenced and constricted and expresses her pre-oedipal but forbidden desires by starving her body and thus attempting to destroy its limiting and restricting effects. The self-starving individual is not completely 'determined' in that she uses and chooses symbolic imperatives against herself to resist phallocentric integration.

Rather than seeing anorexia as an act of conformity to social ideals, it can be seen as an attempt to reappropriate what activity and power she can by constructing a body for herself which is unable to satisfy the dictates of her social and sexual role (ibid.: 67).

Cixous (1981), Irigaray (1985) and Kristeva (1986) went further than Celermajer in developing uniquely feminist psychoanalytic theories. In countering the silencing of women by patriarchal norms, Irigaray deconstructed phallocentricism and explored new spaces where women could see and represent themselves in positive, self-defined terms which challenge patriarchal power (Grosz, 1986: 135). Like Daly (1984), Irigaray (1985) attempted to create a speaking space where women could articulate their needs, desires and knowledge. Such discourses were seen to help develop a woman's sense of self distinct from that defined by patriarchal morphological inscriptions. Irigaray saw the potential for women to develop new ways of understanding their desires which are not based on one organ but are plural and located everywhere. She suggested women need a parody to subvert male discourse (Grosz, 1986). Both self-starvation and binge-purging would seem appropriate contenders for that parody.

Grosz (1987) suggests that the two levels (the individual and the societal) can be reconciled in feminist theory in relation to the body. The phenomenological and psychoanalytic traditions 'explore the subject's corporeal existence from the inside' (Freud, Lacan and Merleau-Ponty are useful here) and the structuralist tradition approaches the corporeal 'from the outside' (ibid.: 10). The first approach provides an account of 'embodied subjectivity', the second a perspective on the corporeal as an 'externality that presents itself to others and to culture as a "writing" or inscriptive surface highlighting the socio-political production of determinate historical bodies' (ibid.: 10). Thus, Grosz argued that, 'the metaphors of the body as a writing surface explain the ways in which the body's interiority is produced through the exterior inscription' (ibid.: 10; see also Part III, this volume).

She saw the need to 'reconceive notions of power' such that the body can be recognised as 'both the means by which power is disseminated and a potential object of resistance to power' (ibid.: 12). Like Daly, Griffin and the French psychoanalytic feminists, Grosz argues for the development of 'other systems of signification and representation (to) describe women in their own terms' (ibid.: 12–13) and goes beyond the 'language' theorists by arguing that, 'it is not new language that is required but, more feasibly, the construction of new knowledges' since 'all knowledges, all discourses are produced by interests, values and political perspectives'.

Theory in the twenty-first century: Contradictions, tensions and multiple 'normalising gazes'

The interviews which I conducted in the 1990s with young women who self-starved and/or binge-purged suggested a tension between subjectivity and asceticism (Eckermann, 1994a). My informants wanted to be 'good' in the eyes of others but also wanted to express their individuality. In a sense, the feelings that they conveyed were embodied in their activities around food and their bodies represented a crystallisation of competing discourses (Bordo, 1988) around rights and obligations of being a late twentieth-century citizen in the first world. However, some did eventually find more satisfying ways of being which were not as life threatening and physically and emotionally debilitating as self-starvation and binge-purging.

Social theorists of the body, Foucault, postmodern and post-structuralist theorists and critical feminist theorists revolutionised the potential to 'read' these contradictory aspects of self-starvation in the late twentieth century. Since then, globalisation theories, based on Beck's (1992) notions of the globalisation of risk, have been used to explain twenty-first century consti-tutions of the self. The relationship between 'disorder' (chaos) and 'order' (discipline) in the constitution of self-starvers mirrors the tensions in con-temporary social theory between assumptions about the 'deregulation of the macro-global level' (Beck's risk society) and Foucault's assertion of further articulation of the 'micro-politics of surveillance and regulation' in the carceral society (Turner, 1997). When applied to self-starvation and binge-purging, critical feminist theories allow us to incorporate both perspectives (Beck and Foucault), as well as a feminist perspective, to deconstruct the apparent contradictions between eating 'orders' (the disciplined, saintly self) and 'disorders' (the chaotic self).

Despite reporting elements of agency and choosing in 'eating dis/orders' (see also Day and Keys, this volume), self-starving individuals whom I interviewed still described a sense of 'loss of certainty' and 'loss of control', especially when unintended consequences emerge from their actions. The physiological sequelae of self-starvation can be quite frightening. For the first time in their lives they feel they have gained control of their bodies, only to find their palpable bodies 'turn nasty on them' at the zenith of their power. Suddenly their body and self are 'perceived as inherently unpredictable and uncontrollable' (Toombs, 1987: 231). The 'body serves as a symbol of evil, as a structural system contrasted with pure spirit which, by its nature, is free and undifferentiated' (Douglas, 1973: 17).

Modernist perspectives tend to assume that the socialisation process of a unitary normalising gaze is all-pervasive, and totalising, and that the resolution of cognitive dissonance is a powerful force at both individual and societal levels in creating coherent selves and societies (Giddens, 1991). How, then, from these perspectives, can any society sustain epidemic proportions of both 'anorexia' and 'bulimia' and any one individual sustain the two modes alternately? These two 'conditions' are presented in the psychiatric and popular literatures as the opposite ends of a discursively constituted binary between honorific absolute bodily control ('anorexia') and pejorative lack of bodily control ('bulimia'), yet some young women defy this dualistic construction (Burns, 2004). The concept of the multiply constituted self, propounded by postmodern theorists, challenges cognitive dissonance theory, bridging 'order' and 'disorder' to explain their co-existence in any one embodied self. This can also be applied at the societal level to explain the contradictory co-existence of selfhood and sainthood in both the culture and the individual (Eckermann, 1994b).

Social systems and individuals encompass remnants of the past, prevailing trends and future emergent trends, all of which have an effect on their configuration. These trends may be logically 'incongruent', yet are tolerated and fostered within the individual or the social formation. One could interpret self-starvation as a sign of our times (Bordo, 1988) or as a yearning for the past (Weedon, 1987) or as a postmodern emergent trend (Celermajer, 1987). Self-starving and binge-purging individuals may symbolise past, present or future disquiet. Sontag's (1983, 1988) analyses of 'illness as metaphor' for social, economic and political processes and ideologies has important implications for deconstructing the variety of symbolic representations of self-starvation over time. Just as AIDS replaces cancer as the metaphor of 'excess', self-starvation replaces TB and chlorosis as the romantic and aesthetic symbol of the ethereal. Self-starvation, like consumption, represents a 'manner of appearing' (see also Malson, this volume). Sontag argues that in the nineteenth century 'it became rude to eat heartily' and 'it was glamorous to look sickly'. The often quoted maxim of the Duchess of Windsor, 'One can never be too rich or too thin', Sontag suggests, reflects the nineteenth-century belief that 'good health was not chic' (Sontag, 1983: 33; see also Probyn, this volume). The symbolic association between illness and affluence was seen as having more contemporary commercial relevance since 'twentieth century women's fashions . . . are the last stronghold of the metaphors associated with the romanticizing of TB' (Sontag, 1983: 33).

Associations between wasting illness and 'being interesting' and 'being creative' are shared by the tubercular and the self-starving. This is reinforced in common responses to reference to 'anorexia': 'I wish I could catch a dose of that.' In twentieth-century western nations, self-starvation crystallised the search for transcendence. Sontag argues that in the West in the late twentieth century, insanity was 'made the index of a superior sensitivity, the vehicle of "spiritual" feelings and "critical" discontent' (ibid.: 39). In the twenty-first century self-starvation has special symbolic significance as a parody of 'healthism', of the ultimate exercise of will-power, and anti-consumerism – not taking up too much space and reducing the carbon footprint literally and metaphorically. Yet, at the same time, self-starvation represents an act of deviance (even death) on many fronts. It stands for the ultimate contradiction between compliance and defiance. 'Heroin chic' is promoted in clothing, make-up and other forms of bodily presentation in the mainstream media and fashion, but 'emo gaunt' and 'dead angels' are valorised on websites such as www.myspace.com and www.pro-ana-nation.com (see also Day and Keys, this volume).

'Anorexia', in its adjectival form, 'anorexic', has 'become a metaphor' (Sontag, 1983: 63) for thrift, exercise of willpower and thinness generally. Thus in contrast to 'syphilitic' and 'cancerous', which are generally used as pejorative terms, 'anorexic' is often used in an honorific sense and to denote thrift: for example, managers are praised for devising an 'anorectic budget'. 'Anorexia', like TB, represents not taking up too much space or using too many resources, 'eating yourself up, being refined, and getting down to the core, the real you' even if that means leaving the body behind (ibid.: 71). In a society where such enterprises are valued, self-starvation can thrive.

The thin body and the fat body represent, respectively, the 'bodily signs of holy grace' and the 'bodily signs of physical disorder' (Goffman, 1986). The self-starving body, although regarded as pathological by the medical profession, acquires honorific ascription; it is a symbol of the positive attributes of willpower, self-control, asceticism and personal strength.

Conclusions

By moving out of our disciplinary boundaries and combining phenomenology with structural theories and postmodern and post-structuralist feminist theories, we can take account of the fact that, '[t]he body is not simply an issue in epistemology and phenomenology but a theoretical location for debates about power, ideology and economics' (Turner, 1984: 59). It is the 'meeting ground of the social and natural worlds'. These more recent theoretical frameworks combine to provide a significant critique of both the biomedical and psychiatric models of illness and the simplistic socio-cultural models of young women as hapless (even 'accidental') victims of the thinness industries (see also Probyn, this volume). Despite the critiques by Callinicos (1989), Rorty (1986) and Habermas (1987), amongst others, mounted against post-structuralism and postmodernism for their alleged 'reckless relativism' and 'abandonment of the emancipatory project of the Enlightenment', these newer theoretical traditions are invaluable to understanding the intricate networks of power operating in the contemporary construction of the female self.

The continuing superior explanatory power of critical feminism, in understanding the practices of self-starvation, comes largely from theorising the gendered body and overriding the dualisms of the modernist tradition (in this case, especially, the mind–body and nature–culture dualisms). The emancipatory agenda of postmodernism comes from its 'allowing' and 'legitimating' a variety of epistemological positions. It overcomes the silencing of intuition, emotion and affectivity evident in much modernist discourse. By incorporating postmodern perspectives into the analysis of self-starvation, one is able to move beyond psychiatric discourse, beyond phallocentric discourse and beyond the confines of western rationality in understanding why people self-starve. Late twentieth-century sociological accounts of self-starvation and binge-purging tended to accept unquestioningly psychoanalytic accounts of these activities as being the result of overprotective mothering (Bruch, 1974, 1980, 1988). Some elements of the postmodern tradition also uncritically accept psychoanalytic mother blaming (Celermajer, 1987). The critical tradition in sociology has tended to emphasise the structural components of 'ill health', blaming media advertising and the fashion industry as key structural and ideological forces producing false consciousness in female consumers (Orbach, 1985; Wolf, 1990). A simplistic theory which points to the institutions of the media and the family as the culprits in the rising incidence of self-starvation and binge-purging in the twenty-first century is limited and ignores the extent to which other factors are deeply embedded in our cultural heritage and contribute to individuals' conceptions of themselves. The phenomenological, post-structuralist and postmodern feminist traditions allow for multiple and contradictory influences on the individual. Furthermore, as Brumberg (2007) points out, the range of body projects that girls are taking on as we approach the end of the first decade of the twenty-first century are expanding well beyond eating dis/orders, to include cosmetic surgery, body piercing and tattooing, and pubic waxing and shaving at ever younger ages.

The body is used by individuals as a symbol, as an individual ritual for dealing with the lack of 'commitment to common symbols' in the cultural milieu generally. The generation of new rituals and new symbols satisfies the yearning of adolescents for symbolic and ritual significance. In this sense, a variety of symbolic ways of 'being thin' are generated. The question arises as to whether self-starving bodies represent super-conformity to, or super-defiance of, the norms of twenty-first century western societies. In an increasingly ascetically-oriented society where moderation and significant lifestyle discipline are emphasised, one could argue, as Bordo (1988) does, that self-starvation represents a bodily crystallisation of that society. However, a consumption-oriented economy with an emphasis on 'health' would regard the self-starving body as 'pathological', as going against the dictates of nature and culture. Maybe resolution of this dilemma is offered by including class, ethnicity and sex/gender as dimensions of significant structural differentiation within societies – producing differing 'determinancies'. Thus combining structural theories with critical feminist and phenomenological theories provides an appropriate framework for deconstructing self-starvation in the twenty-first century as both a private and a public issue.

References

Beck, U. (1992) *Risk Society*, London: Sage.

Bordo, S. (1988) Anorexia nervosa: psychopathology as the crystallization of culture, in I. Diamond and L. Quinby (eds), *Feminism and Foucault; Reflections on Resistance*, Boston, MA: North-eastern University Press.

Bruch, H. (1974) *Eating Disorders: Obesity, Anorexia Nervosa and the Person Within*, London: Routledge and Kegan Paul.

Bruch, H. (1980) *The Golden Cage: The Enigma of Anorexia Nervosa*, Cambridge: Open Books.

Bruch, H. (1988) *Conversations with Anorectics*, edited posthumously by D. Czyzewski and M.A. Suhr, New York: Basic Books.

Brumberg, J.J. (2007) *From Daughters*, newsletter, 1 January.

Burns, M. (2004) Eating like an ox: femininity and dualistic constructions of bulimia and anorexia, *Feminism & Psychology*, 4(2): 269–295.

Callinicos, A. (1989) *Against Post-modernism: A Marxist Critique*, Cambridge: Polity Press.

Celermajer, D. (1987) Submission and rebellion: anorexia and a feminism of the body, *Australian Feminist Studies*, 5.

Chernin, K. (1981) *Womansize: The Tyranny of Slenderness*, London: Woman's Press.

Chernin, K. (1988) *The Hungry Self*, London: Virago.

Cixous, H. (1981) The laugh of Medusa, in E. Marks and I. Courtivron, *New French Feminisms*, Brighton: Harvester.

Daly, M. (1984) *Pure Lust*, London: Women's Press.

Douglas, M. (1973) *Natural Symbols*, Harmondsworth: Penguin.

Eckermann, E. (1994a) *Selfhood/Sainthood: self-starvation and binge-purging as embodiment of cultural ambiguity*, doctoral dissertation, Flinders University of South Australia.

Eckermann, E. (1994b) Self-starvation and binge-purging: embodied selfhood/ sainthood, *Australian Cultural History*, 13: 82–99.

Eckermann, L. (1997) Foucault, embodiment and gendered subjectivities: the case of voluntary self-starvation, in A. Petersen and R. Bunton (eds), *Foucault, Health and Medicine*, London: Routledge.

Featherstone, M. (1987) Lifestyle and consumer culture, *Theory, Culture and Society*, 4: 55–70.

Foucault, M. (1967) *Madness and Civilization: A History of Insanity in the Age of Reason*, London: Tavistock.

Foucault, M. (1970) *The Order of Things*, London: Tavistock.

Foucault, M. (1972) *The Archaeology of Knowledge*, London: Tavistock.

Foucault, M. (1973) *The Birth of the Clinic: An Archaeology of Medical Perception*, New York: Pantheon Books.

Foucault, M. (1977) *Language, Counter-memory, Practice: Selected Essays and Interviews*, edited with an introduction by D.F. Bouchard, Ithaca, NY: Cornell University Press.

Foucault, M. (1979) *Discipline and Punish: The Birth of the Prison*, Harmondsworth: Penguin.

Foucault, M. (1980) *Power/Knowledge*, edited by C. Gordon, Brighton: Harvester.

Foucault, M. (1981) *The History of Sexuality: An Introduction*, Harmondsworth: Penguin.

Foucault, M. (1987) *The History of Sexuality: Vol. 2: The Use of Pleasure*, Harmondsworth: Penguin.

Foucault, M. (1988) *The History of Sexuality: Vol. 3: The Care of the Self*, London: Allen Lane.

Giddens, A. (1991) *Modernity and Self-identity: Self and Society in the Late Modern Age*, Cambridge: Polity Press.

Goffman, E. (1986) *Stigma: Notes on the Management of Spoiled Identity*, New York: Simon and Schuster.

Grosz, E. (1986) Conclusion: what is feminist theory?, in C. Pateman and E. Grosz (eds), *Feminist Challenges, Social and Political Theory*, Sydney: Allen and Unwin.

Grosz, E. (1987) Notes towards a corporeal feminism, *Australian Feminist Studies*, 5: 1–15.

Grosz, E. (1990) *Jacques Lacan: A Feminist Introduction*, Sydney: Allen and Unwin.

Grosz, E. (1994) *Volatile Bodies: Towards a Corporeal Feminism*, Sydney: Allen and Unwin.

Habermas, J. (1987) *The Philosophical Discourse of Modernity*, Cambridge: Polity Press.

Irigary, L. (1985) *This Sex Which is Not One*, Ithaca, NY: Cornell University Press.

Kalucy, R.S., Crisp, A.H. and Harding, B. (1977) A study of 56 families with anorexia nervosa, *British Journal of Medical Psychology*, 50: 381–395.

Kristeva, J. (1986) *The Kristeva Reader*, Oxford: Blackwell.

Lacan, J. (1977) *Ecrits*, London: Tavistock.

Lawrence, M. (1984) *The Anorexic Experience*, London: Women's Press.

Lawrence, M. (1987) *Fed Up and Hungry*, London: Women's Press.

MacLeod, S. (1981) *The Art of Starvation*, London: Virago.

McNay, L. (1992) *Foucault and Feminism*, Cambridge: Polity Press.

Malson, H. (1997) Anorexic bodies and the discursive production of feminine excess, in J. Ussher (ed.), *Body Talk: The Material and Discursive Regulation of Sexuality, Madness and Reproduction*, London: Routledge.

Malson, H. (1998) *The Thin Woman: Feminism, Post-structuralism and the Social Psychology of Anorexia Nervosa*, London: Routledge.

Martin, E. (1989) *The Woman in the Body: Cultural Analysis of Reproduction*, Boston, MA: Beacon Press.

Minuchin, S. (1975) *Families and Family Therapy*, Cambridge, MA: Harvard Press.

Orbach, S. (1978) *Fat is a Feminist Issue*, New York: Berkley.

Orbach, S. (1982) *Fat is a Feminist Issue II*, London: Hamlyn.

Orbach, S. (1985) Visibility/invisibility: social considerations in anorexia nervosa – a feminist perspective, in S.W. Emmett (ed.), *Theory and Treatment of Anorexia Nervosa and Bulimia*, New York: Brunner Mazel.

Palazzoli, M.S. (1985) Anorexia nervosa: a syndrome of the affluent society, *Transcultural Psychiatric Review*, 22: 199.

Place, F. (1989) *Cardboard*, Sydney: Local Consumption Publications.

Probyn, E. (1988) The anorexic body, in A. Kroker and M. Kroker (eds), *Body Invaders: Sexuality and the Post-modern Condition*, Basingstoke: Macmillan.

Rideout, V., Roberts, D. and Foehr, U. (2005) *Generation M: Media in the Lives of 8–18 Year Olds*, Washington, DC: Kaiser Family Foundation.

Rorty, R. (1986) Foucault and epistemology, in D.C. Hoy (ed.), *Foucault: A Critical Reader*, Oxford: Blackwell.

Rosenzweig, M. and Spruill, J. (1987) Twenty years after Twiggy: a retrospective investigation of bulimic-like behaviours, *International Journal of Eating Disorders*, 6(1): 59–66.

Shilling, C. (1993) *The Body and Social Theory*, London: Sage.

Silverstein, B. et al. (1986) Some correlates of the thin standard of bodily attractiveness for women, *International Journal of Eating Disorders*, 5(5): 895–906.

Siochru, S.O. (2004) *Social Consequences of the Globalization of the Media and Communication Sector: Some Strategic Considerations, Working Paper No. 36*, Policy Integration Department, World Commission on the Social Dimension of Globalization, International Labour Office, Geneva.

Sontag, S. (1983) *Illness as Metaphor*, Harmondsworth: Penguin.

Sontag, S. (1988) *AIDS and its Metaphors*, London: Allen Lane.

Spitzack, C. (1987) Confessions and signification: the systematic inscription of body consciousness, *Journal of Medicine and Philosophy*, 12(4): 357–369.

Toombs, S.K. (1987) The meaning of illness: a phenomenological approach to the patient–physician relationship, *Journal of Medicine and Philosophy*, 12(3): 219–240.

Turner, B.S. (1984) *The Body and Society*, Oxford: Basil Blackwell.

Turner, B.S. (1992) *Regulating Bodies: Essays in Medical Sociology*, London: Routledge.

Turner, B.S. (1997) Foreword, in A. Petersen and R. Bunton (eds), *Foucault, Health and Medicine*, London: Routledge.

Weedon, C. (1987) *Feminist Practice and Post Structuralist Theory*, Oxford: Basil Blackwell.

White, M. and Epston, D. (1989) *Literate Means to Therapeutic Ends*, Adelaide: Dulwich Centre Publishing.

Wiseman, C.V. et al. (1992) Cultural expectations of thinness in women: an update, *International Journal of Eating Disorders*, 11(1): 85–90.

Wolf, N. (1990) *The Beauty Myth*, London: Vintage.

3 Feeding the body[1]

Janet Sayers

Introduction

In common with other factors affecting our bodies, feeding is very much socially conditioned. Our bodies are what we feed them. But what we feed them is conditioned by economic, historical, biographical, ideological, and discursive factors. These, in turn, vary systematically with culture, class, and sex. This is particularly evident in conditions of food scarcity and abundance. I will accordingly focus on these conditions in this chapter, beginning with ways in which scarcity has varied, and continues to vary, with class and sex in Europe and Asia. I will then consider how class and sex, as well as ideological and discursive factors, including fantasy, mediate what women and men feed their bodies in conditions of abundance. Finally, I will consider the implications of all this for feminism.

Scarcity

First, then, let us consider how feeding the body is affected by scarcity. Food scarcity is mediated by wealth and power. Even when food is most scarce – even when its scarcity reaches famine proportions – it is available to those who can command it through rights of property, exchange, and employment. Noting this, Mennell (1991) goes on to argue that, from 1750 onwards, the increasing reliability of food production and distribution resulted in famine less often occurring in Western Europe.

Nevertheless, concern about the quantity and quality of food and water supplies continued and still continues in the West. Following the industrial revolution philanthropists and others in the British ruling class, concerned for the welfare of the urban poor, and fearful of contagion by the diseases of urbanization (such as cholera), and wanting to minimize the tax burden of those rendered incapable by illness and disease, pressed for improvements in the supply of food and water. Anxiety about the bodily debility of men recruited to the army during the Crimean, Boer, and First and Second

---

1 A longer version of the following can be found in Evans and Lee (2002).

World Wars also led to pressure to improve the otherwise scant or inadequate diet of the poor. It led, among other things, to the introduction of
meals for children at school. Sociological research also contributed, earlier
in the twentieth century, to increasing pressure to alleviate food scarcity
among the working class. Particularly notable in this respect was Charles
Booth's seventeen-volume study, *The Life and Labour of the People in
London*, published in 1902–1903, and Seebohm Rowntree's (1902) book,
Poverty, A Study of Town Life, in which Rowntree concluded from investigating the calorie requirements of the average working man that:

> The diet of the 'servant-keeping class' is in excess of that necessary for
> health, the food supply for the artisan class is satisfactory if there is no
> 'wasteful expenditure on drink', and the diet of 'the labouring classes,
> upon whom the bulk of the muscular work falls, and who form so large
> a proportion of the industrial population are seriously underfed'.
>   (Rowntree 1902: 28, quoted in Turner 1992: 191)

By the end of the twentieth century, however, some sociologists assumed
that inequalities between classes as regards food scarcity had been elimi-
nated in Europe. In 1991, Mennell claimed that equality and interdepen-
dence between social classes in Western Europe had been achieved to such
an extent that scarcity had become a thing of the past. He maintained there
was now considerably greater equal distribution of food, and similarity of
cuisine between classes, and that there were now considerably less extreme
differences between the food consumed on ordinary and festive occasions.

Yet food scarcity persists in the West. And it continues to be mediated
unequally both by class and sex. In England and Ireland those who are
poorest, as measured by dependence on welfare benefits, often suffer dietary
deficiency, with women often suffering worse deficiency than men. In the
1990s, Lobstein (1991) and Dowler and Calvert (1995) reported that a
significant proportion of women claimant households in London had a diet
deficient in key nutrients. As regards differences between women and men in
what they ate, Hilary Graham (1993) reported that a study, published in
1989, of people living on a Dublin housing estate suffering scarcity of food
because many of the residents were unemployed, demonstrated that women
fared significantly worse than the men in terms of the recommended daily
food allowance (RDA) deemed necessary for optimum health. Three times
as many women as men in the study were found to be consuming less than 75
per cent RDA for vitamin C. And only half the lone mothers achieved even
half the RDA for iron. Men, by contrast, suffered little in this respect.

Graham argues that women's food deficiency relative to men in conditions of scarcity is due, at least in part, to their doing without food in
favour of giving it to their children and men. She quotes one mother in the
above-cited Dublin study and another mother from a study conducted in
1990 saying:

> I'll cut down myself on food. Sometimes if we're running out the back
> end of the second week and there's not a lot for us to eat, I'll sort of
> give the kids it first and then see what's left.
>
> (Graham, 1993: 160)

> I buy half a pound of stewing meat or something and give that to Sid
> and the kiddies and then I just have the gravy – before I used to buy
> soya things and substitutes to meat but I can't afford that now.
>
> (ibid.)

Similar inequalities between women and men, and between upper and lower classes, in conditions of food scarcity prevail in the developing world where, according to McGuire and Popkin (1990), women generally meet a smaller percentage of their current RDA than men, and often consume lower quality vegetable protein, with men often consuming a larger proportion of whatever animal protein is available. This sex difference, report McGuire and Popkin, is particularly marked in Burkina Faso (in the former Upper Volta). Here, women not only consume a lower proportion of what is deemed necessary as regards gross daily protein intake, they also consume only 0.8 grams of animal protein compared to men's consumption of 10.3 grams daily.

McGuire and Popkin also note that women's vitamin and mineral intake in the developing world is inadequate, both absolutely and relative to men's intake. Jiggins (1994) reports similar sex inequalities. She notes that, in self-provisioning households in South Asia, men tend to have preferential access to whatever food is available. Furthermore, she observes, as the amount or quality of food deteriorates, differences in male and female health and nutritional status increase, with women and girls tending to have a lower nutritional and health status than men and boys even in wealthier households. Gittelsohn (1991) reports similar sex inequalities in the distribution of food to women and men (but not to girls and boys) in rural Nepal. And in India one study reports that, while rich women consumed a daily average of 2500 calories, and increased their weight by an average of 12.5 kilograms during pregnancy, poor women consumed a daily average of 1400 calories, and only increased their weight by an average of 1.5 kilograms during pregnancy (Anon, 1985: 43).

Evidence regarding sex inequalities in infant feeding in conditions of food scarcity in the East is more unclear. Harriss (1989) found no differences in South Asia between boys and girls in the amount they were breast-fed, whereas Santow (1995) reports that in rural Uttar Pradesh girls are sometimes breast-fed for a shorter time and less intensely than boys. Chatterjee and Lambert (1989; see also UNICEF, 1988) report similar inequalities in breast-feeding of girls and boys in India and Pakistan generally. There is also evidence in the rural Punjab that, although ordinary food is divided equally between boys and girls, more nutritious food goes disproportionately to boys (Das Gupta, 1987). In another study of children in rural Bangladesh, the calorie consumption of boys exceeded that of girls by 16 per cent in children under five years old, with protein intake averaging 14 per cent more in boys (Chen et al., 1981). On the other hand, while Abdullah and Wheeler (1985) report significantly lower food intake by girls aged one to four years in one village in Bangladesh, Chaudhury (1984) found greater intake of nutrition for pre-school Bangladeshi girls.

The evidence is also conflicting as regards sex differences in infant malnutrition and mortality. One factor contributing to conflicting findings is the effect of the position and number of girls in the family. In Bangladesh, for instance, it was found that the risk of infant mortality was 84 per cent in girls with older sisters compared to a risk of 14 per cent in girls without sisters (Rousham, 1999). Another factor is whether the girl's family own land. Rousham reports that, among two- to six-year-olds in a remote rural area of Bangladesh, girls in landless families had worse nutritional status than all other children during the monsoon, but that this difference was no longer significant following the end of the monsoon and a successful late October rice harvest. Children from landless families still ate significanly fewer meals per day than children from landowning households. But there was no differences between boys and girls in the frequency of their meals. In sum, Rousham's study indicates that cultural bias against feeding girls has a significant impact only at times of food scarcity, when its impact is worst on girls growing up in landless families unable to access and control its supply.

Whatever their impact, sex and class inequalities in feeding persist not only in conditions of food scarcity; they also obtain in conditions of food abundance, as we will now see.

Abundance

In Western Europe, writes Mennell (1991), the economically and socially most powerful classes sought, in earlier centuries, to distinguish themselves from less powerful classes by the quantities they ate; he thus argues that pressure to over-eat was linked to fear of food scarcity. In the past, he notes, the state sought to suppress gluttony: but, he adds, increasing reliability in the abundance and availability of food was more effective in this respect. This led to court cuisine becoming more delicate and refined, and to the middle classes imitating the food delicacy and refinement of the upper class, at least in France.

Food intake in conditions of abundance has also been shaped by what the Marxist theorist, Louis Althusser, dubbed 'ideological state apparatuses', and by what Foucauldians refer to as 'discursive practices'. Particularly important in this respect in the Middle Ages was religious doctrine concerning the virtues of fasting. This doctrine persisted into the Renaissance and beyond. In 1558, for instance, an influential Italian book, *Trattato della vita sobria* (*Treatise on the Sober Life*), preached the virtues of foregoing feasting as defence against the temptations of the flesh. Its author, Luigi Cornaro, who had cured his own ills through dieting and sobriety, recommended the same for his readers. He had learnt, he wrote, 'never to cloy my stomach with eating and drinking, but constantly to rise from table with a disposition to eat and drink still more' (Turner, 1991: 161).

An English edition of the book was published in 1634. It may in turn have been read by George Cheyne, who, in the next century, wrote several books advocating diet which became very influential and popular among the London élite with whom Cheyne lived and worked. He portrayed disciplined food intake as a religious duty, and condemned gluttony as tantamount to suicide. He blamed excessive eating in his class on expanding trade having brought exotic food, drink, spices, and a general surplus of food to England and he condemned, as contrary to nature and digestion, the changing eating habits and cuisine of his class. Attributing the ills of his class to over-abundance and inactivity, he advocated abstinence, temperance, exercise and purging:

> For the 'learned professions', he recommended regular use of his 'domestick purge' – a mixture of rhubarb, wormwood, nutmeg and orange peel . . . Once a proper, regular diet has been established [Cheyne wrote], the professional man has only two further requirements for sound health – (1) 'A Vomit, that can work briskly, quickly and safely' by 'cleaning, squeezeing and compressing the knotted and tumified Glands of the Primae Viae'; (2) 'Great, frequent and continued Exercise, especially on Horseback'.
>
> (Turner, 1992: 189)

Cheyne's claims regarding the healthful effects of dieting spread, in turn, to other social classes by the religious preacher, John Wesley. Wesley's popular 1791 book, *Primitive Physic*, following Cheyne, advocated a regime of regularity and moderation, more as a matter of right conduct than of diet, for which this was hardly relevant, at least for his readers and listeners from the working class, in so far as they were still at risk of famine and starvation. Nevertheless, the emphasis of Cheyne, Wesley, and others on diet, hygiene, and exercise was taken up by all classes, arguably because of its ideological value to the ruling class in inculcating discipline in its workers and their children. As such, it shaped education, work, and health up to our own times, embracing all social classes in what Turner calls 'a framework of organized eating, drinking and physical training' (Turner, 1992: 192).

Alongside discourses of religion and diet, a discourse of taste has also shaped similarities and differences between social classes in what they eat in conditions of food abundance. Pierre Bourdieu, for instance, notes the following class-related effects of this discourse:

The taste of the professionals or senior executives defines the popular taste, by negation, as the taste for the heavy, the fat and the coarse, by tending towards the light, the refined and the delicate . . .

(Bourdieu, 1984: 185; see also Shilling, 1993)

But eating is not only shaped by class-related discourses concerning religion, diet, and taste. It is also shaped by these and other discourses concerning gender, as I will seek to highlight next through turning to women's fasting and feasting, and its medical construction as symptomatic of anorexia and bulimia nervosa.

Fasting and feasting

Fasting is not, of course, confined to women. It has been an ascetic discipline for both sexes in virtually all religions. A frequently quoted example, at least in recent books about anorexia (e.g. Hepworth, 1999), is Catherine Benincasa, who lived from 1347 till 1380. Resisting pressure from her family to marry against her will, she took refuge in fasting, which she justified as divinely inspired, as a means of securing her parents' salvation. She accordingly courted scarcity, and

From the age of fifteen . . . consumed nothing but bread, uncooked vegetables, and water; from the age of twenty-five she simply chewed on bitter herbs, spitting out the substance . . . In the end she refused even to drink water and so, in her early thirties, put an end to her life.

(Cohn, 1986: 3)

While her parents, apparently, construed her fasting as rebellion against them, the Church made her a saint, and it is by her sanctified name – Saint Catherine of Siena – that she is now usually known.

The sociologist, Arthur Frank (1991), argues that this contradictory disapproval and approval of fasting (as in Catherine's case) became general following the Renaissance, with some equating fasting with purity and holiness, and others regarding it as heresy inspired by the devil. In the nineteenth century this religious construction of fasting was gradually supplanted by a scientific medical discourse, which, in the case of fasting, made women its object. Fasting came to be diagnosed as a symptom of hysteria (linked to the wandering of women's wombs).

Addressing a meeting of the British Medical Association in Oxford in 1868, William Gull, a London-based specialist in gastric disorders, spoke of 'young women emaciated to the last degree through apepsia hysterica' (Hepworth, 1999: 2). Later, in 1874, he introduced the term 'anorexia nervosa' to describe women patients in whom there was no evidence of gastric dysfunction, whose emaciation he attributed, not to gastric dysfunction, poverty, or lack of available food, but to loss of appetite due to a morbid mental state. Gull's patients evidently came from the wealthier classes, as in the following case of whom Gull wrote:

> Miss B., aged 18, was brought to me Oct. 8, 1868, as a case of latent tubercle. Her friends had been advised accordingly to take her for the coming winter to the South of Europe. The extremely emaciated look, much greater indeed than occurs for the most part in tubercular cases where patients are still going about, impressed me at once with the probability that I should find no visceral disease. All the viscera were apparently healthy. Notwithstanding the great emaciation and apparent weakness, there was a peculiar restlessness, difficult, I was informed, to control.
>
> (Gull, quoted in Hepworth, 1999: 2)

Just as Gull wrote about women's emaciation in terms of the then received medical discourse, so did Charles Lasègue, a physician in France, who, in 1873, assimilated this symptom of emaciation, as had Gull initially, to hysteria. He called it *l'anorexia hysterique*, and attributed it to sexual frustration or unfulfilled sexual expectations in courtship and early married life. Other doctors, notably Charcot and Freud, similarly linked anorexia to sex. Freud initially attributed it to patients having been sexually abused – or 'seduced', as he called it – in early childhood. Later he described anorexia as expressing, in the form of oral disgust, repressed, and therefore unconscious, sexual desire for oral sex with the father. His immediate followers similarly diagnosed anorexia as an illness, claiming it was the pathological effect of regression from adolescent genital desire to the oral desires of infancy. (For further details, see Sayers, 1988.) Since Freud, psychoanalytically-minded writers have diagnosed anorexia less in terms of genital or oral sexuality, and more in terms of feeding and its control (e.g. Sours, 1980), noting it involves self-imposed scarcity in conditions of abundance. In *The Golden Cage* (1977), for example, Hilde Bruch characterizes anorexia as a form of gilded existence involving disturbed body image, disturbed perception of hunger stimuli, and a paralyzing sense of ineffectiveness. Her characterization of anorexia has, in turn, informed the American Psychiatric Association's (APA) definition of this condition (Busfield, 1996).

Alongside the APA's and WHO's (World Health Organization) medical construction of self-imposed lack of food as evidence of anorexia, both organizations have also constructed bingeing and purging, in scientific and medical terms, as warranting the diagnosis 'bulimia nervosa', 'characterized by repeated bouts of overeating and an excessive preoccupation with the control of body weight' (ibid.: 177). Just as Gull and Lasègue construed anorexia as a female condition, in so far as they characterized it as a form of hysteria, so too does the APA. In its most recent pronouncements on the subject, it notes that anorexia and bulimia are six to ten times more prevalent in women than in men (APA, 2000). And, like Gull and Lasègue, the APA also diagnoses these conditions in scientific, publicly observable, behavioural terms. So, too, do Bruch and other psychoanalytically-minded US ego psychologists. Others, by contrast, understand these conditions in terms of more inward-looking fantasy.

Fantasy

Whereas Freud and his immediate followers linked anorexia with sexual fantasy, post-Freudians, particularly in England, link anorexia and other eating disorders with fantasies they imply are universal in infancy regarding feeding and being fed. In this, they often draw on Melanie Klein's development of Freud's theory. On the basis of her work in pioneering child analysis, Klein hypothesized that, in feeding from the breast or bottle, babies fantasize incorporating the mother as a loved and hated figure within them. They imagine her as super-abundant. They also imagine emptying her. They imagine greedily robbing and scooping her out, and enviously spoiling and destroying everything inside her, thereby voiding her of all goodness, food, and love. This, in turn, gives rise to children's fantasies of their mothers retaliating by devouring them, as in the fairy tale of Hansel and Gretel fed and fattened with all manner of sweets by a witch so she can eat them up.

Explaining eating disorders in these terms, and to illustrate the everyday occurrence of such fantasies, art therapist, Mary Levens, quotes the following conversation:

Dinah: Where did I live before I was born? I don't know.
Mother: In my tummy.
Dinah: And did you eat me up?
Mother: No.
Dinah: And what did I eat?
Mother: Some of my food, because you were in my tummy.

(Levens, 1995: 49)

Levens argues that eating-disordered patients today similarly equate loving and eating with fantasies of destroying and being destroyed to which this equation can give rise. She quotes an anorexic patient imagining her mother ordering herself: 'Eat the child, bind the child, claw the child. . . . Never let it go' (ibid.: 56). Levens notes that the novelist, Margaret Attwood, attributes the following cannibalistic fantasy to an anorexic character in her 1980 novel, *The Edible Woman*:

She cut into the [pink heart-shaped] cake. She was surprised to find that it was pink in the inside too. She put a forkful into her mouth and chewed slowly. It felt spongy and cellular against her tongue, like the bursting of thousands of tiny lungs. She shuddered and spat the cake out into her napkin.

(Levens, 1995: 61)

Levens also quotes a contrary fantasy of this same character baking a cake to resemble a woman's body, and telling it: 'You look delicious . . . very appetising . . . that's what you get for being food' (ibid.). Returning to non-fictional data, Levens quotes a young boy, playing at swallowing his foster mother, triumphantly saying, 'Now you can't talk', and then immediately vomiting her out (ibid.: 62).

But if these fantasies occur in both sexes, why is it that anorexic and bulimic fasting and feasting occur so much more often in girls and women than in boys and men? What does this imply for sexual politics?

Feminism

In *Fat is a Feminist Issue* (1984), the feminist therapist, Susie Orbach, explains sex differences in the incidence of eating disorders as originating in sex inequalities in early infant feeding. Whereas I have cited data from Asia regarding these inequalities (see pp. 24–25 above), Orbach cites data from Italy. She combines this with evidence that buying and cooking food is usually assigned to women and thus becomes part of their role as providers of love, care, and concern for their families, including subordinating their need for food to men and children in their families when food is scarce (see pp. 23–24 above). In England, this is also evident in women cooking what their husbands want rather than what they want, and in their not bothering to cook or even eat when their husbands or children are absent or gone (Murcott, 1983).

Generalizing from such findings, Orbach (1984) argues that women teach their daughters from earliest infancy to subordinate their needs – including their need for food – to others. This results, she says, in girls growing up alienated from, and unconscious of, hunger signals arising within their bodies. Women's fatness, she argues, may be motivated by resistance to this process of socialization through indulging their needs and bingeing on whatever they want. Or, like the suffragettes at the beginning of the twentieth century, they may protest by fasting and going on hunger strike (Orbach, 1986).

But this explanation of women's fasting and feasting poses problems. Orbach advocates combating women's alienation from their need for food by reconnecting them with this need so as to make them conscious of it. But this is to treat our need for food as though it existed within us unaffected by, and divorced from, the social factors which, as we have seen above, in fact shape and condition our feeding of our bodies from earliest infancy. Furthermore, claims Joan Busfield (1996), Orbach over-readily allies anorexic and bulimic starving and bingeing with political protest, although this is rarely their conscious intent.

Orbach's account also does not explain why anorexia, at least until recently, occurred more often in England among young women from upper middle-class, high-achieving families, whereas the prevalence of bulimia was distributed more evenly across all social classes. Nor can Orbach's account explain why, in the US, eating disorders appear to be as common in young Hispanic as in Caucasian women, and appear to be more common in Native Americans and less common among Black and Asian women (see also Bordo, Nasser and Malson, this volume). Nor does it explain why African Americans are more likely to become bulimic than anorexic, nor why they are more likely to purge with laxatives than with vomiting.

These national, ethnic, and class differences can be more adequately explained in terms of the theory of women's eating disorders put forward by Susan Bordo. She argues that anorexia and bulimia are an effect of three dominant discursive practices – or 'axes'– promulgated in Western Europe and the US (Bordo, 1993).

The first axis she identifies is the mind–body dualism associated with the philosophies of Plato and Descartes, which, in effect, repudiates the body as alien to the mind. This philosophy, Bordo implies, contributes to both bulimia and anorexia. It is evident in the bulimic reviling her bingeing as 'an animalistic orgy . . . whoring after food'. The second axis concerns control. Bordo notes western philosophy's celebration of willpower and its control, which, she argues, are expressed in the bulimic's compulsive exercising, and in the anorexic using her scales, as one patient put it, to provide 'visible proof . . . that I can exert control' (ibid.: 149). And, of course, this philosophy of control tallies with the self-control or self-discipline which Turner (1991, 1992), as we have seen, notes writers from the sixteenth century onwards in Europe enjoined on men in the ruling class in urging them to curb and control what they drank and ate.

Bordo's axis of control also tallies with Turner's account of the spread from the upper to the lower class of a discourse of diet and self-control in so far as it suited the interests of the ruling class to have the lower classes control and discipline themselves so as to become effective soldiers in war, and effective workers in agricultural and factory production. Not surprisingly, perhaps, given the greater benefits of this injunction to the ruling class, its effect – in the form of anorexia – first occurred most frequently in this class, and only spread subsequently, through assimilation and globalization, to other cultures and classes. On the other hand, capitalist expansion also enjoins women and men of all classes to increase its profits by indulging themselves as much as they can as consumers. This arguably contributes to the prevalence of 'self-indulging' bulimic bingeing and the remedying of its effects through vomiting as long ago preached by Cheyne to the élite for whom he wrote (see p. 26 above).

To explain why, despite this universalization across classes, controlling bulimic purging and anorexic fasting occur more often in women than men, Bordo singles out a third 'gender–power' axis. Noting the lack of power socially accorded women relative to men, she argues that this makes young women both fearful and disdainful of becoming powerless and oppressed like their mothers and women generally in the generation before them. It also makes them fearful of embodying the misogynist image of women, that is arguably a corollary of women's social powerlessness and oppression: 'the archetypal image of the female as hungering, voracious, all-needing, and all-wanting' (Bordo, 1993: 160). Bordo implies that the way forward lies in feminism combating the social inequalities reflected in this negative stereotype.

Conclusions

Over half a century ago a young social theorist, Simone Weil, died of starvation in Ashford, Kent. Some claimed it was due to anorexia, stemming from a personal biography of poor bodily feeding even as a baby. Others argued that Weil starved herself out of solidarity with the working classes in German-occupied Paris, who were then suffering terrible food shortages. After Weil's death, aged 34, in 1943, the coroner's verdict recorded: 'The deceased did kill and slay herself by refusing to eat whilst the balance of her mind was disturbed.' By contrast the *Kent Messenger* ran a story under the title: 'French Professor's curious sacrifice' (McLellan, 1990: 266).

This contradictory reaction to Weil's death nicely highlights a contradiction in the data I have discussed in this chapter. On the one hand, it indicates personal preoccupations, in conditions of abundance, with feeding and not feeding the body so as to maximize pleasure and health, improve appearance, and distinguish oneself from individuals in other cultures and classes. It also indicates our preoccupation as individuals, from earliest infancy, with fantasies about feeding and being fed. On the other hand, the data I have discussed also testifies to the importance of sociological and collective forces, as opposed to individual factors, conditioning what we eat. It demonstrates the persistence of gross inequalities between East and West, North and South, upper- and lower-class girls and boys, and women and men in what they can and cannot feed their bodies. As I said at the outset: our bodies are what we feed them, but everywhere differently so according to class, culture, and sex.

References

Abdullah, M. and Wheeler, E.F. (1985) Seasonal variations, and the intra-household distribution of food in a Bangladeshi village, *American Journal of Clinical Nutrition*, 41: 1305–1313.
Anon (1985) *Women: A World Report*, New York: Methuen.

APA (2000) Practice guideline for the treatment of patients with eating disorders (revision), *American Journal of Psychiatry (Supplement)* 157: 1–39.

Booth, C. (1902–1903) *Life and Labour of the People in London*, London: Macmillan.

Bordo, S. (1993) *Unbearable Weight*, Berkeley: University of California Press.

Bourdieu, P. (1984) *Distinction: A Social Critique of the Judgement of Taste*, London: Routledge.

Bruch, H. (1977) *The Golden Cage*, Cambridge, MA: Harvard University Press.

Busfield, J. (1996) *Men, Women and Madness*, Basingstoke: Macmillan.

Chatterjee, M. and Lambert, J. (1989) Women and nutrition, *Food and Nutrition Bulletin*, 11: 13–28.

Chaudhury, R.H. (1984) Determinants of dietary intake and dietary adequacy for pre-school children in Bangladesh, *Food and Nutrition Bulletin*, 6: 24–33.

Chen, L.C. et al. (1981) Sex bias in the allocation of food and health care in rural Bangladesh, *Population and Development Review*, 7: 55–70.

Cohn, N. (1986) By love possessed, *New York Review*, 30 January: 3–4.

Das Gupta, M. (1987) Selective discrimination against female children in rural Punjab, India, *Population and Development Review*, 13: 77–100.

Dowler, E. and Calvert, C. (1995) *Nutrition and Diet in Lone Parent Families in London*, London: Family Policy Studies Centre.

Evans, M. and Lee, E. (2002) *Real Bodies: A Sociological Introduction*, Basingstoke: Palgrave Macmillan, pp. 151–156.

Frank, A. (1991) For a sociology of the body, in M. Featherstone, M. Hepworth and B.S. Turner (eds), *The Body: Social Process and Cultural Theory*, London: Sage, pp. 36–102.

Gittelsohn, J. (1991) Opening the box: intrahousehold food allocation in rural Nepal, *Social Science and Medicine*, 33: 1141–1154.

Graham, H. (1993) *Hardship and Health in Women's Lives*, New York: Harvester Wheatsheaf.

Harriss, B. (1989) Excess female mortality and health care in South Asia, *Journal of Social Studies*, 44: 1–123.

Hepworth, J. (1999) *The Social Construction of Anorexia Nervosa*, London: Sage.

Jiggins, J. (1994) *Changing the Boundaries: Women-centered Perspectives on Population and the Environment*, Washington, DC: Island Press.

Levens, M. (1995) *Eating Disorders and Magical Control of the Body*, London: Routledge.

Lobstein, T. (1991) *The Nutrition of Women on Low Income*, London: London Food Commission.

McGuire, J.S. and Popkin, B.M. (1990) *Helping Women Improve Nutrition in the Developing World*, Washington, DC: World Bank.

McLellan, D. (1990) *Utopian Pessimist*, New York: Simon and Schuster.

Mennell, S. (1991) On the civilizing of appetite, in M. Featherstone, M. Hepworth and B.S. Turner (eds), *The Body: Social Process and Cultural Theory*, London: Sage.

Murcott, A. (1983) It's a pleasure to cook for him, in A. Murcott (ed.), *The Sociology of Food and Eating*, Aldershot: Gower.

Orbach, S. (1984) *Fat is a Feminist Issue*, London: Hamlyn.

Orbach, S. (1986) *Hunger Strike*, London: Faber and Faber.

Rousham, E. (1999) Gender bias in South Asia, in T.M. Pollard and S.B. Hyatt (eds), *Sex, Gender and Health*, Cambridge: Cambridge University Press.

Santow, G. (1995) Social roles and physical health, *Social Science and Medicine*, 40: 147–161.

Sayers, J. (1988) Anorexia, psychoanalysis, and feminism, *Journal of Adolescence*, 11: 361–371.

Seebohm Rowntree, B. (1902) *Poverty, A Study of Town Life*, London: Thomas Nelson.

Shilling, C. (1993) *The Body and Social Theory*, London: Sage.

Sours, J. (1980) *Starving to Death in a Sea of Objects*, New York: Aronson.

Turner, B. (1991) The discourse of diet, in M. Featherstone, M. Hepworth and B.S. Turner (eds), *The Body: Social Process and Cultural Theory*, London: Sage, pp. 157–169.

Turner, B. (1992) *Regulating Bodies: Essays in Medical Sociology*, London: Routledge.

UNICEF (1988) *The Lesser Child: The Girl in India*, New Delhi: UNICEF.

Wesley, J. (1791) *Primitive Physic*, Boston, MA: William M. Cornell, 1858.

4 Understanding obesity by understanding desire

Michael Gard

Introduction

Is 'obesity' an eating disorder? Keeping in mind that many people technically classified as obese eat no more than the rest of the population, we might begin answering this question by asking what it means for a person's eating to be 'disordered'. What constitutes 'normal' eating? How are ideas about 'normal' eating formed and to what extent are people culpable for the way they eat? If a person[1] freely and happily chooses to eat what is widely considered an inordinate amount of food, could their eating habits truly be described as 'disordered', and if so, why? Does the term 'disordered' merely indicate that a behaviour fails to conform to social convention rather than being an objective bio-medical health risk? After all, not all obese people are ill or die young. In addition, no discussion of these questions could avoid the ways in which gender relations shape ideas about 'normal' or 'desirable' body shapes and 'appropriate' eating habits.

There are those who argue that moving obesity from the realm of 'social deviancy' into a scientific medical framework will reduce the stigma that obese people endure and will lead to more efficacious solutions to the problems of obesity (Shell, 2002; Vogel, 1999). This chapter wrestles with this convergence of science and social convention in the field of obesity. The proposition that I will put forward is that the scientific study of obesity has delivered no straightforward answers to the questions posed above. This is true not because science itself is inherently evil or a particularly unreliable mode of enquiry; it is neither of these things. Rather, it is true because the nature of obesity – its causes and cures – are not, in the end, scientific matters. How we respond to obesity – what we think and do about it – will be matters of politics and social convention, not science, which is another way of saying that obesity is a moral issue.

---

1 Some argue that many 'obese' people are not in fact 'compulsive over-eaters' but claim that the assumption is nevertheless frequently made and is clearly prominent in understandings of 'obesity' (see also LeBesco, Throsby, both this volume). See also pp. 37–38.

Throughout this chapter I will use the term 'obesity' in the knowledge that its use and meaning are matters of ethical and theoretical dispute. I appreciate that other writers reject the term because of their desire to, amongst other things, de-medicalise fatness. However, my work as a social scientist has focused on engaging critically with the medico-scientific community on its own terms in order to change it. While I acknowledge and admire the work of fat activists, their politics are not my politics. My politics are the politics of knowledge about the scientific category of 'obesity', with all its shortcomings. In the context of this work it would be self-defeating to talk about fatness instead of obesity.

Trap doors and couch potatoes

I began researching obesity science nearly ten years ago because I had a hunch about the disjuncture between growing media comment about childhood obesity and the state of scientific knowledge. I knew that data existed about secular trends in children's physical activity levels and that these showed no obvious decline and, in some cases, showed increases (Pratt et al., 1999). And yet in the final years of the twentieth century, the idea of a 'couch-potato' generation of children was beginning to take root and would soon rapidly spread (e.g. Campbell, 2000; Powell, 2000).

This research produced two – at least for me – unexpected findings. First, in terms of exaggerated claims, hyperbolic language and apocalyptic predictions, there was often little to choose between journalists and scientists. This is not a field where scientists seemed likely to complain about a distorting or sensationalist media. In fact, scientists seemed to explicitly and strategically use doomsday language when speaking to the media in order to get policy makers to react in a certain way. For example, leading obesity scientists seem to have no misgivings whatsoever in equating the magnitude of the risks of obesity with that of global warming (CBS News, 2006). Second, I discovered that obesity science is a kind of Alice-in-Wonderland place where nothing is as it seems. It is a field in which leading researchers repeatedly concede an alarming lack of knowledge about even the most fundamental questions while, often within the same article, making bold and unsupported generalisations about the causes and cures for obesity (see, e.g., Bouchard and Blair, 1999). Part of the reason for this is the uncanny regularity with which 'common sense' ideas about body weight are overturned by research findings. Some examples are in order here.

In 1985 one of the founding figures of modern obesity research and 'obesity epidemic' rhetoric, William H. Dietz, co-authored a paper asking whether modern technology was producing a generation of lazy and overweight children (Dietz and Gortmaker, 1985). Over the next 20 years inconclusive findings were seen as being caused by methodological problems. However, a consensus is now emerging; while there is a low-to-moderate correlation between levels of technology-use and fatness in some (but by no means all) cultures, this appears to have almost nothing to do with physical activity levels (for example, Ekelund et al., 2006). Studies often find that technology use has no bearing on children's fitness or activity levels, and some even find that children who are most physically active are also the most devoted users of technology (for reviews of this literature, see Dugdale and Dixon, 2007; Gard and Wright, 2005; Gorely et al., 2004). Most researchers in this area seem now to concede, albeit grudgingly, that the presence of electronic entertainment in the home is no barrier to physical activity (Grant and Bassin, 2007).

Some experts predicted that the number and proximity of fast-food outlets to the family home would increase the likelihood of childhood obesity. But studies designed to test this idea find no such link (Cummins and Macintyre, 2006). Elsewhere, others suggested that declining levels of physical education or decreasing numbers of children walking to school might be to blame. Again, studies repeatedly find that physical education and walking to school have almost no impact on children's overall activity levels (e.g. Booth et al., 2002; Mallam et al., 2003). A recent study by Wilkin et al. (2006) studied the effect of television viewing, geographic location, school physical education, walking to school, availability of leisure facilities and social class and found that none of these factors seemed to affect children's total physical activity levels. In fact, remarkably, the authors question whether environment has any bearing on childhood physical activity at all. Whether readers are inclined to agree with this conclusion or not, my point here is the bewildering likelihood in this field of study that any apparently reasonable assumption will be contradicted by research findings.

To take an example that is particularly germane to this volume's concern with feminist thought, an enormous amount of research energy has gone into the 'girl problem'; the apparent and progressive disinterest of western adolescent girls in physical activity (Kimm et al., 2002). Some researchers have argued, not implausibly, that girls' consistently lower levels of fitness, physical activity and physical skill – compared with boys – is a pressing public health concern (e.g. Neumark-Sztainer et al., 2003). However, others tell us that western girls and women are less likely to be overweight or obese than their male compatriots (Mokdad et al., 2001) and more, not less, likely to be physically active as they grow older (Telema and Yang, 2000; Van Mechelen et al., 2000). If there is a problem associated with girls' relative disinterest in 'traditional', organised forms of physical activity, forms that often favour the 'traditional' interests and skills of boys, it is not clear what this problem is (see also Rice, this volume).

There is no respite from apparently counter-intuitive research findings if we turn to food. Research into average food consumption across the developed world shows declining levels of fat and total calorie intake since the 1920s (Rolland-Cachera and Bellisle, 2002), a well-known research finding that, nonetheless, is routinely overlooked in scientific journal articles and has generally stupefied journalists, academics and members of the public I have discussed this with over the last five years. So consistent and unsettling has this research finding been that many obesity experts simply dismiss it, arguing that food consumption and restraint have become significant markers of moral superiority in western cultures and, therefore, people lie or are simply incapable of accurately recalling the amount of food they eat (for example, see reviews by Hill and Peters (1998) and French et al. (2001); see also LeBesco, Throsby, both this volume).

In summary, my purpose so far has been to illustrate the field of obesity research as a series of trap doors, a field in which uncertainty and contradiction have made decisive and uncontroversial public policy virtually impossible.

The virus of modern life

One explanation for the uncertainty that dogs obesity science could be that quantitative experimental and quasi-experimental science is not well suited to studying a complex social phenomenon like rising western obesity. To take one final example from the obesity science literature, a recently published study (Christakis and Fowler, 2007) in the *New England Journal of Medicine* tracked the body weights of a cohort of 12,067 Americans over 30 years and found that a person's body weight was most likely to change as the body weight of their friends changed. The statistical effect of friends was much stronger than neighbours and parents and seemed to endure even when people moved to live in another part of the country. A *New York Times* (Kolata, 2007: 1) report of the study quoted other obesity researchers describing the work as 'path breaking', 'unique' and 'extraordinarily subtle and sophisticated' because of the way it pointed to a person-by-person, contagion-style spread of obesity across the United States.

From the point of view of a social scientist, it is difficult to see why this finding should seem so remarkable. People who study social processes know that close friends tend to share similar values, like similar things, behave in similar ways and follow similar social and cultural trends. After all, shared beliefs, tastes and behaviours are an important reason why people become friends in the first place and this probably applies as much to food and physical activity as it does to any other aspect of our lives. And while the study's authors seem to have been surprised to find that change in a person's body weight is more likely to be predicted by the body weight of close friends rather than immediate family, this too seems unremarkable. If, rather than body weight, the researchers had studied, say, tastes in fashion or music or levels of iPod usage, it is difficult to imagine that the results would have been qualitatively different. In other words, if a person's behaviour, and in particular *changes* in their behaviour, are similar to their closest friends, this is simply to say that we live in a social world, a social world in which peer groups are dominant and an important – perhaps the most important – conduit for social change. This is hardly news.

My point here is that obesity science has found its research methodologies ill-equipped to make sophisticated sense of the changing social worlds we inhabit. And while there is a risk of being overly uncharitable – it is no doubt unfair to expect one group of experts to produce exhaustive truths about complex bio-medical problems – obesity science has been resolute in its determination to see obesity as either, on the one hand, an impersonal bio-medical disease and contagion or, on the other, the deplorable personal moral failing of bad parents, lazy children and malevolent corporations. And while the words 'disease' or 'contagion' lack overt moral overtones, they do stoke the flames of 'crisis' and ratchet up the sense of impending doom.

How, though, might we think differently about obesity and, in particular, changing food behaviour? The historian Humphrey McQueen (2001) offers a useful starting point by examining the emergence of twentieth-century western food preferences. McQueen's general thesis relates to the birth of the modern corporation during the nineteenth and early twentieth centuries and its mutating effects on pre-existing forms of capitalism. Using Coca-Cola as his exemplar, he reminds us:

> Although our pleasure for sweetness rests in our physiology, *Homo sapiens* evolved without sugar in the form of sucrose. Food is oxidised to blood sugars but they are not sucrose, any more than we need the latter to produce the former. How far our liking for sugar is gratified and how we satisfy that longing depends on social and economic factors. Addiction to the sweet is a product of the last 200 years, just as the sweet things we consume are now corporate inventions. Americans guzzle fructose-heavy Classic Cokes, while Orientals decline to sweeten their tea.
>
> (ibid.: 286)

In unmistakably structuralist terms, McQueen argues that corporate capitalism has overridden human nature and created a 'second nature' made up of new needs and desires. This is interesting because there are mainstream medical researchers who argue that changing the way humans, but particularly children, eat will be difficult because we are biologically programmed to prefer sweet and salty foods (Schwartz and Puhl, 2003). This deterministic and static view overlooks McQueen's point that tastes have changed already and will continue to do so. Rather than our taste for certain levels of sugar and salt being 'hard wired', they exist in a feedback loop which includes the worldwide over-production of salt and sugar, new efficiencies in the way these products are shipped and stored and, perhaps most important of all, the enormous public relations and advertising campaigns that have sought to convince consumers that these products are indispensable, natural and highly desirable.

McQueen's 'second nature' argument is a useful starting point for moving beyond crudely medico-scientific understandings of obesity but it is not a satisfactory conclusion. Most obvious, its reliance on an unverifiable original human nature means that pre-Victorian European stock must stand for the whole of humanity despite the vast cultural variation in gastronomic preferences across time and space. But a more interesting problem with this argument is that it pathologises modern desires (see also Saukko, this volume). After all, what would be the point of drawing attention to a 'second nature' that produces strange new desires unless these desires are assumed to be inferior or even diseased versions of the real things?

Food and desire

It will be well understood by most readers of this volume that a generation of feminist and postmodernist scholarship has problematised the idea of establishing a set of essential human behaviours and qualities, apart from those most fundamental to physical survival. What, then, are the limits of our desires? What kinds of desires would qualify as 'unnatural' and where do desires come from anyway? At the risk of rushing to my conclusion, my point here is to cast doubt on the salience of categories like 'natural' and 'unnatural' or (*à la* McQueen) 'authentic' and 'fake' when it comes to human desires. This is because, as others have argued, desires are not things, but are rather meaning laden processes of communication embedded in discursive contexts (Lancaster, 2003). If this is right, human desire would be limited only by the physical ability of people to enact their desires, an unsettling prospect indeed for those who believe human morality and, closer to the concerns of this chapter, human health are relatively self-evident states of being. Let me explore this point further in the context of food.

That preparing, consuming and thinking about food are social processes is, I think, self-evident. Were they simply matters of brute survival, why would they manifest themselves with such variation? Although post-structuralism is perhaps the most recent, a number of social science traditions hold that the quality of all social processes depends on the ideas, words, emotions and concepts – what, for shorthand, I will call the 'discursive environment' – people use and are surrounded by (Griffiths and Wallace, 1998; Stacey, 1994).

Perhaps the most significant consequence of thinking about food in this way is that food behaviour can be seen as identity work; we relate to food in ways that say something about who we are and who we want to be. It is well documented that social class, gender, ethnicity and a range of other variables play a significant role in people's food choices (see also Sayers, this volume). For example, there is consistent research that women's role as the primary preparers and monitors of food in the home is changing only slowly in western countries (Murcott, 1998), while some contemporary researchers are still inclined to blame rising childhood obesity on mothers – not fathers – working out of the home (Banwell et al., 2007). Ethnographic research suggests that talk about food and dietary restraint is central to modern white 'girl culture' (Ambjörnsson, 2005; see, however, Bordo, Nasser and Malson, both this volume) and that boys and men are more easily able to access discourses that celebrate bigness and deflect public health pressure to show dietary restraint (Monoghan, 2007). But, as McQueen's work shows, ideas about who we are and want to be are constantly being offered to us by a range of formal and informal institutions like the media, corporations, governments, health authorities and peer groups. The recent history of western food consumption is also, in part, the history of consumer capitalism. From about the 1880s onwards, food was increasingly presented to consumers as an entrée into a particular kind of identity or lifestyle (Stearns, 1997; Sayers, this volume).

That our relationships with food (including foods we consume and refuse to consume) are an expression of individuality and choice is probably a more important point than the details of particular kinds of foods and particular identities. After all, the meaning of specific food types changes. What is more significant in our neo-liberal world is that the flipside of seeing food as an expression of individual freedom and choice is the idea that people are increasingly responsible, and therefore culpable, for their food choices. The discourse of culpability has been particularly resurgent as the panic of obesity has hit fever pitch in western countries (for an especially virulent example, see Esmail and Brown, 2005). In this discursive environment it is much easier for scholars, health authorities and moral conservatives alike to attack 'bad parents' (read 'bad mothers') and to advocate for social policies that punish the obese for their lack of nutritional self-discipline (see also Throsby, this volume). In fact, just as the case against the food production and marketing practices of 'Big Food' has been built by scholars (Nestle, 2002), investigative journalists (Schlosser, 2001) and other commentators (Hutton, 2002) eager to blame rising obesity on the excesses of capitalism, the response of their opponents has been to assert more strongly that nutrition and body weight are matters of individual responsibility and morality (Critser, 2003). In particular, the recent defeat of law suits brought against fast-food companies by obese people have generally been received in the media as victories for common sense and a rare vindication of the primacy of individual responsibility in a world all too happy to blame others for its own misfortunes (Holland, 2004).

In my view, what these debates exemplify is that western capitalisms produce an enduring and probably unavoidable discursive tension between consumption and restraint (see Eckermann, this volume). On the one hand, our economies and our lives are largely driven by the production of new desires and a constant flow of consumers for these desires. Many scholars argue that it is primarily through consumption that we construct our identities (for example, Bauman, 2004; Hamilton and Dennis, 2005) and there is an extensive literature concerning the construction of gendered bodies through consumer capitalism (e.g. Sceats, 2005; Tice, 2006). On the other hand, it is equally true that people's appetite for restraint – for refusing to consume – is a powerful discursive resource in the formation of modern identities and the moral calculus that surrounds food, physical activity and body weight. We should not forget that the pleasure of consuming 'bad' food is no more real than the pleasure of displaying virtuous restraint and self-control to others or oneself. There is clear evidence that similar things can be said about the pleasure of inactivity and the virtuous pleasures of being a person who exercises (Pronger, 2002).

In fact, my argument would be that not only have ideas about pleasure, restraint and self-control been obvious discursive tools in the creation and demarcation of gendered, racial, ethnic, economic and moral boundaries, the discourses of restraint and virtuous self-sacrifice have also played a key role in fomenting obesity hysteria. After all, in the face of equivocal evidence about the economic and medical consequences of rising obesity levels, the obese body has emerged discursively as a self-evident marker of individual moral failing, rampant desire and a society in decline. Our collective hatred of fatness has succeeded where the science has failed.

Conclusions

The 'obesity epidemic' is not a health crisis nor an economic crisis. What it is, is a sign that new forms of desire, pleasure and human embodiment are colliding with older moral codes that have not had time to change. 'Obesity' itself is a category that rests on arbitrary normative judgements about not only what a person should look like but also how they should conduct themselves. Talk of an 'obesity epidemic' and 'social contagions' fails to see that it is human embodiment, the things we feel about and desire for our own bodies, that is shifting; it also locates debate about obesity within a phoney moral universe. In most of my previous writing about obesity I have argued that a war on obesity is not worth fighting, but if fight we must, then it might help to remember that avoiding obesity is not only a matter of reining in desire. It is equally a matter of cultivating new desires.

References

Ambjörnsson, F. (2005) Talk, in D. Kulick and A. Meneley (eds), *Fat: The Anthropology of an Obsession*, New York: Jeremy P. Tarcher/Penguin.

Banwell, C., Shipley, M. and Strazdins, L. (2007) Sin#3: The pressured parenting environment: parents as piggy in the middle, in J. Dixon and D.H. Broom (eds), *The Seven Deadly Sins of Obesity: How the Modern World is Making Us Fat*, Sydney: UNSW Press.

Bauman, Z. (2004) *Wasted Lives: Modernity and its Outcasts*, Cambridge: Polity Press.

Booth, M.L., Okely, A.D., Chey, T., Bauman, A.E. and Macaskill, P. (2002)

Epidemiology of physical activity participation among New South Wales school students, *Australian and New Zealand Journal of Public Health*, 26(4): 371–374.

Bouchard, C. and Blair, S.N. (1999) Introductory comments for the consensus on physical activity and obesity, *Medicine and Science in Sports and Exercise*, 31(Suppl.11): S498–S501.

Campbell, D. (2000) Schools rear crop of couch potatoes, *The Observer*, 27 February, p. 6.

CBS News (2006) 'Obesity an 'international scourge', at: www.cbsnews.com/stories/ 2006/09/03/health/main1962961.shtml.

Christakis, N.A. and Fowler, J.H. (2007) The spread of obesity in a large social network over 32 years, *New England Journal of Medicine*, 357(4): 370–379.

Critser, G. (2003) *Fat Land: How Americans Became the Fattest People in the World*, Harmondsworth: Penguin.

Cummins, S. and Macintyre, S. (2006) Food environments and obesity – neighbourhood or nation?, *International Journal of Epidemiology*, 35(1): 100–104.

Dietz, W.H. and Gortmaker, S.L. (1985) Do we fatten our children at the television set? Obesity and television viewing in children and adolescents, *Pediatrics*, 75(5): 807–812.

Dugdale, A. and Dixon, J. (2007) Sin#4: The technological environment: digital technologies or space to play (up) and belong?, in J. Dixon and D.H. Broom (eds), *The Seven Deadly Sins of Obesity: How the Modern World is Making Us Fat*, Sydney: UNSW Press.

Ekelund, U., Brage, S., Froberg, K., Harro, M., Anderssen, S.A., Sardinha, L.B., Riddoch, C. and Andersen, L.B. (2006) TV viewing and physical activity are independently associated with metabolic risk in children: the European Youth Heart Study, *PLoS Medicine*, 3(12): 2449–2456.

Esmail, N. and Brown, J. (2005) The wrong defense for tackling obesity, *The Fraser Institute*, at: www.fraserinstitute.ca/shared/readmore1.asp?sNav=ed&id=352.

French, S.A., Story, M. and Jeffery, R.W. (2001) Environmental influences on eating and physical activity, *Annual Review of Public Health*, 22: 309–335.

Gard, M. and Wright, J. (2005) *The Obesity Epidemic: Science, Morality and Ideology*, London: Routledge.

Gorely, T., Marshall, S.J. and Biddle, S.J.H. (2004) Couch kids: correlates of television viewing amoung youth, *International Journal of Behavioral Medicine*, 11(3): 152–163.

Grant, B.C. and Bassin, S. (2007) The challenge of paediatric obesity: more rhetoric than action, *New Zealand Medical Journal*, 120(1260): 61–68.

Griffiths, S. and Wallace, J. (eds) (1998) *Consuming Passions: Food in the Age of Anxiety*, Manchester: Mandolin.

Hamilton, C. and Dennis, R. (2005) *Affluenza. When Too Much is Never Enough*, Crows Nest: Allen and Unwin.

Hill, J.O. and Peters, J.C. (1998) Environmental contributions to the obesity epidemic, *Science*, 280(5368): 1371–1374.

Holland, J. (2004) Fat chance to sue food chains in cheeseburger bill, *Sydney Morning Herald*, 6 March, p. 15.

Hutton, W. (2002) Fat is a capitalist issue, *The Observer*, 27 January, p. 30.

Kimm, S.Y.S., Glynn, N.W., Kriska, A.M., Barton, B.A., Kronsberg, S.S., Daniels, S.R., Crawford, P.B., Sabry, Z.I. and Liu, K. (2002) Decline in physical activity in black girls and white girls during adolescence, *New England Journal of Medicine*, 347(10): 709–715.

Kolata, G. (2007) Find yourself packing it on? Blame friends, *New York Times*, 26 July, p. 1.

Lancaster, R.N. (2003) *The Trouble with Nature: Sex in Science and Popular Culture*, Berkeley: University of California Press.

Mallam, K.M., Metcalf, B.S., Kirkby, J., Voss, L.D. and Wilkin, T.J. (2003) Contribution of timetabled physical education to total physical activity in primary school children: cross-sectional study, *British Medical Journal*, 327(7415): 592–593.

McQueen, H. (2001) *The Essence of Capitalism: The Origins of Our Future*, Sydney: Sceptre.

Mokdad, A.H., Bowman, B.A., Ford, E.S., Vinicor, F., Marks, J.S. and Koplan, J.P. (2001) The continuing epidemics of obesity and diabetes in the United States, *Journal of the American Medical Association*, 286(10): 1195–1200.

Monoghan, L.F. (2007) Body Mass Index, masculinities and moral worth: men's critical understandings of 'appropriate' weight-for-height, *Sociology of Health and Illness*, 29(4): 584–609.

Murcott, A. (ed.) (1998) *The Nation's Diet: The Social Science of Food Choice*, London: Longman.

Nestle, M. (2002) *Food Politics: How the Food Industry Influences Nutrition and Health*, Berkeley: University of California Press.

Neumark-Sztainer, D., Story, M., Hannan, P.J., Tharp T. and Rex, J. (2003) Factors associated with changes in physical activity: a cohort study of inactive adolescent girls, *Archives of Pediatrics and Adolescent Medicine*, 157(8): 803–810.

Powell, S. (2000) One in four Australian children is overweight. Slower, stiffer, heavier – they are the cotton-wool generation, *Weekend Australian*, 27–28 May, pp. 6–8.

Pratt, M., Macera, C.A. and Blanton, C. (1999) Levels of physical activity and inactivity in children and adults in the United States: current evidence and research issues, *Medicine and Science in Sports Exercise*, 31(11 Suppl): S526–S533.

Pronger, B. (2002) *Body Fascism: Salvation in the Technology of Physical Fitness*, Toronto: University of Toronto Press.

Rolland-Cachera, M.F. and Bellisle, F. (2002) Nutrition, in W. Burniat, T. Cole, I. Lissau and E. Poskitt (eds), *Child and Adolescent Obesity: Causes and Consequences, Prevention and Management*, Cambridge: Cambridge University Press.

Sceats, S. (2005) *Food, Consumption and the Body in Contemporary Women's Fiction*, Cambridge: Cambridge University Press.

Schlosser, E. (2001) *Fast Food Nation: What the All-American Meal is Doing to the World*, London: Allen Lane.

Schwartz, M.B. and Puhl, R. (2003) Childhood obesity: a societal problem to solve, *Obesity Reviews*, 4(1): 57–71.

Shell, E.R. (2002) *The Hungry Gene: The Science of Fat and the Future of Thin*, New York: Atlantic Monthly Press.

Stacey, M. (1994) *Why Americans Love, Hate and Fear Food*, New York: Simon and Schuster.

Stearns, P.N. (1997) *Fat History: Bodies and Beauty in the Modern West*, New York: New York University Press.

Telama, R. and Yang, X. (2000) Decline of physical activity from youth to young adulthood in Finland, *Medicine and Science in Sports and Exercise*, 32(9): 1617–1622.

Tice, K.W. (2006) For appearance's sake: beauty, bodies, spectacle, and consumption, *Journal of Women's History*, 18(4): 147–156.

Vogel, S. (1999) *The Skinny on Fat: Our Obsession with Weight Control*, New York: W.H. Freeman and Company.

Van Mechelen, W., Twisk, J.W.R., Post, G.B., Snel, J. and Kemper, H.C.G. (2000) Physical activity of young people: the Amsterdam Longitudinal Growth and Health Study, *Medicine and Science in Sports and Exercise*, 32(9): 1610–1616.

Wilkin, T.J., Mallam, K.M., Metcalf, B.S., Jeffrey, A.N. and Voss, L.D. (2006) Variation in physical activity lies with the child, not his environment: evidence for an 'activitystat' in young children (EarlyBird 16), *International Journal of Obesity*, 30(7): 1050–1055.

5   Not just 'a white girl's thing'

The changing face of food and body image problems

Susan Bordo

When you think of eating disorders, whom do you picture?

If your images of girls and women with eating and body image problems have been shaped by *People* magazine and *Lifetime* movies, she's probably white, heterosexual, North American, and economically secure. If you're familiar with the classic psychological literature on eating disorders, you may also have read that she's an extreme 'perfectionist' with a hyper-demanding mother, and that she suffers from 'body-image distortion syndrome' and other severe perceptual and cognitive problems that 'normal' girls don't share. You probably don't picture her as Black, Asian, or Latina. Consider, then, Tenisha Williamson. Tenisha is black, suffers from anorexia, and has described her struggle on 'Colors of Ana,' a website specifically devoted to the stories of non-white women dealing with eating and body image problems. Tenisha, who was raised believing that it was a mark of racial superiority that Black women are comfortable with larger bodies, feels like a traitor to her race. 'From an African-American stand-point,' she writes, 'we as a people are encouraged to "embrace our big, voluptuous bodies." This makes me feel terrible because *I don't want a big, voluptuous body!* I would rather die from starvation than gain a single pound' (Colors of Ana, http:colorsofana.com//ss8.asp).

Also on the 'Colors of Ana' site is the story of 15-year-old Sami Schalk. Sami is biracial, and attended a virtually all-white grade school: 'At school, stick-skinny models were the norm,' she writes, 'and I was quickly convinced that my curves and butt weren't beautiful. Instead of seeking help, I turned to binge and emotional eating, and at around 11 years old began purging after I ate' (ibid.). When Sami's mom finally took her to a doctor, he put her on a 'safer' diet. The diet only made Sami gain more weight – which in turn led to diet pills and laxative abuse.

Eighteen-year-old Jun Sasaki's eating problems developed after her father was transferred from Japan to the United States. Sasaki, who like many Japanese girls was naturally slim, did not have a problem until one day, when she was 12, a friend hit her slightly protruding stomach playfully and said, 'You look like you're pregnant.' Jun was appalled. She intended at first to lose only a few pounds, but when she began to receive compliments from friends and neighbors, she started a regime of 800 calories a day. Ultimately, as Jun describes it, she lost the ability to 'eat normally.' 'I ate from day to night, searching for every piece of food in the house, consuming every piece of fat I could find. I was never hungry, but I ate, I ate and ate and ate' (ibid.).

As someone who has tracked the world of popular culture for the last 25 years, I'm not surprised to see that clinicians are seeing more and more ethnic, racial, and sexual diversity among their anorexic patients (see Renfrew Center Foundation for Eating Disorders, 2003; see also Franko et al., 2007, for discussion of statistics). When I wrote *Unbearable Weight* (1993) however – one of the first multi-dimensional, interdisciplinary studies to take a cultural approach to eating problems (see also pp. 51–52 below for a summary of my arguments) – I was virtually alone in viewing eating and body image problems as belonging to anyone except privileged, heterosexual white girls.

Where did this idea come from? Several factors played a role

As with many other scientific and social-scientific explanations of various disorders, the first paradigms for understanding eating problems were based on populations that were extremely skewed, both in terms of race and in terms of class. Most of the initial clinical data came from the treatment of white, middle- and upper middle-class patients (see also Saukko, this volume). They were the first ones to seek out treatment; the ones with the money to do so; the ones with the cultural support for doing so. And so, the way their eating problems presented themselves became the standard – of diagnosis, profiling, and explanation. This, of course, resulted in a very limited picture. Most of these patients were brought in by their parents, which meant that the problem had become desperate – which is to say, among other things, highly visible, and an enormous source of family struggle. Emaciated, refusing to eat in circumstances of plenty, often engaged in fierce battles with parents at dinner-time, these girls presented with what would become stamped in many people's mind as a rich, spoiled, white girl's disease: anorexia nervosa.

From this initial paradigm, a number of ideas about eating problems flowed. Dysfunctional family dynamics began to be defined as paradigmatic of eating disorders. So did physical, perceptual, and psychological criteria that reflected the extreme nature of the classical anorexic syndrome. Emaciation. Never seeing oneself as thin enough, even when skeletal – a perceptual distortion that came to be picked up in the popular media as the hallmark of this 'bizarre' disease. An 'addiction to perfection'. And so on.

Who was left out of this picture? For one thing, the many young college women, of all races and ethnicities, who looked just fine, but were privately throwing up and abusing laxatives regularly to keep their weight under control. Ultimately, this type of disordered eating became better known. But because of the dominant anorexic paradigm, within which binging and purging was subsumed as a variant – called bulimia nervosa – clinicians failed to see how normative such behavior had become. More than half of all college girls were doing it; and it was still conceptualized as a 'disease' to which only certain kinds of young women – with the expected family profile, 'anorexic thinking,' 'body image distortion syndrome,' and so on – were vulnerable.

Also left out of the picture were the growing numbers of young black women who were struggling with body-image issues. Early research *had* shown a much lower incidence of eating disorders among African American women, and both black women *and* black men, in interviews and studies, have consistently expressed distaste for the hyper-skinny models that many anorexics emulate. From this, many specialists postulated that black women were permanently 'immune' to eating problems. The conclusion was based on a perspective that viewed eating problems as cast in an unchanging mold, rather than the dynamic and shape-shifting phenomena that we have witnessed over the past decade, as more voluptuous styles of bodily beauty that had been excluded from the dominant culture have gained ascendancy, due to the popularity of stars such as Beyonce Knowles and Jennifer Lopez. As video director, Little X, maintains, 'Black folks . . . now have influence, and we're able to set a new standard of beauty. We've flipped the mirror. The old standard of the superskinny white woman doesn't really apply.'

The new standards, however, can be equally self-punishing, and have expanded the repertoire of eating problems from starvation diets and the dream of a body as slender as a reed, to exercise addictions and the dream of a body that is curvaceous but rigorously toned. Probably more college girls today – of *all* races and ethnicities – aspire to some version of this body than they do to the hyper-skinny body. Here, the rise of the female athlete as beauty icon has played as significant a role as racial aesthetics. Ours is now a culture in which our sports superstars are no longer just tiny gymnasts but powerful soccer and softball players, broad-shouldered track stars: Mia Hamm, Sarah Walden, Marion Jones, Serena Williams. It's also a culture, however, in which female athletes are presented as sex goddesses by Nike and *Vogue*, their muscular bodies feminized and trivialized, turned into fashion accessories and erotic magnets for male eyes. The young girls who emulate these bodies are 'passing' – they look great and many may seem to be eating healthfully, too. It's hard to see that there's anything wrong. But the hours spent at the gym are excessive, and when the girls miss a day they are plunged into deep depression. Their sense of self-acceptance, although you can't tell just from looking, in fact hangs on a very slender thread.

In believing Black, Latina, and other ethnicities to be 'immune,' the medical literature often conflated class and race. Poor people didn't get eating disorders – so how could black people get eating disorders, they reasoned – fallaciously. For of course there are plenty of young black women who come from privileged families, attend private schools, and are subjected to the same competitive pressures as their white counterparts – a fact which slipped by those eating disorders specialists who declared eating problems to be 'virtually unknown' in their homogeneous notion of 'the black community.'

Some also may have been unconsciously influenced by the image of the plump, maternal Mammy as the prototype of black womanhood. Only Scarlet has to worry about fitting into a corset; mammy's job is to cook the fried chicken and lace her baby in. Her own girth is of no consequence – she has no romantic life of her own; her body exists only to provide comfort. Does this sound like a relic of a time long gone? In an article in *Essence*, Retha Powers (1989) describes how she went to her high-school guidance counselor, seeking help managing her weight, and was told she shouldn't worry because 'black women aren't seen as sex objects.' It's highly unlikely, of course, that such a comment would be made today in the era of Beyonce and L'il Kim, but many people *do* still believe that just because a woman is black, she has greater cultural permission to be large. Here, generational as well as class differences are being ignored – differences that are highlighted in a piece by Sirena Riley (2002: 358–359):

> As a teenager, I remember watching a newsmagazine piece on a survey comparing black and white women's body satisfaction. When asked to describe the 'perfect woman,' white women said she'd be about five foot ten, less than 120 pounds, blond and so on. Black women described this ideal woman as intelligent, independent and self-confident, never mentioning her looks. After the survey results were revealed . . . the white women stood, embarrassed and humiliated that they could be so petty and shallow. They told stories of starving themselves before dates and even before sex. The black women were aghast! What the hell were these white women talking about?
>
> I was so proud . . . Black women being praised on national television! There they were telling the whole country that their black men loved the 'extra meat on their bones.' Unfortunately, my pride also had a twinge of envy. In my own experience, I couldn't quite identify with either the black women or the white women.
>
> Raised by a single mother, independence was basically in my blood. But in a neighborhood of successful, often bourgeois black families, it was obvious that the 'perfect woman' was smart, pretty and certainly not overweight. As a child, no one loved the 'extra meat' on my bones. I was eight years old when I first started exercising to Jane Fonda and the cadre of other leotard-clad fitness gurus. I now have a sister around that age, and when I look at her and realize how young that is, it breaks my heart that I was so concerned about weight back then.

[. . .] If we really want to start talking more honestly about all women's relationships with our bodies, we need to start asking the right questions. Just because women of color aren't expressing their body dissatisfaction in the same way as heterosexual, middle-class white women, it doesn't mean that everything is hunky-dory and we should just move on. If we are so sure that images of rail-thin fashion models, actresses and video chicks have contributed to white girls' poor body image, why aren't we addressing the half-naked black female bodies that have replaced the half-naked white female bodies on MTV?

Also left out of the 'anorexic paradigm' were compulsive or binge eaters who do *not* purge, or whose repeated attempts to diet are unsuccessful. To have an 'eating disorder,' according to the anorexic paradigm, means being thin – and since most compulsive eaters are overweight, it took a long time for clinicians to recognize that compulsive eaters, too, are suffering from an eating disorder. Class bias played a role here, too, for a growing body of research has shown that people who have gained the most weight in the last decade – and the largest population of bingers – have tended to have the lowest incomes. The reasons, once you know them, make enormous sense: people who work long, hard hours have little time or energy for cooking, and feeding a family at McDonald's, although it may not be the most nutritious way to go, is the most affordable alternative for many people. Processed foods rich in sugar and fat are now far cheaper than fresh fruits and vegetables. In the ads, they beckon with the promise of pleasure, good times, and satisfaction, to lives which have very little of those in any other domain.

I include myself among compulsive eaters. Although I have never binged to the degree of excess represented in media depictions of bulimics, I, like many women, especially those from cultures for whom food represents comfort, safety, home – Black women, Jewish women, Latinas – often find myself unable to control my end-of-day longings to be soothed and pleasured by food. I may not empty the cupboards, but as I watch late night junk-television, my daughter asleep and my immediate pressures dealt with, every commercial becomes a cue to leap up and go to the kitchen. My choices are benign at first – a slice of rolled up lo-fat ham, some leftover tabouli, fat-free chips. Then, a slice of fat-free cheese makes its way into the ham roll-up. I have a couple of those, dipped in honey mustard. Fat free or not, cheese is a trigger for me; soon I am microwaving it with salsa, and dipping the chips, then my fingers, into it. The creaminess unhinges me, and I'm at the freezer, after the Edy's slow-churned (50 percent less fat) French silk ice cream. I eat so much of it that 'less fat' becomes laughable; by the next commercial my rational mind has been put fully on hold. I sprint into my office, open my desk drawer, and make it back to my chair with the chocolate truffles that I bought for my daughter's teacher.

Probably the most significant factor, however, in the failure to conceptualize eating problems in an inclusive way has been ignorance of (or, in some cases, resistance to acknowledging) the awesome power of cultural imagery. Fiji is a striking example of that power. Because of their remote location, the Fiji islands did not have access to television until 1995, when a single station was introduced. It broadcasts programs from the United States, the UK, and Australia. Until that time, Fiji had no reported cases of eating disorders, and a study conducted by anthropologist Anne Becker (Becker et al., 2002, reported in Snyderman, 2002: 84; Becker, 2004) showed that most Fijian girls and women, no matter how large, were comfortable with their bodies (see also Nasser and Malson, this volume). In 1998, just three years after the station began broadcasting, 11 percent of girls reported vomiting to control weight, and 62 percent of the girls surveyed reported dieting during the previous months. Becker was surprised by the change; she had thought that Fijian cultural traditions, which celebrate eating and favor voluptuous bodies, would 'withstand' the influence of media images. Becker hadn't yet understood that we live in an empire of images, and that there are no protective borders.

Asia is another example. Among the members of audiences at my talks, Asian women had for years been among the most insistent that eating and body image weren't problems for their people, and indeed, my initial research showed that eating disorders were virtually unknown in Asia. But when, a few years ago, a Korean translation of *Unbearable Weight* was published, and several translations of chapters appeared in Chinese publications (a Chinese edition of the book is currently in preparation), I felt I needed to revisit the situation. I discovered multiple reports (see also Nasser and Malson, this volume) on dramatic increases in eating disorders in China, South Korea, and Japan. Eunice Park, in *Asian Week* magazine, writes: 'As many Asian countries become Westernized and infused with the Western aesthetic of a tall, thin, lean body, a virtual tsunami of eating disorders has swamped Asian countries' (reported in Rosenthal, 1999).

The spread of eating problems, of course, is not just about aesthetics. Rather, as I argued in *Unbearable Weight*, the emergence of eating disorders is a complex, multilayered cultural 'symptom,' reflecting problems that are historical as well as contemporary, accelerating in our time because of the confluence of a number of factors. Eating problems, as I theorize them, are overdetermined in this culture. They have not only to do with new social expectations of women and the resulting ambivalence toward the plush, maternal body, but also with more general anxieties about the body as the source of hungers, needs, and physical vulnerabilities not within our control. These anxieties are deep and long-standing in western philosophy and religion, and they are especially acute in our own time. Eating problems are also linked to the contradictions of consumer culture (see also Gard, this volume), which continually encourages us to binge on our desires at the same time as it glamorizes self-discipline and scorns fat as a symbol of laziness and lack of willpower. And they reflect, too, our increasing 'postmodern' fascination with the possibilities of reshaping our bodies in radical ways, creating new selves that are unlimited by our genetic inheritance.

The relationship between problems such as these and cultural images is complex (see also Part III, this volume). On the one hand, the idealization of certain kinds of bodies foments and perpetuates our anxieties and insecurities – that's clear. But, on the other hand, such images carry fantasized solutions *to* our anxieties and insecurities, and that's part of the reason why they are powerful. As I argued in *Twilight Zones* (1997), cultural images are never 'just pictures,' as the fashion magazines continually maintain (disingenuously) in their own defense. They speak to young people not just about how to be beautiful but also about how to become what the dominant culture admires, values, rewards. They tell them how to be cool, 'get it together,' overcome their shame. To girls and young women who have been abused they may offer a fantasy of control and invulnerability, and immunity from pain and hurt. For racial and ethnic groups whose bodies have been deemed 'foreign,' earthy, and primitive, and considered unattractive by Anglo-Saxon norms, they may cast the lure of being accepted by the dominant culture. And it is images, too, that teach us how to *see*, that educate our vision in what is a defect and what is *normal*, that give us the models against which our own bodies and the bodies of others are measured. Perceptual pedagogy: 'How To Interpret Your Body 101.' It's become a global requirement.

A good example, both of the power of perceptual pedagogy and of the deeper meaning of images is the case of Central Africa. There, traditional cultures still celebrate voluptuous women. In some regions, brides are sent to fattening farms, to be plumped and massaged into shape for their wedding night. In a country plagued by AIDS, the skinny body has meant – as it used to among Italian, Jewish, and Black Americans – poverty, sickness, death. 'An African girl must have hips,' says dress designer, Frank Osodi, 'We have hips. We have bums. We like flesh in Africa.' For years, Nigeria sent its local version of beautiful to the Miss World Competition. The contestants did very poorly. Then a savvy entrepreneur went against local ideals and entered Agbani Darego, a light-skinned, hyper-skinny beauty. Agbani Darego won the Miss World Pageant, the first black African to do so. Now, Nigerian teenagers fast and exercise, trying to become 'lepa' – a popular slang phrase for the thin 'it' girls that are all the rage. Said one: 'People have realized that slim is beautiful' (Onishi, 2002).

It's incorrect, however, to imagine that this is simply about beauty. When I presented the example at a college whose faculty included a Nigerian, she pointed out that Nigerian girls were dieting well before Agbani Darego won her crown, and that, in her opinion, the allure of western body ideals had to do primarily with the rejection of traditional identities and the system of male dominance that they were anchored in. It was for men, she explained, that Nigerian women were encouraged to be full-bottomed, for men that they were often sent to fattening farms to be plumped into shape for the wedding night. Now, modern young women were insisting on the right of their bodies to be less voluptuous, less domestically 'engineered' for the sexual pleasure and comfort of men. Hearing this was fascinating and illuminating. Here was a major similarity in the 'deep' meaning of slenderness for both the young Nigerian dieters and the first generation of (twentieth-century) anorexics in this country. Many of them, like the young Nigerian women, were also in rebellion against a voluptuous, male-oriented, sexualized ideal – that of the post-World War II generation (see also Saukko, this volume). Significant numbers of them had been sexually abused, or witnessed their mothers being treated badly. To be a soft sexual plaything, a Marilyn Monroe, was their horror; Kate Moss and others (like Agbani Darego for the young Nigerians) provided an alternative cultural paradigm to aspire to.

Clearly, body insecurity can be exported, imported, and marketed – just like any other profitable commodity. In this respect, what's happened with men and boys is illustrative. Ten years ago men tended, if anything, to see themselves as better looking than they (perhaps) actually were. And then the menswear manufacturers, the diet industries, and the plastic surgeons 'discovered' the male body (see Bordo, 1999). And now, young guys are looking in their mirrors, finding themselves soft and ill defined, no matter how muscular they are. Now they are developing the eating and body image disorders that we once thought only girls had. Now they are abusing steroids, measuring their own muscularity against the oiled and perfected images of professional athletes, body-builders, and *Men's Health* models.

Let me be clear here. I've got nothing against beautiful, toned, bodies. I also realize that many people come by their slenderness naturally, by virtue of genetics, and that not all models are anorexics. Nor am I anti-fitness. I know that I am happier and healthier when I'm exercising regularly and trim enough to feel comfortable and confident in the form-fitting clothes that I like to wear when my husband and I, who have been doing ballroom dancing for three years, do our rumbas and mambos. The issue for me is not fat versus fitness, but moderation, realism and appreciation of human diversity versus the excesses, the obsessions, the unrealistic expectations that make people sick and treat others as cultural pariahs. Unfortunately, it's the extremes, excesses, and obsessions that our culture fosters. It's a breeder of disorder.

In 2009, I would think this should be obvious. And yet, the prevailing medical wisdom about eating disorders has failed, over and over, to acknowledge, finally and decisively, that we are dealing here with a *cultural* problem. Initially, in the early 1980s, when I first began attending conferences on the subject, eating disorder specialists were very grudging – and most designers and fashion magazine editors in downright denial, and still are – about the role played by cultural images in the spread of eating and body image problems (see Bordo, 1997, 2004). In the early 1990s, when Kate Moss and Calista Flockhart were in ascendancy, we saw a brief flurry of accusations against the fashion industry and the media. But astonishingly (or perhaps predictably), the more indisputable the evidence of the central role played by culture, the more the medical focus has drifted toward genetic and bio-chemical explanations – as, for example, in this *Newsweek* story on anorexia:

> In the past decade, psychiatrists have begun to see surprising diversity among their anorexic patients. Not only are [they] younger, they're also more likely to be black, Hispanic or Asian, more likely to be boys, more likely to be middle-aged. All of which caused doctors to question their core assumption: if anorexia isn't a disease of A-type girls from privileged backgrounds, then what is it? Although no one can yet say for certain, new science is offering tantalizing clues. Doctors now compare anorexia to alcoholism and depression . . . diseases that may be set off by environmental factors such as stress or trauma, but have their roots in a complex combination of genes and brain chemistry. . . . The environment 'pulls the trigger,' says Cynthia Bulik, director of the eating-disorder program at the University of North Carolina at Chapel Hill. But it's a child's latent vulnerabilities that 'load' the gun.
>
> (Tyre, 2005)

It doesn't make sense; you have to torture logic to come to this conclusion. But although logic is tortured, the empire of images is let off the hook; the culture is merely a 'trigger'; 'it's the child's latent vulnerabilities that load the gun.' Well, I don't buy it. I'd put it this way instead: 'Some studies show that genetic vulnerabilities may play a role in which children develop the most serious forms of eating problems. But the incredible spread of these problems to extraordinarily diverse groups of genetic populations, over a strikingly short period of time, and coincident with the mass globalization of media imagery, strongly suggests that culture is the "smoking gun" that is killing people, and that the situation will not change until the culture does.'

What do I mean by 'the culture'? I mean many things. 'Culture' includes those who made the decision to present an actress like Tony Collete as the 'fat sister' in the otherwise charming film, *In Her Shoes*. Collette gained 25 pounds for that role, and even so, there's nothing remotely fat about her body in the movie. 'Culture' includes directors like David Kelley, who pressure their actresses into losing weight (see Gumbel, 2000; Keck, 2000; Van Meter, 2006). 'Culture' includes the manufacturers of Barbie who, despite a brief flurry of interest some years back in making a more 'realistic' body for the doll, are now making her skinnier than ever. 'Culture' includes those companies that would have us believe that computer-generated thighs are ours for the price of a jar of cellulite control cream. 'Culture' includes

Men's Health magazine, and all the merchandisers and advertisers who have suddenly recognized that men can be induced to worry about their bodies, too (see Bordo, 1999). 'Culture' includes the contradictory and extreme messages we are constantly receiving about eating, dieting, and fitness. Open most magazines and you'll see them side-by-side. On the one hand, ads for luscious – and usually highly processed – foods, urging us to give in, let go, indulge. On the other hand, the admonitions of the exercise and fitness industries – to get in shape, get it together, prove you've got willpower, show that you have the right stuff. And don't settle for mere cardiovascular fitness, but insist on the sculpted body of your dreams – go for the gold, make it your new religion, your life. It's easy to see why so many of us experience our lives as a tug-of-war between radically conflicting messages, and why it's not a 'paradox,' as it is often represented, that we have an epidemic of obesity alongside increases in anorexia, bulimia and exercise addictions in this culture.

'Culture,' is, of course, the fashion industry. The average model is 5'10" and weighs 107 pounds; the average American woman is 5'4" and weighs 143 pounds. With a gap like this, it's a set up for the development of eating disorders, as girls and women try to achieve bodies that their genetics, for the most part, just won't support. It's true that more and more merchandisers are beginning to realize that there are lots of size 12 and over girls and women out there, with money to spend, who will respond positively to ad campaigns that celebrate our bodies. But as potentially transformative images, campaigns that single us out as 'special' still mark us as outside the dominant norms of beauty, requiring special accommodation.

What we need, instead, is a transformation similar to what has been going on in the world of children's movies and books, which have normalized racial diversity far more consistently and strikingly than their adult counterparts. Disney's *Cinderella*, for example, without presenting it as remarkable in any way, has Whoopi Goldberg and Victor Garber – a white actor – married, as the queen and king; their son is Asian. Brandi plays Cinderella; her mother is Bernadette Peters. One of her stepsisters is black and the other is white. This is a movie that tells my Cassie, the biracial daughter of two white parents, that there is nothing unusual or improbable about her own family. From this, and from many of her books, she's learned that families are made in many different ways, and that looking like each other is not a prerequisite for loving each other. I would like to see a visual world that will tell her, similarly, that healthy bodies are made in many different ways, and that looking like Beyonce or Halle Berry – or even Marion Jones – is not a prerequisite for loving oneself. A world in which voluptuous models are not only found in 'Lane Bryant' and 'Just My Size' ads.

Unfortunately, and with a few notable exceptions – such as Dove's Campaign for Real Beauty, for example, and the brave, and quite unique, resistance of teenage television fashionista Raven Simone – instead of this happening, I'm seeing a lot of backsliding among once-progressive forces. *Essence* and *Oprah* magazine used to have fashion spreads that featured a range of bodies; they hardly ever do anymore. In 2002, *YM* magazine, an up-beat fashion magazine for teen readers, conducted a survey that revealed that 86 percent of its young readers were dissatisfied with the way their bodies looked. New editor, Christina Kelley, immediately announced an editorial policy against the publishing of diet-pieces and said *YM* would henceforth deliberately seek out full-size models for all its fashion spreads (www.womensnews.org/article.cfm/dyn/aid/833/context/journalistofthemonth; Carmichael, 2002. For an interview with Christina Kelley, see NPR, 2002). It hasn't.

'The culture' includes parents, too. A study in the *Journal of the American Dietetic Associations* found that five-year-old girls whose mothers dieted were twice as likely to be aware of dieting and weight-loss strategies as girls whose mothers didn't diet (Abramovitz and Birch, 2000). 'It's like trying on Mom's high heels,' says Carolyn Costin, spokeswoman for the National Eating Disorders Association, 'They're trying on their diets, too' (Choi, 2006). But this is even to put it too benignly. 'Self-deprecating remarks about bulging thighs or squealing with delight over a few lost pounds can send the message that thinness is to be prized above all else,' says Alison Field (Field et al., 2001), lead author of another study, from Harvard, that found that girls with mothers who had weight concerns were more likely to develop anxieties about their own bodies.

I've been guilty of this. A lifelong dieter, I've tried to explain to my eight-year-old daughter that the word diet doesn't necessarily mean losing weight to look different, but eating foods that are good for you, to make your body more healthy. But the lectures paled beside the pleasure I radiated as I looked at my shrinking body in the mirror, or my depression when I gained it back, or my overheard conversations with my friend Althea, about the difficulties we were facing, as a Jewish and Black woman respectively, who had habitually used food for comfort. When Cassie saw me eat a bowl of ice cream and asked me if I wrote down my points, I knew she understood exactly what was going on.

So far, Cassie has not yet entered the danger zone. A marvelous athlete, she has a muscular, strong body that can do just about anything she wants it to do; she loves it for how far she can jump with it, throw a ball with it, stop a goal with it. Looking at her and the joy she takes in her physical abilities, the uninhibited pleasure with which she does her own version of hip-hop, the innocent, exuberant way she flaunts her little booty, it's hard to imagine her ever becoming ashamed of her body.

Yet, as I was about to serve the cake at her last birthday party, I overheard the children at the table, laughingly discussing the topic of fat. The conversation was apparently inspired by the serving of the cake. 'I want to get fat!' one of them said, laughingly. But it was clearly a goad, meant for shock and amusement value, just as my daughter will sometimes merrily tell me 'I want to get smashed by a big tank!' and then wait for my nose to wrinkle in reaction. That's what happened at the party. 'Uggh! Fat! Uggh!' 'You do not want to be fat!' 'Nyuh, huh, yes, I do!' 'You do not!' And then there was general laughter and descent into gross-talk, 'Fat! Fat! Big fat butt!' and so on.

No one was pointing fingers at anyone – not yet – and no one was turning down cake – not yet. But the 'fat thing' has become a part of their consciousness, even at eight, and I know it's just a matter of time. I know the stats – that 57 percent of girls have fasted, used food substitutes or smoked cigarettes to lose weight, that one-third of all girls in grades nine to 12 think they are overweight, and that only 56 percent of seventh graders say they like the way they look. I also know, as someone who is active at my daughter's school – a public school, with a diverse student population – that it actually begins much, much earlier.

Already, Cassie sometimes tells me that she's fat, pointing to her stomach – a tummy we all would *die* to have. Recently, we were watching TV, and she sucked in her gut and said, 'This is what I'd like my stomach to look like.' At such moments, the madness of our culture hits me full force. I know that I am up against something that cannot be fought with reason or reassurance alone – or even, I'm afraid, with body-image workshops. As gargantuan as the task may seem, as helpless as we may all feel to do much to change things, we cannot let our culture off the hook.

No one strategy will suffice, because the powers that have created and continue to promote body image disorders – and here I refer to not only eating disorders, but the over-use and abuse of cosmetic surgery, steroids, exercise addictions, our cultural obsession with youth, and on and on – are multi-faceted and multiply 'deployed,' as Foucault would put it. That is, they are spread out and sustained in myriad ways, mostly with the cooperation of all of us. There is no king to depose, no government to overthrow, no conspiracy to unmask. Moreover, the very same practices that can lead to disorder are also, when not carried to extremes, the wellsprings of health and great deal of pleasure – exercise for example. This is one reason why it has been so difficult to create coalitions – for example, between different generations of feminists – to work for change. But there is also tremendous potential for inclusiveness here; for, as I've argued, these are issues that are far from limited to the problems of rich, spoiled white girls, but that reach across race, class, ethnicity, nationality, age, and (as I've shown elsewhere) gender. I don't have a master plan for how to alter or resist what seems to be our inexorable drift into this culture in which it *seems* as if our choices to do what we want with our bodies are expanding all the time, but in which we increasingly exercise those 'choices' under tremendous normalizing pressure. But then, neither do I know what can be done to alter some of the larger social and political injustices, dangers, and absurdities of our lives today. Not knowing what to do about those, however, doesn't prevent people from analyzing, complaining, organizing, protesting, working to create a better world. I'd like to see more of that sort of spirit operating in this arena too – if not for ourselves, then for our children.

References

Abramovitz, B. and Birch, L. (2000) Five-year-old girls' ideas about dieting are predicted by their mothers' dieting, *Journal of the American Dietetic Association*, 100(10): 1157–1163.

Becker, A.E. (2004) Television, disordered eating, and young women in Fiji: negotiating body image and identity during rapid social change, *Culture, Medicine and Psychiatry*, 28(4): 533–559.

Becker, A.E., Burwell, R.A., Herzog, D.B., Hamburg, P., Gilman and Stephen, E. (2002) Eating behaviours and attitudes following prolonged exposure to television among ethnic Fijian adolescent girls, *British Journal of Psychiatry*, 180(6): 509–514.

Bordo, S. (1993) *Unbearable Weight: Feminism, Western Culture and the Body*, Berkeley: University of California Press.

Bordo, S. (1997) Never just pictures, in S. Bordo, *Twilight Zones: The Hidden Life of Cultural Images From Plato to O.J.*, Berkeley: University of California Press.

Bordo, S. (1999) Beauty re-discovers the male body, in S. Bordo, *The Male Body: A New Look at Men in Public and in Private*, New York: Farrar, Straus and Giroux.

Bordo, S. (2004) Whose body is this?, in S. Bordo, *Unbearable Weight: Feminism, Western Culture and the Body*, 10th anniversary edition, Berkeley: University of California Press.

Carmichael, A. (2002) Teen magazine takes stand against diet, weight obsession, *Ottawa Citizen*, 11 February.

Choi, C. (2006) Mother's dieting also affects her daughter, *Lexington Herald Leader*, 11 August, p. B6.

Field, A. et al. (2001) Peer, parent, and media influences on the development of weight concerns and frequent dieting among preadolescent and adolescent girls and boys, *Pediatrics*, 107: 54–60, at: www.pediatrics.org/cgi/content/full/107/1/54.

Franko, D.L. et al. (2007) Cross-ethnic differences in eating disorder symptoms and related distress, *International Journal of Eating Disorders*, 40(2): 156–164.

Gumbel, A. (2000) Survival of the thinnest, *The Independent*, 21 December.

Keck, W. (2000) *Ally McBeal's* Courtney Thorne-Smith says she's fed up with the pressure to be thin, *US Weekly*, 11 December, at http://www.geocities.com/cthorne_smith/us_121100.html.

NPR (2002) On the media, 26 January.

Onishi, N. (2002) Globalization of beauty makes slimness trendy, *New York Times*, 3 October.

Powers, R. (1989) Fat is a black woman's issue, *Essence*, October: 75–78, 134–146.

Renfrew Center Foundation for Eating Disorders (2003) *Eating Disorders 101 Guide: A Summary of Issues, Statistics and Resources*, October, at: http://www.renfrew.org.

Riley, S. (2002) The black beauty myth, in D. Hernandez and B. Rehman (eds), *Colonize This!*, Emeryville, CA: Seal Press, pp. 357–369.

Rosenthal, E. (1999) *Beijing Journal*: China's chic waistline: convex to concave, *New York Times*, 9 December.

Snyderman, N. (2002) *The Girl in the Mirror*, New York: Hyperion.

Tyre, P. (2005) No one to blame, *Newsweek*, 5 December, 52–53.

Van Meter, J. (2006) Disappearing act: how did Portia De Rossi withstand the pressures of Hollywood, *Vogue*, 1 April, at: www.advocate.com/newsdetailektid 28186.asp.

Part II

Interrogating cultural contexts of dis/ordered eating

6 A critical discussion of normativity in discourses on eating disorders

Paula Saukko

Introduction

Eating disorders are widely acknowledged to be fuelled by media and other social discourses delineating normative notions of the female body. In this chapter, I argue that diagnostic discourses on eating disorders themselves delineate normative notions of the female self and discuss an alternative way of making sense of eating disorders. The first part of the chapter briefly discusses historical and contemporary discourses on eating disorders. I will analyse how Hilde Bruch's pioneering research on obesity and anorexia emerged from a specific American historical context between 1930 and 1960. Her pre-war research on the causes of childhood obesity among poor immigrants framed fat children as constrained by the traditionalism of their Eastern European families. Bruch's later research on anorexia interpreted young middle-class self-starving women as falling victim to the post-war, middle-class, suburban mass culture, associated with fascism and communism. Both the obese and the anorexic individual were defined as deficient in relation to the American, liberal or rugged individualism – imagined as male, white and privileged – while articulating specific historical anxieties of their times.

In the second part of the chapter, I challenge the way in which eating disorders have been mobilised to support normative notions of self and society. The anorexic's starving is frequently informed by absolutist ideas of good or ideal ways of being beautiful, strong, independent and fit. Telling her that she is lacking in terms of the very same historically contingent normative ideal of strong individuality merely fuels the quest for more control and strength (see Gremillion, 2003). Furthermore, the classist, racist and sexist undercurrents embedded in the apparently progressive psychological and political critiques of traditionalism or mass culture go unquestioned.

I argue that most theories on anorexia, Bruch's included, are founded on a time-based metaphor, where the anorexic is defined as having 'false consciousness', projecting a development from this state of falsehood toward genuine health and/or emancipation. I propose an alternative, space-based approach for making sense of anorexia (see also Saukko, 2008). The space-based approach does not arrange discourses into linear order from bad to good, but evaluates them 'simultaneously, as if in space, rather than time' (Hermans and Kempen, 1993: 42). This mode of analysis brings into relief the multifaceted or 'multiaccentual' (Volosinov, 1973) nature of discourses, which can be simultaneously politically and personally empowering and disempowering. I will also discuss how this approach helps to understand the way in which political contradictions in the discourses on anorexia translate into intrapersonal paradoxes, such as experiencing critiques of beauty culture as both helpful and humiliating. Rather than seek to resolve these paradoxes, a space-based approach acknowledges them, paving a way for a less simplistically judgemental and more critically reflexive attitude toward all discourses that suggest a way of relating to ourselves, others and the world in which we live.

On American freedom

Hilde Bruch (1904–1984) was one of the most influential psychiatrists on anorexia. Her theory of anorexia as a symptom of lack of autonomy has been integrated into feminist theorising on the topic (e.g. Orbach, 1986) and become part of common sense. Anorexia nervosa had been identified and defined before her time (Brumberg, 1988). Yet, Bruch was responsible for defining the anorexic as someone with an insufficiently autonomous self – a definition which is still alive and well in clinical practice, in self-understandings of anorexic women and in popular culture.

Initially Bruch's research focused not on anorexia but obesity. In the 1930s, soon after escaping from Nazi Germany, Bruch was asked to found an endocrine clinic for obese children in the Babies' Hospital in New York City. Obesity, at that time, was claimed to be caused by endocrine dysfunction and treated with popular glandular injections (Bruch, 1939). The children treated in Bruch's new clinic were mainly immigrants of Eastern European Jewish and to a lesser extent Italian and Irish, families. Bruch's studies refuted the endocrinological theory of obesity (see also LeBesco, this volume). She noted there was nothing wrong with the children's metabolism; they simply ate enormously and were unusually inactive (Bruch and Touraine, 1940). She concluded that the problem was to be found not in the children's biology, but in their families, particularly mothers. Bruch describes the mothers as resentful, 'self-pitying' women, who abused their children and overfed them, partly to pacify them and partly to assuage their guilt. She associated the mothers' behaviour with the recent immigrants' culture and dashed hopes of a life of 'ease and luxury'. She describes the children's familial circumstances. For example:

> The [child's] father is [himself] the youngest of five children. 'He is the unsuccessful one of my children,' says his mother, who resents the presence of his family in her overcrowded apartment. The mother . . .

avoids discussion of her early life except to recount her adolescent popularity. 'I never bothered with my family, I was the one having a good time.' But at 42 years she displays a strong tie to her mother, which supersedes all other personal relationships. She is an immature and unreliable person who covers up real issues and facts in her life, and refuses to face realities, just as she blondines her hair and covers her wrinkles with gaudy make-up.

(Bruch and Touraine, 1940: 158)

Obesity and many other physical and behavioural traits were associated with genes and race in the 1920s and 1930s, and these theories informed strict immigration laws in the US (Jimenez, 1993). As a German-Jewish exile, Bruch may have found these eugenic presuppositions particularly abhorrent, and her work refuted them. However, Bruch also found fault with the Eastern European immigrants, although she did not locate the problem in their genes but in their attitudes and culture. The fat immigrant children became symbols of their families' adherence to traditions such as maintaining extended families and rough child disciplining practices. They were also symbols of the allure of the emerging consumer culture, such as mass-marketed cosmetics and Hollywood dreams of ease and luxury. In short, the obese child became the antithesis to the American, liberal individualism, enshrined in the principles of entrepreneurship and hard work and the emerging middle-class child-rearing practices with 'relaxed methods of child discipline, separate rooms for each child, and educational toys and music lessons' (Mintz and Kellogg, 1988: 187).

Bruch turned her attention to anorexia after the war. At this time, she had undergone psychoanalysis with a fellow German-Jewish exile, Frieda Fromm-Reichmann, and her clientele were now middle-class children seen in private practice. In this new context Bruch again turned her attention to the mothers. She argued that the anorexics suffered from being over-compliant; their lives had become 'an ordeal of wanting to live up to the expectations of their families' (Bruch, 1978: 24). Bruch related this 'perfectionist' desire to be successful and pretty to the mothers' expectations that their daughters would live up to their frustrated dreams as well as to their fathers' more traditional expectations:

The mothers had often been career women, who felt they had sacrificed their aspirations for the good of the family. In spite of superior intelligence and education, practically all had given up their careers when they married. . . . The fathers, despite financial and social success, often considerable, feel in some sense 'second best'. They are enormously preoccupied with physical appearance, admiring fitness and beauty, and expecting proper behaviour and measurable achievement from their children.

(ibid.: 27)

Just like the fat immigrant children, the middle-class anorexic girls were also defined as lacking in terms of the American, rugged individualism, usually imagined as masculine. The young girls were not identified as being constrained by traditionalism but by a new peril in post-war USA: the newly affluent, competitive and consumer-oriented middle-class and its 'mass culture'. Mass culture was strongly associated with the post-war American chief political enemies – fascism and communism – which were both viewed as authoritarian ideologies, rendering people the same and stripping them of their individuality. Bruch's theories resonated with the insights of the Frankfurt School, which criticised post-war America for a social complacency and lack of cultural critique, reminiscent of the Weimar Republic (Adorno and Horkheimer, 1945/1997). The Frankfurt School was particularly interested in culture, arguing that mass-produced, rhythmic and repetitive popular music, for example, numbed the senses and the intellect, unlike classical music, which developed a theme and contained surprises, fostering original thought. The resonances between Bruch and the Frankfurt School were not mere coincidence; Bruch's mentor and psychoanalyst, Frieda Fromm-Reichmann, was the ex-wife of one of the figureheads of the school, Erich Fromm. As noted by Huyssen (1986), the debates on mass culture associated a weak or easily influenced psychological disposition, mass-produced or 'low' culture with conservative politics, and imagined all these qualities as distinctly feminine. The anorexic girl, who had allegedly become mentally ill, because of excess of things and images and middle-class suburban complacency, seemed to epitomise the hallmarks of the psychological, cultural and political decline of the times. Thus, despite the progressive accents of the concern over mass culture, Bruch's work also expressed an intellectualist disdain toward the newly affluent middle-classes and a sexist disregard for things and attitudes associated with femininity, such as the private sphere, consumption, appearance and being directed toward the needs and expectations of others.

Hilde Bruch's theory has since become part of the common sense understanding of anorexia. Anorexics are commonly perceived to be young girls, who try too hard to be pretty and successful, having fallen victim to parental and peer pressures and ubiquitous images of thin models in the media (e.g. Wykes and Gunther, 2005). The notion of the perfectionist 'goody' girl, rendered neurotically compliant by the overly demanding middle-class family was popularised in the media coverage of Karen Carpenter, whose death from complications arising from anorexia in 1983 made the condition widely known. Similar to Bruch's descriptions, the media framed Carpenter's anorexia as revealing not only familial but also underlying political or social pathologies embedded in the return to conservative values during the Nixon and Reagan eras in the 1970s and early 1980s. The Carpenters' romantic and wholesome soft rock seemed to epitomise the neoconservative political agenda focusing on 'family values':

Their parents kept buying them whatever musical instruments they wanted – flute, accordion, drums. They could be whoever they wanted, go as far as their dreams and talent would take them. . . . They were as wholesome as their music in that drug-crazed, politically unrestful time – something you could count on, and stand up and salute. And behind the scenes they were popping pills and starving themselves to death.

(Kitman, 1988)

Bruch's ideas about anorexia as having to do with women's struggle with independence were also appropriated by feminists, who argued that anorexia articulated women's unconscious resistance to limiting gender roles, associated with the voluptuous female body (e.g. Bordo, 1993; Orbach, 1986).

My discussion of the historical context which has given rise to our current conceptions of anorexia as a disorder articulating women's lack of independence, seeks to underline the historical contingency of these ideas. Rather than being universal truths about what is troubling individuals with eating disorders, the notions of a sick, eating-disordered self lacking in autonomy have their origins in very specific historical contexts and projects, such as the 1930s' agonies about Eastern European immigrants, post-war fears of mass culture and later feminist critiques of limiting gender roles. I am not suggesting these ideals and agendas are 'wrong'. Rather, I am questioning the way in which they have shaped accepted 'truths' about anorexia without further interrogation of their contradictory political origins and implications.

Beyond normativity

Recent research has begun to argue that psychiatric discourses on anorexia fuel the same ideas and practices that inform anorexia in the first place (see also Moulding, this volume). Psychiatric treatment for eating disorders defines mental health in terms of strength and fitness, which are the same goals the anorexic sets out to achieve (Gremillion, 2003). Research on the lived experience of women with eating disorders has also found that anorexic women often perceive diagnostic and popular descriptions of them as denigrating, depicting them as 'vain', 'superficial' or 'spoilt brats' (Malson, 1998; Rich, 2006; Saukko, 2000, 2008).

I argue that the problem with diagnostic and popular discourses on anorexia is not only, or even mainly, their content but their form. Bruch's (1978) descriptions, as well as her followers' ideas, are grounded on judgemental normative distinctions between the healthy and the pathological. They also posit a linear temporal development from a state of illness or false consciousness toward recovery and emancipation. The ideal end state is imagined in terms of attaining the bounded, autonomous, masculine self, independent from the influences of tradition, family members, consumer culture and constraining gender roles. There may be much at fault with traditions, families, consumer culture and gender roles. Yet, such judgements about social ways of being remain blind to their own underside, such as the sexism embedded in critiques of mass culture, which frame women as gullible victims of outside influences (Huyssen, 1986), or the one-dimensionality of exultations of autonomy, which deny the value of relations with and respect for others, including kin and social groups (Gilligan, 1991).

Drawing on dialogic theory and narrative therapy (see also Part V, this volume), I suggest a way of making sense of anorexia and the discourses surrounding it based on the metaphor of space rather than time. Both the experience of anorexia and the experience of being diagnosed as an anorexic are informed by multiple discourses, which invite individuals to specific subject positions, such as being a less traditionally feminine, strong woman. Narrative therapy has distinguished between these subject positions and the 'self' of the anorexic woman (see Epston and Maisel, Treadgold et al., Burns et al., all this volume). Rather than viewing the anorexic's psyche as lacking in autonomy, narrative therapy takes the view that women are invited into discourses such as media discourses idealising thinness or diagnostic discourses idealising autonomy. They are thus called to be a particular way by discourses that are social and external to the self (White and Epston, 1990). Thus, narrative therapy does not recommend curing the anorexic's self – by, for example, increasing her autonomy. It suggests instead that the anorexic should gain critical distance from the discourses that have defined her. The intention is to come up with different, more productive discourses about the self that could help the woman to 're-narrate' her self (see also Guilfoyle, this volume).

Narrative therapy has sparked enthusiasm among scholars and practitioners interested in anorexia (e.g. Gremillion, 2003; Maisel et al., 2004). Locating the source of eating disorders in social and historical discourses rather than women's psyches is promising in the light of the historical and political origins of both beauty ideals and diagnostic discourses on anorexia. However, some forms of narrative therapy continue to subscribe to a time-based logic, in that they tend to postulate a path from a state of illness to listening to a healthy, preferred, anti-anorexic, anti-perfectionist, voice. By doing this, they do not sufficiently address the multidimensionality of voices or discourses, in that, for example, perfectionism not only leads to obsession and starvation but can also enable young women to succeed in increasingly competitive educational and professional markets (Evans et al., 2004; Walkerdine et al., 2001).

A slightly different approach to narrative therapy is offered by Hermans and Kempen (1993). They seek to avoid time-based metaphors and linear narratives with a beginning, a middle and an end. They argue for an approach to narrative based on the metaphor of space, which would perceive 'all [voices] as being coexistent and to perceive and depict [voices] side by side and simultaneously, as if in space rather than time' (ibid.: 42). Hermans and

Kempen tell a story of a woman who used to loathe being introverted and began to reflect on the enabling and disenabling sides of both being introverted and extroverted, rather than simply valorise the latter (ibid.: 81–88). In relation to anorexia, this approach would not arrange internal voices in a linear manner into a progression from anorexic sick perfectionism toward an anti-anorexic healthy relaxed attitude. Instead, it would evaluate the multiple – both empowering and disempowering – dimensions of social discourses on, for example, being perfect and successful.

Personal and political space

The dialogic theory of Volosinov (1973) and Bakhtin (1981) offers a useful way of bridging a space-based understanding of intrapersonal voices and similarly a spatially informed analysis of the social and political context. In his 'sociological' definition of consciousness Volosinov argues:

> Consciousness takes shape and being in the material of signs created by an organized group in the process of its social intercourse. . . . The logic of consciousness is the logic of ideological communication, of the semiotic interaction of a social group.
>
> (1973: 13)

Volosinov ascertains that consciousness is constituted by signs, which are created in the interaction of specific social groups and articulates their worldviews and agendas. Thus, intrapersonal voices inviting women to be successful or autonomous are utterly social, having their origins in specific historical time and social contexts. Furthermore, Volosinov elaborates that all signs are 'multiaccentual', which means that they 'refract' existence and reality in many different ways, as they have their origins in the 'intersecting of differently oriented social interests, within one and the same sign community' (ibid.: 23).

Volosinov's notion of social nature and the multiaccentuality of the sign helps to unpack the concept of autonomy, the cornerstone of much theorising on anorexia. In Bruch's research on obesity, the ideal of autonomy was mobilised to affirm the modernist notion of personal independence, specifically in relation to tradition and kin and imagined in opposition to the Eastern European immigrants, who were seen as a threat to American values and lifestyle in the 1930s. The later notion of autonomy in relation to anorexia was propped up in defence of similar rugged, masculine, American individualism. This time it was seen to be encroached upon by the new consumer and mass culture, associated with the Cold War enemies of fascism and communism, and related to the feminised, newly affluent lower middle-classes. Later articulations have made the anorexic's alleged lack of autonomy stand for the pathological nature of 1970s' US neoconservatism and traditional gender roles (e.g. Haynes, 1988).

This analysis illustrates how the concept of autonomy articulates many social and political accents, becoming harnessed into diverse, historically evolving projects from modernist antagonism towards tradition to liberal feminism. Traditional psychiatric and even some feminist research has interpreted autonomy fairly simplistically as an intrinsically fortuitous state, signifying freedom from constraining social forces of, for example, traditions, consumer culture and gender roles. This research, however, remains blind to the underside of these social agendas, such as the classism and racism embedded in the critique of Eastern European traditionalism. Volosinov refers to the drive to seal the meaning of a sign – such as rendering 'autonomy' always good and desirable – as an attempt to suppress the struggle between different social values by rendering it 'uniaccentual', that is, to have one meaning (1973: 23). The uniaccentualism of the sign contributes to the linear approach to eating disorders, which imagines the recovery from eating disorders as a progression towards an unproblematic ideal self such as the autonomous individual.

Volosinov and Bakhtin argue that uniaccentuality articulates the centralising or 'centripetal' quest of one worldview or social group to achieve dominance over others. This is reflected in the idealisation of masculine, American individualism in the discourse on anorexia. They both explore the possibilities of psychological/sociological theorising to bring to the fore the contestations or multiaccentuality and polyvocality within the sign. Bakhtin claims that the modern novel is unique in its artistic ability to do justice to the social struggles at play in language; he argues that:

> [t]he art of prose is close to a conception of languages as historically concrete and living things. The prose art presumes a deliberate feeling for the historical and social concreteness of living discourse, as well as its relativity, a feeling for its participation in historical becoming and in social struggle; it deals with discourse that is still warm from that struggle and hostility, as yet unresolved and fraught with hostile intentions and accents; prose art finds discourse in this state and subjects it to the dynamic unity of its own whole.
>
> (1981: 331)

Novelistic prose, according to Bakhtin, thrives in the tensions and struggles between diverse social accents and forces. This makes a novel operate according to a space-based logic that can simultaneously appreciate diverse social viewpoints as if existing on the same plane rather than ordered according to linear, hierarchical time. From a Bakhtinian perspective, the discourse on autonomy and eating disorders is shot through by social accents, articulating the agendas of diverse social groups, including the high-modernist intellectualist and sometimes left-wing disdain for traditionalism and consumer culture, which is undercut by racism and sexism. The later feminist rearticulations of this agenda seek to harness it to emphasise the limiting nature of traditional gender roles, but they still echo the contradictions of the original ideal of autonomy, which is still usually imagined as masculinist.

An analytical mode grounded on the metaphor of space does not iron out the contradictory social accents speaking through the discourse on autonomy into a simple moral story on pathological and healthy self and society. Bakhtin argues for a literary style – and this applies to analysing eating disorders – that does not impose an overarching unified voice on multiple voices but brings each voice's 'role and actual historical meaning' into relief by contrasting it to other contextual, social understandings so that 'each of them begins to sound differently than it would have sounded "on its own," as it were' (Bakhtin, 1981: 412).

Bakhtin's and Volosinov's theories bridge the personal and political in eating disorders in a manner different from the usual thesis of 'false consciousness'. Volosinov's notion of individual consciousness as constituted by the voices of social groups helps us to understand how social struggles translate into the contested personal universe of the anorexic, whereby women experience therapeutic discourses as both healing and eye-opening as well as humiliating and reactionary (Malson, 1998; Rich, 2006; Saukko, 2000, 2008).

The experience of anorexia is frequently characterised by a fixated pursuit of normative absolutes, such as strength and self-determination. Therapeutic approaches often end up complicit with this pursuit, prescribing more of the same norms, such as strength and self-determination, which may account for the poor recovery rates. A critically reflective approach – imagined in terms of critical exploration of multiple voices on a level plane in space – could pave the way for a more productive approach to making sense of the intrapersonal dynamics of eating disorders. A space-based approach would also facilitate a more nuanced understanding of the political dimension of discourses that inform and discourses that diagnose eating disorders, helping to see both their progressive and retrograde (e.g. sexist and classist) commitments.

Conclusions

In this chapter I have discussed how discourses about anorexia reinforce similar historical normative notions of gendered being, which inform the production of 'eating disorders' in the first place. I argue that the trouble with these discourses is not so much the norms that they support (though some of them are problematic, too) but the logic of setting up dichotomies. The black and white visions of healthy and pathological self and society evident in diagnostic and popular discourses on eating disorders resemble the anorexic dogged pursuit of absolutes. I have also argued that discourses on anorexia frequently and problematically follow a time-based narrative predicated on a movement from sick or inauthentic present to a healthy, genuine future. As an alternative, I have suggested a space-based approach to eating disorders, which could appreciate the multifaceted, tension-riddled nature of discourses. Rather than condemning one discursive position, such as seeking other people's acceptance and approval, it would flesh out both its enabling and disabling dimensions both in terms of personal life and political ideologies. Women with eating disorders frequently report seeking perfection, not only understood as having a perfect body or report card but on a more fundamental level as attaining a pristine, purified or uncontroversial existence. At that level, acknowledging that all norms and discursive positions are contradictory, shot through with problematic as well as exhilarating possibilities, might offer the beginnings of a life philosophy that could lead away from eating disorders. At a political level, being sensitive to the many dimensions of the politics around anorexia, such as the sexism embedded in the intellectualist critiques of mass culture, would contribute to a more nuanced and critically self-reflexive feminist engagement with wider political issues influencing women's relationship with their bodies and selves.

References

Adorno, T. and Horkheimer, M. (1945/1997) *The Dialectic of Enlightenment*, London: Verso.

Bakhtin, M. (1981) *The Dialogic Imagination*, Austin: University of Texas Press.

Bordo, S. (1993) *The Unbearable Weight: Feminism, Western Culture, and the Body*, Berkeley: University of California Press.

Bruch, H. (1939) Obesity in childhood I: Physical growth and development of obese children, *American Journal of Diseases of Children*, 58(3): 457–484.

Bruch, H. (1978) *The Golden Cage: The Enigma of Anorexia Nervosa*, Cambridge, MA: Harvard University Press.

Bruch, H. and Touraine, G. (1940) Obesity in childhood: V. The family frame of obese children, *Psychosomatic Medicine*, 11(2): 141–206.

Brumberg, J. (1988) *Fasting Girls: The History of Anorexia Nervosa*, Cambridge, MA: Harvard University Press.

Evans, J., Rich, E. and Holroyd, R. (2004) Disordered eating and disordered schooling: what schools do to middle class girls, *British Journal of Sociology of Education*, 25(2): 123–142.

Gilligan, C. (1991) *In a Different Voice: Psychological Theory and Women's Development*, Cambridge, MA: Harvard University Press.

Gremillion, H. (2003) *Feeding Anorexia: Gender and Power at a Treatment Center*, Durham, NC: Duke University Press.

Haynes, T. (1988) *The superstar: The Karen Carpenter story*, film, Iced Tea Productions, USA.

Hermans, H. and Kempen, H. (1993) *The Dialogic Self: Meaning as Movement*, New York: Academic Press.

Huyssen, A. (1986) Mass culture as woman: modernism's other, in T. Modleski (ed.), *Studies in Entertainment: Critical Approaches to Mass Culture*, London: Routledge, pp. 188–208.

Jimenez, M.A. (1993) Psychiatric conceptions of mental disorder among immigrants and African-Americans in nineteenth and early twentieth century American history, *Research in Social Movements, Conflicts and Change*, 16: 1–33.

Kitman, M. (1988) Two things on TV make me sick today, *Newsday*, 30 December.

Maisel, R., Epston, D. and Bordon, A. (2004) *Biting the Hand that Starves You: Inspiring Resistance to Eating Disorders*, New York: Norton.

Malson, H. (1998) *The Thin Woman: Feminism, Post-structuralism and the Social Psychology of Anorexia Nervosa*, London: Routledge.

Mintz, S. and Kellogg, S. (1988) *Domestic Revolutions: A Social History of American Family Life*, New York: Free Press.

Orbach, S. (1986) *Hunger Strike: The Anorectic's Struggle as a Metaphor for our Age*, New York: Norton.

Rich, E. (2006) The anorexic (dis)connection: managing anorexia as an 'illness' and an 'identity', *Sociology of Health and Illness*, 28: 284–305.

Saukko, P. (2000) Between voice and discourse: quilting interviews on anorexia, *Qualitative Inquiry*, 6(3): 299–317.

Saukko, P. (2008) *The Anorexic Self: A Personal, Political Analysis of a Diagnostic Discourse*, Albany: State University of New York Press.

Volosinov, V. (1973) *Marxism and the Philosophy of Language*, New York: Seminar Press.

Walkerdine, V., Lucey, H. and Melody, J. (2001) *Growing Up Girl: Psychosocial Explorations of Gender and Class*, London: Palgrave.

White, M. and Epston, D. (1990) *Narrative Means to Therapeutic Ends*, New York: Norton.

Wykes, M. and Gunther, B. (2005) *The Media and Body Image: If Looks Could Kill*, London: Sage.

7 Beyond western dis/orders

Thinness and self-starvation of other-ed women

Mervat Nasser and Helen Malson

Introduction

In challenging the prevailing conceptualisation of 'eating disorders' as individual psychopathologies, critical feminists have been at the fore in re-theorising 'anorexia' (Bordo, 1993; Eckermann, 1997; Hepworth, 1999; Malson, 1998) and, to a lesser extent, 'bulimia' (Burns, 2004; Burns and Gavey, 2004) as culturally embedded, complex and heterogeneous collectivities of discursively constituted subjectivities, experiences and body management practices that can be read as expressing a variety of often gender-specific cultural norms, values and dilemmas. In dismantling the distinction between the normal and the pathological, we have re-theorised and researched both the diagnostic categories and the lived experiences of girls and women diagnosed as 'anorexic' or 'bulimic'; understanding them as being constituted within and by the various regulatory norms of late twentieth- and early twenty-first century western(ised) cultures. Indeed, the notion that societal 'factors', particularly media idealisations of thinness in women, play some part in producing girls' and women's distressed and pathologised body management practices has been widely accepted for some time. The conceptualisation of 'eating disorders' as 'culture bound' (Littlewood and Lipsedge, 1987; Swartz, 1985), as a problem *particular* to contemporary western cultures and, more specifically, to middle-class, white western girls and young women (see Bordo, this volume), thus has some considerable cultural as well as academic currency.

This re-theorisation of 'eating disorders' has been invaluable both in challenging the pathologisation of girls and women and in problematising a diverse array of cultural norms by elucidating their imbrication in girls' and women's 'anorexic' and 'bulimic' experiences and practices (see, e.g., Eckermann, Bordo, both this volume). Powerful and politically useful as they are, however, critical feminist approaches might also produce, at least temporarily, their own lacuna (see also Guilfoyle, this volume). How, for example, when we understand 'anorexia' and 'bulimia' as profoundly embedded in and produced by the socio-historically specific discourses of contemporary western cultures, might we engage with questions about 'eating disorders' amongst girls and women living in cultural contexts other than the predominantly white mainstream cultures of western countries?

Since the 1990s an increasing number of studies have investigated the prevalence of 'eating disorders' amongst girls and women of ethnic minorities in both the US and the UK. Such studies report an increase in 'eating disorders' in African-American, Native American and Hispanic communities in the US (Edwards-Hewitt and Gray, 1993; Williamson, 1998; see also Nichter, 2000; Thompson, 1992) and amongst Asian British and Black British girls and women in the UK (Dolan et al., 1990; Gordon 2001; see also Wardle et al., 1993). Hand in hand with these studies a surge of publications reported epidemiological research from a range of countries, clearly suggesting that disordered eating patterns are increasingly a global phenomenon. Recent research from the Middle East (Abu-Saleh et al., 1998; Apter et al., 1994; El Sayed, 1998; Nabakht and Dezkhan, 2000; Nasser, 1994), South Africa (Szabo and Le Grange, 2001), South America (Meehan and Katzman, 2001), Asia (Lee, 2001) and the Pacific (Becker, 2004; Becker et al., 2002) indicates that 'eating disorders' are now emerging in many non-western societies, with rates that are similar to or even higher than those reported in the West (Nasser, 1997). The majority of these latter studies were community surveys, frequently modelled on those carried out in the West. The quality of this work and their application of western measures in non-western settings may be questionable (see Gordon, 2001; Lee, 2001; Nasser, 1997). Nonetheless, these studies do suggest that distressed and disrupted eating practices are 'not just a white girl thing' (Bordo, this volume) nor even an exclusively western thing (Nasser and DiNicola, 2001).

Despite its limitations, such research thus poses a number of challenges for critical feminist theory and research. How best to understand increasing eating and 'body image' problems amongst girls and women in ethnic minority communities in the West or increased diagnoses of 'eating disorders' across the rest of the world without dis-locating 'anorexia' and 'bulimia' from the (predominantly white mainstream) western cultural contexts in which we have understood them to be constituted; without imposing western meanings on non-western women's experiences (Lee, 2001); and/or without resorting to under-theorised notions of culture-clash (Marshall and Woollett, 2000) or globalisation/westernisation (Meehan and Katzman, 2001; Nasser, 2000; Nasser and DiNicola, 2001)?

Our aim in this chapter is therefore to discuss, from a critical feminist perspective, questions of culture, difference and ethnicity and of 'eating disorders' amongst ethnic minority and non-western girls and women (see also Bordo, Rice, Probyn, all this volume). Our discussion here is inevitably shaped and delimited in some ways by our own gendered, racialised and disciplinary subject positions. Mervat Nasser is an Egyptian consultant psychiatrist who has been living and working in England for 30 years.

Helen Malson is a critical feminist psychologist and a white British mother of a mixed-race daughter.

Theorising the inside/outside of culture

In studies investigating the prevalence of 'eating disorders' amongst girls and women from ethnic minority communities in both the US and the UK, it is often suggested that confusion about ethnic identity or problems of 'culture clash' increase susceptibility to developing eating disorders (Nasser and Katzman, 2003; Timimi and Adams, 1996). From this perspective, 'disordered eating' is seen as resulting from the difficulties of straddling two different cultural worlds, of living up to the 'traditional' expectations of women in the parent/minority culture whilst simultaneously endorsing modern western ideas about women (Katzman and Lee, 1997; Skarderud and Nasser, 2007).

As Katzman and Lee (1997) have argued, experiences of transition, dislocation, and/or racialised oppression might precipitate 'anorexic' or 'bulimic' practices as individual(ised) solutions to socio-political problems. Nasser and Katzman (1999; see also Nasser, 1997) have similarly argued that the distress associated with such experiences may be expressed in 'disordered forms of bodily regulation' – be they 'disordered eating' or otherwise. The notion of culture clash (as an aetiological explanation of 'eating disorders' amongst girls and women from ethnic minority communities) is, however, frequently used in quite problematic ways. This is, firstly, because it tends to be predicated on a conceptualisation of cultures as definable, contained, unitary and relatively stable such that an Asian British girl, for example, is understood as being caught in a collision between two seemingly unitary (and incompatible) cultures, creating distressing tensions and dilemmas in her life, which are then expressed as an 'eating disorder' or some other psychopathology. However, as Bhabha (1996) argues, the notion of culture on which such a view is based is both fallacious and politically suspect precisely because it conceptualises cultures as self-contained unities.

Moreover, it is a view which tends to frame minority cultures as *partial* (in that migrating people are understood as bringing only part of their parent culture with them) in contrast to the alleged wholeness of the dominant 'national' culture. From this perspective, the migration of 'partial' cultures is thus understood as 'generat[ing] borderline affects and identifications, "peculiar types of cultural-sympathy" and "culture-clash"' (ibid.: 54). Yet, as Bhabha points out, the very presence of minority cultures in 'national' cultures clearly indicates 'the impossibility of culture's containedness and the boundaries between' (ibid.: 54). The notion of cultures as self-contained and definable, which underpins the idea of culture clash, entails, then, a disavowal of 'the internal differentiation, the "foreign bodies", in the midst of the nation . . . the double inscription of the part-in-the-whole, or the minority position as the outside of the inside' (ibid.: 57). It can be understood as re-inscribing an exclusionist racialised fantasy of a self-contained British (or American or Australian) culture that might be somehow defined independently of its multicultural past and present.

Further, the notion of culture clash as an aetiological explanation of 'eating disorders' amongst girls and women from ethnic minority communities is also frequently predicated on a somewhat stereotyped notion of minority cultures as 'fixed' and 'traditional' (Nasser, 2000). In contrast with commonplace representations of western cultures as constantly changing, modern and progressive, non-western cultures are often viewed as static, isolated and remote from the forces of change affecting western societies (Nasser, 2000; Robins, 1996). This is particularly evident in representations of non-western women, who are often viewed within a stereotyped framework of unchanging and highly restricted 'traditional' gender roles. For example, 'disordered eating attitudes' amongst Asian girls are often explained in terms of 'perceived parental control' (e.g. Ahmad et al., 1994; McCourt and Waller, 1995). Of course, parental control may well be experienced by (some) Asian girls as a problem (as it might by Caucasian girls (see Bruch, 1974), with whom they are contrasted). However, that 'perceived parental control' is often used as an index of culture clash (Nasser, 1997) suggests a dubious contrast between Asian girls' restrictions and western girls' greater freedoms as if it were simply true that mainstream western gender politics are more egalitarian or less oppressive than the gender politics of other cultures: as if it were perhaps only non-western girls whose lives were restricted and only western women whose lives have changed and who can now 'choose' to live beyond the parameters of traditional domestic femininities.

Yet feminist movements have also arisen in many non-western countries and the social position of many non-western women has changed significantly, with increasing numbers being highly educated and working outside the family (Nasser, 1997). The Egyptian feminist movement, for example, began in the late nineteenth century at much the same time as the Suffragettes in Britain and the feminists in France. The veil and the social seclusion of women were abolished; laws were passed to protect women against discrimination; and women achieved equal rights to education, employment, promotion and equal pay. Similar social changes occurred in Turkey, Lebanon, Syria, Tunisia and Morocco.

Ironically, the stereotyping of non-western women as 'traditionally feminine' – as leading lives untouched by feminism or, indeed, any other form of social change – is particularly pronounced in the case of Moslem women, despite the fact that many Moslem women's lives have changed considerably. Many non-western societies, including Islamic ones, embraced socialism in their post-colonial phase. And, whilst socialist policies prevailed, women were valued for their participation in an overall social project (rather than for adherence to 'traditional' femininities) and their access to education, employment and child care was protected. With later economic liberalisation, however, some of these socialist provisions and protections for women were eroded and it is also important to note that the decline in communism worldwide has coincided with the rise of fundamentalism. Many Moslem women now face new pressures following recent revivals of Islamic ideology encouraging many of them to take up the veil. This 'new veiling' phenomenon is not restricted to Islamic societies but constitutes a global process, the gender politics of which is subject to ongoing debate (see Macleod, 1991; Nasser, 1999, 2000; Watson, 1994). Our point here, however, is to indicate the considerable transitions in non-western societies and in the lives of non-western women.

Recent changes in non-western societies such as those outlined above have inevitably produced a complex, ambiguous, multifaceted and hetero-geneous picture that cannot be said to be adequately comprehended in the unidimensional stereotype of 'the traditional non-western woman' who frequently figures in discussions of 'eating disorders' amongst girls and women from ethnic minorities. In short, we would argue that 'culture clash' explanations of 'disordered eating' are frequently problematic, both in their reliance on a dubious notion of cultures as somehow self-contained *and* in their recourse to often over-simplistic, homogenising and sometimes derogatory stereotypes of non-western cultures and non-western gender norms (Nasser, 1997).

Issues of ethnicity, cultural difference and racialised identity require, then, a different theorisation. Bhabha (1996) and others (e.g. Gilroy, 1993), for example, have re-theorised 'culture' not as whole but as inevitably hybrid, in-between and indeterminate. It is a theorisation which, without glossing over the problematic politics and experiences entailed here, opens up the possibility of positive, creative as well as negative readings of multicultural spaces and subjectivities. It thus forestalls a sometimes too-easy reliance on notions of 'culture clash' as potentially pathogenic. Amin Maalouf (1999) similarly explores the impossibility of 'living in one's own skin' in contemporary western cultures as both a broadly applicable pre-dicament of the postmodern subject and as a specifically racialised issue: an issue expressed by Nitin Sawney on the cover of the CD *Beyond Skin* (1999):

> I am Indian. To be more accurate, I was raised in England, but my parents came from India – land, people, government or self, 'Indian' – what does that mean? At this time the government of India is testing nuclear weapons – Am I less Indian if I don't defend their actions? . . . Less Indian for being born and raised in Britain – For not speaking Hindi? Am I not English because of my cultural heritage? – Or the colour of my Skin? Who decides?

To engage with the ways in which girls' and women's racialised and other-ed subjectivities are articulated with (and against) 'anorexic' and 'bulimic' subjectivities and body management practices requires, we would argue, similarly nuanced theorisations of both ethnicity and culture.

Acculturation, globalisation and the dissemination of western values

The second explanation of increases in 'eating disorders' amongst girls and women both in ethnic minority and multicultural contexts in western countries and in the rest of the world is in terms of increased exposure to and acceptance of dominant, mainstream western norms and values. It is an explanation that is clearly more compatible with a critical feminist perspective and with a theorisation of cultures as hybrid and indeterminate; as 'no longer belong[ing] to any one place or location . . . [and] increasingly inhabit[ing] shifting cultural and social spheres' (Giroux, 1994: 288). Indeed, numerous studies of body dis/satisfaction and eating practices amongst girls and women of ethnic minorities have found significant correlations between levels of body dissatisfaction and acculturation to mainstream western values (Davis and Katzman, 1999; Edwards-Hewitt and Gray, 1993; Pumariega, 1986). And the globalisation of western values, particularly of gendered idealisations of slimness/thinness, similarly feature in explanations of recent rises in dieting, body dissatisfaction and diagnoses of 'eating disorders' across the rest of the world (Katzman and Lee, 1997). As Susan Bordo (this volume, p. 54) argues, 'the incredible spread of these problems to extraordinarily diverse groups . . . over a strikingly short period of time, and co-incident with the mass globalization of media imagery, strongly suggests that [western/globalised] culture is the "smoking gun" that is killing people.'

At the same time, however, as elucidating the articulation of hegemonic western norms and values in the production and regulation of 'eating disordered' experiences amongst girls and women of diverse ethnicities, cultures and countries, it is also clearly important not to flatten out cultural difference and to attend to local specificities in the discursive production and regulation of girls' and women's subjectivities and body management practices (Katzman and Lee, 1997); to the re-inflections of western discourses that may produce locally specific as well as global/western meanings in the re-production of global/western signs (see Dolby, 2000; Marshall and Woollett, 2000). Precisely because it is a racialised (as well as globalised) 'ideal', thinness will inevitably be articulated and experienced as both the same and/but different across different contexts and for differently racialised girls and women (see Lee, 1991; Nasser, 1997; Thompson, 1992). And, indeed, as Katzman and Lee (1997) have argued, an aesthetic of thinness may not always be relevant in understanding the discursive contexts and locally-constituted meanings of women's self-starvation (see also Part III, this volume). In the remainder of this chapter, we shall therefore briefly explore some of this sameness-and/but-difference in meanings of thinness and self-starvation in three narratives of 'eating disorders' in transcultural/ multicultural and non-western contexts.

Global/local meaning-making in three narratives of thinness and self-starvation

The first of these narratives belongs to a young woman, Katie, who was engaged in therapy with the first author. She is of Egyptian/Japanese origin and was educated in the UK. Whilst her family considered her to be Moslem, she regarded herself as 'Zen Buddhist'. In her diary she wrote:

> I wanted to be beautiful when I was 16, when I was deeply insecure about the way I looked in a homogenized race. I wanted to fit in. Being half Egyptian and half Japanese made me feel an outsider whatever I do. I wanted to look fragile and controlled like a Japanese beauty. There is a Japanese saying that is 'the life of a flower is beautiful. Short lived and painful.' So, I decided to fast everyday, I had a strong desire to disappear. I measured the thickness of my legs when standing naked in front of a mirror. I squeezed my legs together, and measured the thickness not by looking at my actual legs but by looking at the negative space in-between my legs. No matter how big the hollow space in between, it was simply not enough.

Katie's focus on the negative space between her legs can be read as expressive of her 'strong desire to disappear'; to become disembodied, invisible. Her account thus resonates with those of other girls and women living in predominantly white mainstream western contexts who have similarly articulated thinness and self-starvation in terms of a pursuit of a disembodied existence and an evasion of visibility (Lawrence, 1979; Malson, 1998, this volume). An 'invisibility' of the emaciated body which at the same time as physically dematerialising 'screams out' its invisibility (Orbach, 1986), becoming all the more visible to the scrutiny of medical, media and public gazes as well as to the woman herself: a body that appears to disappear (Malson, 1999; Nasser, 2004; see also Burns, this volume). A pursuit of invisibility which Katie explicitly racialises.

At the same time, Katie's fast can also be read in terms of religious self-denial resonating with both the Islamic and Buddhist spiritual ideologies[1] of her cultural heritage (see Nasser, 2000; Nasser and DiNicola, 2001). Her account also articulates specifically Japanese cultural notions of beauty and purity, which both coincide with and diverge in important ways from mainstream western constructions of feminine beauty and 'ideal' femininity. Moreover, in the context of her Moslem background, Katie's pursuit of invisibility through 'fasting' might be read in relation to the act of veiling,

---

1 Sufi Islam has, in fact, a lot in common with Buddhism and indeed bodily self-denial features in the majority of religions such that any specificity in the religious connotations of her 'fast' is hard if not impossible to discern.

where both self-starvation and veiling entail a dialectic between the visible and the invisible; between a denial or renunciation of the female body, on the one hand, and a highly visible marking or hyper-embodiment of 'femininity', on the other. These dialectical meanings, in the contexts both of Katie's Egyptian/Japanese heritage and her British education, can also be read in terms of both western and non-western gender politics and the reading of 'anorexic' bodies both as hyper-feminine and as a quasi-feminist rejection of more 'traditional' domestic femininities (see Bordo, this volume; Orbach, 1986).

The second and third narratives we will consider here belong to two young Chinese women participating in Lee's (1995) ethnographic study of 'anorexia' in Hong Kong. Lee argued that these women's thinness was embodied against an absence of 'fat phobia' or any desire to pursue slimness for the purpose of beautification. For one woman, her loss of interest in eating was represented as a loss of voice in an overwhelmingly oppressive world. It signified a loss of power and, paradoxically, an act of empowerment that enabled her to avoid and resist a sexually abusive father at the dining table. According to Lee (2001), this was a profound act of communication by not communicating; an expression of intrafamilial hostility which could nevertheless be located within the parameters of Confucian values of 'demure', non-confrontational female behaviour. Thus, whilst very specifically Chinese in many respects, this woman's narrative also resonates with familiar western feminist debates about 'anorexia' as both (quasi-) feminist protest and/or hyper-conformity to the patriarchal regulation of 'femininity' (e.g. Bordo, 1993; Boskind-Lohdahl, 1976; Chernin, 1983; Orbach, 1986). It resonates too with earlier feminist psychoanalytic theorisations of 'hysteria' as a co-opted feminist protest (e.g. Mitchell, 1974) and with the notion of 'accommodating protest' or 'rebellion through conformity' advanced in Nasser's (2000) polemic on the 'new veiling' among Moslem women as a possible equivalent to 'anorexic' body regulation. In this comparison, both self-starvation and veiling can be read, in the context of cultural ambivalence about 'the proper place' of women, as both a resignation to and rebellion against gendered status quos (Nasser, 2000).

The second woman in Lee's (1995) study lived in a semi-rural context, where she was brought up to expect a 'timely marriage' with a financially dependable man. However, when she reached the 'marriageable' age of 24 her boyfriend left for the UK without any explanation. Her complaints of 'abdominal bloating' and her expressed conviction that she could not eat were interpreted as expressing a profound grief for her 'lost love'. Her food refusal signified her sadness and near-extinguished interest in life. Lee (ibid.; see also Katzman and Lee, 1997) argued that this woman's food refusal and weight loss cannot be construed as 'fat phobia' and that in her local cultural context her abdominal discomfort rather than her thinness was the more persuasive metaphor of her distress. The construction and embodiment of 'anorexia' as an expression of profound distress is clearly apparent in western contexts as well as here, but the specificities of its significations in 'anorexic' bodies may equally clearly differ depending on local context (see Lee, 2001). The western and increasingly globalised cultural loathing of body fat that is so apparent in the discursive production and regulation of western girls' and women's bodies thus appears here rather less prominent than the locally-specific significances of abdominal discomfort.

Conclusions

Our aim in this chapter has been, first, to discuss two frequently used explanations ('culture clash' and acculturation/globalisation) of 'eating disorders' amongst girls and women who, in terms of ethnicity and/or 'nonwestern' nationality, are positioned as 'other' in relation to a predominantly white western mainstream culture. And, second, we have sought to explore some of the variations and discontinuities as well as the continuities in the production and regulation of girls' and women's 'anorexic'/'bulimic' bodies and practices across different multi- and transcultural contexts and countries. The spread of thinness as a master signifier of feminine beauty, promulgated by the mass media and the post-colonial operations of transnational capital, across all sections of western societies and across the world has been devastatingly effective in the 'globalisation' of 'eating disordered' subjectivities and practices (Becker et al., 2002; Bordo, this volume). And, as Katzman et al. (2004) illustrated in their analyses of 'anorexia' in Curaco, other 'western' significations of thinness and food restriction, including success and the assertion of autonomous identity (see also Saukko, this volume), appear similarly to have been exported internationally. Thinness as a gendered body 'ideal' and a signifier of a multiplicity of positively construed 'attributes' can clearly no longer be considered exclusively western or white. To borrow from Giroux (1994: 288), western culture and, hence, the discourses and discursive practices in which 'anorexia' and 'bulimia' are constituted, 'no longer belong to any one place or location . . . [but] increasingly inhabit shifting cultural and social spheres'.

Neither, though, can it be assumed that a gendered aesthetics of thinness is always central to the production of self-starvation – *wherever* it occurs (Katzman and Lee, 1997). Other locally-specific discursive constructions of self-starvation may be more relevant and, as numerous feminist and critical feminist analyses have demonstrated, even in mainstream western and westernised contexts where a cultural preoccupation with 'body image' is so prominent, 'anorexic'/'bulimic' bodies and practices are also expressive of a considerable range of other cultural issues (Bordo, 1993; Katzman and Lee, 1997; Malson, 1998; Orbach, 1986). The discourses and discursive practices in which 'anorexia' and 'bulimia' are constituted may vary from one location to another and the ways in which they are taken up and re-articulated by, on and against girls' and women's differently racialised bodies in different-and/but-same cultural contexts may also vary. Hence, we would argue, we need to attend to both the globalised and the locally-specific in understanding the production and regulation of differently located and differently racialised girls' and women's 'eating disordered' experiences and practices.

References

Abu-Saleh, M., Younis, Y. and Karim, L. (1998) Anorexia nervosa in an Arab culture, *International Journal of Eating Disorders*, 23: 207–212.

Ahmad, S., Waller, G. and Verduyn, C. (1994) Eating attitudes among Asian schoolgirls: the role of perceived parental control, *International Journal of Eating Disorders*, 14(1): 49–57.

Apter, A., Shah, M., Ianco, I., Abromovich, H., Weisman, A. and Tanyo, S. (1994) Cultural effects on eating attitudes in Israeli subpopulations and hospitalised anorectics, *Genetic, Social and General Psychology Monographs*, 120(1): 83–99.

Becker, A.E. (2004) Television, disordered eating, and young women in Fiji: negotiating body image and identity during rapid social change, *Culture, Medicine and Psychiatry*, 28(4): 533–559.

Becker, A.E., Burwell, R.A., Herzog, D.B., Hamburg, P., Gilman, D.B. and Stephen, E. (2002) Eating behaviours and attitudes following prolonged exposure to television among ethnic Fijian adolescent girls, *British Journal of Psychiatry*, 180(6): 509–514.

Bhabha, H.K. (1996) Culture's in-between, in S. Hall and P. du Guy (eds), *Questions of Cultural Identity*, London: Sage.

Bordo, S. (1993) *Unbearable Weight*, Berkeley: University of California Press.

Boskind-Lohdahl, M. (1976) Cinderella's step-sisters: a feminist perspective on anorexia nervosa and bulimia, *Signs*, 2(2): 342–356.

Bruch, H. (1974) *Eating Disorder: Obesity Anorexia Nervosa and the Person Within*, London: Routledge and Kegal Paul.

Burns, M. (2004) Eating like an ox: femininity and dualistic constructions of bulimia and anorexia, *Feminism and Psychology*, 14(2): 269–295.

Burns, M. and Gavey, N. (2004) Healthy weight at what cost? Bulimia and a discourse of weight control, *Journal of Health Psychology*, 9(4): 549–565.

Chernin, K. (1983) *Womansize: The Tyranny of Slenderness*, London: Women's Press.

Davis, C. and Katzman, M. (1999) Perfection as acculturation: psychological correlates of eating disorders in the United States, *International Journal of Eating Disorders*, 25(1): 65–70.

Dolan, B., Lacey, J. and Evans, C. (1990) Eating behaviour and attitudes to weight and shape in British women from three ethnic groups, *British Journal of Psychiatry*, 157: 523–528.

Dolby, N. (2000) The shifting ground of race: the role of taste in youth's production of identities, *Race, Ethnicity and Education*, 3(1): 7–23.

Eckermann, L. (1997) Foucault, embodiment and gendered subjectivities: the case of voluntary self-starvation, in A. Peterson and R. Bunton (eds), *Foucault, Health and Medicine*, London: Routledge.

Edwards-Hewitt, T. and Gray, J. (1993) The prevalence of disordered eating attitudes and behaviour in Black-American and White-American college women, *European Eating Disorders Review*, 1(1): 41–54.

El Sayed, M. (1998) The prevalence and socio-demographic data of eating disorders in a sample of Egyptian adolescent girls, doctoral thesis, Ain Shams University, Cairo, Egypt.

Gilroy, P. (1993) Between Afro-centrism and Eurocentrism: youth culture and the problem of hybridity, *Young: Nordic Journal of Youth Research*, 1(2): 2–12.

Giroux, H. (1994) Doing cultural studies: youth and the challenge of pedagogy, *Harvard Educational Review*, 64: 278–308.

Gordon, R. (2001) Eating disorders East and West: a culture-bound syndrome unbound, in M. Nasser, M. Katzman and R. Gordon (eds), *Eating Disorders and Cultures in Transition*, New York and London: Brunner-Routledge.

Hepworth, J. (1999) *The Social Construction of Anorexia Nervosa*, London: Sage.

Katzman, M. and Lee, S. (1997) Beyond body image: the integration of feminist and transcultural theories in the understanding of self-starvation, *International Journal of Eating Disorders*, 22(4): 385–394.

Katzman, M., Hermans, K., Hoeken, D. and Hoek, H. (2004) Not your typical woman: anorexia nervosa is reported only in subcultures in Curaco, *Culture, Medicine and Psychiatry*, 28: 463–492.

Lawrence, M. (1979) Anorexia nervosa: the control paradox, *Women's Studies International Quarterly*, 2: 93–101.

Lee, S. (1991) Anorexia nervosa in Hong Kong: a Chinese perspective, *Psychological Medicine*, 21(3): 703–711.

Lee, S. (1995) Self-starvation in context: towards a culturally sensitive understanding of anorexia nervosa, *Social Science and Medicine*, 41: 25–36.

Lee, S. (2001) Fat phobia in anorexia nervosa: whose obsession is it?, in M. Nasser, M. Katzman and R. Gordon (eds), *Eating Disorders and Cultures in Transition*, New York and London: Brunner-Routledge.

Littlewood, R. and Lipsedge, M. (1987) Culture-bound syndromes, in K. Granville-Grossman (ed.), *Recent Advances in Psychiarty 5*, Edinburgh: Churchill-Livingstone.

Maalouf, A. (1999) *Les identites meurtrieres*, Paris: Bernard Grasset (Arabic translation by N. Beidon, Damascus: El Guindy publishing house).

Macleod, A. (1991) *Accommodating Protest: Working Women, the New Veiling and Change in Cairo*, New York: Columbia University Press.

Malson, H. (1998) *The Thin Woman: Feminism, Post-structuralism and the Social Psychology of Anorexia Nervosa*, London: Routledge.

Malson, H. (1999) Women under erasure: anorexic bodies in postmodern context, *Journal of Community and Applied Social Psychology*, 9: 137–153.

Marshall, H. and Woollett, A. (2000) Changing youth: an exploration of visual and textual cultural identifications, in C. Squire (ed.), *Psychology and Culture*, London: Routledge.

McCourt, J. and Waller, G. (1995) Developmental role of perceived parental control in eating psychopathology of Asian and Caucasian schoolgirls, *International Journal of Eating Disorders*, 17: 277–282.

Meehan, O. and Katzman, M. (2001) Argentina: the social body at risk, in M. Nasser, M. Katzman and R. Gordon (eds), *Eating Disorders and Cultures in Transition*, London and New York: Brunner-Routledge, pp. 146–171.

Mitchell, J. (1974) *Psychoanalysis and Feminism*, Harmondsworth: Penguin.

Nabakht, M. and Dezkhan, M. (2000) An epidemiological study of eating disorders in Iran, *International Journal of Eating Disorders*, 28: 265–271.

Nasser, M. (1994) Screening for abnormal eating attitudes in a population of Egyptian secondary school girls, *Social Psychiatry and Psychiatric Epidemiology*, 29: 88–94.

Nasser, M. (1997) *Culture and Weight Consciousness*, London: Routledge.

Nasser, M. (1999) The new veiling phenomenon – is it an anorexic equivalent? A polemic, *Journal of Community and Applied Social Psychology*, 9: 407–412.

Nasser, M. (2000) Gender, culture and eating disorder, in J. Ushher (ed.), *Women's Health, Contemporary International Perspectives*, London: British Psychological Society.

Nasser, M. (2004) Dying to live: eating disorders and self harm behaviour in a cultural context, in J. Levitt, R. Sansone and L. Cohn (eds), *Self-harm Behaviour and Eating Disorders, Dynamics, Assessment and Treatment*. New York and London: Brunner-Routledge.

Nasser, M. and DiNicola, V. (2001) Changing bodies, changing cultures: an intercultural dialogue on the body as the frontal frontier, in M. Nasser, M, Katzman and R. Gordon (eds), *Eating Disorders and Cultures in Transition*, New York and London: Brunner-Routledge.

Nasser, M. and Katzman, M. (1999) Eating disorders: transcultural perspectives inform prevention, in N. Piran, M. Levine and C. Steiner-Adair (eds), *Preventing Eating Disorders: A Handbook of Interventions and Special Challenges*, Philadelphia, PA: Brunner/Mazel, pp. 26–44.

Nasser, M. and Katzman, M. (2003) Sociocultural theories and eating disorders: an evolution in thought, in J. Treasure, U. Schmidt and E. van Furth (eds), *Handbook of Eating Disorders*, 2nd edition, Chichester: Wiley, pp. 139–141.

Nichter, M. (2000) *Fat Talk: What Girls and Their Parents Say About Dieting*, Cambridge, MA: Harvard University Press.

Orbach, S. (1986) *Hunger Strike: The Anorexic Struggle as a Metaphor for Our Age*, New York: Norton.

Pumariega, A.J. (1986) Acculturation and eating attitudes in adolescent girls: a comparative and correlational study, *Journal of the American Academy of Child Psychiatry*, 23(1): 111–114.

Robins, K. (1996) Interrupted identities: Turkey/Europe, in S. Hall and P. du Guy (eds), *Questions of Cultural Identity*, London: Sage.

Sawney, N. (1999) *Beyond Skin*, Outcaste Records.

Skarderud, F. and Nasser, M. (2007) Refiguring identities: my body is what I am, in M. Nasser, K. Baistow and J. Treasure (eds), *The Female Body in Mind: The Interface between the Female Body and Mental Health*, London: Routledge, pp. 17–29.

Swartz, L. (1985) Anorexia nervosa as a culture-bound syndrome, *Social Science and Medicine*, 20(7): 725–730.

Szabo, C.P. and Le Grange, D. (2001) Eating disorders and the politics of identity: the South African experience, in M. Nasser, M. Katzman and R. Gordon (eds), *Eating Disorders and Cultures in Transition*, London and New York: Brunner-Routledge, pp. 24–40.

Thompson, B.W. (1992) Eating problems among African-American, Latina, and White women, *Gender and Society*, 6(4): 546–561.

Timimi, S. and Adams, R. (1996) Eating disorders in British-Asian children and adolescents, *Clinical Child Psychology and Psychiatry*, 1(3): 441–456.

Wardle, J., Bindra, R., Fairclough, B. and Westcombe, A. (1993) Culture and body image: body perception and weight concern in young Asian and Caucasian British women, *Journal of Community and Applied Social Psychology*, 3(3): 173–181.

Watson, H. (1994) Women and the veil, personal responses to global processes, in A. Ahmed and D. Hastings (eds), *Islam, Globalisation and Postmodernity*, London: Routledge.

Williamson, L. (1998) Eating disorders and the cultural forces behind the drive for thinness: are African American women really protected?, *Social Work in Health Care*, 28(1): 61–73.

8 Anorexia/bulimia as resistance and conformity in pro-Ana and pro-Mia virtual conversations

Katy Day and Tammy Keys

Introduction

The 'pro-eating disorder' phenomenon on the Internet first came to the media's attention in 2000 (Bell, 2007). Conservative estimates over five years ago put the number of operational sites at around 400 (Dolan, 2003) and these are said to be maintained and accessed mostly by girls and women aged between 13 and 25 (Fraser, 2003). The sites often emphasize the benefits of anorexia and bulimia,[1] for example as ways of coping (Norris et al., 2006), and may provide advice such as 'tips and tricks' on how to maintain a low body weight. There are, however, a number of ways in which these websites vary. Csipke and Horne (2007), for example, make a distinction between 'moderate pro-ED' sites (e.g. Blue Dragonfly) and 'more uncompromisingly pro-ED' sites (e.g. Starving for Perfection). The creators of 'less extreme' sites claim that they avoid providing advice that may be harmful to visitors, such as tips on how to hide an eating disorder (see Mulveen and Hepworth, 2006), a characteristic of some of the more 'uncompromising' sites. Instead, 'moderate' pro-ED sites often concentrate on 'safe' or 'healthy' practices for those with an eating disorder, such as the use of multi-vitamins to supplement an anorexic diet (Fox et al., 2005).

There have been calls for the censorship of such websites on the grounds that they may attract 'normal' girls and women seeking advice on weight loss who then become drawn into a 'pro-Ana' lifestyle (e.g. Doward and Reilly, 2003) and that they might reinforce girls' and women's dysfunctional and destructive 'eating disordered' practices (Jackson and Elliott, 2004). However, to date, there is little research examining the consequences of exposure to 'pro-eating disorder' material on the Internet. One study, by Bardone-Cone and Cass (2006), found that women who viewed a pro-anorexia website experienced decreased levels of self-esteem, appearance

---

1 On the websites, anorexia is often referred to as 'Ana' and bulimia as 'Mia'. References and websites devoted to the former were found to be more common and so the chapter refers mostly to these.

self-efficacy and perceived attractiveness and increased levels of negative affect and perceptions of being overweight. Similarly, Csipke and Horne (2007) found a trend towards a worsening of body image satisfaction as a result of visiting pro-eating disorder sites and reported that participants admitted that these helped them to maintain 'disordered' eating and discouraged them from recovery.

It is important to note, however, that people are not simply passively 'influenced' by the contents of the websites they visit (Mulveen and Hepworth, 2006). Rather, it has been suggested, those who use the Internet deploy critical evaluation when accessing information (Schwartz et al., 2006). In addition, recent research has produced a more complex and nuanced account of pro-eating disorder websites and Internet communities, suggesting that such sites may have multiple purposes or functions. For example, the sites may provide a supportive and non-judgemental environment for girls and women whose behaviours and views are often regarded in mainstream society as unacceptable (see Fox et al., 2005; Mulveen and Hepworth, 2006) and who often feel poorly understood in their encounters with clinicians (Tierney, 2004). Csipke and Horne (2007) found that those who use the chatrooms on such sites and regularly seek support from others are more likely to benefit psychologically and emotionally than 'silent browsers' seeking tips on extreme dieting.

Another apparent function of these sites is their circulation of less readily available meanings of Ana and Mia that are occluded in culturally dominant discourse. One example is the promotion of anorexia as a lifestyle choice rather than as an illness – a noted characteristic of some of the more 'uncompromising' sites (Tierney, 2006). This construction of Ana as a lifestyle is not inconsistent with feminist challenges to the pathologisation of disordered eating and feminist re-theorisations of disordered eating as, instead, a fairly understandable (albeit extreme) response to the socio-cultural pressures to which girls and women are subjected, such as the pressure to be thin (see Hepworth and Griffin, 1995). Similarly, researchers such as Lyons (2000) have also pointed to the Internet as a potential space for feminist activism because of the counter-hegemonic work around femininity and the female body that can occur in on-line spaces. Likewise, Harris (2001: 132) argues that, in cyberspace, young people can be seen 'doing their politics' by resisting culturally dominant ways in which they, their interests and activities are represented. The construction, articulated on some pro-Ana websites, of those who self-starve as active agents or experts of their own 'condition' (Fox et al., 2005) 'or lifestyle', rather than, for example, as passive sufferers of a disease, might then be viewed similarly as an example of girls and women 'rewriting' their actions, experiences and identities in ways that may benefit them or position them in more powerful ways (see, e.g., Eckermann, 1997).

In short, we argue, pro-eating disorder websites can be understood as heterogeneous and as serving a number of sometimes conflicting purposes.

They manifest a considerable complexity and can be understood as being simultaneously both compatible and incompatible with feminist struggles (see Pollack, 2003).

This chapter aims to explore these issues further by examining within a feminist post-structuralist framework the 'meaning making' that occurs between those posting information and messages on 13 'pro-eating disorder' websites (see Day and Keys (2008) for further study details). Our chapter pays particular attention to the themes of conformity and resistance, which we discuss in relation to material from the websites, in debates around the pro-eating disorder phenomenon and in feminist literature. In analysing material from 'pro-eating disorder' websites, we seek to illustrate that the lines between 'conformity' and 'resistance' are extremely blurred and to explore some of the implications of this for feminist understandings of and responses to these websites.

The 'thin ideal' and the 'good anorectic'

A common feature of the material downloaded from these sites was the description and promotion of regimes of disciplining the female body. The 'thin ideal', as promoted by wider mainstream western(ized) culture, was often a central point of discussion, as can be seen in the two posts below:

> If you have a terrible craving, turn on the T.V.! Most likely, SOME sort of show will be on with skinny, gorgeous actresses/models.
>
> (Site 12)

> I [Ana] force you to stare at magazine models. Those perfect-skinned, white-teethed, waif-ish models of perfection staring out at you from those glossy pages. I make you realise that you could never be one of them. You will always be fat and never will be as beautiful as they are.
>
> (Site 8)

Reference was often made on the sites to the media and 'skinny' celebrities. Such cultural images were constructed as pervasive – 'SOME sort of show will be on', as desirable and as providing considerable motivation to restrict food intake. However, these sites also paint a picture of a complex and troubled relationship between posters and such cultural texts. For example, encounters with images of 'skinny' celebrities were often represented as inducing feelings of inferiority and inadequacy in the face of such 'impossible' standards of 'beauty': 'You will always be fat and never will be as beautiful as they are.'

The postings on these sites thus articulated a buying into and conformity to the notion of thinness as ideal. However, at the same time, the thin ideal is critiqued for its unattainability and there is a questioning of the notion – often presented in media such as television, women's magazines and health promotion literature (Bishop, 2001) – that thinness is achievable for girls and women via careful dieting and exercise. In this way, the contents of the pro-eating disorder websites are arguably more critical of the thin ideal than much 'mainstream' media and one purpose of posting on the sites may be the expression of anger about the socio-cultural promotion and pervasiveness of this notion of an *attainable* thin 'ideal'.

Some feminist scholars have suggested that beauty ideals alone are insufficient as explanations of women's distress about their/our bodies and body management (e.g. Bordo, 1993; Eckermann, 1997; Malson, 1992). Our analysis of material from the websites indicates that the practices of those who posted on these sites were understood as having significance and meaning that extended beyond simply attempting to achieve a culturally validated look (which, as discussed above, was sometimes portrayed as unattainable anyway). For example, 'being Ana' was constructed as a feature of a more general way of living and of being a 'good anorectic', characterized on the sites as a super-compliant servant or secular saint (see Eckermann, 1997, this volume) who abides by the 'rules' of the 'pro-eating disorder religion':

> Thou shall not eat without feeling guilty.
> Strict is my diet. I must not want. It maketh me to lie down at night hungry. It leadeth me past the confectioners. It trieth my willpower . . .
> I believe in calorie counters as the aspired word of God . . .
> I believe in bathroom scales as an indicator of my daily successes and failures.
>
> (Site 11)

Such theological-style discourse and imagery was noticeable in much of the material analysed. The rigid and punitive rules articulated above constitute Ana and Mia as 'religions' and imply a necessity of subscribing to these rules in order to be a 'true' member of an Ana/Mia community – constructions which can be seen to conflict with the notions of choice and agency articulated elsewhere on these websites. Indeed, some of the posts, particularly those that are presented as the 'voice' of Ana or Mia (as a sort of leader or even supernatural being) had a distinctly authoritarian and dictatorial tone, positioning those who subscribe as passive followers of these 'religions':

> [The voice of Mia] Your fingers will be inserted down your throat and not without a great deal of pain, your food binge will come up. . . . You fat cow you deserve to be in pain!
>
> (Site 8)

Griffin and Berry (2003), in their discussion of 'holy anorexia' (Bell, 1985), describe how, throughout the ages, 'fasting' and the demonstration of independence from or control of physical needs has often been regarded as a route to salvation for women.[2] This is perhaps because of constructions of femininity as closely bound with the body, with nature, desire and the 'primitive'; things that have come to be devalued (in preference for masculinist notions of rationality and restraint [see also Saukko, this volume]). In this context, feminist writers have often drawn attention to constructions of 'good femininity' in terms of such 'qualities' as self-sacrifice, self-denial and restraint (e.g. Orbach, 1986). In addition, researchers have demonstrated how contemporary discourses around food and healthy eating/living (as evident in various forms of popular media and health promotion literature) continue to bind food consumption with themes of morality, 'holiness' and 'sin' (e.g. Burns, 2004; Griffin and Berry, 2003; Madden and Chamberlain, 2004). And, given the construction of women as guardians of moral virtue (Sied, 1994), this moralization of bodily discipline is clearly a distinctly gendered issue. As Wetherell (1988) argues, within such discursive contexts those (women) who 'fail' to discipline their bodily desires and who eat 'bad' food are still positioned as 'sinners'.

This matrix of discourses has arguably created conditions of possibility whereby good citizenship and, furthermore, good or ideal femininity is achieved via the restriction and control of food intake (Burns, 2004). These conditions of possibility appear to be taken up on the sites where the 'good anorectic' is characterized in ways that embody notions of 'good', compliant and disciplined femininity and where those who pursue and promote Ana appear to be buying into patriarchal constructions of the female body and female desire as requiring control. Thus, whilst, as discussed above, critiques of the thin ideal are evident on the sites, Ana and Mia are also often characterized in terms of conformity to cultural constructions of femininity in ways that also extend beyond this thin ideal.

Ana and Mia as resistance?

As outlined above, one characteristic of the pro-eating disorder websites is the construction of alternative meanings of Ana and Mia within these spaces (Tierney, 2006); for example, that self-starvation represents a lifestyle choice as opposed to sickness or disease (e.g. Pollack, 2003). Thus, we noted during our analysis that Ana and Mia were often described as 'ways of living' or 'lifestyle choices' as opposed to medical or psychological 'conditions'. Indeed, those who are 'pro-Ana' were often portrayed as 'elite' or enlightened:

2 For more detailed discussions of the links between disordered eating and spirituality, see Bell (1985), Malson (1998), Walker Bynum (1991) and Eckermann (this volume).

This is a place for the elite who, through personal determination in their ongoing quest for perfection, demonstrate daily that Ana is the ONLY way to live.

(Site 5)

[. . .] the best we can be is the thinnest we can be. We will not allow those around us to detour our missions. We will do whatever it takes to reach our goals.

(Site 5)

In these extracts, being Ana is constituted as a highly valued 'mission', suggestive of political struggle. It is a construction which challenges or resists more normative and widespread notions of 'anorexia' and 'bulimia' whereby the subject is positioned in a passive role, either as a 'sufferer' of an illness (see Benveniste et al., 1999) or a 'victim' of socio-cultural forces and expectations – as the subject is sometimes cast in feminist analyses (see also Part III, this volume). Thus, girls and women who self-starve and/or binge and purge might 'take up' the normative subject position of, for example, 'the sick self'. But they might also take up positions within discourses that rework and resist such meanings (see Weedon, 1987), as they seem to on these websites. There could be much at stake for them (many of the posters claimed to have been in forced treatment at one time or another), especially if we consider arguments presented by those such as Laing (see Liversidge, 1988) that pathologizing labels and categories are often used to strip people of their civil liberties.

The construction of Ana and Mia as a mission of the elite thus brings with it notions of agency and resistance which converge with notions (promoted by those who support the sites) that 'pro-Ana' ways of living are about demonstrating freedom (see Tierney, 2006) but which run counter to other aspects of these websites, in posts such as *'Ana is the ONLY way to live'* (emphasis in original). The latter posts appear to downplay choice and portray the subject as being compelled by a force, as with Ana 'forcing' the subject to stare at pervasive magazine models.

In addition, where Ana and Mia are constituted as 'missions', issues of both conformity *and* resistance are apparent. The 'mission' of Ana or Mia is very often described as a 'quest', with thinness or 'perfection' as its ultimate goal, rather than as the challenging of widespread beliefs and ideas about disordered eating. However, another goal of 'the mission', as suggested on the sites, which seems rather less indicative of conformity to cultural ideals, is the struggle for independence and control. In contrast to constructions of self-starvation discussed above, such practices are reconfigured here as 'non-compliance' with cultural prescriptions to discipline and control the female body and as resistance to constructions of femininity as passive and controlled:

> Our [anorectics'] authority is our control over our own bodies.
>
> (Site 5)

> I believe in Control, the only force mighty enough to bring order to the chaos that is my world.
>
> (Site 11)

Note that the person posting the message on Site 11 above describes her 'world' as characterized by 'chaos'. And a number of feminist writers have portrayed self-starvation as an attempt to gain control in a patriarchal world of confusing and contradictory expectations that are placed on girls and women (e.g. Lawrence, 1984; Orbach, 1986; see however Saukko, this volume). Women's lack of (right of) control of their own bodies and the control exerted over these by the medical and 'psy' professions, as well as socio-cultural forces more generally, has long been a topic of feminist concern (e.g. Daly, 1978). Accounts posted of experiences of (forced) treatment on the sites can, we argue, be understood from this perspective as accounts of defiant acts, including 'tips and tricks' on how to defeat various 'agents of control':

> If you're in outpatient treatment and have to have your blood tested . . . there are a few ways you can fool the test.
>
> (Site 12)

> Praise fat people and they [parents] will never guess that you're starving yourself into thinness.
>
> (Site 12)

> Stage a conversation over the phone about how you don't think you need to lose weight.
>
> (Site 4)

Foucault (1979, 1980) argued that the surveillance and discipline of bodies within society via institutions such as the media and health professions has created the conditions for self-surveillance and self-discipline. Although Ana and Mia are sometimes construed on these websites as resistance to the control of outside agencies and authorities, this theme of resistance is largely over-written by themes of self-control, self-discipline and self-surveillance, often (though not always) in line with culturally dominant ideals. Issues of agency/control and passivity, resistance and conformity thus become intensely complex. All the more so if, as Foucault (1979, 1980) argued, these micro-processes of disciplinary power are even more powerful when we understand ourselves to be acting out of choice.

Conclusions

In analysing material from pro-Ana/Mia websites, we have sought to illustrate how Ana or Mia are constituted in different and sometimes contradictory ways, focusing in particular on the ways in which issues of conformity and resistance are articulated here. Our analysis thus to some extent converges with Eckermann's (1997, this volume) argument that girls and women who self-starve can be positioned as both 'conformists' (e.g. to the demands of the thin ideal) and as 'rebels' (e.g. defying the dictates of the medical and health professions). We would like to further trouble this issue of resistance/conformity on the pro-eating disorder websites. The promotion of alternative meanings surrounding self-starvation and/or binge-purging evident on these sites might be read as attempts to regain some control over understandings of such practices (see Tierney, 2006). In addition, as discussed above, some of these re-constructions of Ana and Mia were not entirely incompatible with feminist struggles: for example, the critique of the thin ideal as unattainable and the assertion of reclaiming control over the female body. Yet the notions of choice and agency entailed in such constructions simultaneously stand in contrast to constructions of Ana and Mia as forces that compel the subject (e.g. to look at magazine models) and with the positioning of posters as complying with the theologically styled dictates of Ana and Mia.

Moreover, we have also sought to explore how the deployment of meanings that cast self-starvation as resistance (to cultural norms and/or medical interventions) can also be understood as consistent with a conformity to wider cultural requirements. This can be read in terms of a conformity to culturally dominant body and gender ideals. Yet constructions of Ana and Mia as agentic 'missions' and as attempts to gain autonomy, independence and control can, paradoxically, also be read as conforming with cultural requirements that women be autonomous and independent (see also Saukko, this volume). Thus, MacSween (1993) argues that in bourgeois patriarchal cultures, girls and women are often encouraged to be conformist and passive (e.g. conform to beauty ideals). However, at the same time, so-called masculine values of independence and autonomy are promoted and so girls and women are often faced with the task of negotiating a satisfactory feminine identity in a way that incorporates both sets of requirements (see also Burns and Gavey, 2004; Wetherell, 1988). We would therefore agree with Pollack (2003) that, whilst acknowledging the resistance articulated on pro-Ana/Mia websites, feminist theorists should also be hesitant about romanticizing pro-eating disorder websites as political statements.

References

Bardone-Cone, A.M. and Cass, K.M. (2006) Investigating the impact of pro-anorexia websites: a pilot study, *European Eating Disorders Review*, 14: 256–262.

Bell, R. (1985) *Holy Anorexia*, Chicago: University of Chicago Press.

Bell, V. (2007) Online information, extreme communities and Internet therapy: is the Internet good for our mental health?, *Journal of Mental Health*, 16(4): 445–457.

Benveniste, J., LeCouteur, A. and Hepworth, J. (1999) Lay theories of anorexia nervosa: a discourse analytic study, *Journal of Health Psychology*, 4: 59–69.

Bishop, R. (2001) The pursuit of perfection: a narrative analysis of how women's magazines cover eating disorders, *Howard Journal of Communications*, 12: 221–240.

Bordo, S. (1993) *Unbearable Weight: Feminism, Western Culture and the Body*, Berkeley: University of California Press.

Burns, M. (2004) Eating like an ox: femininity and dualistic constructions of bulimia and anorexia, *Feminism and Psychology*, 14(2): 269–296.

Burns, M. and Gavey, N. (2004) 'Healthy weight' at what cost? 'Bulimia' and a discourse of weight control, *Journal of Health Psychology*, 9(4): 549–565.

Csipke, E. and Horne, O. (2007) Pro-eating disorder websites: users' opinions, *European Eating Disorders Review*, 15: 196–206.

Daly, M. (1978) *Gyn/Ecology: The Metaethics of Radical Feminism*, London: Women's Press.

Day, K. and Keys, T. (2008) Starving in cyberspace: a discourse analysis of pro-eating-disorder websites, *Journal of Gender Studies*, 17(1): 1–15.

Dolan, D. (2003) Learning to love anorexia? Pro-Ana websites flourish, *New York Observer*, 3 February.

Doward, J. and Reilly, T. (2003) How macabre world of the web offers fresh insight on anorexics, *The Observer*, 17 August.

Eckermann, E. (1997) Foucault, embodiment and gendered subjectivities: The case of voluntary self-starvation, in A. Peterson and R. Bunton (eds), *Foucault, Health and Medicine*, London: Routledge.

Foucault, M. (1979) *Discipline and Punish*, New York: Random House.

Foucault, M. (1980) *Power and Knowledge: Selected Interviews and Other Writings, 1972–1977*, New York: Pantheon Books.

Fox, N., Ward, K. and O'Rourke, A. (2005) Pro-anorexia, weight-loss drugs and the Internet: an 'anti-recovery' explanatory model of anorexia, *Sociology of Health and Illness*, 27(7): 944–971.

Fraser, M. (2003) Anorexia on the web, at: www.capitalnews9.com/content/health_team_9/?ArID=6973andSecID=17.

Griffin, J. and Berry, E.M. (2003) A modern day holy anorexia? Religious language in advertising and anorexia nervosa in the West, *European Journal of Clinical Nutrition*, 57: 43–51.

Harris, A. (2001) Revisiting bedroom culture: new spaces for young women's politics, *Hecate*, 27(1): 128–138,

Hepworth, J. and Griffin, C. (1995) Conflicting opinions? 'Anorexia nervosa', medicine and feminism, in S. Wilkinson and C. Kitzinger (eds), *Feminism and Discourse: Psychological Perspectives*, London: Sage.

Jackson, M. and Elliott, J. (2004) Dangers of pro-anorexia websites, BBC News International Edition at: http://news.bbc.co.uk/2/hi/health/3580182.stm.

Lawrence, M. (1984) *The Anorexic Experience*, London: The Women's Press.

Liversidge, A. (1988) Interview with R.D. Laing, *OMNI Magazine*, April, pp. 56–63.

Lyons, A. (2000) Examining media representations: benefits for health psychology, *Journal of Health Psychology*, 5(3): 349–359.

MacSween, M. (1993) *Anorexic Bodies: A Feminist and Sociological Perspective on Anorexia Nervosa*, London: Routledge.

Madden, H. and Chamberlain, K. (2004) Nutritional messages in women's magazines: a conflicted space for women readers, *Journal of Health Psychology*, 9(4): 583–597.

Malson, H. (1992) Anorexia nervosa: displacing universalities and replacing gender, in P. Nicolson and J. Ussher (eds), *The Psychology of Women's Health and Health Care*, Basingstoke: Macmillan.

Malson, H. (1998) *The Thin Woman: Feminism, Post-structuralism and the Social Psychology of Anorexia Nervosa*, London: Routledge.

Mulveen, R. and Hepworth, J. (2006) An interpretative phenomenological analysis of participation in a pro-anorexia Internet site and its relationship with disordered eating, *Journal of Health Psychology*, 11(2): 283–296.

Norris, M.L., Boydell, K.M., Pinhas, L. and Katzman, D.K. (2006) Ana and the Internet: a review of pro-anorexia websites, *International Journal of Eating Disorders*, 39(6): 443–447.

Orbach, S. (1986) *Hunger Strike: The Anorectic's Struggle as a Metaphor of Our Age*, London: Faber and Faber.

Pollack, D. (2003) Pro-eating disorder websites: what should be the feminist response?, *Feminism and Psychology*, 13: 246–251.

Schwartz, K.L., Roe, T., Northrup, J., Meza, J., Seifeldin, R. and Neale, A.V. (2006) Family medicine patients' use of the Internet for health information: a MetroNet study, *Journal of the American Board of Family Medicine*, 19: 39–45.

Sied, R.P. (1994) Too 'close to the bone': the historical context for women's obsession with slenderness, in P. Fallon, M.A. Katzman and S.C. Wooley (eds), *Feminist Perspectives on Eating Disorders*, London: Guilford Press.

Tierney, S. (2004) *A Review of the Literature on the Nature and Treatment of Adolescent Anorexia*, University of Exeter: Centre for Evidence-Based Social Services.

Tierney, S. (2006) The dangers and draw of on-line communication: pro-anorexia websites and their implications for users, practitioners, and researchers, *Eating Disorders*, 14: 181–190.

Walker Bynum, C. (1991) *Fragmentation and Redemption: Essays on Gender and the Human Body in Medieval Religion*, New York: Urzone.

Weedon, C. (1987) *Feminist Practice and Poststructuralist Theory*, Oxford: Blackwell.

Wetherell, M. (1988) Fear of fat: interpretative repertoires and ideological dilemmas, in J. Maybin and N. Mercer (eds), *Using English: From Conversation to Cannon*, London: Routledge.

9 How big girls become fat girls

The cultural production of problem eating and physical inactivity

Carla Rice

Introduction

> I was going to be a big kid. I wasn't necessarily going to be fat, though. It became a self-perpetuating cycle of eating to feed myself emotionally because I didn't fit. I became fat because of circumstance. Cultural environment shaped my size.
>
> (Sylvie)

Despite growing dialogue about body diversity, there are many disparaging depictions of people perceived as fat. In contemporary western cultures, overweight and obesity increasingly are interpreted as unattractive, downwardly mobile, physically or emotionally unhealthy, and as a lack of body and self-control (LeBesco, 2004; LeBesco, Gard, both this volume). Throughout public health discourses, obesity is conceptualized as a disease and as an epidemic (World Health Organization, 2000; see also Gard, Probyn, Throsby, all this volume). Consequences of size standards and stereotypes are especially exacting for girls and women, who encounter frequent evaluation of physical appearance as part of their social experience of gender.

Feminist and post-structuralist perspectives emphasize how bodies and identities are shaped and experienced through cultural representations and social relations. Unfinished at birth, bodies are configured over the course of a life through the intermingling of biology, culture and society. For some theorists, physicality, psyche and society play a part in the dynamic process of the body's 'becoming' (Grosz, 1994). From a feminist post-structuralist vantage point, cultural meanings given to bodies also become a basis of identity in social relations (Brah, 2001). In western societies, one location that may be particularly salient in shaping identity is school; a place where perceptions of appearance and difference shape children's belonging and standing (Rice, 2003). Entering peer groups for the first time at school, children grasp how idealized physical features enhance some girls' popularity and social power, and how divergence from cultural standards elicits devaluation of others' differences. This includes fat girls, who may be marginalized by messages about the abject fat female body interwoven throughout interactions.

In North American societies, two competing frames shape current dialogue on obesity and overweight: obesity as an 'epidemic' versus as a 'myth' (Campos, 2004; Gard and Wright, 2005). The first of these dominates public discourse. Yet, as recently as the 1980s, there was active debate about the concepts, causes and consequences of overweight. Feminist theorists in particular provided alternative positions to conventional medical accounts by situating experiences of diversely embodied women within patriarchal social relations (Orbach, 1979). Although many feminist and other critical voices contested medicalizing views, these increasingly have been marginalized by 'obesity epidemic' rhetoric. Initially adopted by the US government, Canadian institutions also embraced this conceptualization, and commissioned reports that framed fatness as a disease of westernized societies (Raine, 2004). In Canada, as in other wealthy countries, obesity epidemic discourses emerged as hegemonic in part because they dovetailed with earlier state efforts to improve the fitness of citizens. From the 1960s onwards, many western governments responded to growing concerns about excessive consumption and sedentary lifestyles by initiating public campaigns calling for more physical activity to prevent fatness and promote fitness, especially for children (Gard and Wright, 2001). Importantly, the efficacy of such interventions has never been established.

Close reading of obesity research reveals empirical uncertainty about its core conviction that obesity is a disease caused by overeating and inactivity (see Gard, this volume). For example, the disease status of fat depends on its correlation with *future* illness (Ross, 2005); a medicalization which can be contested because current size is pathologized here only on the basis of possible future illness. Use of the term 'epidemic' is also challenged for arousing deep-seated fears associated with rapid spread of communicable disease. This may heighten public anxieties and 'rationalize' morally questionable medical interventions into overweight (Gard and Wright, 2005). Despite dissent within obesity science, causes and solutions recurrently converge on people's health practices (Cogan and Ernsberger, 1999). Such a stance not only ignores empirical ambiguity it also erases contextual factors of poverty, sexism, and weightism that constrain individuals' options for eating and activity. Rather than focusing upon stemming the 'epidemic' of fat folk, critical analysis of obesity discourses shifts the emphasis to examining the emergence of an idea – obesity as a dangerous disease – that has captured the cultural imagination. Throughout western history, body size has been a signifier for the health, fitness and status of individuals and nations, with celebration and stigmatization of fat fluctuating at different times among different groups (Stearns, 1997). Despite critical perspectives on fat, the ways in which present-day obesity discourses might affect fat girls' bodies, behaviours and identities remain largely unexplored.

Hence, this chapter draws upon feminist post-structuralist theories of fat to analyse the body histories of women who recount their experiences of becoming 'fat girls' within a Canadian context. Because most body image research analyses white, middle-class, average-sized and non-disabled women's weight and embodiment problems (see also Bordo, this volume), I focus on narratives of diversely-embodied women to explore affinities and disparities in their body experiences. Drawing on feminist insights about the body's 'becoming', I demonstrate 'how the unfit fat body is made from interactions of large bodies, cultural representations and social practices that shape bodies of size' (Rice, 2007: 164). In the analysis below, I draw on participants' accounts to illustrate how harmful consequences of weight stereotyping crystallize in a tendency to avoid physical activity and adopt problematic eating. For participants of diverse races, ethnicities and abilities, negative perceptions of fatness create a difficult double bind by blocking opportunities for claiming credible (feminine or tomboy) identities. In light of recent warnings about the 'obesity epidemic' among children, the analysis concludes with a discussion of the implications of this for feminist praxis.

Methodology and interpretation

This analysis emerges from qualitative research I undertook to understand the role of bodies in women's identity acquisition between early childhood and late adolescence (see Rice, 2007, for details). The project followed participants' creation of body images and their initiation into body practices as attempts to give symbolic and material form to received and preferred accounts of themselves. My central research question was: *How do women negotiate cultural meanings given to bodies and use these interpretations in shaping their identities, subjectivities and sense of life possibilities?*

To attract participants with a range of appearances and differences, I combined snowball and strategic sampling (Strauss and Corbin, 1998) and crafted an open-ended, semi-structured interview guide to capture experiences they considered significant. After analysing the data to formulate themes that explained the role of the body in identity formation, I moved to capture, through narrative analysis, the complexities of identity and agency embedded in women's accounts. I found that constant comparative coding combined with post-structuralist narrative analysis shed light on social processes underpinning participants' personal accounts, while illuminating their abilities to craft a self in the context of disparaging images and daily intrusions.

The participants were women aged 20 to 45 years, who described themselves as Northern European (28%), African-Caribbean (20%), South-Asian (14%), Southern and Eastern European (13%) and Asian (10%) Canadian. These percentages roughly reflected the ethno-racial makeup of the

Canadian city where the study was conducted.[1] Their mobility and sensory disabilities included cerebral palsy and blindness; their facial and physical differences consisted of craniofacial conditions and scoliosis; and their chronic illness ranged from rheumatoid arthritis to reproductive disorders. While women described growing up in middle- (43 percent) and working- or welfare-class households (40 percent), at the time of the interview a majority (61 percent) reported that their income situation was 'limited'. This analysis includes the accounts of 21 women who had formed a fat identity by the end of childhood and/or who witnessed effects of anti-fat attitudes on other children.

Producing physical and social 'unfitness'

> My mom would ask me to go to the store. I had so much anxiety about that . . . I think it was because of being overweight and people commenting even though that's not what I thought consciously. All I knew was that it was uncomfortable to go outside.
>
> (Salima)

Women recounted how they were rendered as physically and socially unfit through the on-going dialogue of their social relations. This included the symbolic systems, physical environments, and visual, verbal and physically violent exchanges, which taught them that they transgressed the culturally normal (feminine, fit and flawless) body. Negative perceptions of fatness became increasingly commonplace as contributors moved through childhood, and occurred at home, on the street and especially at school. When memorable anti-fat cultural representations gained meaning and momentum in social interactions, these had significant implications for participants' developing sense of bodily self.

Participants told how critical comments from friends and family were the most memorable sources of cultural knowledge about size. For most, including Aurora, family members first imparted the significance of size differences through body-based comparisons with sisters, cousins and female friends:

> My sister is chubbier. They'd always make that distinction. I was 'la flaca' [the thin one], and she was 'la gorda' [the fat one]. Together, we

---

1 The 'visible minority' population in Canada had grown from 5 percent of the population in 1981 to 13.4 percent in 2001, mainly due to changes in racist immigration policies (Boyd and Vickers, 2000). In 2001, South Asian, Asian and African Canadians comprised the largest racialized groups, and were concentrated in metropolitan areas of Toronto, Vancouver and Montreal (Chard and Renaud, 1999).

make the perfect ten. It was terrible. They're lavishing on me and disregarding her . . .

(Aurora)

As a result of such body-based comparisons, many women acquired consciousness of unequal values given to different sizes. Stories of Catherine and many others further suggest that gendered power relations operating in encounters with fathers, brothers and other boys frequently opened up big girl bodies to a particularly gendered critical gaze:

My brother started to give me the nickname Moose or Cow. Those names hurt. But I wasn't aware of it [being big] and it wasn't negative until people started to comment.

(Catherine)

Through harsh and harassing comments, boys and men dictated anti-fat attitudes that informed women's perceptions of their bodies and selves. For many, designation of their bodies as 'fat' laid the foundation for their forced accommodation to an unfit identity that, in turn, negatively shaped their embodied being.

FIT FAT
August, 1979

Figure 9.1 Fit-Fat.

Source: ParticipACTION Canada.

In Canada, memorable messages for many women interviewed were state-sponsored fitness tests delivered through school curricula and public service announcements (PSAs) disseminated through popular media. In one PSA, from the 1970s, entitled 'Fit-Fat' (see Figure 9.1), an ungainly, chubby 'a' cartoon character was contrasted with an able, slim 'i' figure (Lagarde, 2004).[2] By linking fitness with thinness and positioning fat as opposite to fit, such messages conveyed that fatness and fitness could *not* coincide within the same body. While few participants could recall the specific contents of these messages, Maude recounted their consequences, which included instilling a nascent sense that her body was in some way bad or wrong:

> I remember this feeling of dread when the ads came on TV. Once my father and I were watching and I remember a man's voice saying, 'This year fat's not where it's at.' This made me so self-conscious because I was already feeling bad about my body . . .
>
> (Maude)

Women told how body standards and stereotypes were conveyed everywhere at school, including through furniture design and dress codes, playground interactions, but especially, in gym classes. While most participants enjoyed physical education, many described how their continual framing as 'fat', rather than according to their potential or actual abilities, eroded their physical agency. When teachers and students rooted assessments of fat girls' abilities in stereotypical notions concerning their size, as Iris explained, they produced girls' presumed lack of skill:

> Once I was a fat kid, there's limitations on your abilities. You're unfit basically. . . . NO, I lost confidence in that. I didn't like sports or gym. Not because I couldn't actually perform the sports. It's because I didn't like being taunted.
>
> (Iris)

Within recent feminist research, experiences of gender, race and weight-related harassment emerge as a major obstacle to girls' participation in physical activity at school (Bauer et al., 2004; Larkin and Rice, 2005). For participants in this study, routines and requirements of physical education such as fitness testing, public performance, weight measurements and revealing clothes also increased their exposure to the evaluative gaze and potentially harassing commentary and practices of others:

> My teacher commented on how I was gaining weight, when I was about 10. He said that I had poor eating habits. When we had to run in the

---

2 Thanks are extended to ParticipACTION Canada and the late Russ Kisby for permission to reprint the Fit-Fat graphic analysed in this chapter.

gym, he said I had problems running. . . . It didn't feel very good in front of everybody.

(Isobel)

My body became a source of torment. This is why I HATE my grade 5 teacher: he had the practice of letting kids divide up teams for sports. My best friend and I were always picked last.

(Gayle)

According to the women's narratives, pedagogical practices that under-mined fat girls' sense of ability often dissuaded them from participation in physical activities. By exposing big girls' bodies to others' critical gaze, school dress codes and open changing rooms frequently instilled a negative body image, giving rise to stressful strategies to conceal size differences:

I loved school, but I hated the students and I hated the interaction. I hated gym class. I hated changing in the change rooms. I didn't want them to see my body.

(Yolanda)

By framing participants first (and primarily) as 'unfit' and only secondarily as girls with other characteristics, abilities and aspirations, fat for many became a dominating identity in childhood. Combined racial, disability and weight-related harassment made it difficult for some racialized women to distinguish which physical differences were being devalued within interactions. Yet when fatness was framed as a personal flaw or moral failure at home and school, as Leigh testified, it became a recurring source of shame:

I was the only Chinese kid in class. I didn't know: 'Are they picking on me because I'm Chinese or are they picking on me because I'm bigger?' . . . More from my family that I was given all these comments and made to feel bad about myself. People talk about overweight people being shamed into losing the weight. That's what my mom did. My siblings heard her taunts. That's what bothered me the most: they learned this from my mother.

(Leigh)

Failing at femininity

These women's narratives illustrate how conforming to culturally appro-priate expressions of gender was central for self-definition in childhood. However, rather than being a stable or unitary influence, the salience of gender shifted in social situations and in its intermingling with other identities (Thorne, 1999). While gender fluidity was a significant feature of their accounts, gendered identities frequently took a negative direction via a devaluing of their size differences. Many fat women, including Gayle, told how they were perceived as possessing a body that 'other-gendered' them as 'improper', 'odd' or 'not' girls:

> Because of my fat . . . I was made to feel like an improper female if I showed signs of femininity. In grade 3, I liked a boy. There was nothing remotely sexual. 'Look, he's your boyfriend!' 'Oooh, you like him!' That was a shock to me, having to watch your actions so that they can't be construed as you like someone. . . . My 'fat, ugly' label stuck and I was a loser, weird Gayle.
>
> (Gayle)

Black and other racialised women indicated that images of an attractive female body spanned a broader range of sizes in their communities than in mainstream contexts (see also Bordo, this volume). However, these women grew up during a time when communities of colour comprised less than 5 percent of the Canadian population (Statistics Canada, 2003). Subjected to racial othering and isolation within the social landscapes of childhood, many lacked a community context in which to develop a critical consciousness of racist beauty ideals or to imagine an alternative body aesthetic (Poran, 2002). In addition, racialized women told how negative perceptions of their colour combined with negative perceptions of their size to disqualify their gender:

> I didn't feel like a girl. Do girl things. I was not a girl, not a boy, just someone existing. Then compound that with being a black female. You feel: 'I'm nowhere.' It's bad enough being a white girl and you're fat. But when you're fat and you're black, that's the lowest.
>
> (Sharon)

Black feminists have analysed how black women are seen as more aggressive and athletic within dominant discourses of femininity (Hammonds, 1999). Some African-Caribbean Canadian participants suggested that constructions of female blackness as more masculine may intermingle with meanings of fatness as less active and less able such that they become positioned as neither masculine nor feminine girls.

For many women, 'failing' at femininity often opened up other possibilities for performing gender and, with this, space to contest received constructions of otherness and to thus improvise alternative identities. The in-between status of 'tomboy' enabled girls to express attributes – such as athleticism, curiosity and strength – that were disallowed in 'feminine' girls. Once given the attribution of 'fat', however, they found their status as tomboy difficult to sustain. When cultural meanings of boy bodies as wiry, gutsy and strong conflicted with interpretations of fat bodies as inert, inept and weak, participants perceived as fat frequently faced disqualification from tomboy identities through their exclusion from tomboy pursuits. As Sylvie's narrative indicates, exclusion often occurred through boys' aggressive challenges to big girls' physical abilities and strength:

> I remember my 'fall from grace' from being one of the boys. . . . When I was a kid I was stronger than they were. I didn't throw like a girl, I didn't run like a girl, I didn't fight like a girl. I can remember when the boys started to become stronger than me. They would gang up on me so I couldn't beat them up any more. So I got banished. . . . I became the classic fat kid. I went from being a powerful kid to totally despised . . .
>
> (Sylvie)

Many social commentators, following Foucault (1980), have argued that power in modern society operates through creating a desire to conform to a 'normal' body. Katerina testified that girls' compliance with gendered size norms is also secured through direct, repressive and often violent control of their bodies:

> I'll never forget this, she [a girl perceived as fat at Katerina's school] was walking home. . . . A bunch of boys got together and they spit all over her. Her jacket was covered in spit.
>
> (Katerina)

As Sylvie and Katerina's stories powerfully illustrate, because girls' fatness was made to signify their failure to conform to cultural standards of the feminine *or* the fit tomboy body, it was treated as a symbolically significant and threatening state of embodied being.

Enforcing problem eating practices

In a westernised Canadian culture that equates a person's merit and morality with body conformity, the women's narratives show how fatness became a bodily sign of physical and social unfitness. Many recounted how adults (re)produced prescriptive bodily ideals, by imposing punitive dieting routines to discipline fat children's bodies and behaviours deemed as unruly, greedy and weak. At Gina's school for children with disabilities, for example, staff regulated the eating of students perceived as fat. Segregation of fat students with disabilities created an identifiable group of others, who were multiply marginalized by perceptions that they were incapable of maintaining control over their bodily abilities or appetites:

> They had this institutional attitude about kids with disabilities. They stuck kids that they perceived to be too big or too fat on the cafeteria

diet table. For years, myself and my friends were on this diet table. That was very damaging because it was at public school and peer pressure [was intense] . . .

(Gina)

For women with disabilities, cultural messages about the disabled body, such as bodily fragility, vulnerability and dependency (Rogers and Swadener, 2001), intersected with gendered messages about the fat form, including incapacity, overindulgence and lack of restraint or willpower. Although both bodily differences were interpreted as impairments that needed fixing, cultural treatment of disability as an inherent attribute contrasted sharply with the framing of fatness as an intentional act (also see Throsby, this volume). Appetites of fat disabled kids were regulated because their fatness was seen as a deliberate action that further impaired an already unfit form. Fatness signified surrender of the disabled child's self to excessive appetites that could be restrained only through greater control of the already incapacitated body.

Most participants without disabilities did not experience such disturbing and overt institutional enforcement of cultural size norms through disciplining or disruption of their eating. Yet when those perceived as fat failed to 'qualify' as girls, their doctors, mothers and others encouraged and enforced dieting routines as a strategy for re-making their bodies to fit gendered size norms.

Medical concerns about dieting and weight intersected with other anxieties regarding girls' adherence to a conventionally feminine body. As Sharon illustrates, messages about healthy weights augmented messages about femininity to enforce adherence to both imperatives:

I was 8 or 9. My doctor said, 'You should lose weight. Don't you want to go to your high school prom?' He said that boys don't go out with fat girls. . . . My mother was there when he said this. She had brought me to him to help me to lose weight. . . . They put me on pills. They just made me sleep. . . . That was when I started to hide the food . . .

(Sharon)

According to participants, regulation of size through enforced dieting resulted in lifelong struggles with food. Like Sharon and Gina, some developed compulsive, binge or secretive eating practices in childhood in response to adult interventions. Others talked of taking up 'disordered' eating during adolescence as a result of pressures to appear desirable. When participants, perceived as too plain, unattractive or ethnically different, were positioned as 'other than female' in the passage to womanhood, many adopted problem eating to escape their labelling as deviant: 'At least I felt normal enough and desirable enough [when bulimic] that I could actually contemplate a sexual relationship' (Gayle). Whether they started secretive eating in childhood to resist restrictive diets or later adopted 'disordered' eating to amend size differences disqualifying of their desirability, it is noteworthy that *all* participants perceived as fat eventually talked of taking up problem eating practices.

Conclusions

Over the past three decades fat has been reframed as a disease of epidemic proportions. Yet designation of obesity as a threatening disease may have serious negative consequences for women and girls perceived as fat. The women in this study suggested that by framing big bodies as fat and unfit, anti-fat attitudes, commonplace in the 1970s and 1980s, contributed to their problematic eating and exercise and may have caused them to gain weight. According to their accounts, being a big girl was not the same as being a fat girl. Instead, their bigness became fatness within environments that produced their physical and social 'unfitness', leading to exercise and eating practices typically associated with fat. Fat became a problem for participants through a multiple marginalizing of big girls' bodies within social relations that refused to see female physical and social fitness as embodied by anything but a thin, able-bodied and white form.

This analysis suggests that, with renewed focus on fatness prevention through fitness promotion, today's obesity epidemic proponents likewise may be leading a new cohort of big children (especially girls) to adopt problem eating and exercise, possibly contributing to another generation's struggles with identity and with weight. Rather than endorsing policies and practices with such potentially harmful effects, a preferred path may be to adopt a 'body equity' approach that would advocate for greater acceptance of diverse bodies, enhanced opportunities for enjoyable activities and expanded options to make good food choices (Rice and Russell, 2002). This might open up new ways to approach the relationship of fatness to fitness and health, for instance by moving away from cultural practices of enforcing body norms and toward more creative ways of exploring the abilities and possibilities unique to different bodies.

Acknowledgements

I want to thank the women who generously agreed to participate in this research, from whom I have learned so much. I also wish to acknowledge and thank my colleagues Claire Carter, Sheila Gill, Margaret Hobbs, Colleen O'Manique, Jennifer Nelson, Lorna Renooy and Hilde Zitzelsberger as well as Natalie Beausoleil, Maree Burns, Eithne Luibheid, Helen Malson and Jan Wright, whose perceptive comments contributed to strengthening ideas developed in this chapter.

References

Bauer, K., Yang, W. and Austin, B. (2004) How can we stay healthy when you're throwing all of this in front of us?, *Health Education and Behaviour*, 31(1): 36–46.

Boyd, M. and Vickers, M. (2000) 100 years of immigration in Canada, *Canadian Social Trends*, 58, 2–12.

Brah, A. (2001) Difference, diversity, differentiation, in K.-K. Bhavnani (ed.), *Feminism and 'Race'*, New York: Oxford University Press, pp. 456–478.

Campos, P. (2004) *The Obesity Myth*, New York: Gotham Books.

Chard, J. and Renaud, V. (1999) Visible minorities in Toronto, Vancouver, and Montreal, *Canadian Social Trends*, 54: 20–25.

Cogan, J. and Ernsberger, P. (1999) Dieting, weight, and health: reconceptualizing research and policy, *Journal of Social Issues*, 55(2): 187–205.

Foucault, M. (1980) *Power/knowledge: Selected Interviews and Other Writings* (translated by C. Gordon), New York: Pantheon Books.

Gard, M. and Wright, J. (2001) Obesity discourses and physical education in a risk society, *Studies in Philosophy and Education*, 20: 535–549.

Gard, M. and Wright, J. (2005) *Obesity Epidemic: Science, Morality and Ideology*, New York: Taylor and Francis.

Grosz, E. (1994) *Volatile Bodies*. Bloomington: Indiana University Press.

Hammonds, E. (1999) Toward a genealogy of black female sexuality, in J. Price and M. Shildrick (eds), *Feminist Theory and the Body*, New York: Routledge, pp. 93–104.

Lagarde, F. (2004) Keys to ParticipACTION's success, *Canadian Journal of Public Health*, 95(S2): S20–S26.

Larkin, J. and Rice, C. (2005) Beyond 'healthy eating' and 'healthy weights': harassment and the health curriculum in middle schools, *Body Image*, 2(3): 219–232.

LeBesco, K. (2004) *Revolting Bodies?*, Boston: University of Massachusetts Press.

Orbach, S. (1979) *Fat is a Feminist Issue*, New York: Berkley Books.

Poran, M. (2002) Denying diversity: perceptions of beauty and social comparison processes among Latino, Black and White women, *Sex Roles*, 47(1/2): 65–81.

Raine, K. (2004) *Overweight and Obesity in Canada*, Ottawa: Canadian Institute for Health Information.

Rice, C. (2003) Becoming women: body image, identity, and difference in the passage to womanhood, unpublished doctoral dissertation, York University, Toronto.

Rice, C. (2007) Becoming the 'fat girl', *Women's Studies International Forum*, 30: 158–174.

Rice, C. and Russell, V. (2002) *Embodying Equity: Body Image as an Equity Issue*, Toronto, Canada: Green Dragon Press.

Rogers, L. and Swadener, B. (eds) (2001) *Semiotics and Dis/ability*, Albany: State University of New York Press.

Ross, B. (2005) Fat or fiction: weighing the obesity epidemic, in M. Gard and J. Wright (eds), *Obesity Epidemic*, New York: Taylor and Francis, pp. 86–106.

Statistics Canada (2003) Visible minority groups and sex for population, for Canada, provinces, territories, census metropolitan areas and census agglomerations, 2001 Census (Statistics Canada Catalogue No. 97F0010XIE2001002), at: http://www.statcan.ca/bsolc/english/bsolc?catno=97F0010X2001002.

Stearns, P. (1997) *Fat History*, New York: New York University Press.
Strauss, A. and Corbin, J. (1998) *Basics of Qualitative Research: Techniques and Procedures for Developing Grounded Theory*, Thousand Oaks, CA: Sage.
Thorne, B. (1999) *Gender Play*, New Brunswick, NJ: Rutgers University Press.
World Health Organization (2000) *Obesity: Preventing and Managing the Global Epidemic*, Geneva, Switzerland: WHO.

Part III
In/visible bodies and embodiment

10 Fat, feelings, bodies

A critical approach to obesity[1]

Elspeth Probyn

Introduction

I always feel big in cities. In some cities this is understandable. For instance, in Hong Kong I feel elephantine. While the shop assistants are sweet, they concur that none of their jeans would ever fit me. In London I feel extended by the knowledge of the millions that swell into the city centre to work each day. The battle to cross the road forces me into uncomfortable contact with bodies rendered pasty and bloated by commuter travel. In Sydney, especially as the temperatures hit the high thirties, clothing sticks and I try to hide in loose shirts that make me billow and wilt in the hot and humid blasts of air. In the urban US, I feel fat by contagion and feel myself physically trying to withdraw into some small space.

By western standards, I am a fairly normal size, although normal is an increasingly dubious notion. My sensitivity to size is fed by a project on youth cultures of eating that underpins some of my ideas here. There's nothing like being immersed in literature about obesity to make you feel somewhat strange in your body. It also makes you acutely aware of the bodies around you.

There seems to be no question that, in general, everyone is getting bigger. But some demographic groups are increasing faster than others. The old adage attributed to Mrs Wallis Simpson (that scrawny American divorcee who married a king) seems to hold: you can never be too rich or too thin. It seems that now if you are a rich woman, you are more likely to be thin. However, if you are a middle-class working mother, beware. A report – widely and sensationally circulated in the British tabloids – by the Institute

---

1 As a background to this chapter, I am drawing on an ongoing three-year project entitled 'Youth Cultures of Eating'. This project is explicitly formulated to try to provide another way of approaching the question of child and youth obesity (Elspeth Probyn and Jennifer O'Dea, *Youth Cultures of Eating: a comparative cultural analysis of youth obesity, gender, class, ethnicity and age*, Australian Research Council Discovery Project, 2006–09). This is a quantitative survey of some 6000 Australian school boys and girls with an accompanying qualitative study of 250 high primary and high school students.

of Child Health at University College London and Great Ormond Street Hospital has shown that obesity increases in direct correlation with family income. And in higher-income households the longer the mother works each week, the greater the chances of her child being overweight (Davies, 2007).

The question I want to pose is how can we approach this phenomenon from a feminist cultural studies perspective? To briefly situate my research, I see feminist cultural studies as an engaged analysis of individual and group material practices, understood as embedded within the social structures of class, ethnicity, gender, geo-location, and so forth. In terms of weight, obesity and eating practices, there is no possible way of understanding the phenomenon and problematic without centrally focusing on social class. Equally, and as we will see, the unequal global distribution of discourses surrounding bodies, fat and feelings must be central.

Much of cultural studies has attended to the politics of representation, especially media and other popular cultural forms. My own work in this area spans some 20-odd years and has continually returned to questions about gender and embodiment. My very first academic work was an historical analysis of anorexia, which I traced back to case studies published in the *Lancet* in the late 1880s. Published as an article (Probyn, 1987), I attempted to intervene in the increasingly hysterical analyses of anorexia as the result of 'bad' media images of women. Anorexia, I argued, is about the desperate attempt to control something in one's life, and in dire circumstances one of the only options open to young women (and increasingly now young men) is to control their bodies through physical starvation.

Over the years, I have been astonished to see that a certain line about 'body image' has continued to flourish, even though it is often grounded in weak scholarship. To use the Foucauldian concept of discourse, one can say that the 'body image' discourse is now a rarefied and pervasive form of knowledge, spreading across government programs (in Australia, the 'Body Think' initiative in Victoria; in the UK, the 'Body Image' summit), hospital treatment programs for eating disorders, school curricula and education programs, academic analyses in several disciplines (many not equipped with any expertise in media analysis) to, of course, the media itself.

To be schematic, the fixation on the image tends to fix bodies in the sense it renders understandings of bodies as static – and here I intend the double sense: the analyses themselves are static and they produce bodies as static, something that is image but not feelings, emotions and affects. Translated into identity politics, this imparts a hyper-surveillance on what bodies look like in regards to other idealised bodies, and obviates the different feelings bodies experience both in terms of intra-experience (background, personal history, etc.) and inter-experience (in terms of insults, praise, etc.) (see also Burns, this volume).

An unevenly distributed worldwide phenomenon of increased weight, and the widely reported medical effects of this – such as Type II diabetes – now further complicate the insistence on body image (see also Gard, LeBesco, Throsby, all this volume). In what follows, I discuss some of the implications of this phenomenon, and then turn to specific programs around 'youth obesity'. My argument is that an image-based feminist response is insufficient to understand, let alone intervene in, this problematic.

Is obesity a global epidemic?

Much of the debate centres on whether obesity and youth obesity constitute a global epidemic. The terms 'obesity' and 'epidemic' are problematic. Within the rarefied spheres of epidemiology, there is considerable debate about whether obesity is an epidemic and whether the epidemic is worldwide (Campos et al., 2006; Flegal, 2006). As I will describe later on, nonetheless it is clear that something very worrisome is going on in terms of eating patterns, as well as ideas about food.

The WHO (2003) thinks there is a global epidemic, but the Bush Administration didn't like the WHO's recommendation for government intervention. The American think tank, the Center for Science in the Public Interest (2004), argues that 'the US is protecting the food industry, not public health'. For different reasons, I'd argue that the WHO's recommendations focus too narrowly on the government regulation of television advertising, especially for children's television. While arguments about children's 'pester power', referring to their supposed influence gained from fast-food ads over parents' actions, continually circulate in the media, there is still little hard evidence that a causal link exists between the viewing of fast-food advertisements and obesity.

From around the world, and in places with little access to western television, there are reports on growing numbers of overweight people. Some of the reports are quite shocking. For instance, the African nation of Gambia is in an early transition from a rural based to an urban and increasingly globalised economy. Andrew Prentice, an international nutrition expert at the London School of Hygiene and Tropical Medicine, and Felicity Webb conducted research, which includes a striking photo essay. They argue that due to the fact that rural lifestyles are unsustainable because of the collapse of the groundnut crop (due to external competition), Gambians are moving to urban areas. 'This encourages . . . sedentary occupations and plentiful high-fat diets' (Prentice and Webb, 2006: 24). Cheap imported vegetable oils containing trans-fats are resulting in obesity, which was traditionally reserved as a badge of honour for the chief and his wives. Their report provides a snapshot of the complicating factors. On the one hand, there is a traditional privileging of what is called 'having body'. As one of their informants says, 'Both my wife and I had body. . . . Bigger people are thought to be rich. I was proud to be called fat.' His daughter, however, is humiliated when she is called fat. In Gambia, malnutrition and obesity can be found together, although increasingly it is the complications arising from obesity that take up most of the limited medical resources. Diabetes is ten-fold higher than in the UK and the amputation of diabetic feet is the most common medical procedure.

Here, we see a situation that can be called global urbanisation, whereby economic forces drive internal migration into the cities. The destruction of local and rural economies is largely due to the importation of cheap and poor quality cooking oil. This then combines with local values that are themselves in transition, caught between local and national values of 'having body' as a testimony to prosperity, and western aspirational images of thinness, as well as the importation of mainly unhealthy western food-stuffs. As one woman puts it: 'It's not good, everyone who has body doesn't want it. Everything makes you tired when you are fat . . . so much, so much pain' (Prentice and Webb, 2006: 30). Another effect of globalisation is that changed local economies of labour may mean that there is less manual labour in the fields and more service industries, commonly associated with women's work. With women working long hours, traditional ways of preparing food become scarcer, even if there were the desire and the products from which to prepare traditional meals.

Closer to home, in Hong Kong, it again seems that the globalisation of national economies is having effects on bodies that are also gendered. Sing Lee, from CUHK, has found that women especially increasingly complain of feeling fat and fatigued (1999). He argues that it would be simplistic to blame women's changing body image on the West. China's open door policy and an unlimited supply of cheap labour have shifted Hong Kong's labour force from manufacturing to a service-based economy, which favours women employees. As Lee (1999: 61) explains, young women increasingly have very different opportunities from their mothers: 'With their own earnings, they become unlimited consumers for a dizzying panoply of beauty products and services, which commodify the body and fluidize their identities.'

What is particularly interesting about Lee's research, albeit slightly dated, is that young women *feel* fat even if they are not. And indeed studies show that in the past 15 years women in Hong Kong have tended to become slimmer while the men have become fatter. In 2002, the Hong Kong Association of Obesity found that 38 per cent of men were overweight and 4.3 per cent were considered obese; 22 per cent of women were overweight and 29 per cent underweight (*China Daily*, 2004).

As with feeling fat, Lee (1999: 63) posits that feeling fatigued provides the women with 'a sociomoral experience [and language] that resists medical-isation'. In other words, it allows for a communal language of embodiment with which to express solidarity with other young women, as well as indi-vidually giving voice to the anxieties that accompany modern urban life. When he conducted his research, it was rare that young women would work out. He quotes a 23-year-old who says, 'I understand that regular workout may enhance my health, but that makes me too tired to go to work the next day. I would rather relax by taking a nap or window shopping' (ibid.).

While I'd rather jog (which I loathe) than shop, this presents an intriguing picture. Under radically different conditions than their mothers, educated and relatively affluent young women have constructed a language through which to link what may be a western-influenced complaint amongst women ('I feel fat') to a localised response to objectively changed conditions and subjective experience of those changes (see also Nasser and Malson, this volume). And this is a very embodied reaction to the changes in the macro-structures of society.

Is fat still a feminist issue?

I now want to turn to a seminal text about feelings and fat. Susie Orbach's *Fat is a Feminist Issue*, first published in 1978 focused on 'fat in the mind'. As Orbach recently reiterated, 'Eating today is a real problem for many because it is inflected with guilt, confusion, regret and worry' (Orbach, 2006: 68). Her point of attack continues to be the body-image industries, which, as she says, 'operate as a negative force on girls', and women's, and increasingly boys' and men's self-experience'.

When *Fat is a Feminist Issue* was first published, it was extraordinary. Its enduring legacy can be seen in the ways in which its title has thoroughly entered the English language as a catch phrase. For instance, a recent blog writer, 'Pasta Queen', was astonished to find out that it was the title of a book. However, writing in the 1970s, Orbach took up many contemporary feminist methods and concerns. She had been involved in women's con-sciousness raising groups, and she writes that she felt 'overwhelming relief to be in a group with women, fat and thin . . . where they could discuss a subject that had been so hidden and so private' (Orbach, 1978: 10). Let me be clear that Orbach's commitment and verve were and remain impressive, and her current objective of attack – the diet industry – is well aimed.

Coming from a feminist inflected psychoanalytic framework, Orbach went beyond 'reducing overeating and obesity to character defects' (ibid.: 17). Her central theme is that 'fat is about protection', protection from society's sexual stereotypes and limited options for women. She turned around the usual articulation of why are women fat, and asked 'what is it about women's position in society that leads them to respond by getting fat?' (ibid.: 19). Her response is that, 'fat is a way of saying no to powerlessness and self-denial' (ibid.: 33). The main point of the book is that women use fat to protect themselves from a hostile and sexist society. Orbach's main thesis is that, '[b]eing fat isolates and invalidates a woman' (ibid.: 16).

It is undeniable that many, many women found solace in her message. And it is still being taken up. But I want to argue that it may well be that a misreading of Orbach's message has been translated into the idea that the goal is acceptance (see also LeBesco, Rice, both this volume). Her original argument that it is not in women's interest to be fat still stands. However, especially in the US, the fat-acceptance movement has become powerful and directly draws its inspiration from feminism. Drawing on much the same tactics as other identity politics, including queer, the end point is often simplistically seen as accepting and celebrating super-sized female bodies. In feminist media studies, a constant theme is the analysis of television and other media to determine that fat bodies are not acceptable in the mainstream media. This refrain, variously theorised or not, is repeated in feminist journals. For instance, in 2005 *Feminist Media Studies* – that often publishes good material, and I am on their editorial board – published a section on 'Gender and the plus-size body'. The overall tone was directed to the advancement of fat acceptance. As Melinda Young (2005: 251) argued, using the tactics of semiotic reversal in regards to 'fat', 'Feminism could use this technique to advance fatness as a culturally viable, uncontested form.' In another article, Natalie Wilson (2005: 252) is outraged at the fact that, 'in New Zealand, an official proposal to tax food based on fat content was put forward'.

What's a feminist to do?

These are, of course, selected quotations. They are, however, indicative of something quite worrying. In other words, I do not think that it is a viable strategy for feminism to 'reclaim fat and use it as a political strategy' (to quote Young, from above). There is over a decade of critique in cultural studies, which argues against a simplistic model of politics based in semiotic reversal (Mercer, 1994). The examples that Wilson cites range widely: her denunciation of the New Zealand proposal is posed in an unproblematised list along with examples such as the seriously stupid and perhaps damaging reality show, *The Swan*, where fat is surgically removed from contestants.

Part of the theoretical problem here is that the attention to the cultural in feminist cultural studies has fostered too much emphasis on the politics of representation. It's hard to believe that 30 years of quite sophisticated theoretical debates are now reduced to complaints about the lack of images of 'plus-sized' women or to the outcry at the emaciated state of catwalk models. This has been accompanied by a pervasive argument, which drew on a very narrow reading of Foucault's ideas about power and discipline. The refrain of 'docile bodies', passively awaiting discursive inscription, and the accompanying obsession with resistance closes down more than it illuminates. To be schematic, fat becomes objectified as a mode of resistance. While this may provide limited vocabularies, for instance in terms of, most often, American-based fat acceptance identity politics, as a viable strategy for social intervention it is limited. In a paradoxical manner, the focus on image and fat acceptance reduces women's being to that of 'fat woman'. Whether she is a proud fat woman or not, this is a limited way to understand human subjectivity.

I am also not convinced that such tactics can overturn the shame and emotional damage that many women who are overweight regularly face. If anything, fat is becoming increasingly laden with a highly moralistic set of assumptions and popularised on television as a source of comedy. Take as an example the proposed new BBC3 reality show called 'Fat Teens Can't Hunt'. Produced by Big Brother's Endemol, the premise is mind-boggling. Ten overweight British teenagers are to be taken to Australia to live with Aboriginal Australians. 'If they want to eat they must feast on plants, grasses and fruit as well as trap, kill, and cook any animals or insects they find' (Nathan, 2007: 29). As Sara Nathan, the TV writer for *The Sun*, sums up the idea: 'if they do not tuck into the traditional tucker, they go without' (ibid.).

Obviously Endemol is seeking to offend as many as possible. It also seems that they have taken this idea from an episode of *Survivor* filmed in Australia, where one of the challenges involved eating 'bush tucker'. From the looks on their faces, one would have thought they were being asked to eat each other. The producer of Endemol's farce seemingly is serious when she states that, 'this experiment gives our teenagers a unique opportunity to address their dysfunctional relationships with food once and for all before they reach adulthood' (Nathan, 2007).

The ways in which the current situation regarding obesity is being framed in terms of race, class and geo-location is, to say the least, evident. Against the demonisation of the working class and the poor, or the overt racism of the depiction of Aboriginals as primitive and the horror and disgust of traditional bush foods,[2] it is hard to see what a simplistic model based on the vague and untheorised notion of fat acceptance can offer. This focus has radically limited how feminist cultural studies can respond to what is both a social problem and an issue that affects large numbers of individual women, men, girls and boys.

I want to return to the question of *feeling* big, or in other words, to the question of embodiment rather than representation. As you will know, embodiment or corporeality has been a sustained thread of inquiry within feminist cultural studies. But, as I alluded to above, the focus on the image (see also Burns, Malson, both this volume) may have shifted the question of how and where bodies feel.

Dynamic bodies

The focus on the body as image renders bodies static. And by this I mean that the body is detached from the social forces, which mould how bodies feel and with what consequences. How some bodies feel or are made to feel disgusting, out of place or conversely – and rarely – *bien dans sa peau* (at ease with oneself) and comfortable, is of necessity a topic that compels

---

2 I have discussed elsewhere (Probyn, 2000) how racism is effected through representations of what others are thought to eat, and thus to be.

awareness of economics and geo-political positioning, as well as localised and globalised notions about gendered bodies. As Lee's (1999) research suggested, when Hong Kong women say they feel fat, they may also be saying something profound about their situation in a changed political and familial realm. Or, in a quite different context, as Gambians are caught in a generational shift from valuing body to deploring fat, they are also responding in an embodied way to the tremendous economic and social changes they are living through. As Marcel Mauss would have put it, these expressions demand a 'total' approach to the question, which is at once psychological, social, economic and physiological.

In a more recent take on this, geographers such as Joyce Davidson, Liz Bondi and Mick Smith (2005) have argued for accounts of social life that focus on the inherently dynamic and relational geographies of modern life. To make this more explicit, this places the body in relation to different structural factors and seeks to draw out how bodies come to feel global-isation as it rearranges local bodies.

The challenge is to devise a frame of analysis and modes of intervention that can hold together the subjective ways in which bodies are imbricated in large-scale economic changes that are transforming our cities and the bodies that inhabit them. By way of conclusion, I want to briefly turn to a French program, which may have a chance of rendering the relation of bodies to their multiple contexts more dynamic. EPODE, which stands for '*Ensemble, prévenons l'obésité des enfants*' ('Together we will prevent child obesity'), brings together ten towns around France. Children are taken to the markets, taught how to cook and are allowed an occasional treat – *une journee de gourmandise*. They are also encouraged to walk and cycle around their towns, and programs are set up to make this safe. The input from towns is crucial to this project. The mayors must compete to be a part of the network, which is conducted with other groups such as *Les villes cyclables*. The financial contribution of commercial partners also means that the program costs local inhabitants one euro per day. For this, they get family breakfasts with a dietician, a program of walking to school, and educational sessions for parents. Each month there is a focus on a different seasonal food, and a farmer may be brought in to school classes, the cafeteria will focus on the product and local supermarkets distribute free recipes. The results are encouraging: in five towns the rate of overweight or obese children has stabilised and in five it has dropped.

While this program seems promising, there are obvious drawbacks both to its implementation and conceptualisation. It tends to place a normative family at the centre, with parents able to undertake the various educational and physical activities. It may also depend on the French 35-hour work-week, now being totally revamped by the current French government. One wonders how exactly differences in ethnicity can be incorporated, as well as those of class – although a healthy respect for food cultures spans French society.

More broadly, the French are resisting the increasing homogenisation of food and tastes created by a supermarket culture. In a fascinating ethnographic study, Wendy Leynse (2006: 130) charts the ways in which French school children are being socialised as 'informed and situated eaters'. Through the school system, children are taught why and how 'terroir' matters. Terroir, which is usually associated with wine, is broadened to include the interrelation of soil, climate, topography and the cultural history of food production and consumption. Through field trips on bicycles, children are given a 'taste education', recognising that 'to learn to differentiate smells and tastes, one must have experience and references (of sensory memory) to different smells/tastes' (ibid.: 141).

As Leynse (ibid.: 141) puts it, 'this is an argument to taste things starting young'. I want to turn briefly to another program, which also gets kids when they are young and teaches them the pleasures of taste. Stephanie Alexander's Kitchen Garden project has been running for several years in the Australian state of Victoria. Alexander is a highly respected cook and food writer. Concerned by the widespread ignorance of children about food (for instance, studies in the UK show that a large percentage of children do not know where bacon or yoghurt come from), Alexander set up a garden at a school in Melbourne's working-class suburb of Collingswood. There, children grow different vegetables and then learn to cook with them. It's a simple and brilliant idea that gets kids' hands dirty in the soil, teaches them about why and how different things grow, and then gets them proudly making their own food.

These programs may initially seem like a long way from the theoretical ideas I have raised. However, their rationales and results are opposed to an obsessive attention to images of bodies. Importantly, they offer a glimpse of how to respond in a practical way to the demands of a dynamic and relational emotional geography, that children have little resources to navigate.

Given this messy and complicated issue, what can feminist cultural studies do? First, we must move away from a form of analysis and critique based on a simplistic model of images and the politics of representation. Arguing for increased representations of 'plus-size' bodies and for fat acceptance will do little to change a situation where class, gender and location overdetermine who becomes overweight or obese (see also LeBesco, Rice, both this volume). Nor will it do anything to effect change in improving ideas about what to eat.

At a fundamental level, we need to listen to the voices of those caught within a complex matrix of changing global and local conditions (see also Nasser and Malson, this volume). In this chapter, I have tried to point to the ways in which transitions caused by globalisation and what I've called global urbanisation reveal conflicting beliefs and ideas. The Gambian woman who cries out that, 'Everything makes you tired when you are fat . . . so much, so much pain', is one instance of an embodied response to the profound shift in how bodies feel. The Hong Kong women who use a language of feeling fat can be seen as another instance of an embodied language that responds to changing cultural and economic contexts. These voices are hardly to be celebrated – as within a fat acceptance model. They are, however, to be accounted for.

As distressing is the widespread confusion that we hear from many of the young girls and boys we have interviewed in our research on youth cultures of eating. Particularly in the case of girls, and thanks in great part to the feminist-fuelled panics over anorexia, there is no language with which to sensibly talk about eating and bodies. As one girl puts it: 'it's really hard to talk about in school, do you know what I mean? Like so many people say they are fat and people don't really know how to tell them if they are or not 'cause like they are so sensitive about it.' As Fanny Ambjörnsson (2005) also found in her ethnographic research with Swedish girls, there is 'a normalisation of dissatisfaction [which] seems to be the result of the victimization discourse of the 1980s and '90s'. As she argues (ibid.: 119), the constant attention to eating disorders, and I would add the hyper-surveillance of girls' bodies and eating, 'appears to have ended up conveying that dissatisfaction is a normal female state'.

I realise that my critique of feminist approaches may be harsh, but how is it that after years of privileging the body, we have a whole generation who literally cannot talk about their bodies? As Matti Bunzl (2005: 210) argues, in his critique of the politics of focusing on images and representation, 'in the interests of formulating truly progressive strategies as fat and queer people, we might do better to start with the world as it actually is.' We urgently need new ideas about how to intervene. The reason I find the French program promising is that it promises to defuse and de-sensitise food and bodies. Incorporating the whole town, and through the various educative measures, may allow individuals to talk to each other about how their bodies feel. It may create a web wherein a language can be created and at each point – the supermarket, the restaurant, schools, family, people on the streets walking or cycling – individuals are reassured in their bodies. I realise that this is a big ask, but that is the challenge I see for our discipline.

References

Ambjörnsson, F. (2005) Talk, in D. Kulick and A. Meneley (eds), *Fat: The Anthropology of an Obsession*, New York: Penguin.

Bunzl, M. (2005) Chasers, in D. Kulick and A. Meneley (eds), *Fat: The Anthropology of an Obsession*, New York: Penguin.

Campos, P., Saguy, A., Ernsberger, P., Oliver, E. and Gaesser, G. (2006) The epidemiology of overweight and obesity: public health crisis or moral panic?, *International Journal of Epidemiology*, 35: 55–60.

Center for Science in the Public Interest (2004) Bush Adminstration fights WHO obesity report, at: www.cspinet.org/new/200402181.html.

China Daily (2004) Hong Kong men become fatter while women slimmer, at: china.org.cn.

Davidson, J., Bondi, L. and Smith, M. (2005) *Emotional Geographies*, London: Ashgate.

Davies, C. (2007) Middle class fuelling child obesity, *The Telegraph*, 23 July, at: www.telegraph.co.uk/news/main.jhtml?xml=/news/2007/07/23/nantidep323.xml.

Flegal, K. (2006) Commentary: the epidemic of obesity – what's in a name?, *International Journal of Epidemiology*, 35: 72–74.

Lee, S. (1999) Fat, fatigue and the feminine: the changing cultural experience of women in Hong Kong, *Culture, Medicine & Psychiatry*, 23: 51–79.

Leynse, W.L.H. (2006) Journeys through 'ingested topography': socialising the 'situated eater' in France, in T.M. Wilson (ed.), *Food, Drink and Identity in France*, Amsterdam: Rodopi.

Mercer, K. (1994) *Welcome to the Jungle: New Positions in Black Cultural Studies*, London: Routledge.

Nathan, S. (2007) Fat's entertainment: reality show forces tubby teens to find food, *The Sun* 13 April, p. 29.

Orbach, S. (1978) *Fat is a Feminist Issue . . . How to Lose Weight Permanently – Without Dieting*, London: Hamlyn.

Orbach, S. (2006) Commentary: here *is* a public health crisis – it's not fat on the body but fat in the mind and the fat of profits, *International Journal of Epidemiology*, 35: 67–69.

pasta.queen.com (2007) Fat is a feminist issue.

Prentice, A. and Webb, F. (2006) Obesity amidst poverty, *International Journal of Epidemiology*, 35: 24–30.

Probyn, E. (1987) The anorexic body, in M. Kroker and A. Kroker (eds), *Body Invaders: Panic Sex in America*, New York: St. Martin's Press.

Probyn, E. (2000) *Carnal Appetites: FoodSexIdentity*, New York and London: Routledge.

Wilson, N. (2005) Vilifying former fatties: media representations of weight loss surgery, *Feminist Media Studies*, 5(2): 252–255.

WHO (2003) Controlling the global obesity epidemic, at: www.who.int/nutrition/topics/obesity/en/index.html.

Young, M. (2005) One size fits all: disrupting the consumerized, pathologized, fat female form, *Feminist Media Studies*, 5(2): 249–252.

11 Bodies as (im)material?

Bulimia and body image discourse

Maree Burns

I wouldn't want what I may have said or written to be seen as laying claims to totality. I don't try to universalize what I say; conversely, what I don't say isn't meant to be thereby disqualified as being of no importance . . . I like to open up a space of research, try it out, and then if it doesn't work, try again somewhere else . . . My books aren't treatise in philosophy or studies of history; at most, they are philosophical fragments put to work in a historical field of problems.

(Foucault, 2000: 224)

Ever since the late 1980s when the first feminist postmodern analyses of dis/ordered eating began to emerge, there has been an ideological division of sorts between feminists who are interpreted as emphasising the inscriptive nature of cultural imagery and those who emphasise embodiment or the body as experienced. As a scholar, activist and therapist working within the field of dis/ordered eating, I am interested in how postmodern theories of the discursively constituted body might be deployed in ways that trouble the constructed divisions between interior/exterior, experience/discourse, agency/passivity and embodied practice/image. Employing bulimia as a case in point, and drawing upon the work of critical feminists, this chapter engages with ideas about disordered eating, as an outcome of the inscriptive power of cultural representations, and of the body as the site of lived experience engaged in body management practices that may or may not have anything to do with idealised (western) images of slenderness.

Since the late 1980s, a number of feminist academics (e.g. Bray, 1996; Bray and Colebrook, 1998; Eckermann, 1994; Lester, 1997; Probyn, 1988, 1991, this volume) have cautioned against those postmodern analyses of disordered eating which they have interpreted as overly emphasising the inscriptive power of cultural images of thinness. The critique goes as follows: by focusing upon the external surfaces of bodies as inscribed (by media images), and by interpreting varied body management practices as the outcome of the consumption of representations of the thin ideal, such approaches miss an important opportunity to theorise other meanings that might be (re)produced by the performance and experience of various bodily practices. Such analyses potentially render persons as passive and docile rather than (also as) engaging with, resisting and potentially transforming the discourses embedded within those images. Certainly, while critical feminist analyses locate disordered eating in many cultural contexts – not just idealised thin media images – media is usually identified as (an often central) part of the relevant discursive context (especially within westernised cultures). And, it is important to note that even within critical feminist writing, there remains a tendency to focus analyses on the eating disordered (and this is usually the 'anorexic') body as already produced and on the ways in which that body is/has been constituted by discourses (see also Probyn, this volume). This focus is often at the 'expense' of theorising embodiment, experiences and practices whose 'purposes' might not be to alter the surface of the body, its appearance or shape. Even if – as I believe – these critiques of feminist analyses which focus on images of the thin ideal are sometimes misplaced, it is nevertheless important to consider these discussions in order to refine postmodern feminist theories of the discursive production of the material (eating disordered) body.

So, playing devil's advocate, if, in our theories about the mobilisation of dis/ordered eating we were to focus mainly upon the negative effects of the almost ubiquitous image (in westernised cultures) of idealised thinness, then our interrogation of disordered eating would be constrained in particular ways. Such a focus would risk privileging pathological image consumption (Bray and Colebrook, 1998) as 'causal' in these pathologised experiences, and would reify exteriority and the body as a sign. And therefore, thirdly, it would potentially de-emphasise the importance of the 'experience' or embodiment of certain body management practices (e.g. food restriction, bingeing, compensating, exercising) for our interpretations of them, and their activation in women's lives (e.g. Baeveldt and Voestermans, 1996; Brain, 2002; Bray, 1996; Bray and Colebrook, 1998; Eckermann, 1994; Lester, 1997, Probyn 1988, 1991; Squire, 2002, 2003). In the following pages, I will discuss these potential effects, extrapolating from the arguments utilised by the critics cited above.

Without a careful theorisation of embodied subjectivity, Probyn (1991: 117) has suggested, a focus on the (eating disordered) body as 'a disembodied and ideologically interpellated subject position' risks (re)producing dualistic constructions of the self in which mind and body, inside and outside, are once again split. This division occurs, according to Brain (2002), because in the charge to insert the body as the site of gendered material forces of power, some feminist accounts of eating disorders potentially reduce subjectivity to (just) the discursive body, producing it as the effect of a collision of discourses: as a surface of cultural inscription (Radley, 1995). This focus, Brain (2002) suggests, (re)produces the arbitrary theoretical distinctions that continue to be made between the realms of the body as lived (the 'extra' discursive) and the body as inscribed (the discursive). By focusing upon the body as the site/sight of meaning, critics have warned that there is a risk of weighting our focus too heavily in the direction of the latter (e.g. Baeveldt and Voestermans, 1996; Brain, 2002; Bray, 1996; Bray and Colebrook, 1998; Eckermann, 1994; Lester, 1997; Probyn 1988, 1991; Squire, 2002, 2003). Eating disorders are then rendered primarily 'interpretable' via our theorisation of the (visible) bodies of eating disordered women, potentially excluding any notion of the self, embodiment or experience, from analysis. This, they argue, simply reverses the Cartesian mind–body split and produces, not a disembodied self, but rather, a 'deselfed body' (Lester, 1997: 481). Brain (2002: 152) has suggested that this works to render the body-as-experienced 'out of sight' and indeed irrelevant in theorising eating disorders.

As I have mentioned, sole emphasis on cultural imagery of the body as a normalising strategy involved in both the production and interpretation of 'docile' (eating disordered) subjectivities/bodies and practices has been described (Bray and Colebrook, 1998) as potentially reinforcing a notion of women as 'susceptible' to phallocentric representations. This renders less visible to critical scrutiny the myriad other facets of cultural contexts that are involved in the production of identity and practice and women's engagement with these (Brain, 2002; Bray, 1996; Bray and Colebrook, 1998; Eckermann, 1994; Grosz, 1994; Lester, 1997, Probyn, 1988). It risks positioning women with disordered eating, as victims. Bray (1996) cites the following excerpt from Bordo (1989) as representative of what she sees as the tendency of some feminist theorists to overemphasise and present as monolithic and universally oppressive, representations of slenderness for the bodies of young women:

> watching the commercials are thousands of anxiety-ridden women and adolescents . . . And watching the commercials is the anorexic, who associates her relentless pursuit of thinness with power and control, but who in fact destroys her health and imprisons her imagination. She is surely the most startling and stark illustration of how cavalier power relations are with respect to the motivations and goals of individuals, yet how deeply they are etched on our bodies, and how well our bodies serve them.
>
> (Bordo, cited in Bray, 1996: 420)

In countering the above analysis, Bray and Colebrook (1998: 43) have argued,

> Eating disorders, for example, might not possess a single relation to representation nor could they be exhaustively accounted for through some general theory of signification and its relation to the signified. Representation is one factor among others in ethical problems of the body; it neither determines nor saturates the field. The body is a

negotiation with images, but it is also a negotiation with pleasures, pains, other bodies, space, visibility and medical practice; no single event in this field can act as a general ground for determining the status of the body.

So, for Bray (1996: 421), 'to privilege the mass media as the most effective means of moulding minds is to ignore the multiplicity of social contexts operating in the everyday' which inform and constitute women's subjectivities. Although I consider this to be a misrepresentation of the complex and groundbreaking contributions of Bordo's work,[1] I do wonder about what constraints are operating when we *only* think about eating disorders in terms of their inscriptive relation to female slenderness (whatever that might be theorised to represent, e.g. control, individualism, beauty), or indeed to fatness, as Probyn (this volume) argues. Suggestions to incorporate a more (albeit critical) phenomenological analysis alongside a focus on interpreting representations of slender femininity are appealing. Such an approach seems especially salient when we turn our attention towards the category 'bulimia' given some of the unique challenges involved in theorising the 'invisibly' bulimic body from the 'outside'.

In what are rare examples of critical analyses of bulimia, Squire (2002, 2003) has usefully highlighted the problematics of a theorisation of eating disorders that begins with (or is only concerned with) cultural representations of the physical body. She has argued that this tendency to decipher the *surface* of women's ('eating disordered') bodies in order to unravel their discursive production is one reason for bulimia's (relative to anorexia) absence within feminist discourse. Indeed, based upon my own research with women described as 'bulimic', I would agree that reading bodies as texts is rendered inadequate by this particular 'expression' of pathologised body management. Unlike anorexia, which can be interpreted via the visibly emaciated body as, for example and among other meanings, 'an attempt at disembodiment through negation'[2] (Squire, 2003: 18), bulimia as a visual text remains inscrutable (see also Vice, 1996). Bulimia's invisibility in both critical and mainstream feminist writings about eating disorders might then be understood (in part) as an outcome of its failure to provide a cultural script, in the form of a visually 'different' body, for decoding 'since its status

---

1 As far as I can see, Bordo has concentrated upon examining the ideologies of femininity represented in cultural images of the slender female body *as well* as other sociocultural currents or 'axes' that find their expression in women's disordered eating. Perhaps where she is vulnerable to critique is in those places where she has been interpreted as suggesting eating disorders are 'caused' by these representations/axes, thereby inadvertently positing a somewhat deterministic and *inevitably* oppressive, process.

2 Both Ellman (1993) and Spitzack (1993) have analysed anorexia as a 'performed' spectacle of femininity that gains its meaning via the audience's visual consumption of the visibly emaciated body.

as a normal weight body renders it camouflaged, if not entirely invisible'[3] (Squire, 2003: 18). Unlike the extremely thin 'anorexic' body that demands attention, and which Squire (ibid.: 18), citing Probyn, suggests has been claimed by feminists as 'proof of an unjust society' and the 'feminist emblem of powerlessness', the 'bulimic' body appears unremarkable. Instead of providing an obvious visual statement, bulimia might therefore be more readily conceptualised as an experience 'of immersion in the body and its processes' (ibid.). It thus presents a challenge to theorists who would read its meanings off the body's surface rather than through its practices and experiences.

A couple of examples from my research interviews are possibly instructive in this regard. The accounts below construct bulimic practices, not in relation to a visibly slender body but rather as a collection of practices that (a) are a pleasurable 'secret' and (b) position the woman as 'controlled':

(a) I liked the idea – I know I liked the feeling of, of being able to do something and it was my secret. That's what I really remember about it. I mean [.][4] I know that I liked having something that nobody could take away from me [long pause] no-one could do anything about it, no-one knew about it . . . um it was like I was doing something for myself.

(b) I know I'm definitely in control when I'm throwing up, definitely/ MB: and after that's happened how does that feel?/ I just get back to life [laughing] it's fine. Um [long pause] I feel relieved I guess [laughing]/ MB: That it's over?/ Yeah, that it's over 'cos it's horrible [long pause] but it's just, yeah, I just carry on. Definitely control when I'm vomiting. Control when I'm not eating, and very proud of myself [laughing] controlled when I'm throwing up.

In order to adequately theorise bulimia, these extracts require, as Squire (2002, 2003) has suggested, that we reconceptualise it 'as a specific embodied habitual practice' (2003: 17) rather than, or possibly as well as, an 'attempt' at being thin (whatever thinness is held to represent). This might involve, according to Brain (2002: 152), beginning with 'narrative accounts of bodily becoming' from women engaging in 'bulimic' practices rather than with an *a priori* interpretation of the body's 'visualised surface'. Indeed, despite it being more amenable to a visual decoding, others have also made this suggestion with reference to anorexia (e.g. Lester, 1997; Probyn, 1991). They have pointed out that it is in theorising the *doing* of

---

3 This adds an interesting and complex layer to reflections upon the body's 'visibility', when considered alongside Malson's (this volume) discussion of the increasing 'visibility' of the paradoxically disappearing 'anorexic' body.

4 [.] indicates removed interview text.

anorexia – analysing its practices and women's experiences of them – that we might be able to more fully conceptualise it as a particular style of 'being', a project concerned with the production of a particular kind of self (see also Malson, 1998).

Bray and Colebrook (1998) have also suggested that this approach, which disrupts a notion of the observed or representational body as foundational (see also Baerveldt and Voestermans, 1996; Probyn, 1988, 1991) has the potential for theorising eating distress in a multiplicity of (potentially contradictory) ways; as exemplifying a point of agency and activity *as well as*, potentially, collusion or capitulation. They have argued for a feminist theory of the body in which it is understood in terms of a series of practices and regimens in which it takes on meaning:

> a critical approach to ethical problems of the body might question the idea of the body as an effect of image consumption and would do so by looking to the body's various effects and forces, rather than its capacities to be a sign, theatre or image.
>
> (Bray and Colebrook, 1998: 52)

For Bray (1996) it is important to locate women's eating distress on a continuum of body/food management practices within the contexts within which they are given meaning by those experiencing them. She uses the example of nutritional and exercise knowledge/regimens within which the body is inscribed as a quantifiable and manageable source of energy, the management of which overlaps with discourses of health and fitness (see also Gremillion, 2002). She has suggested that within these discourses, it is then possible to understand problematic eating practices within the context of an ethics of self-care rather than as a pathologi/cal/sed response to idealised feminine body norms. Here, transformation of the self and 'the measurement of corporeal activities is coded as a moral activity' (Bray, 1996: 425), and engaging in the minutiae of bodily regulation are continuous with other normative forms of body management.

Like Bray (1996; Bray and Colebrook, 1998), Lester (1997), Probyn (1988, 1991) and Saukko (2000) have also utilised the Foucauldian notion of 'technologies of the self' – 'an art of existence, a theoretical project, an ensemble of meaningful practices worked on the body which both constitute and transform the self' (Lester, 1997: 482) – in their analyses of anorexia. This work concentrates more on later Foucauldian analyses of the productive nature of power rather than the notion of it stamping its influence upon docile bodies. It therefore offers a conceptualisation of power that can account for women's participation in shaping their own existence by their adoption of and 'resistance' to various discursive/social practices via efforts to transform the embodied self. Rather than positioning the body as a potentially passive and docile object awaiting inscription, embodiment in Foucault's 'technologies of the self' can be understood in terms of meaningful practices through which selves/bodies are (re)constituted. For Foucault (1984), these practices (technologies of the self) are integral to people's subjective experiences. These technologies are therefore deployed in the service of producing a 'style' of embodied existence and the repetition of these practices in turn shape a body/self that articulates a socially meaningful position.

Drawing upon this theory in relation to disordered eating, Lester (1997) suggests that far from being 'detached' from their material being, women with dis/ordered eating are positioned – and position themselves – in ways that contribute to an acute 'awareness' that within westernised cultures women 'exist' as little more than their bodies. Body management, then, can be understood as 'the conscious and deliberate shaping of the self according to a particular philosophy of living and through a given set of culturally meaningful bodily practices' (ibid.: 482). Within this reading, eating distress does not 'exist' (only) as a desperate attempt to be thin, but as an attempt to embody and convey a 'self' (i.e. an embodied identity) via embodied practices that are characterised by, for example, 'competence, self-control and intelligence' (ibid.: 486), as suggested in extract (b) above. Of course, in line with Bordo's (e.g. 1993) thesis, it is problematic to suggest that these practices *actually* or only provide competence, self-control and intelligence (given their potentially health-compromising effects (see also Bordo, 1997)) but rather that they might be 'experienced' as such by a woman who participates in them, just as they might be by other women practising less 'extreme' body management such as dieting and exercising.

Of course, theorising the type(s) of selves that such practices might convey necessarily involves focusing critical feminist analyses at a more specific level: that of women's accounts of their 'disordered' eating practices and experiences (e.g. Saukko, 2000), as well as at the meanings embedded in cultural images that we may wish to deconstruct. This focus has the potential to reinsert and take seriously the 'lived experiences' of such women and, in so doing, guards against a tendency to 'collapse very real voices and bodies into mere matter to be appropriated by discourse' (Probyn, 1988: 201). This also counters any inclination to seek and impose generalisable meanings for women's eating distress (Eckermann, 1994), which, as has been highlighted throughout this volume, is essential. Foucault's technologies of the self (and feminist appropriations of these (e.g. Grosz, 1994; Probyn, 1991; and see Eckermann, this volume)) offer an approach that is able to theorise bodies in these ways as at once, both interiority and exteriority or, put another way, that can complicate and transgress the body–self dualism. I believe that critical feminist work in the field of dis/ ordered eating might usefully turn its attention to issues of practice, experience and embodiment, finding ways to research the body as simultaneously 'experienced' and as 'discursively produced', thus providing fruitful avenues for theorising women's (and indeed men's) 'experiences' of their bodies and body management (see also Probyn, this volume).

In a deconstructive analysis of her own account of bulimia, Squire (2002) contributes to such a retheorisation, moving away from the dualism of mind and body, inside and outside. She offers a description of bulimia that is not (only) concerned with its ability to produce a particular type of body (and therefore a generalisable cultural text). She focuses upon her lived experiences of bingeing and purging, narrating them as repetitive or habitual practices that are productive of a particular style of embodied subjectivity. She does not suggest that these accounts offer the truth about bulimia or her body but, rather, that they provide a number of different positions through which to articulate her experiences:

> I found that bulimia was a way of managing anxiety in the absence of other forms unavailable to me. My weight gain in the early stages of my mother's illness, and subsequent weight loss prior to, and following, her death, provided a context which was unlike the tales I had read of teenage girls dieting and starving themselves in an effort to be slim. I began to understand my bulimia in terms of grief, as it was situated within a broader mother–daughter separation process. . . . In the numbness of grief, bulimia was also an attempt to feel less empty through an intensely embodied and psychically invested practice. Bulimia was also, in this sense, only one of a number of practices I carried out in an excessive manner in the absence of an embodied mourning ritual.
>
> (ibid.: 61)

On the basis of this account, it would seem inappropriate to theorise bulimia (only) in relation to cultural representations of slender femininity (and other body 'images'). What would perhaps be particularly interesting here is to focus upon Squire's reported experience and understanding of her practices as part of a grief process. Here, for example, we might investigate gendered ideologies that constitute 'appropriately' and 'inappropriately' feminine expressions of grief, anxiety and loss, and the ways in which they are deployed and function to legitimise, normalise and mobilise practices such as binge eating and vomiting. Put another way, we would be examining the meanings and experiences of the practices rather than the meanings of the body (image) as an end-product. From such a vantage point, we might theorise that the kind of self/body being articulated in this account is deployed in the service of building an 'identity' that effectively manages mourning, emptiness and anxiety.

Although my suggestion that theorising about the complex meanings of eating dis/orders might be complemented by an approach that takes more seriously the lived experiences of women who practise/experience so-called anorexia and bulimia, I want to emphasise again (see Burns, 2006) that I am not suggesting that these accounts are unmediated 'facts' about embodied experience. Like Probyn (1991: 113), who has expressed frustration that she has had trouble speaking *from* her body given that 'they [other theorists] seem to agree that what I want[ed] to do with my body was to tell a truth', I am not suggesting that narratives about or experiences of the body or its practices tell *the* truth. Rather, these accounts of embodiment, and indeed the experiences upon which they 'reflect', are partial truths produced in discourse, like the representations of slenderness that play a fundamental role in critical feminist theorising about gendered bodies and eating difficulties.

As I move towards a conclusion of this chapter, I wish also to emphasise that in my view questioning and critically examining what various body management practices mean to women – how they are 'felt' – does seem to shift our analytic focus in helpful ways. It allows us to incorporate critical analyses of culturally produced practices in ways that enable a richer theorisation of these practices as meaningful in their own right, rather than simply as routes to achieving a particular 'type' of body (image) – whatever that body might be theorised to represent. I wonder what it is we occlude when we set out to do critical research informed by assumptions about *the* relationship between women's eating distress and cultural representations of slenderness and other body 'images' (see also Eckermann, this volume). In this endeavour, we risk participating in the construction of anorexia/ bulimia and food refusal/bingeing/compensating, as 'phenomena' that are always or only concerned with the production of the slender 'outer' body – an approach that can disallow the multiplicity and complexity of body management and which may be a homogenising and western-centric project. As several chapters in this volume demonstrate, theorising the meanings/experiences of body practices (as well as body images) allows for a more contextualised, local and culture-specific analysis (see also Bordo, Nasser and Malson, Probyn, all this volume).

As I have discussed, an enduring emphasis upon the body's textuality might be due in part to a tendency to avoid 'experience' and focus upon the discursive (Radley, 1995). Or it may be due to a dearth of approaches transgressing this implausible divide (Barnard, 2000). A focus on the body as an inscriptive site, however, might be preventing us from theorising eating distress in other fruitful ways. I concur with Probyn's (1991: 119; see also Probyn, this volume) conclusion when she has argued that, 'simply put, it is not enough (although it is always important) to critique it's [the body's] exteriority, nor is it possible within feminism to be only preoccupied with a phenomenology of its interiority'. The kind of analysis that attempts to negotiate this (constructed) 'separation' has perhaps been largely missing from critical feminist research upon women's eating and body difficulties. Such a re-focusing at once involves a retheorisation of bodies as embodied subjects rather than 'body texts'. Or, put another way, it imagines the pro- duction of bodies as a process of subjectification as well as objectification.

In summary, and taking Foucault's notions of technologies of the self as a framework, I want to argue for a both/and approach, one that acknowledges the imbrication of 'the empire of images' (Bordo, this volume: 54) and the body as inscribed, but which does not reduce body management practices to the inevitable pursuit of and outcome of these. Incorporating and critically analysing the accounts of women speaking about their binge eating, purging and food refusal without an *a priori* hypothesis that they are attempting to mirror a certain body *image* potentially protects against a tendency to interpret their behaviours (only) according to this theory. This may open up other possibilities for theorising body management and embodiment that do not simultaneously (re)produce the body as only its exterior surface.

References

Baerveldt, C. and Voestermans, P. (1996) The body as a selfing device: the case of anorexia nervosa, *Theory and Psychology*, 6(4): 693–713.

Barnard, S. (2000) Construction and corporeality: theoretical psychology and biomedical technologies of the self, *Theory and Psychology*, 10(5): 669–688.

Bordo, S. (1989) The body and the reproduction of femininity: a feminist appropriation of Foucault, in A. Jagger and S. Bordo (eds), *Gender/Body/Knowledge*, New York: Routledge, pp. 133–156.

Bordo, S. (1993) *Unbearable Weight: Feminism, Western Culture and the Body*, Berkeley: University of California Press.

Bordo, S. (1997) *Twilight Zones*, Los Angeles: University of California Press.

Brain, J. (2002) Unsettling 'body image': anorexic body narratives and the materialization of the 'body imaginary', *Feminist Theory*, 3(2): 151–168.

Bray, A. (1996) The anorexic body: reading disorders, *Cultural Studies*, 10(3): 413–429.

Bray, A. and Colebrook, C. (1998) The haunted flesh: corporeal feminism and the politics of (dis)embodiment, *Signs*, 24(1): 35–67.

Burns, M. (2006) Bodies that speak: examining the dialogues in research interactions, *Qualitative Research in Psychology*, 3(1): 3–18.

Eckermann, E. (1994) Self-starvation and binge-purging: embodied selfhood/sainthood, *Australian Cultural History*, 13: 82–99.

Ellman, M. (1993) *The Hunger Artists: Starving, Writing and Imprisonment*, Massachusetts: Harvard University Press.

Foucault, M. (1984) *The History of Sexuality*, Volume II) (translated by R. Hurley), Harmondsworth: Penguin.

Foucault, M. (2000) *Power. Essential Works of Foucault: 1954–1984, Volume 3* (edited by James D. Faubion and translated by Robert Hurley et al.), New York: New Press.

Gremillion, H. (2002) In fitness and in health: crafting bodies in the treatment of anorexia nervosa, *Signs*, 27(2): 381–414.

Grosz, E. (1994) *Volatile Bodies: Towards a Corporeal Feminism*, Indianapolis: Indiana University Press.

Lester, R.J. (1997) The (dis)embodied self in anorexia nervosa, *Social Sciences and Medicine*, 44(4): 479–489.

Malson, H. (1998) *The Thin Woman: Feminism, Poststructuralism and the Social Psychology of Anorexia Nervosa*, London: Routledge.

Probyn, E. (1988) The anorexic body, in A. Kroker and M. Kroker (eds), *Body Invaders: Sexuality and the Postmodern Condition*, New York: St Martin's Press, pp. 201–211.

Probyn, E. (1991) This body which is not one: speaking an embodied self, *Hypatia*, 6(3): 111–124.

Radley, A. (1995) The elusory body and social constructionist theory, *Body and Society*, 1(2): 3–23.

Saukko, P. (2000) Between voice and discourse: quilting interviews on anorexia, *Qualitative Enquiry*, 6(3): 299–317.

Squire, S. (2002) The personal and the political: writing the theorist's body, *Australian Journal of Feminist Studies*, 17(37): 55–64.

Squire, S. (2003) Anorexia and bulimia: purity and danger, *Australian Journal of Feminist Studies*, 18(40): 17–26.

Spitzack, C. (1993) The spectacle of anorexia nervosa, *Text and Performance Quarterly*, 13: 1–20.

Vice, S. (1996) The well-rounded anorexic text, in T. Armstrong (ed.), *American Bodies: Cultural Histories of the Physique*, Sheffield: Sheffield Academic Press, pp. 196–203.

12 Appearing to disappear

Postmodern femininities and self-starved subjectivities

Helen Malson

> I think um a lot of doctors tend to just focus on: somebody looks that thin, they're actually *wanting* somebody to see what's going on. . . . And the actual um, the physical appearance is much more to do with um *not* wanting to be seen in in some ways, um. There's sort of a a feeling there of wanting to just fade into the background literally.
>
> (Mandy, quoted in Malson, 1998: 174)

Introduction

Even whilst such notions as cognitive distortion, predisposing personality, a gene for anorexia, a biopsychological vulnerability of female bodies and so forth continue to jostle for position in academic, clinical and popular accounts about the causes of 'eating disorders', the idea that 'eating disorders' are 'culture-bound' (Littlewood and Lipsedge, 1987; Swartz, 1985) has nevertheless become widely accepted. 'Culture', however, or perhaps more precisely, that which is considered pathogenic about culture and hence 'bound' to 'eating disorders', tends all too often to be understood *only* as idealised media images of thin women and the concomitant prescription – for girls and women in particular but increasingly for boys and men too – to 'diet' (see also Probyn, Burns, both this volume). 'Culture' here is thus often reduced to the media, fashion and diet industries such that everything else of culture appears to be 'let off the hook' and in a bizarre but – in my experience, oft-repeated turn of conversation – these industries may then be further reduced to individuals such as Kate Moss, Victoria Beckham, Gianni Versace or Jean Paul Gaultier, who can stand as metonyms of fashion. So that finally, in this scheme of things, it is not culture at all but a handful of famous thin fashion models and (usually gay[1]) fashion designers who are

---

1 That fashion designers seem so often in this context to be explicitly referenced as *gay* men is, I think, indicative not only of the prevalence of anti-gay sentiment but also of the individual-isation of aetiological explanations of 'eating disorders' whereby any misogynistic toxicities of fashion are understood in terms of particular alleged attitudes of specific individual designers rather than, for example, as symptomatic of the patriarchal heteronormativity of the 'fashion system'.

held culpable for the spread of 'eating disorders'. And, with 'cultural cause' thus reduced to a few guilty celebrities and/or to images in the pages of women's magazines, those diagnosed as 'anorexic' or 'bulimic' are made to appear as the ultimate fashion victims; as (already pathologically vulnerable) 'super-dieters' (Polivy and Herman, 1985) who, because of their own *individual* predisposition or vulnerability, have (irrationally) *over*-internalised an idealised *image* of female beauty as thinness.

It would, I think, be foolish to argue that the world would not be a better place without mass-media saturation of images dictating 'ideals' for women's bodies. The weight of mainstream research alone demonstrating the pernicious effects of such images (see e.g. Grogan, 1999; Halliwell et al., 2005), even if often epistemologically dubious and over-simplistic in its conceptualisations of cause and consequence (Blood, 2005), seems to me to be nevertheless persuasive enough. My point here, however, is not so much about whether or to what extent ubiquitous idealised media images of thin women are implicated in the production of normative orders and pathologised 'disorders' of eating and body management. It is, rather, that 'anorexic' and 'bulimic' subjectivities, experiences and practices cannot be adequately understood *only* in terms of a hyper-conformity to a culturally dominant, media-promulgated idealisation of female slenderness (see Coleman, 2008; see also Probyn, Burns, LeBesco, Nasser and Malson, all this volume) and that culture's culpability in the production of eating dis/orders is considerably more far-reaching and complex. As Katzman and Lee (1997) have argued, to focus on 'anorexia' as a problem of body image is to occlude the broader contexts, the varied meanings and much of the inequalities of gendered power relations that are articulated in girls'and women's self-starvation.

Feminist and critical feminist analyses of 'anorexia' and, to a lesser extent, of 'bulimia' (see Burns, 2004) have, I think, been at the fore in elaborating this point. Since the 1970s feminist analyses elucidated the *various* ways in which 'the thin female body' can be read as signifying a patriarchally proscribed and subordinated femininity (Boskind-Lohdahl, 1976; Chernin, 1983; Fallon et al., 1994; Orbach, 1993). They have, for example, shown how the extreme control exerted in 'anorexic' practices of body management could be understood as a culturally (patriarchally) produced response to the lack of control afforded to girls and women in other aspects of their/our lives (Lawrence, 1984). Moreover, in attributing a range of gendered meanings to 'anorexia', these feminist analyses also illustrated the polysemic nature of 'anorexic' bodies, theorising 'anorexia' as, for example, an ambivalence about or rejection of traditional femininity (Orbach, 1993), as well as a hyper-conformity to a contemporary cultural ideal of (thin) femininity (Boskind-Lohdahl, 1976).

These analyses thus clearly demonstrated the necessity of going beyond an overly simplistic view of 'eating disorders' as 'only' an exaggerated adherence to cultural prescriptions about dieting and ideal body weight and shape; that

... the image of anorexia as a transitory, self-inflicted problem developed by young women lost in their world of fashion and calorie restricting is a belittling stereotype that may mask women's real worries. By emphasizing slenderness, the dominant imagery about eating concerns misnames as much as it discounts real biases against women and their limited access to other forms of power of self-expression beyond corporeal power. As Thompson (1994) writes, 'in countries [celebrating] glorified images of youth, whiteness, thinness and wealth, it makes painful sense that dissatisfaction with appearance often serves as a stand-in for topics that are still invisible.'

(Katzman and Lee, 1997: 389)

More recently, since the late 1980s (e.g. Bordo, 1988; Brumberg, 1988; Probyn, 1987), critical feminist analyses have explored how a multiplicity of contemporary western cultural discourses that constitute and regulate normative femininities are also central to the discursive production and regulation of girls' and women's eating dis/ordered experiences and practices (e.g. Bordo, 1993; Burns, 2004; Gremillion, 2002; Hepworth, 1999; Malson, 1998). Eating dis/orders are thus theorised here not as distinct clinical entities but as complex, heterogeneous and shifting collectivities of socio-historically located subjectivities, bodies and body management practices that are constituted within and by (rather than outside of) the normative discursive contexts of contemporary western cultures. They can be understood as graphic cultural statements about the conditions of 'being a woman' in contemporary western cultures (Bordo, 1993; Gremillion, 2003; Malson, 1998) and, moreover, as expressive of a diverse range of sometimes contradictory societal values, concerns and dilemmas (Bordo, 1992; Brumberg, 1988; Malson, 1999; Turner, 1992).

Thus, for example, critical feminists *have* theorised and researched 'anorexic' bodies in terms of contemporary cultural prescriptions of feminine beauty as thinness and of 'the gender–power axis' (Bordo, 1992, 1993; Malson, 1998). And, in addition to this, they have illustrated how 'anorexia' and 'bulimia' are *multiply* constituted, expressing, for example, the Cartesian ideal of bodily control (Bordo, 1993; Malson and Ussher, 1996); cultural concerns with individualistic competitiveness and personal display (Brumberg, 1988); the tensions entailed in inhabiting the antithetical identities of self-controlled, disciplined worker and self-indulgent consumer (Bordo, 1990; Turner, 1992); cultural values associated with postmodernity (Malson, 1999; Probyn, 1987) and so forth.

And, just as the 'anorexic' body has been read as both a hyper-embodiment of the cultural ideal of thin femininity *and* conversely as a 'boyish' body expressing a rejection of femininity (Bordo, 1993), so it has also been read in other discursive contexts as expressive of, for example, both self-production and self-destruction, an ethic of anti-consumption and simultaneously a conformity to the values of mass-consumer culture

(Malson, 1999) within which being hyper-thin is constituted as 'hyper-cool' (Turner, 1992: 221); a search for selfhood and, in conflict with this, for sainthood (Eckermann, 1994, this volume); and as a conformity to current 'healthist' orthodoxies of 'healthy' weight management as well as a pursuit of unhealthy/damaging practices of body management (Burns and Gavey, 2004).

Critical feminist analyses have thus elucidated a myriad of ways in which eating dis/orders are constituted within and by the normative discourses and discursive practices of contemporary western cultures. And, in theorising eating dis/orders as a culturally over-determined, heterogeneous and shifting collectivity of discursive constructions, these analyses have also thereby illustrated the inadequacy of reductively explaining 'anorexia' and 'bulimia' only in terms of the hegemonic idealised image of thinness as beauty.

At the same time, however, as Elspeth Probyn (this volume, see also Burns, this volume) suggests, critical feminist analyses have perhaps tended to focus on the 'anorexic' body as an image or inscribed surface to be read at the expense of analysing other less visible aspects of embodiment such as feelings, emotions and (privately conducted) practices. Indeed, as Burns (this volume) suggests, that 'bulimia' is not so noticeably, visibly inscribed on the body as 'anorexia' so clearly is, may well explain the relative lack of analyses of 'bulimia' compared with the attention accorded 'anorexia' in the critical feminist literatures on eating dis/orders.

Postmodern dis/appearing bodies

This critical feminist work on eating dis/orders, like critical feminist work in other areas, has in the main drawn heavily on Foucauldian theory (see Eckermann, this volume) within which, of course, 'the body' features prominently. The body is central to Foucault's theorisation of power/knowledge. It is, he argued, the site upon which 'discipline' is exercised and it is precisely the *visibility*[2] of the always-already discursively constituted and regulated body which renders it/us subject to the workings of disciplinary power (Foucault, 1977a, 1977b). For Foucault, then, the body can never precede discourse, and discourses, he argued, discipline the body through 'a multiplicity of minor processes of domination' (1977a: 138). They constitute the body in particular ways, 'exercising upon it a subtle coercion, obtaining holds upon it at the level of the mechanism itself – movements, gestures, attitudes, rapidity: an infinitesimal power over the active body' (ibid.: 137).

---

2 This is not to suggest that, from a Foucauldian perspective, the general purpose of disciplinary regulation is to affect the body's appearance nor to suggest that the production of disciplined bodies should be equated with a construction of the body-as-image but, rather, that disciplinary regulation of embodied subjects operates in a field of vision as a judgemental scrutiny of subjects against a raft of normative values surrounding not just bodily appearance but virtually every aspect of our lives.

Foucauldian theory thus provides a framework in which the discursive production of bodies can be understood as much more than the regulation of surface appearance (see also Probyn, this volume). And, as Bordo (1998: 91) has argued, '[t]hose discourses [in which "ideal" bodily appearance is constituted] impinge on us as fleshly bodies, and often in ways that cannot be determined from a study of representation alone.' But, in exploring the various ways in which 'anorexic' and 'bulimic' bodies are discursively constituted and regulated within and by the normative discursive orders of contemporary culture, we have perhaps considered the body as 'the inscribed *surface* of events . . . totally imprinted by history' (Foucault, 1977a: 148) more than we have considered the body as a lived-in, active body such that eating dis/ordered experiences, feelings and practices that are not visibly inscribed on the body's surface might have not yet received the critical feminist attention they require (see also Probyn, Burns, both this volume).

It is clearly important to address non-surface aspects of eating dis/ordered embodiment and practice. At the same time, privileging the surface of the body as a focus of analysis might, I think, be understood not so much as an accidental (or theory-driven) oversight than as a response to a particular socio-historically specific form of embodiment. That is, the construction of the body-as-image is a highly prominent aspect of postmodernity and of the ways in which our embodied subjectivities are produced and regulated in late capitalist consumer culture (Featherstone, 1991; Lupton, 1996; see also Bordo, 1992). Within this context, it has been argued, the body of the consumer subject is no longer constituted, experienced or managed as a *natural* body but as a 'floating sign-system' (Kroker and Kroker, 1987: 21) or 'sign-commodity', an always imperfect but perfectible *spectacle* to be worked upon in the pursuit of a better *look*, which might better represent a more marketable self (Featherstone, 1991). As Kroker and Kroker (1987: 21–23) suggest:

> If today, there can be such an intense fascination with the fate of the body, might it not be because the body no longer exists: . . . In technological society, the body has achieved a purely rhetorical existence . . . Indeed, why the concern over the body today if not to emphasize the fact that the (natural) body in the postmodern condition has already disappeared, and what we experience as the body is only a fantastic simulacrum of body rhetorics?

Bodies, it has thus been suggested, are reconfigured in postmodernity, not as 'natural', active or lived-in but as plastic images requiring constant maintenance and 'enhancement' in the pursuit of a certain look, of a surface that is inscribed with the required rhetorics. Surface image becomes all that matters because all that matters – identity, sexuality, moral worth, intelligence, taste, economic success, health and so forth – is signified by the body and, more precisely, by the body as surface image. And, thus reconstituted as image or text, 'the body *qua* body', the body as organic, lived in or active, the corporeal experience of sensate embodiment (see also Bordo, 1992) is erased, disappearing under a deluge of body images (Featherstone, 1991).

Inscribing/erasing 'anorexic' bodies as postmodern bodies

As argued elsewhere (Malson, 1999; see also Probyn, 1987), 'anorexia' can be understood as a particularly intense expression of this postmodern reconfiguration of bodies and embodiment in late capitalist consumer cultures. 'Anorexia' is, as noted above, repeatedly associated in both popular and academic media with images of (thin female) bodies and is stereotypically understood as a 'body image' problem (Katzman and Lee, 1997). The bodies of girls and women diagnosed as 'anorexic' become progressively more visible, subject to the increasing scrutiny of family and friends, of medics and other health care workers, of the woman herself and of the popular media (Malson, 1999) within which the 'anorexic' body is repeatedly constituted as a highly visible spectacle – as a visually arresting *image* of 'misguided femininity' (see also Bordo, 1993).

But at the same time as 'anorexic' bodies are made more visible they also become less visible. Like 'the (natural) body in the postmodern condition' (Kroker and Kroker, 1987: 23), the 'anorexic' body seems to disappear both literally and figuratively. Self-starved bodies are, quite literally, physically erased as they become progressively smaller. And, as Mandy, quoted at the start of this chapter, illustrates, 'anorexic' bodies signify, amongst other things, a desire to fade away or hide from view:

> I think um a lot of doctors tend to just focus on: somebody looks that thin, they're actually *wanting* somebody to see what's going on. . . . And the actual um, the physical appearance is much more to do with um *not* wanting to be seen in in some ways, um. There's sort of a a feeling there of wanting to just fade into the background literally.

'The thinness', she suggests, cannot be understood only or even primarily in terms of the production of a particular body *image* because it is also paradoxically 'to do with um *not* wanting to be seen': 'the physical appearance' signifies a desire 'to just fade into the background literally'. Thus, on the one hand, the 'anorexic' body is constituted here precisely in terms of its *appearance*: it is articulated (and analysed) *as* surface image. Yet, on the other hand, this 'anorexic' appearance is about disappearance, about fading away and no longer being visible. In addition, then, to the myriad of other discursive locations and significations, 'anorexic' bodies might also be understood as inscribed, in the context of postmodernity, as bodies that appear to disappear.

This analysis of 'anorexic' bodies as bodies that appear to disappear can undoubtedly be seen as (yet) another instance of critical feminist analyses which take the inscribed surface of the body as their site of enquiry (see also Probyn, Burns, LeBesco, all this volume). It is undeniably an analysis of how the body *looks* rather than of how it feels or moves or of what it is like to live *in* such a body. At the same time, however, I want to argue that this discursive, corporeal production of 'anorexic' bodies as dis/appearing bodies also raises a number of important issues about the relationships between 'anorexic' bodies, images of bodies and bodies-as-images (see also Coleman, 2008); about the relationships between bodies as lived-in, organic, active bodies and bodies-as-surface-image; and about the ways in which issues of power, including gender–power relations, can be understood as playing out on girls' and women's dis/appearing 'anorexic' bodies.

The production of 'anorexic' bodies as dis/appearing bodies can, I would argue, be understood as expressive of a particularly intense and, in the context of postmodernity, perhaps unresolvable tension created in the juxta-positioning of the (unavoidable) corporeality of embodied subjectivity and the experience of living with the body-as-surface-image. 'Anorexic' bodies can, I think, be understood as expressing a paradoxical and contradictory relationship to the culturally prominent construction of the body-as-image. They *can* be read as signifying *par excellence* a production of the body-as-image; requiring (and signifying) a denial of the corporeality of embodied subjectivity. Yet, they are also, simultaneously, a highly determined evasion of the body's visibility: an evasion which, through the literal erasure and destruction of the body, can in turn be read as an insistence on corporeality; on the impossibility of living in/with the body-as-image. Thus, as noted above, 'anorexia', as it is articulated by Mandy, is constituted in terms of 'physical appearance': it is about *looking* thin. But it is also at the same time about '*not* wanting to be seen' and *literally* fading away.

This relationship between corporeal 'anorexic' bodies and 'anorexic' bodies-as-image, implicit in what Mandy says, is, I think, emphasised further by Nicki and Tricia, as quoted below:

> It's just a way of like trying to disappear. . . . I mean I just wanted to die anyway /HM: mm/ so not eating, becoming smaller is very relevant to that.
>
> (Nicki)

> I remember sort of [.][3] looking in the mirror and actually being surprised that I saw a form in the mirror /HM: right/ and not just a nothingness.
>
> (Tricia)

---

3 [.] indicates a pause.

Both Nicki and Tricia articulate this construction of 'anorexic' bodies as dis/appearing bodies and, in her remembrance of 'looking in the mirror', Tricia perhaps further emphasises the imagistic nature of this dis/appearing body. But both Nicki and Tricia also, I would argue, draw attention to an impossible and dangerous relationship between bodies-as-image and bodies as lived (or died) in. In Nicki's association of 'trying to disappear' with 'want[ing] to die' and in Tricia's surprise that she has any body left to see in the mirror, the corporeal consequences – death and nothingness – of inscribing dis/appearance on the body, of producing a body-as-image are made very apparent. And, as Penny's and Laura's comments below suggest, the corporeal destruction entailed in the (discursive but nonetheless extra-textual) production of dis/appearing 'anorexic' bodies brings with it an erasure of the (embodied) subject as well as of the body itself:

> Penny: it's kind of [.] /HM: I don't/ anger and the fear were kind of just [.] of being Penny I think, of being me . . . I think it was a fear of being me /HM: mm/ totally . . . I just wanted to fade away (inaud)=
> =Laura: I avoided being me. I didn't want to know what me really was so I thought that if I just sort of [.] you know go along like this, just sort of hiding, I think I was just sort of hiding from myself.
>
> (Malson, 1999: 145)

The fading away of the 'anorexic' body thus signifies an evasion of sub-jectivity as much as it does an evasion of the body's visibility, a figurative as well as potentially literal death of the subject (Malson and Ussher, 1997) *because* that subject is embodied. And that this subject is almost invariably a girl or woman is undoubtedly overdetermined by culturally dominant ideologies of gender. Not only are girls and women the prime targets of cultural prescriptions of bodily 'ideals' but, as Irigaray (1988; see also Eckermann, this volume) has argued, the problematics of 'feminine' identity in patriarchal cultures can be understood in terms of an annihilation of 'woman'. In producing 'woman' only as the negatively signified Other of 'man', defining her only in terms of what she is not, patriarchal cultures, Irigaray (1988; see also Minsky, 1996) asserts, rob women of any positively constituted identity and thus 'bury women alive'. Amongst the numerous ways in which woma/en are 'buried alive', the dis/appearing 'anorexic' bodies of girls and women in late capitalist consumer culture can, I would argue, be understood, amongst their many meanings, as being 'buried alive' under a deluge of body images (see Featherstone, 1991).

Conclusions

My argument here does, of course, raise the danger again of reducing 'anorexia' to the 'belittling stereotype' of 'young women lost in their world of fashion and calorie restricting' (Katzman and Lee, 1997: 389) by re-articulating that commonplace association between 'anorexia' and media images of thin women. What I have been seeking to explore here, however, is not the construction of 'anorexia' as a re-articulation of the culturally dominant ideal (image) of female beauty as thinness but rather a construction of 'anorexia' as expressing a specifically postmodern (and highly gendered) problem of embodiment – of which these ubiquitous media images are symptomatic. I have sought to suggest that 'anorexia' expresses an intensely paradoxical relationship towards the culturally prevalent construction of bodies-as-images and indicates the potentially fatal impossibility for embodied subjects of living in/with a body-as-image. That 'anorexia' can be understood as a surface inscribed to excess; as a corporeal production of a hyper-real ideal or image. But at the same time – precisely because it is inscribed so thoroughly and to such excess as an *appearance* requiring the denial and destruction of the lived-in, organic body – it can also be understood as asserting (as well as denying) the lived-in, organic nature of (embodied) subjects, just as it can be understood as becoming less as well as more visible.

I think it is pertinent here that the media-saturating, idealised images of women's bodies with which 'anorexia' is so frequently associated might also be read in terms of this problematic of postmodern embodiment and the gender politics articulated therein: that what is most visually striking about this media spectacle of hyper-real female bodies is the very lack of female flesh; that these images speak volumes about a cultural obsession with bodies (as image), which is at the same time an equally obsessive cultural repudiation of (fleshly, lived-in organic, active) bodies.[4] And equally, I think, they speak volumes about the gender politics of late capitalist consumer culture: of the power relations entailed in the inscription, the playing out – or perhaps more appropriately the *stamping out* – of this cultural tension of dis/appearance on women's bodies. In short, I think these media images of thin, sometimes very thin, female bodies have a cultural significance that goes well beyond their prescriptive function of a fashionable but (mostly) unrealistic/hyper-real body (as image).

However such images are read, though, they are nevertheless images, highly visible media spectacles, and, as I have sought to argue in this chapter, 'anorexic' bodies for all their visibility are also bodies which 'fade into the background literally'. If, as Foucault argued (1977a), visibility is a trap, the field in which we are subjected to the normalising regulations of disciplinary power that are inscribed upon the body (as an active, useful body as much as an inscribed surface), then, I would argue, 'anorexia' ought to be understood not only as the pursuit of an appearance but also a

---

4 Hence also, perhaps, the global obsession with attaining or acquiring a 'perfect' body image (in terms of normative body weight) as an (alleged) means of avoiding the (organic) bodily intrusion of poor health (see also LeBesco, Rice, Gard, Throsby, all this volume).

disappearance; as paradoxically not only a practice of destroying girls' and women's bodies in pursuit of a particular visual body rhetoric but also a practice of resistance (see also Eckermann, Saukko, Burns, Day and Keys, all this volume) and evasion of that disciplinary power exerted on female bodies (as [destroyed in the service of] image), a subversive stance against normative postmodern configurations of embodiment and gender.

References

Blood, S.K. (2005) *Body Work: The Social Construction of Women's Body Image*, London: Routledge.

Bordo, S. (1988) Anorexia nervosa – psychopathology as the crystallization of culture, in I. Diamond and L. Quinby (eds), *Feminism and Foucault: Reflections on Resistance*, Boston, MA: North-eastern University Press.

Bordo, S. (1990) Reading the slender body, in M. Jacobus, E. Fox Keller and S. Shuttleworth (eds), *Body/Politics*, London: Routledge.

Bordo, S. (1992) Anorexia nervosa – psychopathology as the crystallization of culture, in H. Crowley and S. Himmelweit (eds), *Knowing Women: Feminism and Knowledge*, Cambridge and Oxford: Polity Press/Open University Press.

Bordo, S. (1993) *Unbearable Weight*, Berkeley, CA: University of California Press.

Bordo, S. (1998) Bringing body to theory, in D. Welton (ed.), *Body and Flesh: A Philosophical Reader*, Boston, MA: Blackwell, pp. 84–97.

Boskind-Lohdahl, M. (1976) Cinderella's step-sisters: a feminist perspective on anorexia nervosa and bulimia, *Signs*, 2(2): 342–356.

Brumberg, J.J. (1988) *Fasting Girls: The Emergence of Anorexia Nervosa as a Modern Disease*, Cambridge, MA: Harvard University Press.

Burns, M. (2004) Eating like an ox: femininity and dualistic constructions of bulimia and anorexia, *Feminism and Psychology*, 4(2): 269–295.

Burns, M.L. and Gavey, N. (2004) 'Healthy weight' at what cost? Bulimia and a discourse of weight control, *Journal of Health Psychology*, 9(4): 549–565.

Chernin, K. (1983) *Womansize: The Tyranny of Slenderness*, London: Women's Press.

Coleman, R. (2008) The becoming body, *Feminist Media Studies*, 8(2): 163–179.

Eckermann, E. (1994) Self-starvation and binge-purging: embodied selfhood/sainthood, *Australian Cultural History*, 13: 82–99.

Fallon, P., Katzman, M.A. and Wooley, S.C. (eds) (1994) *Feminist Perspectives on Eating Disorders*, London: Guilford Press.

Featherstone, M. (1991) The body in consumer culture, in M. Featherstone, M. Hepworth and B.S. Turner (eds), *The Body: Social Process and Cultural Theory*, London: Sage, published in association with *Theory, Culture and Society*.

Foucault, M. (1977a) *Discipline and Punish: The Birth of the Prison*, Harmondsworth: Penguin.

Foucault, M. (1977b) Nietzsche, genealogy, history, in D.F. Bouchard (ed.), *Language, Counter-memory, Practice: Selected Essays and Interviews*, New York: Cornell University Press, pp. 139–164.

Gremillion, H. (2002) In fitness and in health: crafting bodies in the treatment of anorexia nervosa, *Signs*, 27(2): 381–596.

Gremillion, H. (2003) *Feeding Anorexia: Gender and Power at a Treatment Center*, Durham, NC: Duke University Press.

Grogan, S. (1999) *Body Image*, London: Routledge.

Halliwell, E., Dittmar, H. and Howe, J. (2005) The impact of advertisements featuring ultra-thin or average-size models on women with a history of eating disorders, *Journal of Community and Applied Social Psychology*, 15: 406–413.

Hepworth, J. (1999) *The Social Construction of Anorexia Nervosa*, London: Sage.

Irigaray, L. (1988) Luce Irigaray, in H.E. Barruch and L.J. Sorrono (eds), *Women Analyse Women: in France, England and the United States*, New York: Harvester Wheatsheaf.

Katzman, M.A and Lee, S. (1997) Beyond body image: the integration of feminist and transcultural theories in the understanding of self starvation, *International Journal of Eating Disorders*, 22(4): 385–394.

Kroker, A. and Kroker, M. (1987) Thesis on the disappearing body in the hypermodern condition, in A. Kroker and M. Kroker (eds), *Panic Sex in America*, New York: St Martin's Press.

Lawrence, M. (1984) *The Anorexic Experience*, London: Women's Press.

Littlewood, R. and Lipsedge, M. (1987) Culture-bound syndromes, in K. Granville-Grossman (ed.), *Recent Advances in Psychiatry 5*, Edinburgh: Churchill-Livingstone.

Lupton, D. (1996) *Food, the Body and the Self*, London: Sage.

Malson, H. and Ussher, J.M. (1996) Body poly-texts: discourses of the anorexic body, *Journal of Community and Applied Social Psychology*, 6: 267–280.

Malson, H. (1998) *The Thin Woman: Feminism, Post-structuralism and the Social Psychology of Anorexia Nervosa*, London: Routledge.

Malson, H. (1999) Women under erasure: anorexic bodies in postmodern context, *Journal of Community and Applied Social Psychology*, 9: 137–153.

Malson, H. and Ussher, J.M. (1997) Beyond this mortal coil: femininity, death and discursive constructions of the anorexic body, *Mortality*, 2(1): 43–61.

Minsky, R. (1996) *Psychoanalysis and Gender: An Introductory Reader*, London: Routledge.

Orbach, S. (1993) *Hunger Strike*, Harmondsworth: Penguin.

Polivy, J. and Herman, C.P. (1985) Dieting and binging, *American Psychologist*, 40(2): 193–201.

Probyn, E. (1987) The anorexic body, in A. Kroker and M. Kroker (eds), *Panic Sex in America*, New York: St Martin's Press.

Swartz, L. (1985) Anorexia nervosa as a culture-bound syndrome, *Social Science and Medicine*, 20(7): 725–730.

Turner, B.S. (1992) *Regulating Bodies: Essays in Medical Sociology*, London: Routledge.

13 Weight management, good health and the will to normality

Kathleen LeBesco

Introduction

Feminist scholarship in the social sciences and humanities has long taken anorexic or bulimic bodies produced variously by starvation, bingeing and purging as a focal point in the domain of body politics; key works have suggested that these eating practices are responses to gender-based disempowerment. Similarly, and more recently, feminist scholars have addressed fat bodies as symptomatic of the hegemony of gender and, conversely, as spectacles of resistance to gender norms. Yet because the vast majority of the scholarly literature on eating disorders emerges from this medical paradigm, the politics of the normalization project remain largely invisible. Discourse analysis from a critical feminist perspective provides a much-needed antidote and this chapter, written by a Communication scholar with a feminist cultural studies perspective, attempts to shed light on this normalization process.

This chapter portends to examine a number of key questions surrounding fatness and exceptional thinness and the body management practices that western culture advocates for their erasure: What is at stake in understanding fatness and thinness as forms of corporeal resistance (see also Probyn, this volume)? How can a feminist movement concerned with wanting the best for its constituents respond to health-based claims about fat, anorexic, and bulimic bodies? What are the ideological underpinnings and political ramifications of our pervasive mandate for good health?

Thinness, fatness and feminism

Fatness and thinness are linguistic antonyms, but much is lost in seeing them as mere opposites when it comes to understanding the relationships among medicalized and pathologized versions of each (see also Gard, Rice, Probyn, Throsby, Burns et al., all this volume). Fatness is variously described as overweight or obesity in a medical context, and taken to be an undesirable property of bodies with too much adipose tissue; exceptional thinness in a medical context is often named as the result of anorexia nervosa or bulimia. Often, a fear of fatness is assumed to underpin the disordered eating practices that lead to exceptional thinness; instructively, some researchers point out that such practices are more likely to reflect perfectionism or loss of appetite rather than fat phobia as their motivation for restricted eating or purging (Tareen et al., 2005). Such research provides a clue to the possibilities of understanding fatness and exceptional thinness not as opposites but as linked in intriguing ways. In fact, Maree Burns points out that conceptualizing constructs of 'over-' and 'under-'eating as profoundly tied to notions of appropriate womanhood 'might also function to break down the dangerous idealization of abstinence and restriction that have become exemplars of feminine control and strength' (2004: 290).

Feminist literature accounting for eating disorders and feminist literature about fatness share a concern about the symbolic power of eating practices in a patriarchal environment (see also Probyn, this volume). Eating disorders have been interpreted as being about women striving for cultural ideals of attractiveness, but they're also evidence of and responses to women's subordination and norms of feminine self-sacrifice (Bordo, 1989; Chernin, 1985; Counihan, 1992; Killian, 1994; Orbach, 1986; Thompson, 1994). Likewise, fatness has been variously understood as an outright corporeal rejection of the ideal of slenderness, an act of mothering oneself, as well as protection from the objectifying male gaze (Orbach, 1978). Tapping into this repository of meaning, which situates eating practices and bodies in a larger political context, encourages us to begin to think through the stakes in our cultural rules and ideals about women's bodies.

In a close study of the food journals of college students, anthropologist Carole Counihan (1992: 55) reveals students' heightened concern with 'individual free choice in diet and self-control towards food so as to be thin, moral, and admirable'. Counihan names anorectics and fat people as subverters of these rules surrounding food, but points to health problems (in the first case) and low self-esteem caused by stigma (in the latter) as circumstances which mitigate our cultural capacity to applaud these acts of transgression (ibid.: 63). This discussion anticipates more recent articulations of concern about the limits of reading fatness and exceptional thinness as acts of resistance against patriarchy: namely, the health issue. Political resistance may be all well and good until we realize that women are sometimes physically and/or emotionally suffering as a by-product of this resistance – a resistance that they themselves do many times *not* embrace or recognize as such. Philosopher Susan Bordo (1989: 21; see also Probyn, Sayers, Day and Keys, all this volume) reproves any rejoicing at protest, emphasizing 'the counterproductive, tragically self-defeating (indeed, self-deconstructing) nature of that protest'. That women may lose attractiveness or status is less problematic for critics of the very system that would grant such things on the basis of an approved level of abstinence or self-sacrifice. That women would lose their health or their lives is of much greater concern.

One discursive dilemma that we must attend to before moving further in this analysis is the noun–verb distinction in the subjects of our discussion. Part of what makes fatness and eating disorders complicated to talk about in the same breath, as we are attempting to do in this volume, is their quite different linguistic and discursive positioning. We usually talk about 'obesity', 'anorexia nervosa' and 'bulimia' as food/body/eating problems. But 'obesity' (or the non-pathologizing term 'fatness', which I prefer to use) does not tread the same ground as 'anorexia nervosa' or 'bulimia', conditions which describe particular practices surrounding eating, restricting food or purging. Fatness is a state of being; it does not describe any particular *action* (see Throsby, this volume). It is typically, reductively and mistakenly boiled down to the equivalent of 'compulsive overeating', a semantic collapse that does far more harm than good. In a critique of Overeaters Anonymous, Katherine Van Wormer contends that 'compulsive overeating' and 'eating disorder' are terms bandied about in harmful ways, and she argues that reckless use of these labels has a debilitating political effect that restrains women from action: 'since problems are internalized, their external and political dimensions are obscured' (1994: 292, see also Throsby, this volume). Although anorexia nervosa and bulimia have themselves been pathologized as disordered eating practices, their emphasis on *actions* rather than *bodies* is more productive for empowerment projects.

The aesthetic focus is one sure obstacle to empowering women around issues of food and eating and it needs to be addressed if feminists want to successfully promote the well-being of women. Medical professionals typically confine their exploration of a patient's body size (and its seeming implications for health) to a read-off of the number on the scale. '120' pounds garner congratulations, '155' a raised eyebrow and a gentle admonition, and '200' (or, heavens forbid, above!) a stern talking-to for a woman of average height. The fat body itself is pathologized, usually independent of what that body actually *does* with food or movement. Furthermore, the average-sized body is taken to be healthy regardless of whatever detrimental practices may have been required to bring it into effect (see also Burns, this volume). Doctors who see fat patients typically respond as if they know everything important there is to know by looking at weight, failing to ask for (or to believe, if they do ask) the patient's accounts of her eating practices and movement habits (Jutel, 2005). Some patients may be fat because of compulsive overeating, but not most (see also Gard, this volume): the US National Institutes of Health (NIH) itself has recognized that 'overweight is multifactorial in origin, reflecting inherited, environmental, cultural, socioeconomic, and psychological conditions' (NIH Technology Assessment Conference Panel, 1993: 764). Thus, the incorrect assumption that fatness (noun) equals compulsive overeating (verb) provokes bias and misunderstanding, foisting inappropriate treatment plans on many people whose fatness is simply another human variation rather than the result of disordered eating. The oversimplistic equation of fatness with compulsive overeating, and of average size with healthy eating, also misdirects attention away from the sedentariness that proves a *far* greater predictor of ill health than does body weight.

Another key issue of interest for feminists is that of free will and culpability relative to one's body weight. William DeJong (1980: 75) argues that the derogation of a physically deviant person depends on whether or not that person can be blamed or found culpable for his or her appearance. DeJong concludes from his study of high school girls' perceptions of fat and thin peers, with various explanations for their appearance, that it is not their physical deviance that causes derogation by peers, but rather it is the sense that people are responsible for their deviance that matters. He argues in favor of disseminating information that 'obesity is a complicated disorder' not simply caused by overeating or lack of exercise (ibid.: 85). The pathologization of fatness here is not necessarily useful, but DeJong's attention to changing public attitudes toward fatness is instructive.

Extending this logic, scholar Julie Ferris (2003: 257) notes that media attention to bodies and physical practices deemed excessive functions to reinforce a sense of what a 'normal' body is and how it performs. In studying popular cultural artifacts, she argues that fat female bodies and anorexic female bodies have merged to signify an excess in strong need of taming. 'These two cultural constructs, the anorexic and the obese, are equally marginalized by our culture in an attempt to sustain a center that works to keep bodies constantly in process, never complete' (ibid.: 261). However, Ferris points out that despite similar discursive constructions, there is a distinct split between anorexia and obesity 'when it comes time to incorporate one or the other and its set of processes into the cultural center' (ibid.). Anorexia tends to be portrayed as an external victimizer, something the anorectic cannot control but must battle.[1] In contrast, fatness is something that women or girls do to themselves, and their efforts to battle it (while culturally mandatory) are often deemed inappropriate if seemingly too easy (as in the case of weight-loss surgery; see also Throsby, this volume). Both fat and extremely thin bodies exceed cultural limits, but blame is placed differently – a significant distinction.

Scholars in the field of public health have begun to urge feminist scholars to consider obesity alongside anorexia, though not exactly in the vein of Ferris' deconstructive work. Antronette Yancey, Joanne Leslie and Emily Abel, all public health researchers, believe that women's studies scholars have been remiss and somewhat irresponsible in paying so much attention to anorexia and so little to obesity, pointing out that 'the health consequences of the cultural promulgation of female thinness (bulimia, anorexia) affect only a small minority of women' (Yancey et al., 2006: 426). I would suggest that there are benefits in looking at both corporeal situ-

---

1 Other feminist scholars argue that biases against the gender, class and race skew of people with eating disorders means that they are 'thought to be decadent, self-absorbed, and heavily implicated in their own troubles' (Thompson 1994: 1), in contrast to Ferris' notion that only fat women are implicated in their own situation.

ations from a feminist perspective without necessarily buying the argument that fatness always has deleterious health consequences. Yancey et al. want to make people healthier and wonder aloud how that can happen while avoiding the stigma that often surrounds fatness in the context of such endeavors. On the face of things, it is difficult to argue with such an agenda, but an exploration of the moralizing function of health discourse is in order before signing on to it.

Health, morality and the will to normality

Our contemporary era is characterized by the widespread phenomenon of biomedicalization, wherein medicine becomes a dominant institution of social control, an arbiter of truth, 'a moral exercise used to define normality, punish deviance and maintain social order' (Lupton, 2003: 9). Public health thus becomes a new morality system in which people are compelled to take responsibility for their own risks and the risks of the environment, and in which experts are increasingly entitled to intervene in private lives for the good of both the individual and the social body (Clarke et al., 2003; Petersen and Lupton, 1996). Whereas old public health strategies centered almost exclusively on public hygiene issues, now the conduct and appearance of the individual body is fundamental to today's public health strategies. The healthy body as a signifier of moral worth in this scheme apparently displays a subject's virtues of self-control, discipline, denial and willpower, values similar to those of the Protestant work ethic that Weber tied to the rise of capitalism: the rational actor with a body that maximizes profit, and with no room for excess, is idealized (Petersen and Lupton, 1996: 25, 15). (Seemingly in direct conflict is the parallel edict that, under capitalism, good citizens must also be willing and voracious consumers; they simply may not wear evidence of their consumption practices on their bodies.) The healthiest citizen, then, is the best worker. Fat and exceptionally thin bodies are read as failures in this framework – as morally unworthy, poor workers, having either consumed too much or too little.

Statistics are the handmaidens of contemporary public health discourse. They first became linked to moral topographies in the nineteenth century, turning unruly populations into more easily manageable entities (Rose, 1990: 6). Turned in the service of values like efficiency, social order, consumption and profitability, these statistics provide criteria by which as individuals we can evaluate ourselves and, if we are good citizens, subsequently adjust ourselves as well. For Rose (ibid.: 11), theorist of governmentality,

> the government of the soul depends upon our recognition of ourselves as ideally and potentially certain sorts of person, the unease generated by a normative judgment of what we are and could become, and the incitement offered to overcome this discrepancy by following the advice of experts in the management of the self.

Within this context of biomedicalization and governmentality, fatness registers as a dire predicament when statistics are interpreted in alarmist tones. However, the 'epidemic' moniker is far from a neutral way of naming the situation of fat people (see also Gard, Throsby, both this volume). Researcher Annemarie Jutel (2005) explores how longstanding cultural values – a preference for trusting sight over the other senses, a belief that appearance reflects one's true inner self, and a preoccupation with the moral value of food – combine to produce a misleading overreliance on weight as a chief indicator of health. Jutel slyly notes that, 'the paradox of the aesthetic of virtuous health is that it leads both individuals and medical policy-makers to focus on normative appearance rather than on health, and to presume moral deviance (gluttony, sloth) in the presence of deviant form' (ibid.: 120).

Of course, telling the difference between honest-to-goodness medical problems and moral panic is not always an easy chore, but it is a necessary one for those who are truly interested in health promotion. Pushing women toward diet and exercise in the name of weight loss as part of a normalization project will continue to fail; to their credit, our bodies are notoriously resistant to such efforts. As even Katherine Flegal of the Centers for Disease Control and Prevention sardonically notes, 'Yes, obesity is to blame for all the evils of modern life, except somehow, weirdly, it is not killing people enough. In fact that's why there are all these fat people around. They just won't die' (cited in Kolata, 2006).

Hilde Bruch, an early authority on the emotional aspects of eating disorders, was skeptical about the labeling of obesity as pathological (see also Saukko, this volume). Bruch (1973: 111) recognized that, despite dissent among nutritional researchers, most seemed bent on labeling any deviation from an arbitrarily selected weight norm as abnormal. Luckily, she noted, the damage of stigmatization was minimized by the decision of most fat people to ignore it. Since her writing nearly 40 years ago, fat people seem to have become far more invested in normalization projects, perhaps a testament to the ever-extensive reach of biomedicalization. Bruch herself resisted arbitrary thin ideals, and was instead comfortable with thinking a fat person could be doing well if his/her weight was stable for a long period, if s/he functioned adequately, and generally felt well (ibid.: 114). Were this the case, Bruch pointed out little motivation for advocating weight reduction – and not in a resigned, defeated, 'we can't get them to diet!' sense at all. Hers was more like a 'pick your battles if you really care about health' sense.[2] Instead of seeing fat people as weak or self-indulgent

2 Still, Bruch's own language choices when describing fat bodies are regrettable – 'ungainly, awkward, and slow . . . misshapen . . .' in contrast to the 'grace and liveliness' of slim bodies (1973: 119). Although Bruch does claim that obesity is an abnormal state of nutrition, she is careful to think through what is lost by efforts to pathologize fatness.

for eating too much, Bruch asked readers to consider the 'selfishness and self-indulgence involved in a life which makes one's appearance the center of all values, and subordinates all other considerations to it. I do not know how often people are aware of the emotional sacrifice of staying slim' (p. 198). With this move, she unearths the moral sensibilities that underpin our concepts of 'normal' healthy bodies, a necessary step on the road to the material reality of good health.

Moving forward

Thinking about health against the backdrop of the kinds of moral imperatives outlined earlier in this chapter requires a shift in focus when it comes to weight management. For feminists, the question of how to move forward productively – respecting the political and symbolic functions of women's various eating practices and body shapes, while critiquing docility and gender normalization and intervening in disempowering material realities – is a challenging one. Despite their many points of intersection, scholars who focus on anorexia nervosa move in a somewhat different direction here from many who focus on fatness.

For instance, Julie Hepworth (1999: 3; see also, especially, Eckermann, this volume) argues against the popular view of anorexia nervosa as psychopathology: 'my central thesis is that the dominant psychiatric definition of anorexia nervosa is socially constructed through discourse or . . . regularly occurring systems of language'. She aims to think through new prevention treatment strategies without reproducing the unproductive practices that have been in place. In this sense, she is aimed in a somewhat different direction from many fat activists, who want to disavow any sense of a problem or a need for treatment. Apart from members of the pro-Ana movement, a highly criticized, primarily on-line community of support for women in pursuit of exceptional thinness (see Day and Keys, this volume), there are very few who would suggest that anorexia or bulimia are good, positive or empowering practices.[3] In terms of fatness, however, some fat activists, mindful of the distinction between what a body *is* and what a body *does*, are careful to reject *any* claims linking fatness causally to ill health. In the quite necessary move to question that all-too-easy slide from aesthetic or moral deviance to ill health, they may be throwing out the baby with the bathwater. It almost seems as if any admission at all of ill health related to body weight is an invitation to censure and thus to the collapse of

---

3 Deborah Pollack (2003) conceptualizes pro-anorexia websites as an effort to resist the discourse of the disease model popularized by medical and psychiatric institutions. 'By reversing the flow of medicalized terminology from oppressive to agentic, the pro-eating disordered subject's public attempts to embrace the disorder can be seen as a complex political action' (ibid.: 249). Yet Pollack is wary of romanticizing this agency, noting that 'their choice of medium for protest is one that has a 20 percent long-term mortality rate' (ibid.).

a project of subjectivity for people of all shapes and sizes, and so the defenses come up.

I wonder: How can fat people own their realities – that sometimes fat is healthy and sometimes it isn't – and still keep their political agenda intact?[4] This is a serious question that is worth exploring. How can we maintain health – how can we encourage women to thrive – without the vagaries of psycho/biomedical discourse that have been roundly problematized by feminists? We can start by questioning that which we are asked to do with our bodies, maintaining what feminist philosopher Susan Bordo (1989: 28) calls 'a skeptical attitude toward the seeming routes of liberation and pleasure offered by our culture'.

One space where I see this happening currently is the Health At Every Size (HAES) movement. HAES proponents question the equation of fatness with pathology, and instead emphasize approaches that produce health benefits independent of weight loss. Realizing that shame is neither an appropriate nor an effective tool in the struggle for better health, proponents claim that 'shifting the focus from weight and dieting to enhancement of quality of life and health is radically different from the 'before-and-after' school of personal transformation' with which women are so well acquainted these days (Burgard and Lyons, 1994: 214). The kinds of things that HAES advocates urge women to do with their bodies include: overcoming weight-based prejudice to practice size acceptance; listening to and trusting their own bodies about what, when and how much to eat, rather than bowing to externally promoted anxieties associated with dieting; engaging in pleasurable physical movement rather than exercising for weight loss; and accessing size-friendly health care environments (Robison, 2001). Intuitively, these practices sound far healthier *and* more politically useful for women of *all* sizes than those advocated within regimes of biomedicine, and thus they offer feminist movements concerned with the politics of women's health a less imperiled set of on-the-ground practices.

References

Bordo, S. (1989) The body and the reproduction of femininity: a feminist appropriation of Foucault, in A.M. Jaggar and S.R. Bordo (eds), *Gender/Body/Knowledge: Feminist Reconstructions of Being and Knowing*, New Brunswick, NJ: Rutgers University Press, pp. 13–33.

Bruch, H. (1973) *Eating Disorders: Obesity, Anorexia Nervosa, and the Person Within*, New York: Basic Books.

Burgard, D. and Lyons, P. (1994) Alternatives in obesity treatment: focusing on

4 Michel Foucault might ask: *Should* we work toward a political agenda that seeks to reposition fatness in relation to the concept of health? Or is that merely buying into health-focused discourse?

health for fat women, in P. Fallon, M.A. Katzman and S.C. Wooley (eds), *Feminist Perspectives on Eating Disorders*, New York: Guilford Press, pp. 212–230.

Burns, M. (2004) Eating like an ox: femininity and dualistic constructions of bulimia and anorexia, *Feminism and Psychology*, 14(2): 269–295.

Chernin, K. (1985) *The Hungry Self: Women, Eating and Identity*, New York: Harper Perennial.

Clarke, A.E., Mamo, L., Fishman, J.R., Shim, J.K. and Fosket, J.R. (2003) Bio-medicalization: technoscientific transformations of health, illness, and U.S. biomedicine, *American Sociological Review*, 68(2): 161–194.

Counihan, C.M. (1992) Food rules in the United States: individualism, control and hierarchy, *Anthropological Quarterly*, 65(2): 55–66.

DeJong, W. (1980) The stigma of obesity: the consequences of naïve assumptions concerning the causes of physical deviance, *Journal of Health and Social Behavior*, 21: 75–87.

Ferris, J.E. (2003) Parallel discourses and 'appropriate' bodies: media constructions of anorexia and obesity in the cases of Tracey Gold and Carnie Wilson, *Journal of Communication Inquiry*, 27(3): 256–273.

Hepworth, J. (1999) *The Social Construction of Anorexia Nervosa*, Thousand Oaks, CA: Sage.

Jutel, A. (2005) Weighing health: the moral burden of obesity, *Social Semiotics*, 15(2): 113–125.

Killian, K.D. (1994) Fearing fat: a literature review of family systems under-standings and treatments of anorexia and bulimia, *Family Relations*, 43(3): 311–318.

Kolata, G. (2006) For a world of woes, we blame cookie monsters, *New York Times*, 29 October, at: www.nytimes.com/2006/10/29/weekinreview/29kolata.html?ex= 1319774400anden=9908af1ae7053a2fandei=5088andpartner=rssnytandemc=rss.

Lupton, D. (2003) *Medicine as Culture: Illness, Disease and the Body in Western Societies*, 2nd edition, Thousand Oaks, CA: Sage.

NIH Technology Assessment Conference Panel (1993) Methods for voluntary weight loss and control, *Annals of Internal Medicine*, 119(7): 764–770.

Orbach, S. (1978) *Fat is a Feminist Issue: A Self-help Guide for Compulsive Over-eaters*, New York: Berkley Press.

Orbach, S. (1986) *Hunger Strike: The Anorectic's Struggle as a Metaphor for Our Age*, New York: Norton.

Petersen, A. and Lupton, D. (1996) *The New Public Health: Health and Self in the Age of Risk*, Thousand Oaks, CA: Sage.

Pollack, D. (2003) Pro-eating disorder websites: what should be the feminist response?, *Feminism and Psychology*, 13(2): 246–251.

Robison, J. (2001) Size-friendly health care, *First Do No Harm: An Alternative Approach for Assisting Clients with Eating and Weight-related Concern*, at: www.jonrobison.net/FDNH/INDEX.HTM.

Rose, N. (1990) *Governing the Soul: The Shaping of the Private Self*, New York: Routledge.

Tareen, A., Hodes, M. and Rangel, L. (2005) Non-fat-phobic anorexia nervosa in British South Asian adolescents, *International Journal of Eating Disorders*, 37: 161–165.

Thompson, B.W. (1994) *A Hunger So Wide and So Deep: American Women Speak Out on Eating Problems*, Minneapolis: University of Minnesota Press.

Van Wormer, K. (1994) Hi, I'm Jane; I'm a compulsive overeater, in P. Fallon, M.A. Katzman and S.C. Wooley (eds), *Feminist Perspectives on Eating Disorders*, New York: Guilford Press, pp. 287–298.

Yancey, A.K., Leslie, J. and Abel, E.K. (2006) Obesity at the crossroads: feminist and public health perspectives, *Signs*, 31(2): 425–443.

Part IV

Critiquing the discourses and discursive practices of treatment

14 Food for thought
Embodied slimness and nursing within an eating disorders unit

Ruth Surtees

Introduction

Turning from side to side, I peer at different parts of my body reflected in the mirror. I ask my partner, anxiously: 'Does my butt look too skinny in this?' She says, sighing, 'You look fine, just go to work before you're late.'

This small vignette can undoubtedly be understood within contemporary cultural pre-occupations of many western(ized) women concerning the body's weight and shape (Bordo, 1993a, 1993b; Hepworth, 1999; Malson, 1998; MacSween, 1993). The vignette is an inversion, however, of the much-cited old dictum 'One can never be too thin . . .'. It highlights the heterogeneity of, and complexities for, individual women who are positioned both materially and discursively as subjects/objects of particular forms of embodiment. My contribution to this book foregrounds a critique of my own complex and multiply-embodied experiences of 'slimness' in my role as a nurse in an in-patient Eating Disorders (ED) unit. I first briefly describe the unit I work in. I then discuss aspects of my (auto/bio)ethnographic discourse methodology, before providing just a small taste of one particular aspect of work undertaken by ED nurses and some other clinicians in our team, that of taking part in the practice of supported eating. Finally, I explore how some forms of embodiment and talk about bodies, for these 'professionalized bodies', may come to parallel those of 'pathologized bodies' in the reinforcement of the micro-management of bodily regulation within discourses of 'health'.

The regional ED unit I work in serves the whole of the South Island of Aotearoa/New Zealand, that is, a population of approximately one million people. I work as an in-patient (IP) nurse within the multi-disciplinary team (MDT). Patients may be admitted for various short-stay (two to four weeks) medical, stabilization or assessment admissions, or the much longer (approximately six months to one year) Weight Restoration Programme. Our unit has six in-patient beds and one emergency bed. We broadly utilize a cognitive-behavioural therapy model across the disciplines; a multi-dimensional approach incorporating psychotherapeutic, psychoeducational, biomedical and behaviourist paradigms. This occurs within a 'lenient flexible approach' premised on theories of operant conditioning, and arising from behaviouralist discourses and practices (Snell, 2005; Surtees, 2007). The unit IP programme strives primarily to develop and maintain therapeutic alliances with patients and their whanau/families, consistent with our milieu of leniency, flexibility and partnership.

Eating disorders and me(thod/ology)

Many critical and post-structuralist theorists and nursing scholars foreground the centrality of bodies and embodiment in ethnographic writing, working and researching (Britzman, 2000; Burns, 2006; Coffey, 1999; Ellis and Bochner, 1996; Fine, 1994; Richardson, 1997). Nursing scholars have in this way explored various concepts of embodiment (Lawler, 1997; Shakespeare, 2003; Surtees, 2003; Walker, 1997). This includes the experience of 'embodied largeness' (Carryer, 1997). However, I am unaware of nursing scholarship concerning 'embodied slimness'. My exploration of embodied differences, silences and paradoxes within ED MDT discourses and practices means that I ask questions such as: how can ED nurses and other team clinicians talk of our bodies? What statements can be made about us? What embodied subject positions can be taken up, negotiated and contested? What knowledges are produced, with which effects?

The importance of postmodern discursive understandings and methodologies for therapeutic practice and intervention in the field of EDs is confirmed in a local study (Surgenor et al., 2003). Issues of MDT practice and intervention are always embedded within wider networks of disciplinary and professionalized power, surveillance and (self-)regulation, nested within the discourses and practices of over-arching neo-liberal approaches to health care in New Zealand (Fougere, 2001; Larner, 1997).

In traditional western psychiatry and psychologies, the 'real truth' of the un/healthy body/psyche is assumed to lie deep within the (binarized) body or mind, rendered visible and penetrable by 'objective' medical discourses and practices (Burns, 2004; de Ras and Grace, 1997; Grosz, 1994, 1995; Foucault, 1973; Fournier, 2002). Post-structuralist methodologies utilized by Burns (2006), Gremillion (1992, 2003), Malson (1995, 1998, 1999), Surgenor et al. (2003), and other social scientists in many different disciplinary fields, contest the notion that there can ever be any objective or scientific 'truth', hidden inside bodies awaiting discovery (Grace, 1998). As such, an autobio/ethnographic methodology is only ever concerned with 'partial truths' as they are (re)produced in language (Britzman, 2000). My term 'me(thod/ology)' signals the autobio-ethnographic nature of my inquiry. This chapter itself constructs a partial and subjective (t)ruth, rather than uncovering some kind of 'real' truth about different ED clinicians (including myself), patients or eating disorders.

Many partial (t)ruths and multiple subject positionings all produce my embodiment(s) at work. I explore some of these ambiguities, neither as a retrospective nursing reflection on practice, nor a 'confessional' inwardly navel-gazing narration (Gilbert, 2001). Rather, I partially and subjectively observe and discuss some of the micro-politics at a work-site where my embodiment invokes a set of uncertainties and paradoxes which are highlighted at certain 'governing interfaces' (Burchell, 1996, after Foucault, 1979), or nodes within networks of institutionalized and professionalized power, such as times of eating and talking with others.

While I am currently a practicing clinical nurse, my academic background encompasses critical sociologies of gender, health and medicine. Health clinicians are expected to conform to layers of governance at the national, managerial and unit levels, as well as at the levels of disciplinary professional bodies and our own individual bodies, as part of the processes of 'professionalization' (Fournier, 1999). At the same time, we nurses are required at 'expert' levels of nursing practice, to 'analyse and appropriately question (your) unit's nursing systems and procedures'.[1] I feel keenly the tensions noted by sociologists of health and medicine and other academic nurses as we return to the field to practise or undertake more formal ethnographic research in the field. These tensions involve negotiating an ongoing balance between 'appropriately questioning' and simultaneously conforming to a normalizing nursing disciplinary governance (Allen, 2004; Anspach and Mizrachi, 2006).

While I theorize about everything we do at work, Walker notes that his borderlands positioning of 'living the slash' (Fine, 1994; Walker, 1997), between 'theory/practice' was ultimately an experience of 'unhappily confused identity in the unit' (Walker, 1997: 5). He states that the culture of clinical nursing can at times be 'inexorably conservative', and that:

> difference, novelty, ambiguity and uncertainty constitute sometimes profound challenges to clinical nursing culture, which has historically [and] institutionally been constructed so much around markers of homogeneity, tradition, fixity and certainty . . .
>
> (Walker, 1997: 5)

Walker's words resonate for me in terms of inhabiting an uncertain body at times – ambiguous, ambivalent, androgynous, and 'living the slash' from moment to moment on the ED unit. This multiple borderlands positioning is as much in regard to my 'living/inhabiting the slash' of 'practitioner/academic', as it is 'slim/thin' (that is, 'professionalized/pathologized'). Located in an already culturally privileged body (middle-class, educated,

---

1 Canterbury District Health Board, 'Professional Development and Recognition Programme' (2006).

pakeha[2]) and as a critical sociologist of health and illness, what might I be thinking about our programme and its basis in traditional, western psychiatry and psychology (Bell, 2006; Crowe, 2000)? What might I be thinking, with a post-structuralist feminist orientation to theory, as the mother of a daughter, and as a team member, about our team approaches to identity, individuation, and certain sorts of femininities, that are reproduced in different ways to give rise to the concept of either an unhealthy, anorexic body, or a healthy, non-anorexic body (Gremillion, 1992, 2003; Moulding, 2003, 2006)?

I walk a 'thin line', inhabiting the slash, embodied ambiguously in these ways at work. A personal/professional split inscribes my body spatially – outside the work space its exterior is read variably as 'athletic', 'slim', 'skinny', 'healthy' 'fit-looking', 'thin' or 'vegetarian'. These assumptions and statements are made and enabled in the context of public fear around 'fatness', sanctioned by public health discourses of what constitutes 'health' (Braziel and LeBesco, 2001; see also Gard, LeBesco, both this volume). But as the opening vignette to this chapter suggests, the moment I step over the threshold from private to professional life, public space to professional/ medical space, my embodied sense of self changes perceptually from 'slim' to 'thin', and back again when I go home. The presence of thin bodies is always already troublesome in a medical/psychiatric ED unit, because an objective, inner truth is not visible; hence both eating – and/or not eating – can act as signs of an eating disorder. This paradox is because disordered eating is not necessarily always visible (see also Burns, this volume) – unless of course, an anorexic[3] body is particularly emaciated.

The sign of the body – whatever its anatomically visible shape and size – bears an arbitrary relationship to the signifiers 'anorexia' or 'bulimia' (Burns and Gavey, 2004; Squire, 2003; see also Malson, this volume), indeed as it does to 'health' at all. Interestingly, a bulimic body may be even more ambiguous, given that it is less open to literal, visual interpretations (Squire, 2003; see also Burns, this volume). If a thin – but professional – body is troublesome visually, then ironically a bulimic – but professional – body may remain 'invisible'. The visibly conforming 'normal' sized or 'healthy weight' bodily surface is beyond question – it is authorized by particular public health discourses that reify it as healthy and desirable. This is despite the simultaneous sanctioning and normalizing of quasi-bulimic disciplinary

---

2 The term 'pakeha' refers to a non-Maori person of European descent, born in Aotearoa/New Zealand. The term Maori refers to the indigenous people of Aotearoa/New Zealand. These names signify the colonial relationship between 'Maori' and 'Pakeha', the non-indigenous settler population (Tuhiwai Smith, 1999).

3 I refer to 'anorexia' generally here as it covers broadly the spectrum of in-patients in the unit, whether AN- restricting or purging sub-types, or Eating Disorder Not Otherwise Specified (EDNOS). Similarly, I use the female pronoun as almost all in-patients are female. All the nurses on our team are also female.

bodily practices that include compensatory measures for overeating (Burns and Gavey, 2004; Squire 2003). I now go on to explore aspects of one of the micro-managed bodily practices performed in my work roles – the practice of supported eating with the patients.

Rules for supported eating

During my first few weeks working on the unit, and conscious that I appeared relatively slim/thin vis-à-vis many members of the MDT, I made sure I could be seen to be eating regularly and 'normally', particularly during the context of supported eating. This half-hour meal, three times per day, with three 10–15-minute snacks in between, is attended by most patients on the unit. Each supported meal and snack is attended also by a clinician, usually a nurse (because of shift and weekend work), but some-times a psychologist, physiotherapist, social worker or occupational ther-apist. Staff announce when the half-hour meal will start and finish, and any late-comers must generally finish at the same time as the others who may have started.

Even as a supportive intervention, the shared meal can often be fraught with tensions, which the clinician acts to mediate in their role as support person and role model of 'normal eating'. Some patients watch the second-hand of the clock agonisingly. Some patients watch each other, or stare at the food on other patients' plates. Some patients stare fixedly down at their own plates, or at cue cards or written reminders they have given themselves as encouragement for eating. Some patients seek eye contact with particular other patients for different reasons, or with the nurse, or avoid eye contact with any others at all. My first few meals in my role attending supported eating were indeed tense, as I endeavoured to think what might constitute 'normal eating' for a nurse who may or may not be particularly hungry at that set time. Hungry or not, I ate everything following the written 'rules for supported eating for staff', in ways designed to give the outward appearance of normal eating; chewing well, relishing a variety of foods, not eating too fast or too slow, eating food in the right order, not mixing or over-chopping food, and presenting a facial appearance of smiling enjoyment, chatting blithely about mundane issues (talk of food is not encouraged but patients may speak of their feelings or indicate that they need verbal support to continue), and generally performing a repertoire of bodily practices or 'technologies of the self' (Foucault, 1986) that demon-strate that, as an ED nurse, I am a healthy, normal eater/person.

In some of those earlier days, I remember a particular group of patients that used non-verbal communication a great deal. On one occasion, the kitchen mistakenly delivered me a meal that was markedly smaller than most of the patients' meals. As we unloaded our trays onto the table, I became aware that the group were catching each other's eyes, directing their gazes onto my plate, and then returning the gaze meaningfully towards each other. What should I say and do, the professional One caught in the gaze of the pathologized Other? Although I was not especially hungry, and knew I could eat more in the nurses' office, or once at home, or indeed at any other time that I was hungry, I made a statement to the effect that 'this would not be enough for me', and called for another nurse to find me some more food. This happened, and with a sense of relief the meal continued. The surveillance that clinicians who are slim/thin may encounter from some patients at different governing interfaces was something that began to interest me from then on, and I began to discuss these issues with other clinicians, particularly nurses, in order to see if any of my experiences were shared.

These shared conversations over time between several slim clinicians within the MDT and myself broadened to include modes of dressing and talking at work, and focused largely on the paradox (that some patients find disturbing) that, while a thin clinician may not have an eating disorder, a patient's body that is outwardly larger than a professional body remains the pathologized 'eating disordered' body. Further, a clinician with a 'healthy BMI' between 20–25 may well maintain this outwardly 'normal' appearance through technologies of the self which may include many compensatory behaviours, yet remains unremarkable against the 'thin' and hence marked 'abnormal' body (Squire, 2003; see also Burns, LeBesco, both this volume). This is largely because of the belief that EDs are also about what is 'inside' the psychological body, in terms of (irrational) thoughts and beliefs about body image and self-esteem, and particular traits such as perfectionism and desire for control (Hardin, 2003c; Malson, 1998).

While the visual boundaries between the professionalized One and the pathologized Other may be slippery and porous, much clinical work involves striving to maintain distinct psychological and physical dualisms between the two. We do this consciously, in our talking, body language, communications and writing with patients, as well as eating with them, to model the differences between 'not-normal' and 'normal' eating, thinking, and feeling that we hope the patients will learn. However, the dichotomy of the professionalized One and pathologized Other can itself be deconstructed in the words of Trinh Minh-ha:

> Not quite the same, not quite the Other, she stands in that undetermined threshold place where she constantly drifts in and out. . . . When she turns the inside out or the outside in, she is, like the two sides of a coin, the same impure, both-in-one insider/outsider. . . . Differences do not only exist between outsider and insider – two entities – they are also at work within the outsider or the insider – a single entity.
>
> (1991: 74–76)

So from where – and how – do I speak/write? How am I, and other team members, able to conduct ourselves, how to think and talk? Differences –

ontologically as well as epistemologically – exist within the subject of knowledge, as well as between subjects of knowledge. As Trinh Minh-ha suggests above, not only am I neither one nor the other, I am never properly One, nor the Other, but an impure, both-in-one, insider/outsider. What assumptions are made about my body that act, consciously or unconsciously, to reinforce this? How might patients/team members speak about my body when I am not present? What assumptions and statements do I, in turn, make about the bodies of different patients and clinicians, in order to create them as Other to me (Allen, 2004; Fine, 1994)?

The nurses' station – surveillance, silences, sublimations

After supported eating, the attending nurse returns to the main office, a large central nursing station which comprises a panoptic visual space (Cheek, 2000; Foucault, 1973). Here, nurses and other members of the MDT spend portions of the day, discussing treatment plans or different patients' progress, working on computers, tending to all sorts of administrative tasks. The office is also a hybrid space, where our personal as well as professional lives are often discussed among us. Windows are on all four sides of the walls. Nurses can observe visitors entering the ward, and patients leaving the ward, or observe the particular ward boundaries different patients may need to adhere to for different reasons. We watch patients line up outside the clinic for their medication after meals. We watch them walk back and forth, signalling non-verbally that they are present and need our help in some way. We can see the bedroom reserved for the sickest patient. We watch them standing or walking briskly about, when we know they should be on bed-rest after breakfast for an hour. We watch them watching us, either to catch our eyes, or to avoid our gaze. We see them watch us talking and eating in the office at times. Each observes the Other.

This visual and mutual surveillance between embodied subjects of knowledge via the windows determines who is professionalized, and who is pathologized. We clinicians may enter any ward space, but the patients may not enter the office space. We clinicians know, because we are in the office looking out, that we are the professionalized, 'normal' subjects, compared to the pathologized Others who we watch closely for signs of transgression, or redemption. This surveillance is a disciplinary technique premised on confining or restoring individuals to the 'norm' – a 'calculated and calculable norm beyond which anything or anyone is "Other"' (Cheek, 2000). However, as Trinh Minh-ha suggests in her quote above, differences exist not only between outsider and insider – two entities – they are also at work within the outsider or the insider – a single entity. So how do clinicians inside the office space know what is 'normal', both between, and within, our own embodied selves?

If we shift discussions of pathologized or professionalized individuals to discussions of ways of saying and knowing, then what can be thought and said, and the statements that can be made, or must be left unsaid, about our own (and other) bodies by differently-positioned clinicians in the office, is opened up as a space for inquiry. What claims are made about particular bodies? What kinds of language have we inherited? Which knowledges become subjugated? Who may speak, with which authority, about the bodies of Others? It is easy for those of us in the space of the office to distance ourselves from the Others in the ward, with all the authority of medicine and psychiatry at our disposal. But in what ways do we differ from each other? ED clinicians, like ED patients, are not a homogenous group. Nurses, for example, do not represent a fixed, unified, rational, theoretical, disembodied and objective 'body of nursing'. We are instead a heterogeneous, polyvocal group of women who share a role – that of being a professionalized nurse; in this case, an ED nurse.

Nurses are complex, multiple subjects; inhabiting fragmented problematic, passionate, transgressive, embodied selves, just as all subjects do (Bordo, 1993b; Fournier, 2002; Grosz, 1994). We nurses partake in informal discussions in the office about many aspects of the programme, and about ourselves. Some of these discussions have included the usefulness of the BMI as a determinant of health for generally teenaged women, and ways to respond to those patients who may ask us about the rationale for this, or what our own BMIs are. One nurse stated to me that she had 'never weighed herself regularly until working here'; still others do not weigh themselves at all. Certainly, I had never thought to work out my own BMI, of 18 or thereabouts, before I began work in the unit.

Another nurse and myself discussed feelings of mild anxiety about appearing 'too skinny' at work in some clothes which we would readily wear at home or in public. Some of us utilize a subversive sense of humour at times, making jokes about 'bingeing', for example, if we have brought food in to share, or at Christmas or New Year when over-eating followed by compensatory body management is publicly sanctioned (Burns and Gavey, 2004; Squire, 2003). Interestingly, while we may joke about compensatory body management behaviours, we would probably not joke in a similar fashion about being 'anorexic'. We generally do not discuss each other's weight overtly. We explore our embodiment in other ways, where actual issues of weight, shape and body image may become sublimated within other discourses.

The predominant discourses amongst nurses concerning our own embodiment which are articulated in the hybrid space of the office generally concern sets of paradoxes. We are at once set up as professionalized subjects of ED clinical knowledge concerning 'healthy eating/living', which 'should be regular', 'should include breakfast', and 'should resemble the healthy food pyramid', for example. But, as shift workers, we nurses negotiate the 'regimes of truth' (Foucault, 1986) we inhabit in multiple ways. We might discuss how difficult it is to maintain regular meal times on shift work; that we might skip breakfast, how night duty interferes with sleeping, eating, appetite, mood and digestion. While not wishing to comment directly on one another's weight or shape, many of us discuss clothing, fashions and the politics of bodily aesthetics readily. Among many other things, we discuss aging, whether we would ever have cosmetic surgery, how to lower cholesterol, increase walking, drink more water, have less coffee, whether we should go to the gym or not, stop smoking or not, issues around menopause, and how to counteract the negative effects of short-rotational shift-work in the already highly stressful and increasingly litigious environment that constitutes our profession as 'health providers'.

We do all this talk about our embodied selves primarily within a discourse of 'healthism' that increasingly pervades the bodily management of everyday life, and can be seen as a response to the 'medicalization' of this everyday life (Armstrong, 2001; Gastaldo, 1997; Lupton, 1997). While espousing health and positive body image on the ward in our professionalized roles, we can often succumb to a discourse of humorous self-depreciation in the office between ourselves that necessarily remains individualized and privatized. Perhaps there is a public presupposition that health providers such as nurses are always already 'healthy', when in fact individual clinicians do not lie outside of – disembodied from – cultural and political discourses concerning the body and its self-management. ED clinicians, like everybody else, are not exempt from contemporary disciplinary regimes of truth regarding the regulation and disciplinary normalization of bodies (Bordo, 1993b; Foucault, 1973, 1986, 1988). Indeed, it is possible that the unit and the office space, both materially and discursively, can be seen as a heightened and intense microcosm of New Zealand public health discourses that both consumers and providers are embedded within.

In this sense, while at once wanting to avoid conversation between ourselves as ED nurses that directly addresses issues of weight, size and shape, we are often acutely attuned to ways of managing our bodies – and negotiating body-talk – in particular ways that are sanctioned by different discourses drawn from the fields of ED work itself, as well as from those of public health policies, liberal feminisms, consumerism, and both medical and media portrayals of female body image. The reinforcement of the micro-management of our own bodies is paradoxically (re)produced and subverted through its very disavowal. This reinforcement occurs through various 'technologies of the self' (Foucault, 1986) – the 'doing' (and disruption) of gendered, professionalized selves, that might be seen as paralleling the bodily micro-management which post-structuralist theorists have already demonstrated occurs in pathologized ED inpatients (Bell, 2006; Gremillion, 1992, 2003; Hardin, 2003a, 2003b; Malson, 1998; Moulding, 2006; Surgenor et al., 2003).

These issues for ED clinicians occur within neo-liberal health regimes of self-surveillance and self-governance in the current context of surveillance medicine (Armstrong, 2001; Bordo, 1993a, 1993b; Burchell, 1996; Rose, 1993, 1994). These and similar paradoxes within the fields occupied by 'health consumers' extend now to the liberal governance of 'health providers' such as nurses. We are at once exhorted to become increasingly professionalized and 'auditable subjects' (Surtees, 2003), in part, by questioning the epistemological frameworks from within which we work. We then also find ourselves negotiating complex fields of risk (to our jobs, to our credibility, to our patients), vis-à-vis this responsibility (Gastaldo, 1997; Lupton, 1995, 1997; Surtees, 2004).

At times in the ED unit I work to destabilize institutional preconceptions of what it means to be a postmodern feminist practitioner, in what feels like part of an 'on-going, flexible and dynamic postmodern game' (Richardson, 1997). As Fine (1994: 81) suggests: 'silence, retreat, and engagement all pose ethical dilemmas . . . all are entangled with ethics of knowing, writing, and acting.' To one who appears visually as neither One, nor the Other, the game/work of psychiatric ED nursing requires an ability for fluid capitulation to contextually and temporarily constructed identities. These identities throw into sharp relief for me the issues under scrutiny for postmodern ethnographers. These include, as Britzman (2000: 30) suggests; the ways in which experience and truth are such unstable constructs, how and why certain practices and bodies are valorized; others repressed, discounted, impossible or unimaginable. Yet in opening up for inquiry the hybrid, paradoxical nursing spaces we inhabit, we can analyse not so much what and who is/not 'normal', but increase our focus instead on what bodies can *do*, rather than focus on what they *look* like; a focus on diversity, difference and plurality, and on polymorphous pleasures and desires.

Acknowledgements

Many thanks go to my nursing supervisor, Associate Professor Marie Crowe, and friend Kate Yeoman, for 'chewing the fat' with me about these issues, and for reading early drafts.

References

Allen, D. (2004) Ethnomethodological insights into insider–outsider relationships in nursing ethnographies of healthcare settings, *Nursing Inquiry*, 11(1): 14–24.

Anspach, R. and Mizrachi, N. (2006) The field worker's fields: ethics, ethnography and medical sociology, *Sociology of Health and Illness*, 28(6): 713–731.

Armstrong, D. (2001) The rise of surveillance medicine, in M. Purdy and D. Banks (eds), *The Sociology and Politics of Health*, London: Routledge, pp. 144–150.

Bell, M. (2006) Re/forming the anorexic 'prisoner': inpatient medical treatment as the return to panoptic femininity, *Cultural Studies/Critical Methodologies*, 6(2): 282–307.

Bordo, S. (1993a) *Unbearable Weight: Feminism, Western Culture, and the Body*, Berkeley: University of California Press.

Bordo, S. (1993b) Feminism, Foucault and the politics of the body, in C.

Ramazanoglu (ed.), *Up Against Foucault: Explorations of Some Tensions between Foucault and Feminism*, London: Routledge, pp. 179–202.

Braziel, J.E. and LeBesco, K. (2001) *Bodies out of Bounds: Fatness and Transgression*, Berkeley: University of California Press.

Britzman, D.P. (2000) 'The question of belief': writing poststructural ethnography, in E. St. Pierre and W.S. Pillow (eds), *Working the Ruins: Feminist Poststructural Theory and Methods in Education*, New York: Routledge, pp. 27–40.

Burchell, G. (1996) Liberal government and techniques of the self, in A. Barry, T. Osbourne and N. Rose (eds), *Foucault and Political Reason: Liberalism, Neoliberalism and Rationalities of Government*, London: University College London Press, pp. 19–36.

Burns, M. (2004) Eating like an ox: femininity and dualistic constructions of bulimia and anorexia, *Feminism and Psychology*, 14(2): 269–295.

Burns, M. (2006) Bodies that speak: examining the dialogues in research interactions, *Qualitative Research in Psychology*, 3: 3–18.

Burns, M. and Gavey, N. (2004) 'Healthy weight' at what cost? 'Bulimia' and a discourse of weight control, *Journal of Health Psychology*, 9(4): 549–565.

Carryer, J. (1997) The embodied experience of largeness: a feminist exploration, in M. de Ras and V. Grace (eds), *Bodily Boundaries, Sexualised Genders and Medical Discourses*, Palmerston North, NZ: Dunmore Press.

Cheek, J. (2000) *Postmodern and Poststructural Approaches to Nursing Research*, San Francisco, CA: Sage.

Coffey, A. (1999) *The Ethnographic Self: Fieldwork and the Representation of Identity*, London: Sage.

Crowe, M. (2000) Constructing normality: a discourse analysis of the DSM-IV, *Journal of Psychiatric and Mental Health Nursing*, 7(1): 69–77.

de Ras, M. and Grace, V. (eds) (1997) *Bodily Boundaries, Sexualised Genders and Medical Discourses*, Palmerston North, NZ: Dunmore Press.

Ellis, C. and Bochner, A.P. (eds) (1996) *Composing Ethnography: Alternative Forms of Qualitative Writing*, Lanham, MD: AltaMira Press.

Fine, M. (1994) Working the hyphens: reinventing self and other in qualitative research, in N. Denzin and Y. Lincoln (eds), *The Handbook of Qualitative Research*, New York: Sage, pp. 70–82.

Foucault, M. (1973) *The Birth of the Clinic: An Archaeology of Medical Perception*, New York: Vintage Books.

Foucault, M. (1979) Governmentality, *Ideology and Consciousness*, 6: 5–21.

Foucault, M. (1986) *The Care of the Self*, Harmondsworth: Penguin.

Foucault, M. (1988) *Madness and Civilization: A History of Insanity in the Age of Reason*, New York: Random House.

Fougere, G. (2001) Transforming health sectors: new logics of organising in the New Zealand health system, *Social Science and Medicine*, 52(8): 1233–1242.

Fournier, V. (1999) The appeal to 'professionalism' as a disciplinary mechanism, *Sociological Review*, 47(2): 280–307.

Fournier, V. (2002) Fleshing out gender: crafting gender identity on women's bodies, *Body and Society*, 8(2): 55–77.

Gastaldo, D. (1997) Is health education good for you? Re-thinking health education through the concept of bio-power, in R. Bunton and A. Peterson (eds), *Foucault, Health and Medicine*, New York: Routledge, pp. 113–133.

Gilbert, T. (2001) Reflective practice and clinical supervision: meticulous rituals of the confessional, *Advanced Journal of Nursing*, 36(2): 199–205.

Grace, V. (1998) Researching women's encounters with doctors: discourse analysis and method, in R. Du Plessis and L. Alice (eds), *Feminist Thought in Aotearoa/ New Zealand: Differences and Connections*, Auckland: Oxford University Press.

Gremillion, H. (1992) Psychiatry as social ordering: anorexia nervosa, a paradigm, *Social Science and Medicine*, 35(1): 57–71.

Gremillion, H. (2003) *Feeding Anorexia: Gender and Power in a Treatment Centre*, London: Duke University Press.

Grosz, E. (1994) *Volatile Bodies: Toward a Corporeal Feminism*, Sydney: Allen and Unwin.

Grosz, E. (1995) *Space, Time and Perversion: The Politics of Bodies*, Sydney: Allen and Unwin.

Hardin, P. (2003a) Shape-shifting discourses of anorexia nervosa: reconstituting psychopathology, *Nursing Inquiry*, 10(4): 209–217.

Hardin, P. (2003b) Constructing experience in individual interview, autobiographies and on-line accounts: a post-structuralist approach, *Journal of Advanced Nursing*, 41(6): 536–544.

Hardin, P. (2003c) Social and cultural considerations in recovery from anorexia nervosa: a critical poststructuralist analysis, *Advances in Nursing Science*, 26(1): 5–16.

Hepworth, J. (1999) *The Social Construction of Anorexia Nervosa*, Thousand Oaks, CA: Sage.

Larner, W. (1997) 'A means to an end': neoliberalism and state processes in New Zealand, *Studies in Political Economy*, 52: 7–38.

Lawler, J. (ed.) (1997) *The Body in Nursing*, Sydney: Churchill Livingstone.

Lupton, D. (1995) Perspectives on power, communication and the medical encounter: implications for nursing theory and practice, *Nursing Inquiry*, 2: 157–163.

Lupton, D. (1997) Consumerism, reflexivity and the medical encounter, *Sociology of Science and Medicine*, 45(3): 373–381.

MacSween, M. (1993) *Anorexic Bodies: A Feminist and Sociological Perspective on Anorexia Nervosa*, London and New York: Routledge.

Malson, H. (1995) Anorexia nervosa: discourses of gender, subjectivity and the body, *Feminism and Psychology*, 5(1): 89–93.

Malson, H. (1998) *The Thin Woman: Feminism, Post-structuralism, and the Social Psychology of Anorexia Nervosa*, New York: Routledge.

Malson, H. (1999) Women under erasure: anorexic bodies in postmodern context, *Journal of Community and Applied Social Psychology*, 9: 137–153.

Moulding, N. (2003) Constructing the self in mental health practice: identity, individualism and the feminization of deficiency, *Feminist Review*, 75(1): 57–65.

Moulding, N. (2006) Disciplining the feminine: the reproduction of gender contradictions in the mental health care of women with eating disorders, *Social Science and Medicine*, 62(4): 793–804.

Richardson, L. (1997) *Fields of Play: Constructing an Academic Life*, New Brunswick: Rutgers University Press.

Rose, N. (1993) Government, authority and expertise in advanced liberalism, *Economy and Society*, 22(3): 283–298.

Rose, N. (1994) Medicine, history and the present, in C. Jones and R. Porter (eds),

Reassessing Foucault: Power, Medicine and the Body, London: Routledge, pp. 48–72.

Shakespeare, P. (2003) Nurses' bodywork: is there a body of work?, *Nursing Inquiry*, 10(1): 47–56.

Snell, L. (2005) Behavioural treatment to promote weight gain, Lecture for Eating Disorders Paper, Postgraduate Health Science Course, University of Otago, Christchurch School of Medicine and Health Sciences.

Squire, S. (2003) Anorexia and bulimia: purity and danger, *Australian Feminist Studies*, 18(40): 17–26.

Surgenor, L., Plumridge, E. and Horn, J. (2003) 'Knowing one's self' anorexic: implications for therapeutic practice, *International Journal of Eating Disorders*, 33: 22–32.

Surtees, R. (2003) *Midwifery as Feminist Praxis in Aotearoa/New Zealand*, published PhD thesis, University of Canterbury, Christchurch, New Zealand, at: http://hdl.handle.net/10092/1662.

Surtees, R. (2004) Midwifery partnership with women in Aotearoa/New Zealand: a poststructuralist feminist perspective on the use of epidurals in 'normal' birth, in M. Stewart (ed.), *Pregnancy, Birth and Maternity Care: Feminist Perspectives*, Oxford: Elsevier Science.

Surtees, R. (2007) Developing a therapeutic alliance in an eating disorders unit, *Kai Tiaki Nursing New Zealand*, 13(10): 14–15.

Trinh Minh-ha (1991) *When the Moon Waxes Red: Representation, Gender and Cultural Politics*, London: Routledge.

Tuhiwai Smith, L. (1999) *Decolonizing Methodologies: Research and Indigenous Peoples*, Dunedin, NZ: University of Otago Press.

Walker, K. (1997) Cutting edges: deconstructive inquiry and the mission of the border ethnographer, *Nursing Inquiry*, 4: 3–13.

15 The anorexic as femme fatale

Reproducing gender through the father/psychiatrist–daughter/patient relationship

Nicole Moulding

Introduction

The idea that health care intervention is based on objective knowledge is central within western medicine and, with the vigorous embrace of the evidence-based approach, this assumption has never been stronger. However, post-structuralist and social constructionist analyses demonstrate that medical intervention (see also Surtees, Throsby, Epston and Maisel, all this volume) like health and illness themselves (see Eckermann, Malson and Burns, both this volume), is socially constructed and culturally situated. Psychiatric interventions used in the treatment of eating disorders perhaps betray their cultural antecedents most starkly because the relationship between the 'helped' and the 'helper' is especially gendered: most patients are young women and girls and senior treating psychiatrists, at least until fairly recently, are typically older men.

Feminists have drawn attention to the gender–power dynamics historically structuring medical intervention around the knowing, acting male doctor and the unknowing, passive female 'patient' (cf. Ussher, 1991). In exploring the gendered aspects of psychiatric treatment for eating disorders, this chapter will demonstrate that gender–power dynamics do not only arise from the fact that relatively powerful male doctors treat less powerful female patients. My discursive research into psychiatric treatment for eating disorders reveals that the operation of 'gender' extends beyond the facts of who is treating who and is bound up with profoundly gendered cultural assumptions about heteronormative femininity.

Feminist research into the treatment of eating disorders

Despite extensive medical and psychological research, eating disorders remain poorly understood within medicine and psychiatry (Hepworth, 1999) and treatments are largely ineffective (Ben-Tovim et al., 2001; Steinhausen, 2002). This fact moved me to explore how traditional models of treatment endure despite poor efficacy, and more specifically to examine the continuing focus on psychopathology and related assumptions about eating disordered women. It is widely acknowledged that psychological theories and interventions make pretensions to gender neutrality, but are in fact based on profoundly gendered assumptions about mental health and illness in women and men (see Broverman et al., 1972; Chesler, 1974; Ussher, 1991). While there has been extensive analysis of the gendered discourses within eating disorder practices themselves (e.g. Bordo, 1990; Burns, 2004; MacSween, 1993; Malson, 1998), there have been few explorations of their operation within the health care interventions used to treat them (although, see Gremillion, 2004).

As part of a larger research study exploring health care workers' constructions of eating disorders and associated health care interventions, I interviewed ten psychiatrists (six men and four women) and two clinical nurses (both women), based in three Australian capital cities, who were involved in the treatment of anorexia and bulimia. I used discourse analysis to explore the ways that patients were positioned in practitioners' talk, particularly attending to how gender was understood and 'practiced' (see Burman and Parker, 1993; Parker, 1992). Discourse analysis is a powerful tool for revealing the interrelations between power and knowledge because it invites us to dispense with the veneer of truth and interrogate knowledge specifically for its power effects (Foucault, 1977). However, while the research on which this chapter is based draws on a post-structuralist perspective that acknowledges the role of language in the discursive production of multiple social realities (Foucault, 1972), it also brings a feminist approach which acknowledges that gender involves wider social dynamics and power relations (McNay, 1992). This reflects my disciplinary background within sociology and, more specifically, gender studies. Within this perspective, then, the discursive practices constituting interventions for eating disorders are understood to involve power relations where truth and subjectivity are at stake (Foucault, 1977).

Father/psychiatrists and daughter/patients

A powerful idea to emerge from the interviews with psychiatrists was that the psychotherapeutic relationship between the senior male psychiatrist and the young eating disordered woman is analogous to that of a father and daughter. This idea of the father/psychiatrist–daughter/patient emerged within a wider situating of the inpatient treatment team as a symbolic 'family', with mother/nurses undertaking the day-to-day work of weighing and feeding patients, while largely absent father/psychiatrists oversee treatment and undertake the more valued, specialised work of individual psychotherapy. As has been previously noted, this arrangement potentially reproduces the model of the controlling mother and absent father charged with causing eating disorders in the first place (e.g. Gremillion, 2004; Moulding, 2006; Ryan et al., 2006; Warin, 2006).

My analysis will now turn to the construction of the father–daughter relation in therapy as natural or inevitable, followed by an unpacking of the specific ways in which the father–daughter axis of the therapeutic family was constructed. I will focus in particular on the way it rests on a contradictory discourse of 'hyper-femininity', where stereotypically feminine characteristics such as dependence and sexual innocence are exaggerated and used alongside other contradictory and supposedly feminine traits such as being manipulative and sexually provocative. I will also show how these hyper-feminine characteristics are encapsulated in three related female archetypes that populated participants' discourse: (1) the *ingénue*, (2) the *femme fatale* and (3) the *fille d'Eve* (daughter of Eve), with the *femme fatale* the most pivotal of the three. I will then discuss how this discourse (re)produces power and authority in the position of the male therapist via a 'father knows best' imperative.

Playing the father–daughter game

Psychiatrists initially presented the father/psychiatrist–daughter/patient relationship as 'natural' and 'expected' in the context of a young female patient receiving treatment from an older male clinician:

> I'm dealing with adolescent girls and young women, so I play the sort of paternal role. I have over the last ten or fifteen years and spend a lot of my time not talking about the anorexia, talking about other things.
>
> (John)

> it's not transference . . . [patients] will treat you, I mean, it's probably just my age, I suppose, it's like a parent.
>
> (Philip)

Adopting a fatherly approach is presented as completely natural if, as an older male clinician, you are treating adolescent girls and young women. The invitation to take up this role also emerges directly from patients, for example, as Paul says, because they 'become keen to please you'. Moreover, the father/psychiatrist–daughter/patient relation extends beyond a focus on 'anorexia' to 'other things' in the young woman's life. In a continuation of this theme, the father/psychiatrist's role includes providing guidance about issues other than food and weight:

> I mean they'll say things like, 'That wasn't very good, was it?' And I say, 'No, no, it's awful really, and I wouldn't say that again if I was you.' So there's a lot of humour involved as well, you know . . .
>
> (Philip)

Interaction between the psychiatrist and patient is portrayed as light-hearted, involving 'a lot of humour' in the way the patient is playfully reproached. John also describes himself as 'playing' the paternal role. The gender identities played out in the father/psychiatrist–daughter/patient relationship might therefore be thought of as a 'game' or 'performance', a 'doing' which constitutes 'the identity it is purported to be' (Butler, 1990: 25). Thus, for the protagonists, the identities arise 'naturally' as a result of pre-existing and real age and gender differences, but are in fact performed within a specific historical, institutional and cultural context.

The idea of this relationship also brings to mind the psychoanalytic concept of 'transference', which Philip was aware of when he said 'it's not transference but . . .'. For Freud, transference reflected a young female patient's 'wish to be received as a favourite daughter' by an older male psychiatrist: a tendency he viewed as positive because it 'clothes the doctor in authority' (Freud, 1973: 495, 498). I am not suggesting that 'transference' explains the dynamics under examination here. However, I will show how these psychiatrists used the idea of the father/psychiatrist–daughter/patient to position themselves as father/authority figures.

The anorexic *ingénue*

As noted earlier, a discourse of hyper-femininity involving exaggeration of stereotypically 'feminine' characteristics emerged in the way psychiatrists talked about their anorexic patients, and this was pivotal to the establishment of the father/authority figure. One aspect of this involved constructing patients as unassertive (Philip) and wishing to please (Paul). Philip goes on to further develop this idea:

> I can remember one lovely kid that I looked after who was brought up in [the country] . . . [.] . . . she arrived at the [university] and you could just imagine, it was just completely overwhelming, lost, and she developed severe anorexia . . . [.] . . . she was so naïve you see . . .[1]
>
> (Philip)

In the above account, the young woman is naïve, unworldly and over-whelmed. In the next extract, another patient is extremely sexually naïve – an *ingénue* – against the assumed sexual experience of the man she is dating:

> she came down to see me one day and she was all flushed . . . [.] . . . Her neck is all red and she said, 'I've met a bloke' and I said, 'That's nice and how old is he?' She said, 'Thirty-two' and she was eighteen, so I said, 'What's he do?' And then she said, 'Do you think it's alright if I hold his hand?' and I thought, 'My God, this bloke has probably had

---

1 [.] indicates removed interview text.

at least four or five important long term relationships and she wants to
hold his hand!' . . . So I had to take her all through that, you know,
what you can and can't do, and how you handle it, and all that stuff.
So that's the kind of protectiveness . . .

(Philip)

The psychiatrist describes taking up a protective fatherly role in asking
questions such as 'what's he do?' and in guiding the young woman's behaviour. Again, the role of the father/psychiatrist extends beyond the confines
of the clinic. There is also an assumption of heteronormative female sexual
behaviour, which involves 'neither too much nor too little' (see Burns, 2004;
McKinley, 1999) and which must be managed correctly by the young
woman with an appropriate level of knowledge and skill.

Another way that the anorexic was constructed as *ingénue* was through
the idea that she regresses to become a kind of 'woman/child' who is
vulnerable (John) and who retreats from adult responsibilities (Paul). More
significantly, Eric and Philip focus on the loss of secondary sexual characteristics thought to distinguish regression:

I do think that [.] the young woman has in many ways a kind of phobia
of maturation . . . [.] . . . she suddenly becomes sexually attractive, she
has an unpleasant sexual experience, she doesn't want it to happen
again . . . [.] . . . well, a way of backing out of it is to not be a sexual
object.

(Eric)

Anorexia actually works . . . you lose weight and the normal biology of
[female] weight loss is that you lose your hormonal status. [It] changes
back to that of childhood. So all that chaos and disorder of adolescence
just disappears . . .

(Philip)

In Eric's account, regression functions as a way to prevent further unwanted
sexual experiences. Later, Eric describes allocating a senior nurse to 'mother'
the anorexic woman/child back to adulthood and, presumably, into 'normal'
female sexuality. In Philip's account, the loss of hormonal status returns the
anorexic to child so that the 'chaos' of adolescence disappears. The regression theory of anorexia nervosa, first put forth by Arthur Crisp (1980),
suggests that, while 'normal women . . . face adulthood with equanimity',
deficiencies in the anorexic render sexuality frightening (MacSween 1993:
31). Philip goes on to question whether the regressed anorexic should be
regarded as an autonomous adult, arguing that he works with the family
during regression and only with the patient in her own right when she
'becomes biologically a young woman again'. The idea that women's mental
function is determined by their hormones has a long and powerful history in

medicine (Gannon, 1998). What is particularly interesting here is the way this discourse is used to justify paternalistic intervention based on the idea that, despite her age, the anorexic is to all intents and purposes a child.

The anorexic *femme fatale*

The notion of the anorexic as *ingénue* is extended in the following accounts to include the idea that these qualities lead to increased risk of sexual abuse and harassment. In portraying the anorexic in this way, she becomes a *femme fatale* figure who has the 'fatal power' to attract men and unconsciously bring adversity (Menon, 2006: 5):

> I've come across quite a few patients who've been sexually harassed or abused in some way or other and . . . [.] . . . one reason is that a patient regresses and they become very vulnerable looking . . . and I think they also get very dependent.
>
> (John)

> These are very vulnerable kids and they do get sexually victimized . . . [.] . . . I mean like at work somebody makes some kind of suggestion and they might blush, but they don't say 'I don't want to talk about that' . . . [.] . . . so the perpetrator takes that as some kind of signal . . . [.] . . . and then suddenly you find one of them on the phone to you saying all these awful things are happening . . .
>
> (Philip)

In both of these extracts, the hyper-feminine traits of the *ingénue* (blushing, passivity, being 'vulnerable looking' and 'dependent') are made problematic not only because they are implicated in causing anorexia, but because they invite abuse. In being unable to manage the attention she unwittingly attracts, the anorexic *femme fatale* is in need of protection. The idea of the *femme fatale* has a long history in western thought and can be traced to Genesis and the story of Eve, who ultimately brought about the downfall of all human kind through her surrender to carnal appetites (Menon, 2006). Menon (ibid.: 5) and others argue that the *femme fatale* 'has come to be known as an archetypal woman' who unconsciously brings destruction not only to the men she attracts but also to herself because of her inability to control herself.[2] In the next account, the idea of the anorexic *femme fatale* is extended to include the power to attract sexual adversity from within as well as outside the clinic:

2 There are many famous *femme fatales* in nineteenth-century English fiction, such as *The French Lieutenant's Woman* and *Tess of the D'Urbervilles*.

I've seen several [patients] who have been dealt with inappropriately by previous psychiatrists . . . I wouldn't say abused, but dealt with inappropriately. . . . It's not that I think [the patients] are provocative as such. I don't think they are. I think they are very vulnerable. And I think it's that which provokes predatory action on some people's part.

Nicole: So how does this [vulnerability of anorexic patients to abuse] influence your practice with them, then? How do you sort of get around, deal with, address these sorts of problems?

Well, I suppose, sadly, as I've got older it's . . . I've adopted a much more paternalistic role . . . [.] . . . I think most of my patients see me [.] very much as a grandfather figure . . .

(John)

The *femme fatale* anorexic is almost perversely attractive to men, including to some male psychiatrists. John is also saying in a wry way, that, 'sadly', as he has gotten older, his patients see him as an asexual grandfather figure which positions him in a protective rather than sexual relation to his patients. John is establishing himself in a humorous way as outside of the problematic sexual dynamics of the *femme fatale* anorexic.

The anorexic *fille d'Eve*

A final feature of the hyper-femininity discourse I have identified is the way eating disordered patients, including bulimic patients, were constructed as 'not all they seem', as 'two-faced' and as 'having another side' to their natures. In an earlier account from Philip, a young anorexic woman is *ingénue* – completely naïve and innocent – in the face of her boyfriend's assumed sexual experience. However, Philip goes on to say that, 'on the other side of the coin', the young woman purposely kept her weight low to retain the therapeutic relationship:

it's very interesting, this whole ethical issue of control and power and use of relationships and so, no, [anorexics are] not without dubiousness in a funny way. I mean she knew [low weight] was her ticket to the relationship and help continuing . . .

(Philip)

This 'dubiousness' of the anorexic refers to the idea that, while they seem innocent and powerless, they can also be controlling and manipulative. The construction of anorexic women as 'two-faced', as at once passive and dependent *and* controlling and manipulative, is very common in the eating disorder literature (e.g. Bruch, 1978; Sohlberg and Strober, 1994; Vitousek et al., 1998). In another version of the idea that anorexics are not all they seem, Philip describes the naïve country girl returning to treatment after some weeks away:

> in through the door she comes, she's got her hair dyed black, and all spunky [sexy], and she's got diamonds in her nose, and a ring through her lips and, you know, and a kind of see through sort of nightie thing that she was wearing and all that sort of stuff. It turned out that she'd been sitting up all night drinking coffee and too much alcohol and she'd got into sex in a big way and she was smoking heavily . . .
>
> (Philip)

The young woman is transformed in this account from 'ingénue' to 'tramp', her hair, jewellery and clothes all signifying sexual availability. The psychiatrist then steps into the fatherly role when he describes saying to her:

> 'Well, it's not very good is it?' and she burst into tears and sobbed her little heart out . . . [.] . . . anyway she went home . . . [.] . . . stopped doing all this stuff [and after] two weeks of her admission to hospital she was a normal weight, not depressed and kind of fine . . .
>
> (Philip)

The gentle but firm father/psychiatrist reprimands the contrite daughter/ patient and her subsequent recovery is because she regains control of herself. The idea of two opposing sexualities in Philip's account reproduces the historical discourse of the virgin and the whore (MacSween, 1993: 178), represented through the archetypes of 'Madonna' and 'Eve' (Menon, 2006): the virgin/Madonna is passive and innocent, while the whore/Eve is desirous, dangerous and out of control (MacSween, 1993; Menon, 2006).

Prior to the nineteenth century, the virgin and the whore were seen to reside in different women, that is, the virgin (the Madonna) in the wife and mother and the whore (Eve) in the prostitute (Menon, 2006). However, with the rise of the women's movement in nineteenth-century France, this was displaced by the idea that both virgin and whore reside in all women, hence use of the term *'filles d'Eve'* (daughters of Eve) to describe women in general (ibid.). In the above account, the *ingénue* indeed reveals herself to be *fille d'Eve*, the very embodiment of the *femme fatale*, with her inherent sexual dangerousness (ibid.). The account is also underscored by an assumption of heteronormative female sexuality that is neither virgin nor whore. Thus, when this young woman is 'virgin' she is 'abnormally' naïve and vulnerable and when she is 'whore' she is 'out of control' and 'off the rails'. A 'normal' female sexuality therefore involves neither too much nor too little sexual desire, just as 'normal' eating should involve neither too much (bulimia) nor too little (anorexia) food (Burns, 2004).

The dualism of the virgin and the whore was also woven into the way some psychiatrists juxtaposed anorexic and bulimic women, with the former sexually innocent and repressed, and the latter flagrantly sexual and out of control. (This is also common in the eating disorder literature. See, for example, Tice et al., 1989, and Kaltiala-Heino et al., 2003.) In this construction, the virgin and whore reside in the opposition of 'good' anorexic and 'bad' bulimic (Burns, 2004). Philip elaborates on the idea of the 'bad' bulimic when he says that they 'have hysteria [and] come in and sort of look at me' with 'apparent sexuality that isn't real, . . . [.] . . .wearing green eye shadow, and lots of jewellery, and looking like they're just going to a disco'. Thus, the bulimic only *plays* the bad girl because her 'apparent sexuality', including her flirtatious behaviour with the father/psychiatrist, 'isn't real'. Ultimately, a normative, healthy female sexuality is not to be found in either the anorexic/virgin or the bulimic/whore because the eating disordered woman isn't a 'real' (that is, 'normal') woman at all.

The idea of the father/psychiatrist–daughter/patient clearly hinges on profoundly gendered and contradictory assumptions about eating disordered women. On the one hand, the anorexic is constructed as *ingénue* and *femme fatale*, her sexual innocence and naïvety fatally and perversely alluring. On the other, both the anorexic and bulimic can take the more troubling form of the *fille d'Eve*/whore. Each of these incarnations is positioned as lying outside heteronormative femininity, which involves the 'right' amount of sexual desire. Feminist scholars have argued that under-pinning this heteronormative construction of female sexuality is the fear of the all-consuming, voracious woman (Bordo, 1993; MacSween, 1993). It is ironic, then, that the idea of the father/psychiatrist–daughter/patient is predicated on the reproduction of this discourse because anorexia and bulimia (themselves as forms of pathologised body management) can be understood to represent an attempt to control the unruly, appetitive female body where food is a metaphor for, among other things, sexual desire (MacSween, 1993). Thus, psychiatry unwittingly reproduces the specific gender discourses that lie at the heart of eating disorders themselves.

Father knows best: power and authority

The above accounts position the psychiatrist in a fatherly, protective stance in relation to the hyper-feminised *femme fatale* patient. Other accounts involved a more implicit paternalism in describing interventions, with patients required to comply with the psychiatrist's view of their problem and surrender to treatment regimens. In the first of these, the psychiatrist is completely authoritative about the anorexic's problems and needs:

> we would be promoting ourselves now saying, 'We provide you with a resource. We've got an understanding of what the condition is. This is

what you need to do to get better'. . . [.] . . . often there is a sense of relief when the patient feels that someone has taken responsibility away, that somebody else has actually taken control for a while . . .

(William)

The anorexic patient takes on a stereotypically feminine form in 'surrendering' herself to the more powerful, knowledgeable male authority figure. In Philip's extract, the patient must capitulate to the united front of the father/psychiatrist and her actual family:

the family couldn't cope with her being home. They fought all the time. It sounds unfeeling, but it was a very complex issue. So we all decided that she would have to go to boarding school . . .

(Philip)

This echoes the nineteenth-century Victorian practice of sending 'hysterical' young anorexic women away because families were seen to lack moral control over them (Brumberg, 1988). In a continuation of the theme of father/psychiatrists 'taking charge', Robert argues that the psychiatrist must look authoritative:

you have to look as though you have authority . . . you can't do it any other way . . . [.] . . . these conditions are very distressing and disturbing . . . [.] . . . you have to say [to patients], 'I can contain this . . . you can put the bad person into me and I'll look after it for you if you like, don't worry' . . .

Robert confides that, in his view, neither he nor other psychiatrists actually know how to help anorexic patients, but that they must nevertheless *appear* to be authoritative. Again, the father/psychiatrist–daughter/patient relation is performative. In talking about helping patients give up control, Robert offers to 'look after' the 'bad person' that patients believe resides within. In all of these extracts, the psychiatrist comes to the rescue of the anorexic patient, who is really her own worst enemy: while she must be protected from the sexual maelstrom she causes, ultimately, she must be saved from herself. The anorexic therefore becomes the quintessential *femme fatale* while the father/psychiatrist is in charge of the situation and of her. Through its controlling *modus operandi*, then, psychiatry paradoxically reproduces the idea that the anorexic is indeed outside her own control and once again reinforces rather than challenges the gendered cultural discourses that lie at the heart of eating disorders (see Bordo, 1993; MacSween, 1993).

Interestingly, none of the female psychiatrists or the two female nurses in this study described treatment in these paternalistic terms, nor did their explanations draw on sexualised and contradictory ideas of female sexuality. While they tended to portray eating disordered women as deficient in autonomy and control (see Moulding, 2003; see also Saukko, this volume), they also described intervention as a more collaborative exercise, and one even saw male psychiatrists' attempts to control anorexic patients as a central cause of patient resistance to treatment.

Conclusions

This chapter has demonstrated how psychiatry reproduces, through the discursive regime of the father/psychiatrist–daughter/patient, a particular version of heteronormative femininity. I have also demonstrated how the specific archetypes used by the psychiatrists to construct eating disordered women, particularly the *femme fatale*, (re)produce power and authority in the position of the psychiatrist through a 'father knows best' imperative. Most significantly, though, this reliance on a dualistic discourse about female sexuality and a controlling approach to intervention reproduces the gendered cultural discourses that underpin eating disorders themselves. Psychiatry has been stubbornly resistant to critical self-reflection on its role in the social construction of eating disorders. However, mounting evidence from discursive research such as this reveals in different ways its collusion in the social reproduction of gender. Psychiatry needs to engage with the inherently gendered nature of eating disorders and reflect on the way it uncritically harnesses and reproduces these same discourses within treatment. Only then will there be scope for this discipline to actively participate in challenging the gendered cultural dichotomies that enable disordered eating.

References

Ben-Tovim, D.I., Walker, K., Gilchrist, P., Freeman, R., Kalucy, R. and Esterman, A. (2001) Outcome in patients with eating disorders: a 5-year study, *The Lancet*, 357: 1254–1257.

Bordo, S. (1990) Reading the slender body, in M. Jacobus, E.F. Keller and S. Shuttleworth (eds), *Body/Politics: Women and the Discourses of Science*, New York: Routledge, pp. 83–112.

Bordo, S. (1993) *Unbearable Weight: Feminism, Western Culture and the Body*, Berkeley and Los Angeles: University of California Press.

Broverman, I.K., Vogel, S.R., Broverman, D.M., Clarkson, F.E. and Rosenkrantz, P.S. (1972) Sex-role stereotypes: a critical appraisal, *Journal of Social Issues*, 28: 59–78.

Bruch, H. (1978) *The Golden Cage: The Enigma of Anorexia Nervosa*, Cambridge, MA: Harvard University Press.

Brumberg, J.J. (1988) *Fasting Girls: The History of Anorexia Nervosa*, New York: Penguin.

Burman, E. and Parker, I. (1993) *Discourse Analytic Research: Repertoires and Readings of Texts in Action*, London: Routledge.

Burns, M. (2004) Eating like an ox: femininity and dualistic constructions of bulimia and anorexia, *Feminism and Psychology*, 14(2): 269–295.

Butler, J. (1990) *Gender Trouble: Feminism and the Subversion of Identity*, London: Routledge.

Chesler, P. (1974) *Women and Madness*, New York: Avon Books.

Crisp, A.H. (1980) *Anorexia Nervosa: Let Me Be*, London: Academic Press.

Foucault, M. (1972) *The Archaeology of Knowledge*, London: Tavistock.

Foucault, M. (1977) *Discipline and Punish: The Birth of the Prison*, Harmondsworth: Penguin.

Freud, S. (1973) *Introductory Lectures on Psychoanalysis*, Harmondsworth: Penguin.

Gannon, L. (1998) The impact of medical and sexual politics on women's health, *Feminism and Psychology*, 8(3): 285–302.

Gremillion, H. (2004) Unpacking essentialisms in therapy: lessons for feminist approaches from narrative work, *Journal of Constructivist Psychology*, 17(3): 173–200.

Hepworth, J. (1999) *The Social Construction of Anorexia Nervosa*, London: Sage.

Kaltiala-Heino, R., Rissanen, A., Rimpela, M. and Rantanen, P. (2003) Bulimia nervosa and impulsive behaviour in middle adolescence, *Psychotherapeutic Psychosomatics*, 72: 26–33.

MacSween, M. (1993) *Anorexic Bodies*, London: Routledge.

Malson, H. (1998) *The Thin Woman: Feminism, Post-structuralism and the Social Psychology of Anorexia Nervosa*, London: Routledge.

McKinley, N.M. (1999) Ideal weight/ideal woman: society constructs the female, in J. Sobal and D. Maurer (eds), *Weighty Issues: Fatness and Thinness as Social Problems*, New York: Aldine de Gruyter, pp. 97–115.

McNay, L. (1992) *Foucault and Feminism: Power, Gender and the Self*, Oxford: Polity Press.

Menon, E. (2006) *Evil By Design: The Creation and Marketing of the Femme Fatale*, Urbana and Chicago: University of Illinois Press.

Moulding, N.T. (2003) Constructing the self in mental health practice: identity, individualism and the feminisation of deficiency, *Feminist Review*, 75: 57–74.

Moulding, N.T. (2006) Disciplining the feminine: the reproduction of gender contradictions in the mental health care of women with eating disorders, *Social Science and Medicine*, 62(4): 793–804.

Parker, I. (1992) *Discourse Dynamics: Critical Analysis for Social and Individual Psychology*, London: Routledge.

Ryan, V., Malson, H., Clarke, S., Anderson, G. and Kohn, M. (2006) Discursive constructions of 'eating disorders nursing': an analysis of nurses' accounts of nursing eating disorder patients, *European Eating Disorders Review*, 14(2): 125–135.

Sohlberg, S. and Strober, M. (1994) Personality in anorexia nervosa: an update and a theoretical integration, *Acta Psychiatrica Scandinavica*, 89(Suppl. 378): 1–15.

Steinhausen, H. (2002) The outcome of anorexia nervosa in the 20th century, *American Journal of Psychiatry*, 159: 1284–1293.

Tice, L., Hall, R.C., Beresford, T.P., Quinones, J. and Hall, A.K. (1989) Sexual abuse in patients with eating disorders, *Psychiatric Medicine*, 7: 257–267.

Ussher, J. (1991) *Women's Madness: Misogyny or Mental Illness?*, Harlow: Prentice Hall.

Vitousek, K., Watson, S. and Wilson, G.T. (1998) Enhancing motivation for change in treatment-resistant eating disorders, *Clinical Psychology Review*, 18: 391–420.

Warin, M. (2006) Reconfiguring relatedness in anorexia, *Anthropology and Medicine*, 13(1): 41–54.

16 'There's something in my brain that doesn't work properly'

Weight loss surgery and the medicalisation of obesity

Karen Throsby

Introduction

Rising obesity rates globally are routinely figured in contemporary popular, policy and medical representations and debates as being of 'epidemic' proportions, constituting a problem against which 'war' has been declared. The rapidly proliferating anti-obesity interventions in the arenas of health and food policy, advertising, education and medicine that constitute the 'war on obesity' are founded on the assumption that obesity represents a significant, and expensive, threat to health, both nationally and globally (James et al., 2001; NAO, 2001; NICE, 2006; WHO, 2000; see also Gard, Rice, Probyn, Burns et al., LeBesco, all this volume). The 'obesity epidemic', therefore, is articulated through the rhetoric of crisis; as an urgent problem against which action must be taken (see Gard, this volume). Alongside this increasingly emphatic construction of obesity as a problem of urgently 'epidemic' proportions are the sporadic panics within the developed world, both in the media and in the policy context, around extreme thinness (see, for example, Goodchild and Woolf, 2006). This has occurred most recently in relation to concerns over ultra-thin catwalk models, and the potential role of Size Zero clothing in the production and exacerbation of eating disorders, particularly among girls and young women. However, while some authors and journalists have articulated links between anti-obesity educative strategies and the development of anorexia (Atkins, 2007; Evans et al., 2004; Rich and Evans, 2005), and while both obesity and extreme thinness can be seen as occupying extreme positions on a continuum of body size, it is also problematic to view obesity and eating disorders like anorexia as simple opposites (see also LeBesco, this volume).

This is firstly because, although the range of people considered to be at risk of developing anorexia continues to expand, it is primarily girls and young women who are considered to be vulnerable to it and who dominate the patient population. However, in the case of obesity, *everybody* is deemed at risk, and exhortations to 'watch your weight' are universally applied; indeed, the management of body weight is increasingly figured as an act of good citizenship for all (Herndon, 2005). But secondly, and more importantly in the context of this chapter, the criteria for diagnosing anorexia differ significantly from those which determine that an individual can be categorised medically as obese. The DSM-IV lists four diagnostic criteria for anorexia nervosa: (1) the refusal to maintain body weight over a minimum normal weight for age and height; (2) intense fear of gaining weight or becoming fat even though underweight; (3) disturbance in the way in which one's body weight, size or shape is experienced, undue influence of body shape and weight on self-evaluation, or denial of the seriousness of low body weight; and (4) in females, the absence of at least three consecutive menstrual cycles when otherwise expected to occur (American Psychiatric Association, 1994). Obesity, on the other hand, does not appear in the DSM-IV, and is very straightforwardly defined as a Body Mass Index of over 30 kg/m^2 [1] – a 'diagnosis' that relies entirely on body size, exclusive of specific pathologised behaviours or psychological disturbances (see also Rice, LeBesco, both this volume). From this diagnostic perspective, the fat body itself is pathologised regardless of current health status, function, aetiology or individual perception, and is rendered the legitimate object of medical 'treatment' on that basis.

While obesity is 'diagnosed' by a BMI calculation, issues of causation remain the subject of considerable uncertainty and the underlying mechanisms of weight loss and gain remain poorly understood (Keith et al., 2006). Indeed, critics of the 'war on obesity' have argued that claims around causation are underpinned by moral judgements rather than objective science (Campos, 2004; Campos et al., 2006; Gard, this volume; Gard and Wright, 2005), and that it is possible to be 'fit and fat' (Cooper, 1998; Lyons, 1989; Wann, 1998). Nevertheless, a range of psychological, environmental and biological factors have been taken up as potentially contributing to weight gain and then targeted in specific weight loss interventions. For example, psychotherapeutic interventions presume a psychological aetiology; the recent banning of the direct advertising of junk food to children presumes an environmental cause; and weight loss pharmaceutical research is increasingly focusing on the regulation of specific hormonal mechanisms thought to affect appetite and satiety (Chiesi et al., 2001; Gura, 2003; Weigle, 2003). However, while interventions of this kind attempt to address a specific causative element, the intervention which currently stands as the 'last resort' in the catalogue of anti-obesity strategies – weight loss surgery (WLS)[2] – constitutes a significant departure from this approach. Weight loss surgery is an umbrella term for a constellation of surgical interventions into the fat body which aim to restrict stomach size and (or)

---

1 For the UK Department of Health definitions of overweight and obesity, see http://www.dh.gov.uk/PolicyAndGuidance/HealthAndSocialCareTopics/Obesity/fs/en.
2 For details of the different WLS surgeries and their attendant risks, see Ackerman (1999), Flancbaum (2003) and Janeway et al. (2005).

intestinal length in order to limit the body's capacity to consume and absorb food. Consequently, WLS can be seen as circumventing suggested first causes rather than attempting to identify and treat them – a move which is perfectly aligned with a diagnostic criterion that is only concerned with body size.

But while WLS is an intervention which operates largely independent of theories of causation, for the patients, the aetiology of their obesity (see also Gard, this volume) is highly significant. The fat body is highly derogated in contemporary society and those who are visibly obese are routinely subjected to social exclusion, discrimination and public and private humiliation on the basis of their size (Cooper, 1998; Puhl and Brownell, 2001; Wann, 1998; see also Rice, LeBesco, both this volume). Consequently, in the contemporary social and cultural context of a morally and ideologically driven 'war on obesity' (Campos, 2004; Gard and Wright, 2005; Oliver, 2006), it becomes important for people to be able to demonstrate, firstly, that body size is beyond the control of the individual, and secondly, that in spite of these difficulties, the individual is prepared to take responsibility for the body and its management. These two elements constitute the primary arbiters of the extent to which obesity can be 'forgiven' socially. However, as a dramatic intervention which physically restricts consumption, WLS always risks being read by others as an opting out of the everyday work of body management – as 'cheating'. This exposes individuals to the negative moral evaluation of others, both for having become obese in the first place and for not tackling their obesity using the morally privileged strategies of bodily discipline and surveillance in relation to diet and exercise. It is this exposure, and the concomitant need to manage its consequences, that makes those who have engaged with WLS a particularly important focus for sociological research into the social and cultural context within which obesity is given meaning.

Drawing on a series of interviews with men and women who had had (or were waiting to have) WLS, this chapter explores the discursive work involved in the rebuttal of these negative evaluations. In particular, this chapter argues that this discursive work involves the construction of WLS as medically necessary in their case, and of obesity as being caused by innate biological dysfunction, and as therefore unamenable to 'lifestyle' interventions. As such, the work of accounting for WLS can never be separated from the work of negotiating fat embodiment (see also Rice, LeBesco, both this volume). These discursive strategies enabled the participants to construct their own surgery not as the abnegation of responsibility for the management of the body but, rather, as an act of taking responsibility in the form of proportionate action. However, while this discursive work enables the participants to rebut the moral judgements of others, it also reiterates dominant constructions of the fat body as unacceptable and unhealthy and as a problem whose resolution lies within the medical domain. This both reflects and contributes to the production of new obligations of bodily management for those who are medically categorised as obese, highlighting the ways in which the surgical treatment of obesity remains circumscribed by the moral and ideological discourses which constitute the 'war on obesity'.

The interviews on which this chapter draws were conducted in 2005–06, with six men and 29 women, all of whom had undergone or were waiting to undergo WLS. They were recruited through the online discussion forums of one of the only organisations in the UK providing advice, information and support for those seeking, undergoing and living with WLS, and all participants had been (and in many cases still were) categorised medically as obese or morbidly obese. The interviews ranged from 45 minutes to over three hours and were mostly carried out at the participants' homes. I also had the opportunity to speak to many family members in the course of the interviews, and I conducted one focus group discussion at a support group meeting in the north of England at the beginning of the project. The interview and focus group data was transcribed orthographically (Wood and Kroger, 2000) and analysed using a discourse analytic approach (Gill, 1996, 2000): that is, by exploring what Foucault described as the 'tactical polyvalence' (1976: 100–102) of discourse. As such, my interest is not in passing judgements on what people do with or to their bodies but, rather, to gain sociological insight into the discursive resources and strategies available to those performing those material and discursive actions.

'I'm going to die anyway'

The prevailing representation of obesity in the medical, policy and popular domains is of it as both a disease in its own right (Rossner, 2002) and as causing chronic diseases such as heart disease, stroke and diabetes (NAO, 2001; WHO, 2000). This underpins the 'war on obesity', which is driven by concerns about future health costs and lost productivity (Campbell, 2003; James et al., 2001; NICE, 2006). Obesity in this context is rendered a proxy for other diseases (see also Gard, Rice, LeBesco, all this volume), and relies on the presumed certainty of a causative link between obesity and ill-health. This is an assumption that is, however, contested in the critical obesity literature, which challenges the 'war on obesity' as ideologically rather than scientifically driven, and questions the grounds upon which claims equating obesity with ill-health are made (Campos, 2004; Gard and Wright, 2005; Monaghan, 2005; see also Rice, Gard, LeBesco, all this volume). However, this resistant voice was entirely absent from the interviews, and the causative link between obesity and ill-health remained discursively intact. This constitutes a fundamental element in the construction of surgery as imperative, both in terms of participants' own well-being and the broader social and economic costs of obesity. Julie, for example, suffered from Type II diabetes, and envisaged a future of inevitable health decline without surgery:

You know, I can't stay like this. I'm going to die anyway from, you know, the diabetes and stuff 'cause I got such poor control of it. And my parents having diabetes, both of them are going blind, they can barely walk and it's an absolute nightmare to go and see them and think that's going to be me if I do nothing.

For Julie, the decision to 'do nothing' equates to consigning herself to the 'nightmare' that her parents are experiencing; this configures surgery as a risk that *has* to be taken, and which is proportionate to the dangers that she perceives herself to be facing. While Julie envisaged incremental health decline, for others, this 'risk' was expressed in terms of sudden catastrophe. Rachel, for example, described herself as 'sitting on a ticking time bomb', and Charles observed: 'My sister's an occupational therapist who special- ises in strokes and every time she saw me, she said "stroke victim". You know, she was very clear that she knew what the indicators were.' Even among those who had no current health problems, the perceived certainty of future health decline combined with anticipated incremental weight gain, was volunteered as evidence of the urgent need for surgery, arguing that it is better to have surgery at a lower weight while you are in good health than at a higher weight with health problems. This sense of urgency is entirely concordant with the rhetoric of the 'obesity epidemic', where the associ- ation between obesity and ill-health has congealed into certainty.

Central to the mobilisation of present and future health problems in accounting for the decision to have surgery is the construction of surgery as an efficient use of public funds. This not only counters directly the always- potential refusal of primary care trusts to pay for surgery, but also provides individuals with the opportunity to position themselves both as good patients and as good citizens. Anne, for example, countered her GP's initial reluctance with extensive and carefully presented research:

And I got all the information that I could possibly get, and I actually went back to see my own GP three weeks later armed with a folder of . . . I put dividers in it, and I put all about the different surgeries. I'd even put an estimate. I'd found some research about how much money was saved for the NHS . . . you know, for a diabetic person to see a nurse, and a podiatrist, and the medication, what it would actually cost.

In the first instance, the folder made the financial case for surgery, rebutting the GP's concerns about costs. However, it also served to demonstrate her commitment to the procedure – a point appreciated by her GP, who noted on receiving the folder that she'd obviously 'really thought about this'. This enables her to counter any accusations that she is rushing into surgery as a 'quick fix' or 'easy option', as well as positions her as an expert, relative to the GP, who readily admitted that he knew very little about weight loss surgery when she first approached him (see also Fox et al., 2005). But significantly, in Foucauldian terms, the documented desire for surgery performs a confessional function (Foucault, 1976), offering legitimacy and inclusion in exchange for a demonstrable determination to take corrective action (see also Lupton, 1995). This repudiates the pejorative characterisation of people who are obese as slovenly, selfish and lazy (see, e.g. Latner and Stunkard, 2003; Murray, 2005) and the cost-saving calculation allows individuals seeking surgery to position themselves not as the stigmatised objects of the 'war on obesity' but as its participatory subjects (Throsby, 2008). However, by pathologising the individual body, participants precluded any questioning of the certainty of weight-related health decline.

'There's something in my brain that doesn't work properly'

The reiteration in the interviews of a causative relationship between obesity and ill-health is a key element in the construction of surgery as a proportionate and necessary measure in the 'war on obesity'. However, participants also identified obesogenic bodily dysfunctions and deficits in accounting for how they had become obese in the first place, mobilising accounts of innate biological dysfunction in order to distance themselves from the moral judgements that easily attach to those who are visibly obese. Significantly, none of the participants attributed their obesity to an eating disorder but, rather, sought out non-specific, individually-held biological explanations for the weight gain.

The recourse of those experiencing obesity to biological explanations is not exclusive to the WLS context; Ogden et al. (2003), for example, observed that while GPs' favoured 'lifestyle' explanations in relation to their obese patients, patients relied on a biological model in accounting for obesity. Most obviously, this facilitates the refusal of blame and the moral censure that attaches itself so readily to obesity by attributing it to a biological cause which they are unable to control. However, in the case of WLS, there is a further inflection to this strategy of discursive resistance since it also provides a basis from which individuals can rebut suggestions that they have opted out of the work of weight management by having surgery. Instead, the discursive mobilisation of obesogenic bodily dysfunction positions the body as *unable to be helped* by 'lifestyle' interventions, forcing them to turn to surgery as the only remaining option. This positions surgery not as an opting out but, rather, as *opting in* via the only remaining means.

For some, this was articulated through the discourse of genetics, with the propensity to gain weight determined by the family 'fat gene' (Throsby, 2007). But, for others, the inability to lose weight was explained in terms of more generalised bodily dysfunctions and deficits. Anna, for example, argued that: 'I just think there's something in my brain that doesn't work properly, and that's a life-long thing, and my band's[3] there to make that bit in my brain . . . what's a deficit there, it works down there now.' Michael's account was even less specific, but relies on the same argument that obesity is not about lack of knowledge or effort but, rather, an unknown cause that is not amenable to change:

> You ask any fat person what they should be eating, they'd be able to give you an absolutely perfect diet. If only they could do it, but there's some reason why they can't.

These claims were endorsed across the interviews by lengthy recounting of years, and often decades, of soul-destroying cycles of weight loss and regain, demonstrating both a long-term commitment to weight management, and an enduring inability to sustain weight loss in spite of that commitment.[4]

The discursive invocation of non-specific physical dysfunction can easily be (mis)construed as a shirking of responsibility by attempting to shift blame onto the biological body (as distinct from the self in this construction). However, as an explanation, it is highly concordant with the contemporary trend for locating physical and behavioural problems within the body, particularly in the context of genetics and the concept of the 'gene for' (Peterson, 2001). Moreover, given the profound lack of scientific understanding, and the intense debates within obesity medicine surrounding obesity aetiology (Keith et al., 2006; see also Gard, this volume), these claims are not only not easy to refute, but also entirely within the realms of the possible. Consequently, an alternative, and less recriminatory, reading of these explanations of bodily deficit and dysfunction would be to read them not as a refusal of responsibility, but as a genuine attempt to make sense of their own embodied experiences of intractable obesity (Throsby, 2007).

For some participants, obesity emerged not as the direct consequence of an obesogenic bodily deficit but, rather, as a side effect of other identified medical problems. This is an inversion of the more conventional rhetoric of the 'obesity epidemic', which is seen as *causing* rather than being *caused by* disease. These explanations deviate from the model of innate biological dysfunction, but retain the central idea of the body as out of their control, as opposed to their being unwilling to control the body. This included, for

---

3 Anna had a gastric band fitted – a silicone band which fits around the stomach, creating a small pouch at the top, and then a narrowed entrance into the rest of the stomach, thereby limiting consumption.

4 Significantly, the failure of 'lifestyle' interventions of diet and exercise to achieve sustainable weight loss is not confined to those experiencing extreme obesity, but rather, is evident in the vast majority of all weight loss attempts (Aphramor, 2005; Campos, 2004; Oliver, 2006). Indeed, the argument that 'diets don't work' occurred repeatedly in the interviews.

example, disabling accidents, depression, rheumatoid arthritis and thyroid problems. In addition, there were iatrogenic factors to weight gain for several participants, including the use of medication that caused them to put on weight, or in one case, the severing of a nerve during surgery for a congenital hip problem, leading to partial paralysis. For many of the women, pregnancy was also an important factor. For Anne, for example, weight gain during a series of miscarried pregnancies was central to understanding her obesity as something beyond her control. She explained this as she recounted her decision to leave the commercial slimming group of which she had been a member:

> And then the leader [of the group] left and this new woman . . . it was . . . she was awful. I actually . . . I feel I can't . . . you know, she was racist and she made comments about black Africans. . . . You know, I didn't like the way she was in class. And you know, 'You can't blame medical reasons for putting on weight, you know, it's just pure greed.' And I thought, how many people who are sitting here have put weight on because of being on steroids, or like I did, with pregnancies, you know. Medical reasons.

The unacceptability of the new leader's views on obesity and moral culpability is reinforced by the potent parallel drawn between her fat-phobic views and her racism. However, it is also important to note that Anne does not challenge the idea that obesity can be the result of 'pure greed', but instead, focuses on the fact that there might also be people in the room (including herself) whose obesity was the result of 'medical reasons'. This highlights the highly contested and moral nature of debates surrounding the causes of obesity and the concomitant centrality of aetiology to the construction of a 'forgiveable' path to obesity. This, in turn, provides the justification of the decision to undergo WLS, which is constructed, via this medicalised discourse, not as an 'easy option' or a piece of dietary 'cheating' but, rather, as a necessary and proportionate 'last resort', given the inevitable failure of alternative 'lifestyle' interventions.

Conclusions

In this chapter, I have argued that those undergoing WLS strategically pathologise their own bodies, both in terms of the perceived negative health impacts of obesity and in terms of the causes of obesity. Through this discursive work the participants sought to distance themselves from the negative moral judgements of others – both for becoming obese in the first place, and for seeking surgery in order to lose weight. By locating their own obesity firmly within the medical domain (and yet outside of full medical understanding), participants constructed the normatively prescribed 'lifestyle' measures of diet and exercise as ineffectual and inappropriate in the face of their own innate, biologically-grounded inability to control their weight. The medicalised discourse, therefore, becomes a means of negotiating the social stigmas attached to both obesity and (by extension) WLS.

The simplicity of a medical definition of obesity based entirely on body size (as opposed to behaviours or self-perception), the contemporary trends towards the location of physical and behavioural problems within the biological body, and entrenched assumptions about the causative relationship between obesity and ill-health all create space for those experiencing extreme and intractable obesity to counter the moral judgements that attach so easily to the fat body. These discourses are strategically integrated (Foucault 1976: 102) into the participants' accounts in order to produce a 'forgiveable' account of obesity which rebuts its derogated social status. However, it is also the case that this discursive work reiterates and reinforces the unacceptability of the fat body and the impossibility of being 'fit and fat' and works to normalise WLS as an appropriate medical response to obesity. This is not to argue that WLS is necessarily an inappropriate intervention, or that individuals should not engage with it. Instead, this discursive work highlights the extent to which individual pathology remains the dominant means of accounting for obesity (and, by extension, WLS), obscuring the morally-infused social and cultural context within which all weight management decisions and interventions are delivered, experienced and accounted for.

References

Ackerman, N.B. (1999) Fat No More: *The Answer for the Dangerously Overweight*, New York: Prometheus Books.

American Psychiatric Association (1994) *Diagnostic and Statistical Manual of Mental Disorders*, 4th edition, Washington, DC: APA.

Aphramor, L. (2005) Is a weight-centred health framework salutogenic? Some thoughts on unhinging certain dietary ideologies, *Social Theory and Health*, 3: 315–340.

Atkins, L. (2007) Too much, too young, *The Guardian*, 29 February.

Campbell, I. (2003) The obesity epidemic: can we turn the tide?, *Heart*, 89(Supplement 2): ii22–ii24.

Campos, P. (2004) *The Obesity Myth: Why America's Obsession with Weight is Hazardous to Your Health*, New York: Gotham Books.

Campos, P., Saguy, A., Ernsberger, P., Oliver, E. and Gaesser, G. (2006) The epidemiology of overweight and obesity: public health crisis or moral panic?, *International Journal of Epidemiology*, 35: 55–60.

Chiesi, M., Huppertz, C. and Hofbauer, K.G. (2001) Pharmacotherapy of obesity: targets and perspectives, *Trends in Pharmacological Sciences*, 22(5): 247–254.

Cooper, C. (1998) *Fat and Proud: The Politics of Size*, London: Women's Press.

Evans, J., Rich, E. and Holroyd, R. (2004). Disordered eating and disordered schooling: what schools do to middle class girls, *British Journal of Sociology of Education*, 25(2): 123–142.

Flancbaum, L. (2003). *The Doctor's Guide to Weight Loss Surgery: How to Make the Decision That Could Save Your Life*, New York: Bantam Books.

Foucault, M. (1976) *The History of Sexuality. An Introduction*, Harmondsworth: Penguin.

Fox, N.J., Ward, K.J. and O'Rourke, A.J. (2005) The 'expert patient': empowerment or medical dominance? The case of weight loss, pharmaceutical drugs and the Internet, *Social Science and Medicine*, 60: 1299–1309.

Gard, M. and Wright, J. (2005) *The Obesity Epidemic: Science, Morality and Ideology*, London: Routledge.

Gill, R. (1996) Discourse analysis: practical implementation, in J.T.E. Richardson (ed.), *Handbook of Qualitative Research Methods for Psychology and the Social Sciences*, Leicester: BPS Books, pp. 141–158.

Gill, R. (2000) Discourse analysis, in M.W. Bauer and G. Gaskell (eds), *Qualitative Researching with Text, Image and Sound: A Practical Handbook*, London: Sage, pp. 172–190.

Goodchild, S. and Woolf, M. (2006) Dying to be thin, *The Independent*, p. 1.

Gura, T. (2003) Obesity drug pipeline not so fat, *Science*, 299: 849–852.

Herndon, A.M. (2005) Collateral damage from friendly fire? Race, nation, class and the 'war against obesity', *Social Semiotics*, 15(2): 127–141.

James, P.T., Leach, R., Kalamara, E. and Shayeghi, M. (2001) The worldwide obesity epidemic, *Obesity Research*, 9(Supplement 4): 228S–233S.

Janeway, J.M., Sparks, K.J. and Baker, R.S. (2005) *The Real Skinny on Weight Loss Surgery: An Indispensible Guide to What You Can Really Expect*, Onondaga, MI: Little Victories Press.

Keith, S., Redden, D., Kazmarzyk, P., Boggiano, M., Hanlon, E., Benca, R., Ruden, D., Pietrobelli, A., Barger, J., Fontaine, K., Wang, C., Aronne, L., Wright, S., Baskin, M., Dhurandhar, N., Lijoi, M., Grilo, C., Deluca, M., Westfall, A. and Allison, D. (2006) Putative contributors to the secular increase in obesity: exploring the roads less travelled, *International Journal of Obesity*, 30: 1585–1594.

Latner, J.D. and Stunkard, A.J. (2003) Getting worse: the stigmatization of obese children, *Obesity Research*, 11(3): 452–456.

Lupton, D. (1995) *The Imperative of Health: Public Health and the Regulated Body*, London: Sage.

Lyons, P. (1989) Fitness, feminism and the health of fat women, in L.S. Brown and E.D. Rothblum (eds), *Overcoming Fear of Fat*, New York: Harrington Park Press, pp. 65–78.

Monaghan, L.F. (2005) Discussion piece: a critical take on the obesity debate, *Social Theory and Health*, 3: 302–314.

Murray, S. (2005) (Un/be)coming out? Rethinking fat politics, *Social Semiotics*, 15(2): 153–163.

NAO (2001) *Tackling Obesity in England*, London: National Audit Office.

NICE (2006) Obesity: the prevention, identification, assessment and management of overweight and obesity in adults and children, NICE guideline, first draft for consultation, March.

Ogden, J., Bandara, I., Cohen, H., Farmer, D., Hardie, J., Minas, H. et al. (2003) GPs' and patients' models of obesity: whose problem is it anyway?, *Patient Education and Counselling*, 40: 227–233.

Oliver, J.E. (2006) *Fat Politics: The Real Story Behind America's Obesity Epidemic*, New York: Oxford University Press.

Peterson, A. (2001) Biofantasies: genetics and medicine in the print news media, *Social Science and Medicine*, 52: 1255–1268.

Puhl, R. and Brownell, K.D. (2001) Bias, discrimination and obesity, *Obesity Research*, 9(12): 788–805.

Rich, E. and Evans, J. (2005) 'Fat ethics' – the obesity discourse and body politics, *Social Theory and Health*, 3: 341–358.

Rossner, S. (2002) Obesity: the disease of the twenty-first century, *International Journal of Obesity*, 26(Supplement 4): S2–S4.

Throsby, K. (2007) 'How could you let yourself get like that?' Stories of the origins of obesity in accounts of weight loss surgery, *Social Science and Medicine*, 65: 1561–1571.

Throsby, K. (2008) 'Happy re-birthday': weight loss surgery and the 'new me', *Body and Society*, 14: 117–133.

Wann, M. (1998) *Fat!So? Because You Don't Have to Apologise for your Size*, Berkeley, CA: Ten Speed Press.

Weigle, D.S. (2003) Pharmacological therapy of obesity: past, present, and future, *Journal of Clinical Endocrinology and Metabolism*, 88(6): 2462–2469.

WHO (2000) Obesity: Preventing and Managing the Global Epidemic: Report of a WHO Consultation, *WHO Technical Report Series*, Geneva: World Health Organization.

Wood, L.A. and Kroger, R.O. (2000) *Doing Discourse Analysis: Methods for Studying Action in Talk and Texts*, London: Sage.

17 Therapeutic discourse and eating disorders in the context of power

Michael Guilfoyle

Introduction

This chapter takes aspects of a systemic view of power, as articulated by Foucault (e.g. Foucault, 1980, 1990; Honneth, 1991) and developed by Laclau and Mouffe (e.g. Laclau and Mouffe, 2001; Mouffe, 2005; Torfing, 1999), to explore certain power-related issues that might be considered when working with eating disordered clients from a feminist-oriented perspective. My interest in this issue is connected to my work in narrative therapy and discourse theory and analysis, and the hope that these fields might help practitioners, firstly, to empathise more meaningfully with those diagnosed with eating disorders and, secondly, to facilitate resistance against noxious aspects of contemporary power arrangements.

I begin by touching on some key aspects of these theorists' conflict-oriented views of societal context, before discussing some implications for the availability and longer-term viability of the politicised subject positions, or identity options, that feminist-oriented therapists might facilitate with their clients.

Power in the social field

According to Foucault, the social arena is infused with power relations from which we cannot escape. As we shall see, this will have significant implications for therapy with eating disordered clients. Whether a therapist or a client, one has no choice but to play society's 'games of power' (Foucault, 1980: 298). Laclau and Mouffe (e.g. 2001) extend Foucault's notion of an inherently strategic social world, arguing that democratic society is shaped up by a more or less organised network of 'social antagonisms'. Difference, conflict or antagonism make choice available to us and also create space for the Other. Thus, antagonism is not something to be overcome or reconciled, but is necessary for proper democratic process. This societal condition of pervasive antagonism has a stabilising function, giving people heterogeneous spaces within which to belong. It thereby 'constitutes and sustains social identity' (Torfing, 1999: 131). These spaces pertain to identity, location or community, within which we can situate ourselves. But such 'homing' inevitably also produces exclusions. For instance, a thin woman, deemed self-disciplined and other-oriented, is more valued in contemporary, heterosexist societies than a fat woman, who might be considered appetitive, lazy and self-oriented (see Rice, Saukko, Throsby, LeBesco, all this volume).

Foucault, Mouffe, Laclau and others indicate that power functions to lend order to this system of inclusions and exclusions. Social antagonism entails difference, but it does not guarantee a tolerance of or respect for such difference. Rather, power tends to suppress difference (Laclau and Mouffe, 2001). Norms are thereby produced and sustained by the circulation of discourses that define ideals about personhood. The implication for identity politics is that there is an almost invisible set of social rules regarding what kinds of identities we can legitimately inhabit, or claim for ourselves, and under what conditions. We are thereby 'ordered' into, and given a place within, the societal network. Power seems to limit, although it does not determine, our choices regarding who we can be and how others will treat us.

Thus, discourses of personhood are currently arranged in such a way that the thin woman is given more room than her larger counterpart to inhabit culturally favourable identity options. For example, enculturated persons are predisposed towards seeing this person as self-disciplined, hard-working, dedicated, healthy and attractive, and as having used her mind – her character, her willpower – to take charge of, or even to deny, the more animalistic, primal, base appetites of the body (e.g. Halse et al., 2007; Malson and Ussher, 1996). These attributes are highly valued in the western world, and such constructions make it more reasonable for a thin woman than a fat woman to *think of herself* as strong, as having achieved, as successful, as socially valuable, and so on. On the other hand, it becomes harder – though not impossible – for the larger woman to assume this kind of identity and to have such a sense of self legitimised by the world around her. She is in some respects 'excluded' from such a valued position, and might have her attempts to construct herself in socially valued ways derogated or undermined (see Rice, this volume). Instead, she is more comfortably included elsewhere in the discursive landscape, called upon to construct herself as lazy, as deficient in self-discipline or willpower, as unattractive, and as having 'lost a battle' with her body; a shameful loss considering the increased cultural salience of 'healthism' (Halse et al., 2007). Despite its negative valuation, numerous forces conspire to make this sort of position seem 'right' or 'reasonable' for her. Her exclusion from one domain (a socially valued space) leads to the production of other spaces in which she is seen to belong (in this case, a devalued psychological and social space). As long as this is accepted, the power arrangements remain in place.

However, these positions are not quite totalising. Torfing (1999) interprets Laclau and Mouffe's later work as suggesting that social antagonisms might arise from splits following attempts to install a hegemonic system; as a response to consequent exclusions, or what they call 'displacement'. The value of social antagonism is that it hints at the possibility of a rearrangement – or at least it tries to keep in dynamic motion and prevent the sedimentation – of society's system of inclusions and exclusions. Resistance against power thereby becomes thinkable and actionable. Indeed, a core tenet of these discursive approaches is that discourse and its subject positions never capture a person's identity in total fashion. It is always possible, for instance, for a larger woman to have positive regard for herself and her social value. As Foucault (e.g. 1980) consistently maintained, resistance against prevailing power arrangements is always possible. From the perspective of power adopted here, it is precisely this observation that makes it possible for us to think of something like a feminist-oriented therapy for eating disorders.

Feminist therapy, eating disorders and the disruption of power

It is interesting, then, to note the vast and diverse body of feminist ways of understanding and addressing eating disorders that has emerged in the therapeutic domain (e.g. Fallon et al., 1994; Gentile, 2007; Heenan, 2005; Nylund, 2002; Orbach, 1978). Clearly, there is no singular 'feminist therapy' for eating disorders. Rather, we find feminist ideas integrated with object relations, relational psychoanalysis, systemic therapy, narrative therapy, cognitive therapy and a range of other therapies. Despite this diversity, these practitioners seem to share an orientation to a core idea: the personal is political (Evans et al., 2005; Rader and Gilbert, 2005). This idea expresses recognition that individuals – anorexic, bulimic, binge-eating or obese clients – are both shaped by the political landscape and also contribute to the shape of that landscape. It is an idea that creates space for us to think of various ways – hence the different feminist therapies – of making therapeutic work 'an act of political resistance' (Brown, 2000: 378). In doing this, it seems that feminist therapies have brought much needed antagonism – in Laclau and Mouffe's sense – to the therapeutic domain. Feminism has interrupted and problematised therapy's historical inclination to embrace individualising and micro-perspectives on eating disorders.

Specifically, the therapeutic domain has tended to separate the personal from the social and political domains; as if they were independent aspects of life. Consider, for example, the following sorts of formulations of eating disorders, which remain persuasive in therapeutic literature and practice: eating disorders arise from self-loathing and low self-esteem (e.g. Björck et al., 2007); from negative thoughts and problematic core beliefs (e.g. Waller, 2003); from experiences of sexual, emotional or physical abuse (e.g. Hodes, 1995); or from underlying personality disorders and dynamics (e.g. Farrell, 1995). What is striking about these formulations is that they emphasise local, individual factors, drawing attention away from the contextual power issues that feminist authors have highlighted. On the other hand, feminist scholarship and practice, while not denying the reality of self-hatred, negative thinking, abuse and so on, emphasise that our formulations should highlight the person–politics relationship in order to attend to the social context that provides the conditions for eating disorders in the first place. So, for example, Bartky (1988) draws on Foucault's discussion of the Panopticon to understand women's subjection to patriarchal discourses. Here, eating disorders (and other distress) can be seen as related to a woman's internalisation of discourses of femininity, to her consequent obsession with appearance (see, however, Probyn, Burns, Nasser and Malson, all this volume), and to her becoming a 'self-policing subject, a self committed to a relentless self-surveillance' under the influence of patriarchy (Bartky, 1988: 81).

Another idea is that heterosexism – the socially constructed core organising principle of social and gendered interaction – places specific requirements on women: to be selfless and to shape self-awareness, body size and shape, and interpersonal conduct in accordance with heterosexist expectations (see Moulding, this volume). Eating disorders are thereby fostered (Thompson, 1992). A third idea is that the powerful Cartesian mind–body division, which still influences our thought and action, promotes a view that the mind should be in control of the body (Malson and Ussher, 1996). This discourse persuades us – as mentioned above – that the larger person is lazy, undisciplined and morally weak whilst persons who restrict their food intake – even those diagnosed as anorexic – are to be admired for their self-discipline, either overtly or covertly (Hardin, 2003).

Certainly, such formulations might not be embraced in the therapeutic world, but it seems that their very existence – as carriers of the personal in political discourse – contributes to the limitation of therapeutic power, and to the vitalisation of therapeutic antagonisms, in at least three ways. First, they add another set of voices to the numerous challenges against the individualising, normalising and pathologising discourses that remain so powerful in psychological and therapeutic practice. As Mouffe and Laclau suggest, 'differences' (e.g. between the various critics of individualising practices) can be transformed into temporary and strategically motivated 'equivalences' when agents are faced with a power system bent on unification and standardisation. For example, the differences between feminist theories and narrative therapy might, in certain instances, be less important than their 'equivalence' such as their shared interest in undermining the decontextualised views, mentioned above, of eating disorders that are common in the clinical arena (cf. Nylund, 2002; see also Gremillion, this volume). Second, feminist formulations make available alternative practice frameworks for clinicians, and thereby facilitate a valuable spreading of therapy's ideological base. And third, they make available alternative and more culturally and politically sensitive subject positions for clients. For example, eating disordered clients are no longer limited to such narrow self-positions as 'disturbed' or 'personality disordered', despite the prevalence of such notions in both professional and lay discourse (e.g. Holliday et al., 2005).

In such ways feminism seems to have usefully contributed to the fracturing of therapeutic power, and helped to maintain a power *dynamic* in the therapeutic world, thereby subverting movement toward the crystallisation or hypostatisation of therapeutic power. It is interesting to note, in this regard, that certain feminist authors call for feminist therapy to retain its diversity; to keep bringing its 'diverse ideas and discourses . . . into abrasive interaction' (Marecek and Kravetz, 1998: 17). Social antagonism – 'abrasive interaction' – helps prevent totalising forms of domination. It is likely that feminist practice might thereby maintain its own dynamism.

The existence of 'standpoint' therapists (Gergen, 1999) – such as feminist practitioners – itself invites a reformulation both of the person and of therapy. Therapeutic professionals can now think of ways to participate in challenging systems of power 'out there', rather than just work within those systems. Furthermore, the existence of the radical, feminist therapist figure already helps circulate the view that while eating disorders are tied up with the socio-cultural power network, the client is capable of resisting the demands placed on her by that network.

A case example

Consider the case of Lisa, aged 42, referred to me after she had been diagnosed with bulimia nervosa. My clinical work is informed by narrative and discursive theory, wherein eating disorders are seen as fundamentally tied up with societal gender and power dynamics (e.g. Lock et al., 2005; Nylund, 2002). One of the issues that emerged in this case was Lisa's gendered self-perception and ways of relating to others. She spoke of being patronised by a plumber whom she had hired to do some work in her home. She reported angrily that he had crafted some story together about why extra work – and thus an extra fee – had been necessary. She felt that he saw her not as 'a person, but as a stupid woman', and tried to take advantage of her. Given that she displayed such competence and resilience in other aspects of her life, I was interested to know how she would respond to someone who – discursively – 'called out to her' to step into a feminine position of docility and naivety.

Of interest here is the background cultural presence of a more or less ordered network of social antagonisms that, on the one hand, help all of us to 'read' this kind of interaction (between Lisa and her plumber), and, on the other hand, offer guidance to both Lisa and the plumber in their engagement. Listening to Lisa's narrative, it seemed that she had a sense of two different sets of discourses about what it means to be a woman. On the one hand is the career-minded, assertive, self-oriented kind of figure; and on the other hand is the 'little girl', the compliant, naive, diminutive figure who strives to please others. Her eating conduct seemed to bear some relation to the latter position, as she understood it in terms of trying to be attractive, to be small, and to seek approval. In many respects, Lisa was struggling to find herself somewhere in relation to these positions, but reported some historical comfort with the latter. This was also where, it seemed, the plumber positioned her. Power functions to claim subjects, partly by ascribing identity, and so we might interpret the plumber to be a (perhaps unwitting) spokesperson of a discourse inscribing docility, seeking to claim Lisa as an example of its own truths – at least in those few moments. The more successful it is at claiming women (and men), the more powerful this discursive production of docile femininity becomes. Put another way, the more examples we see of its functioning, the more difficult it is to oppose. Lisa's accession to the plumber's invitation – in the moment she went along with it and paid him his exorbitant fee, 'giggling like a stupid schoolgirl' – is an indication of the enduring power of this discourse and of its appeal. But, at the same time, she felt ashamed and angry with herself. Regardless of how she acted in that situation, and of her history of being enculturated into various positions of docility, she would not totally accept that she 'belonged' in that culturally available category of person. Her anger and shame themselves alluded to the possibility of alternative – absent but implicit – subject positions, which she could potentially occupy.

Her internal resistance against the imposed, or invited, dominant category of womanhood created the need for a search for other ways of thinking about who she was or would like to be. Narrative therapists call these hints of new ways of thinking 'unique outcomes' (e.g. White and Epston, 1990). And indeed, there were many events in Lisa's life that seemed to challenge this narrative of docility and compliance. She outlined her many successes in her professional career, noting that she had attained an award for outstanding work. She had removed herself from a physically and emotionally abusive relationship and had started a new relationship that she was determined would be different. We explored how her anger at complying with the plumber's expectations connected with these historical competencies.

At stake here is the nature of Lisa's participation in society's network of power relations. All of us are political participants. One of the considerations for feminist therapists is to make sense of the nature of the client's – and our own – participation. This might involve questioning the domains from which the eating disordered person might be excluded and in which she is included or made to feel welcome; and then perhaps questioning the finality or utility of these arrangements. For example, the anorexic woman might, in most parts of western society, be excluded from the category of 'normal', and she might be invited instead to belong to some marginalised group, such as 'the disturbed' or the pro-anorexia community (see Day and Keys, this volume).

In Lisa's case, the most salient question in this regard seemed to orient around how to belong in the world as a woman. Would she continue to identify with – and thereby strengthen and 'thicken' – the culturally available account of women as docile, compliant figures whose function is partly to please the Other? Or would she resist the temptations of this position, and occupy a stance that permits more interpersonal competence, and an awareness of and respect for her own needs and interests? Or, can she create some new and more personal set of positions that allows her more freedom than either of these two poles seem to allow? From the perspective of power adopted here, it seems that these last two possibilities might involve Lisa contributing to an imbalance in societal power arrangements around women's identities. While society's systems of power are obviously not overturned in the process, she might thereby participate in their destabilisation. Thus, at the one extreme, she does not contribute to the reification of gender inequality, stereotyping, and (for instance) woman's compliance; and at the other extreme, she does not necessarily contribute to something like a gender revolution. Rather, her daily practices might contribute, in her own local sphere of sociality, to the maintenance of, precisely, a power *dynamic* – a movement or dialogue of force relations (cf. Falzon, 1998) characterised by the sort of fluid system of social antagonisms to which Laclau and Mouffe refer.

To clarify, in line with the warnings of Ali (2002), Freedman and Combs (1996), and others, I am not suggesting that Lisa should be asked to sign up to some political cause. Rather, I am suggesting that a model of power might be useful in furthering our analyses of the political, power related, effects of our work. But an examination of societal power dynamics can also help us to identify some of the difficulties in seeing our work as critical in the political sense.

The first difficulty is that both clients' and therapists' discourses are vulnerable to the shaping effects of power dynamics. They are themselves part of a system of antagonisms, which is evident even within sessions. For example, my interest in Lisa's competencies seemed to make her feel that she was being inconsistent in how she was talking about herself ('I'm sorry, I'm contradicting myself'). In our discussions, and in contrast to feminist-narrative discourse, she appeared to invoke an arguably more powerful, more widely circulated and more recognisable commonsense discourse of truth/falsity, in order to make sense of the competencies that I thought of as unique outcomes. Thus, she initially interpreted her discussions of competency as a contradiction in her own speech, and went on to interpret her achievements as merely a 'mask' covering up the weakness that she felt characterised her 'true self'. Indeed, there are powerful anti-constructionist discourses available in the culture (e.g. commonsense versions of science, of truth, of expertise and so forth), which might be more accessible and acceptable to clients. We should therefore expect that our ideas will be appropriated and absorbed into more definitive, scientific and realist discourse. Lisa also felt that my job (as a therapist) was 'to try and be positive', and so she thought I was being 'nice' in my attempts to draw out a part of her that she experienced not as real, but as a fantasy of herself. My own conversational clumsiness aside, the point is that our own formulations exist in a power network that might lend shape to, or even distort, the formulations themselves. The sheer force of life experience and ordinary social interaction can sometimes overwhelm – render invisible, naive or otherwise problematic – the therapeutic stances we take and the discourses we use to organise our thought and action.

This applies obviously to clients' understandings and subject positions as they engage with the world outside of therapy, where they will inevitably encounter counter-formulations and more easily accessible subject positions. The changes realised in and through therapy can be hard to maintain when clients' subtly altered sense of self jars with dominant discourses and practices in their social world. In this regard, many feminists and narrative practitioners have become acutely aware of the need for a community basis for eating disordered persons who develop views on themselves and their conduct that are not widely supported (e.g. Freedman and Combs, 1996). For example, anti-anorexia groups provide a place for anorexics and their loved ones to join forces in combating not just anorexia, but the social conditions that contribute to its power (see Burns et al., this volume). In Canada, the Chrysalis programme brings together women who have been diagnosed with personality disorders, but who also have difficulties with eating and body image. Here, community is emphasised as women work together to question their cultural socialisation, the objectification of their bodies, and gendered social prescriptions (Rivera, 2002).

The maintenance of alternative subject positions, which seem to run counter to dominant cultural prescriptions, is helped enormously by the identification or production of a community wherein one side of a social antagonism (e.g. challenging oppressive constructions of women) can be contained and reproduced. This amounts to a way of finding inclusion; of finding a social space where one can belong and contribute, but without having to do so in the spaces typically made available to eating disordered persons in our culture: such as within the category of the mad, the sick or the disturbed; or within other destructive spaces, such as the pro-anorexia community (see also Day and Keys, this volume). Community is increasingly recognised as a vital consideration in therapeutic attempts to support and reproduce alternative, preferred self positions.

In Lisa's case, she felt trapped between the positions of weak and compliant woman, and 'bitchy and aggressive' woman. This duality softened somewhat as we worked towards identifying a community of persons who might disagree with her perception that her competencies were 'false' or 'incidental'. She immediately identified her aunt – a powerful figure during Lisa's childhood – as someone who had always believed in Lisa, and who had described Lisa as having 'a backbone of steel'. This series of recollections enabled Lisa to begin to construct elements of a history of competence that had the tinge of pride carried in her aunt's words, rather than the tinge of 'bitchy' which Lisa sensed in the culture. Thus, she was able to imagine taking up a different subject position, aided by a small community – eventually including myself – who noticed and validated her competence as a person.

Conclusions

Katzman (1997) suggests that, instead of looking at gender as the critical variable in eating disorders, perhaps we should be looking at power. Indeed, the language of power can be useful in facilitating examination of the relationship between therapeutic practice and the socio-cultural context in which eating disordered persons find themselves. My aim here has been to highlight the point that our clients, their problems, and our actions all inevitably enter – or are entered into – societal power dynamics, both inside and outside of the consulting room. They will always exist within some strategic or 'antagonistic' situation. Some of these situations are already being examined in the therapeutic domain. For example, there is increasing recognition that in the absence of some form of holding community – some form of inclusion – persons, together with their therapeutically altered positions, are always at risk of being overwhelmed and recuperated, simply by virtue of their desire to be included somewhere, and to make sense of their experience within some containing narrative.

Various questions are raised: What forms of identity or inclusion are most available and accessible to the various eating disordered persons in our current cultural context (e.g. as mad and/or as part of a pro-anorexia community), and from which subject positions are they excluded (e.g. as a rational, competent individual)? What potential forms of community are 'absent but implicit' in the words of our clients? To what extent can our empathy involve hearing, within clients' speech, the various social antagonisms in which their actions participate, and the forms of inclusion and exclusion that these imply? How can we combat the tendency of power operations to capture and tame our discourses (a problem noted by numerous feminist authors, e.g. Burman, 1999; Heenan, 1996), and to lay discursive claim to clients' conduct and identity once they leave the consulting room?

References

Ali, A. (2002) The convergence of Foucault and feminist psychiatry: exploring emancipatory knowledge-building, *Journal of Gender Studies*, 11(3): 233–242.

Bartky, S. (1988) Foucault, femininity, and the modernization of patriarchal power, in L. Quinby and I. Diamond (eds), *Feminism and Foucault: Reflections on Resistance*, Boston, MA: Northeastern University Press, pp. 61–86.

Björck, C.K., Clinton, D., Sohlberg, S. and Norring, C. (2007) Negative self-image and outcome in eating disorders: Results at 3-year follow up, *Eating Behaviours*, 8(3): 398–406.

Brown, L.S. (2000) Feminist therapy, in C.R. Snyder and R.E. Ingram (eds), *Handbook of Psychological Change: Psychotherapy Processes and Practices for the 21st Century*, New York: Wiley, pp. 358–380.

Burman, E. (1999) Whose construction? Points from a feminist perspective, in D.J. Nightingale and J. Cromby (eds), *Social Constructionist Psychology: A Critical Analysis of Theory and Practice*, Buckingham: Open University Press, pp. 159–175.

Evans, K.M., Kincade, E.A. and Marbley, A.F. (2005) Feminism and feminist therapy: lessons from the past and hopes for the future, *Journal of Counselling and Development*, 83: 269–277.

Fallon, P., Katzman, M.A. and Wooley, S.C. (eds) (1994) *Feminist Perspectives on Eating Disorders*, New York: Guilford Press.

Falzon, C. (1998) *Foucault and Social Dialogue*, New York: Routledge.

Farrell, E.M. (1995) *Lost for Words: The Psychoanalysis of Anorexia and Bulimia*, London: Process.

Foucault, M. (1980) *Power/Knowledge: Selected Interviews and Other Writings, 1971–1977* (edited by C. Gordon), New York: Harvester Wheatsheaf.

Foucault, M. (1990) *The History of Sexuality, Vol. 1*, Harmondsworth: Penguin.

Freedman, J. and Combs, G. (1996) *Narrative Therapy: The Social Construction of Preferred Realities*, New York: Norton.

Gentile, K. (2007) *Creating Bodies: Eating Disorders as Self-destructive Survival*, Mahwah, NJ: Analytic Press.

Gergen, K. (1999) *An Invitation to Social Construction*, London: Sage.

Halse, C., Honey, A. and Boughtwood, D. (2007) The paradox of virtue: (re)thinking deviance, anorexia and schooling, *Gender and Education*, 19(2): 219–235.

Hardin, P.K. (2003) Shape-shifting discourses of anorexia nervosa: reconstituting psychopathology, *Nursing Inquiry*, 10(4): 209–217.

Heenan, C. (1996) Feminist therapy and its discontents, in E. Burman, G. Aitken, P. Alldred, R. Allwood, T. Billington, B. Goldberg, A.J. Gordo Lopez, C. Heenan, D. Marks and S. Warner (eds), *Psychology Discourse Practice: From Regulation to Resistance*, London: Taylor and Francis, pp. 55–71.

Heenan, C. (2005) A feminist psychotherapeutic approach to working with women who eat compulsively, *Counselling and Psychotherapy Research*, 5(3): 238–245.

Hodes, M. (1995) Anorexia nervosa and bulimia nervosa in adolescents, *Continuing Medical Education*, 13(5): 481–488.

Holliday, J., Wall, E., Treasure, J. and Weinman, J. (2005) Perceptions of illness in individuals with anorexia nervosa: a comparison with lay men and women, *International Journal of Eating Disorders*, 37(1): 50–56.

Honneth, A. (1991). *The Critique of Power: Reflective Stages in a Critical Social Theory*, London: MIT Press.

Katzman, M. (1997) Getting the difference right: it's power not gender that matters, *European Eating Disorders Review*, 5(2): 71–74.

Laclau, E. and Mouffe, C. (2001) Hegemony and socialist strategy: towards a radical democratic politics, 2nd edition, New York: Verso.

Lock, A., Epston, D., Maisel, R. and de Faria, N. (2005) Resisting anorexia/ bulimia: Foucauldian perspectives in narrative therapy, *British Journal of Guidance and Counselling*, 33(3): 315–332.

Malson, H. and Ussher, J.M. (1996) Body poly-texts: discourses of the anorexic body, *Journal of Community and Applied Social Psychology*, 6: 267–280.

Marecek, J. and Kravetz, D. (1998) Putting politics into practice: feminist therapy as feminist praxis, *Women and Therapy*, 21(2): 17–36.

Mouffe, C. (2005) *The Return of the Political*, London: Verso.

Nylund, D. (2002) Poetic means to anti-anorexic ends, *Journal of Systemic Therapies*, 21(4): 18–34.

Orbach, S. (1978) *Fat is a Feminist Issue*, London: Paddington Press.

Rader, J. and Gilbert, L.A. (2005) The egalitarian relationship in feminist therapy, *Psychology of Women Quarterly*, 29(4): 427–435.

Rivera, M. (2002) The Chrysalis Program: a feminist treatment community for individuals diagnosed as personality disordered, in M. Ballou and L.S. Brown (eds), *Rethinking Mental Health and Disorder: Feminist Perspectives*, New York: Guilford Press, pp. 231–261.

Thompson, B.W. (1992) 'A way outa no way': eating problems among African-American, Latina and White women, *Gender and Society*, 6(4): 546–561.

Torfing, J. (1999) *New Theories of Discourse*, Oxford: Blackwell.

Waller, G. (2003) Schema-level cognitions in patients with binge eating disorder, *International Journal of Eating Disorders*, 33(4): 458–464.

White, M. and Epston, D. (1990) *Narrative Means to Therapeutic Ends*, New York: Norton.

Part V
Critical interventions

18 Anti-anorexia/bulimia

A polemics of life and death

David Epston and Rick Maisel

Introduction

The following is excerpted from a document sent by Kristen to her therapist and, subsequently, to David Epston. We include it here to exemplify the pontifical judgment so characteristic of what, as narrative therapists, we refer to as anorexia's 'speech'.

Saving a life
By Anorexia, a friend to Kristen Webber

I am a friend of Kristen Webber, her best friend. I have unselfishly dedicated myself to save her life. The thoughts I give her help her to become a better person. Since I am the only one who tells her the truth and really wants her to be happy, I am her only friend.

The most important thing she needs to realize is that she is 50 pounds overweight. She is the fattest person I've ever met. I'm the only one who tells her the truth, even if it hurts. Anyone who tries to get Kristen to eat just wants to see her get fatter and fatter . . . their secret wish is to hurt her and see her in pain.

Being such a fat person, she is worthless and awful. If she were to lose weight, she would become a worthwhile person who deserves to be happy and treated with respect. People respect, admire and are proud of her when she can have enough self-control to resist the temptation to eat and drink. She cannot eat in front of anyone without them thinking she is greedy and selfish. I save her from making others hate her.

There is something about Kristen that makes people want to hurt her. She has already been hurt by males because she was not smart and was very careless. She is safer when she doesn't eat because people don't feel like they need to hurt her. I'm just trying to protect Kristen.

Kristen deserves to die if she doesn't listen to me. She might as well just kill herself if she disobeys me because she'll never find happiness. I have the answer to her happiness. I care about Kristen very much. I only want the best for her. Nothing can go wrong by listening to me. I dedicate myself to her. This is my unselfish mission – to save Kristen's life.

Above, anorexia, in a manner of speaking, expresses itself through a voice of strong moral judgment.[1] In our conversations with those (whom we refer to as 'insiders') who struggle first-hand with the problem of anorexia and bulimia, when we distill the voice of anorexia/bulimia[2] (a/b) we typically hear this kind of strong moral rhetoric. A/b, it appears, arrogates to itself the sole right to pronounce one a 'somebody' or a 'nobody', 'worthy' or 'worthless'. For those at the mercy of a/b's cruel judgments (without recourse to re-valuing counter-moralities), a/b's moral judgments can transform their lives into life-sentences, or all too often, a death sentence.

In the first half of this chapter, we intend to conceptualize a/b as a distinctly heinous morality of personhood, one that is remarkably successful in exploiting many dominant contemporary cultural values (e.g. thinness, self-discipline, self-control, individual achievement) in order to appeal to people's vulnerabilities and aspirations. We propose that a/b, playing on the hopes and fears of those under its spell, co-opts and twists moral discourses to achieve its immoral ends (see Lock et al., 2004). In the second part of the chapter, we explore the implications of a/b as a moral (as opposed to a medical) concern, proposing a way for therapists to take up the moral task of bearing witness to its appalling cruelty in contrast to the more detached position of the objective professional/spectator. In addition, we will briefly introduce therapeutic practices – informed by narrative therapy (see Epston, 1998, 2008; Epston and White, 1992; Freeman et al., 1997; Monk et al., 1997; White, 1995, 1997, 2000, 2004, 2007; White and Epston, 1990; White and Morgan, 2006) – that expose a/b's immoral claims and provide some means for sufferers to contest them and, by doing so, reclaim their lives.

The (im)moral jurisdiction of a/b: claims and implications

For many years, we have endeavored to comprehend how a/b could transform highly intelligent and in many respects 'model' girls and women

1 The second half of the chapter will take up our narrative-therapy informed 'manner of speaking' and thinking about anorexia, one that conceives of it as an external influence as opposed to an internal disease or disorder of the self.
2 We acknowledge the important differences between anorexia and bulimia, but as both problems rely heavily, in our view, on moralistic arguments, we use the term a/b to refer to both problems simultaneously when appropriate.

(and sometimes boys and men) into unwitting bystanders and accomplices to their own torture and impending death while remaining convinced that they are being perfected and 'goodened'? Our enquiries with insiders into the tactics of a/b have exposed the ingenious means by which this rhetoric turns many of our conventional moralities on their head. To put it simply, 'bad' becomes 'good' and 'good' becomes 'bad'.

In 'Anorexia's letter' to Kristen, presented above, we can see how a/b, playing off dominant western notions of beauty and competitive individualism, appeals to Kristen's desire to distinguish herself as successful by becoming thin. A/b asserts that the most important thing is that she is 'fat', because 'being such a fat person, she is worthless and awful'. Given that, in reality, Kristen was in a state of nutritional crisis and life-threatened, we can surmise that a/b has asserted an unattainable standard of thinness, one that equates having fat with being fat. Consequently, a/b can claim that unless Kristen is the thinnest person she knows, it means that she has some body fat and therefore *is fat*. From there, it is a simple matter for a/b to transform the 'bad' of starvation and inevitable death into the moral 'good' of 'self-control', earning her the respect, admiration and pride of others. Were Kristen to resist her execution and allow herself to eat and drink, the 'good' of Kristen's self-care and sustenance would be transformed by a/b into the 'bad' of 'being greedy and selfish'. These moral attributions make a/b's next claim credible to Kristen, as outrageous as it is – that if Kristen allows herself to eat (and by doing so prevents her tragic demise) those who love her and care about her would 'hate' her.

In this fashion, a/b is able to cleverly turn dominant cultural specifications to its own ends. Moral measures – e.g. selflessness, self-abnegation, self-control and so forth – are merged with the contradictions of a 'ruthless individualism', driven by an ethic of individual achievement and policed by scores, marks, weights and other 'objective' assessments. By lashing women (and some men) with a figurative 'whip' braided from both the traditional power of moral judgment and the more modern disciplinary power of normalizing judgment, a/b's moral claims become almost irrefutable.

Conceptualizing a counter-morality

Because a/b's prosecution takes place within the domain of its own moral jurisdiction, we believe that a viable defense can only be mounted within the domain of a counter-morality. This rival morality often takes shape by way of contesting a/b or building bridges back to other moral frameworks that have been overridden by a/b (e.g. those moral perspectives derived from 'nature' or 'spiritualities'). Anti-a/b is not fixed by adherence to any particular extant psychological or moral code but is 'defined' only by its existence as a rival to a/b.

Such rival moralities allow a/b's pronouncements of what or who is good or bad to be interrogated, quarreled with and finally repudiated. In the absence of such a rival morality, breaches of a/b's dogma are invariably interpreted within a/b's moral framework as heretical and shameful. We have referred to this counter-morality and the practices of living associated with it as 'anti-anorexia/anti-bulimia' (see Maisel et al., 2004; see also www.narrativeapproaches.com/antia/b%20folder/anti_a/b_index.htm).

Before a/b's (im)moral rhetoric can be countered, the rhetoric itself must become the object of scrutiny rather than the person the rhetoric is aimed at. In other words, the therapist must find a means by which to help the insider consider a/b's pronouncements not as truths but as tactics. In order for this critical enquiry into the tactics and strategies of a/b to proceed, it is imperative the conceptual distinction between a/b and the person under it's influence be maintained (see also Saukko, Guilfoyle, Burns et al., all this volume). This 'externalizing' conceptual framework and most of the clinical practices we use are derived from narrative therapy.

Narrative therapy

Narrative therapy emerged in the early 1980s out of the longstanding friendship and collaboration of Michael White (in Adelaide, Australia) and David Epston (in Auckland, New Zealand). They were brought together by their shared commitment to the political 'wing' of family therapy resulting from their disquiet with psychological/psychiatric thought and practice. In the mid-1980s, they engaged with the 'early' and 'middle' Foucault and the narrative metaphor (Lock, et al., 2005; White and Epston, 1990: 1–37). The first provided the means of critique through 'the insurrection of local knowledges' (Foucault, 1980: 82) and, as its consequence, the 'solidarity' between those who suffer and those who aspire to assist them. The narrative metaphor provided a 'map' for therapy that emphasized the socially constructed and fluid character of identity, and envisioned therapy as a process of 're-authoring'. In 1990, White and Epston published their classic text *Narrative Means to Therapeutic Ends*.

One of the distinguishing characteristics of narrative therapy is its emphasis on separating the person from the problem through 'externalizing conversations'. In such a 'manner of speaking', considerations of discourse, gender, history and culture can be brought to bear. These conversations subvert taken-for-granted (especially by the 'psycomplex') understandings of problems as residing in and emanating from the disordered 'self' of the person.

We regard 'anti-a/b' (both in the sense of a style of living and a set of therapeutic practices) as a variant of narrative therapy. Because a/b is so effective at co-opting the identity of the people it seeks to subordinate, merging its voice with theirs and making it nearly impossible for them to distinguish between them, anti-a/b adopts the externalizing language of narrative therapy and pushes it to its linguistic extremes. In fact, anti-a/b can be considered a radical form of externalization. Due to the centrality of the practice of radical externalization in unmasking a/bs immorality, in the following section we further elaborate on the differences between internalizing and externalizing conversations (see 'Internalizing versus externalizing discourses' in Epston, 1998: 39–60).

A linguistic turn

How, as therapists, can we bear moral witness to the appalling cruelty of a/b and the heinous suffering it inflicts and continue to engage with therapy practices that expose a/b's (im)moral claims as such and provide some means for insiders to contest and defrock them? We have found that to do so requires thinking and speaking against the grain of most 'professional', medicalized approaches which strip problems of their moral implications. Arthur Kleinman, the Harvard psychiatrist/anthropologist, examined the moral implications of medical practice that 're-creates human suffering as human disease'. He concluded:

> The professionalization of human problems as psychiatric disorders . . . causes sufferers (and their communities) to lose a world. . . . Experts are far along in the process of inauthenticating social worlds, of making illegitimate the defeats and victories, the desperation and aspiration of individuals and groups that could perhaps be more humanely rendered. We, each of us, injure the humanity of our fellow sufferers each time we fail to privilege their voices, their experiences.
>
> (Kleinman, 1995: 117)

It is primarily through internalizing conversations, the practice of thinking and talking about a/b as something 'within' themselves, something that they 'have' or 'are', that this 'professionalization' occurs. This way of thinking about the problem is reflected in common ways of speaking about people, such as 'I have bulimia' or 'she's an anorexic'. This linguistic and conceptual practice, in effect, constructs these problems as psychological and/or medical and imports them into the domain of the professional experts to assess, diagnose and treat. If eating disorders are presumed to originate from within the psyche, then the root causes of eating disorders are presumed to reside within the disordered mind/self of the person (see Malson and Burns, Eckermann, both this volume) or else to be genetically encoded into the body.

These bio/psychological accounts all too easily obscure the interpersonal, social and historical contexts that are so often implicated in the difficulties people experience. These explanations are almost exclusively couched in terms of deficiencies or excesses in relation to norms that such psychological theories have established.

Unfortunately, a/b thrives on such deficit accounts of people, painting a portrait of people as flawed from a lack of 'desirous' attributes, or, as Julie (an insider) points out, thriving on 'judgments of excess (i.e. as too fat, too greedy, too arrogant, too desiring, too loud, too much)'. By directing these young women and men to scrutinize themselves rather than the meaning and discourses that circulate in the social realm, they are turned away from addressing the injustices they may have experienced in their lives as well as those seemingly self-inflicted injustices perpetrated by a/b.

When psychiatrists, physicians, therapists, dietitians and so forth view a/b as internal, they run the risk of inadvertently ushering the insider into an even stronger identification with a/b. As long as they view a/b as entwined with the 'self', they will be more likely to ask questions or make statements that assume the insider is attracted to, needful of or committed to their 'eating disorder' or, at best, they will confine the problem to the 'anorexic self' while entertaining the possibility that there remains a part of the self that is still 'healthy' and seeking 'recovery'. Such enquiries, wherein insiders' thoughts, feeling and actions (rather than the tactics and strategies of a/b) are scrutinized, can easily support a/b's attempt to rob these women and men of their own identities by getting them to think of themselves as 'anorexic' or 'bulimic'.

The lines of enquiry that proceed from such a view make it extremely difficult for someone to distinguish their own (not their 'true' but, rather, preferred) voice – one that captures their lived experience and is in alignment with their larger values and purposes in life – from the voice of a/b. Asking a young woman who is caught up in a/b's spell to reflect on a/b is tantamount to asking her to look in the mirror – all she sees is herself. This is because a/b operates as a modern regime of power (Lock et al., 2005; Maisel et al., 2004; White and Epston, 1990), keeping the spotlight on the person while its power and influence remain hidden in the shadows or entirely invisible. Thus, they may speak not *about* a/b but *through* (or *as*) a/b, claiming that s/he is fat, ugly, guilty, undeserving, unworthy and so forth, often with the conviction associated with an indisputable truth.

Because conventional forms of thinking and speaking about a/b construct a/b as internal, as a disease they 'have', were a person suffering from a/b to tire of their enslavement and seek a better life, what choice would they have but to indict themselves at the same time they indict a/b? An anorexic trap is inadvertently laid such that when they begin to think in opposition to a/b (to 'come out of their denial'), they step into a view of themselves as 'sick' or 'disordered'. From there it is a relatively easy matter for a/b to co-opt this fledgling rebellion and exploit this idea of the person-as-problem to tighten its grip by reminding them of their worthlessness and inadequacies.

In sum, our conversations with insiders have led us to conclude that conceptualizing a/b as internal to the person has several disadvantages, including the fostering of deficit accounts of persons, the encouraging of insiders' identification with a/b, and the facilitation of a/b's attempts to co-opt anti-anorexic resistance. Below, we present a conceptual and linguistic alternative to the medicalized and internalized discourses of conventional treatment, one which we believe provides a foundation for the perception of the (im)morality of a/b, and a means by which to resist it.

A new manner of speaking: externalizing conversations

> Before I just talked with doctors about anorexia. No one ever taught me that you have to talk against her. Before, all I was told was that you have to get over it. It's more than that! When I talk against anorexia there's more of a chance of getting free because I can start hating her and when I do, I can let her go.
>
> (Heather-Anne, 1991)

If a/b is going to take root and flourish, the language of a/b must deny its own presence and conceal itself as the speaker. This camouflaging of a/b would not be possible were it not for the fact that the worldviews, practices and values that breathe life into a/b are pervasive in western culture via, for example, discourses that champion individual achievement, self-control and (especially for women), self-sacrifice, and the importance placed on appearance in general and the valuing of thinness/fitness in particular (see e.g. Bordo, Guilfoyle, Burns et al., all this volume). A/b harmonizes its voice with, indeed is an intensified echo of, these larger cultural voices, eventually appropriating and distorting them, turning them into grotesque caricatures.

It is through what are referred to as 'externalizing conversations' (Lock et al., 2005; White and Epston, 1990) that the presence and operations of a/b can be flushed into the open. Prior to this conceptual and linguistic twist, there is no language available to insiders to represent a/b, but only those vocabularies of self-blame, self-reproach, self-hatred and guilt, which a/b employs to represent people. Externalizing conversations reverse this process, linguistically and conceptually constructing a/b as an influence separate from the person, and inviting the identification, objectification and critique of a/b and its voice. At the same time, the radical externalizing or personifying of a/b also creates space for people to recognize and give voice to their own experience. As one anti-anorexic veteran put it, 'I guess I imagine this quite literally – that as you pull the problem out from the person you actually leave space for the person to inhabit their own body and have their own thoughts.'

Externalizing conversations bring a/b into a sharper focus, reconnect persons to their own bodies and lived experience, and heighten the distinction between their 'own' (i.e. preferred and embodied) voices and the voice of a/b. All of this contributes to the identification of potential avenues of resistance to a/b and fosters a sense of direction and hope.

Counter-moralities as a foundation for counter-stories

Anti-anorexia/anti-bulimia considers a/b to be a form of human cruelty and agrees in principle with the feminist philosopher, Maria Pia Lara, that 'the problem of inflicting suffering through cruelty belongs to the realm of morality and it should be restricted to moral agency' (Pia Lara, 2007: 28). Anti-a/b re-authors lives by means of what the feminist narrative ethicist Hilde Lindemann Nelson refers to as 'counter-stories' of a particular kind: 'A story that resists an oppressive identity and attempts to replace it with one that commands respect which can provide a significant form of resistance to the evil of diminished moral agency' (Lindemann Nelson, 2001: 7).

Below, Judy, aged 30, illustrates how a redemptive and exculpating counter-story can emerge from a moral critique of anorexia, one that exposed anorexia's 'evil' while revealing her own 'innocence':

> As I learn all the ways devised by evil – 'anorexia' – to devour my life, I paradoxically learn my own innocence. I think of how sweet is a little girl who skips down a path singing to herself, oblivious to evil . . . totally unconcerned with evil . . . totally concerned only with whom she will love. You [DE] asked me if I knew evil was being done to me. If I didn't, it is because some of the innocence never left me. But the tragedy is that to know evil, one must give that up. And one must know evil to realize one's innocence. Tragic irony!

> I told you I felt all these years like a silent Jew, forsaken by god, everyone and everything. Whereas they [the Jews of the Holocaust] knew evil was being done to them [and] they didn't deserve it, anorexia gets people to go to the torture chamber smiling, grateful even.

> Anorexia tells me I can never atone for my part in its creation. That in other words I am evil. Fortunately, I know 'you are mine forever' to be a ruse. If I were evil for not resisting evil when I didn't know I could, then could there be any good in the world?

Exposing the immorality of a/b through moral and ethical enquiries

Elucidating an anti-anorexic/bulimic counter-morality provides a foundation for the critique of a/b and its (im)moral claims. When scrutinized through the lens of a rival morality, a/b's arguments appear intended to deceive rather than to enlighten and uplift, and its promises of a 'heaven on earth' are exposed as a ruse leading to a 'hell on earth'. Furthermore, the vantage point of anti-a/b betrays a/b's claim of 'moral goodening' and reveals the extent to which a/b is a manifestation of the very evil to which these young women are so opposed.

What are the domains of such moral and ethical enquiries that such a 'trial for one's life' might canvass? Specific questions with insiders might be raised in relation to what a/b is saying, the effects of a/b's 'voice', the intentions that might be inferred from these effects, and ultimately about the '(im)morality' of a/b. Through questions which expose a/b's (im)morality and reconnect a person to anti-a/b counter-moralities, a/b's inculpating finger, in a manner of speaking, can be bent back in the direction of a/b itself.

Expressions of moral outrage

Once the inhumanity of a/b's 'morality' is unveiled, counter-moralities often become apparent or are reclaimed, giving rise to expressions of moral outrage. Moral outrage can be highly sustaining of a person's anti-anorexic resistance and serve as an anti-anorexic shield for a/b's 'slings and arrows'. The previously demoralized person can now find themselves 'remoralized' (Frank, 2004), whereby their resistance to a/b is founded not only on a desire for a better life (which a/b can so easily twist into 'selfishness') but also for a better world (something akin to 'justice').

David, aged 12, after being assisted to view anorexia through a counter-morality, recognized the injustice of anorexia's reign in his life and wrote himself the apology from anorexia he knew he deserved but would never receive:

Apology from Anorexia to myself

I am writing this apology to myself because I know that even though I may dream about it. Even though I thoroughly deserve it. Even though you have stolen every pleasure that I had in my life. I know that you are so heartless, so shallow and so ruthless that you would never have the compassion or decency to ever make the apology that you have for so long owed me.

Here it is:

I am sorry that I have stolen your life away from you. I am sorry for turning every pleasure you once had in your joyful life into an unbearable torture, from your pleasure in eating to your pleasure in good company and sport. I made you hate yourself and see fault in everything that you were and did. I took away all your happiness and turned everything you found into a horrible ordeal. I sapped all your strength, turning you into a lifeless body without a soul. I deprived you of all the tastes you enjoyed and stole from you x kilograms, turning you into an unhappy skeleton. I lied to you, telling you that I would make you happy and an overall better person. When you did what I said, I was ruthless and pushed your face into the mud, making you hate yourself and blame yourself for things that I had forced and tortured you into doing.

It is obvious that it would be impossible to fix what I have done. There is no way that I can take back what I have done because I terribly scarred and mutilated you. All I can do is apologize and leave you and your family alone forever.

Yours truly sorry,
Anorexia

(March 26, 2006)

The therapist as moral witness

If we, as therapists, hope to engage the people who have been ensnared in a/b's web in an exposé of it's fraudulent munificence, we ourselves must surrender any claim to the professional distance that 'recreates human suffering as human disease' and, instead, reposition ourselves as moral witnesses. We resonate strongly with the anthropologist Scheper-Hughes' (1995) call for a morally engaged position of 'witness' as opposed to the more detached and traditional position of 'spectator'. Viewing a/b as a culturally and historically situated (im)moral 'force' rather than a medical disorder positions us (and those who share this view) as 'witnesses' not 'spectators'.

Scheper-Hughes goes on to differentiate these two positions and locate them within different traditions of thought and practice:

> If 'observation' links anthropology to the natural sciences, 'witnessing' links anthropology to moral philosophy. Observation, or the anthropologist as 'fearless spectator,' is a passive act which positions the anthropologist above and outside human events as a 'neutral' and 'objective' (i.e. uncommitted) seeing I/eye. Witnessing, or the anthropologist as companheira, is the active voice, and it positions the anthropologist inside human events as a responsive, reflexive, and morally committed being, one who will 'take sides' and make judgments, though this flies in the face of anthropological nonengagement with either ethics or politics.

(ibid.: 442)

Abby, an insider, who first drew our attention to the work of Scheper-Hughes, eloquently sums up our viewpoint:

> I consider Scheper-Hughes' distinction a very useful way of thinking about the different stances people can adopt in relation to the sufferings of the 'Other'. More specifically, in relation to anorexia, I think that many conventional health professionals and treatment providers take the position of 'spectator'. As such, those struggling with anorexia are viewed as fundamentally different and 'separate' from themselves – as inescapably 'Other'. Thus, while they may work with those struggling with anorexia day in and day out, and would be aware, at least

intellectually, of the immense suffering anorexia engenders, they don't engage with it on a moral level. Hence they fail to see how, as both treatment providers and members of societies in which anorexia flourishes, they are inextricably involved in that which is profoundly political and of great moral import.

In stark contrast, 'anti-a/b' engages right at the heart of 'moral matters'. By actively 'bearing witness' to the anguish and torment a/b inflicts and by pursuing lines of inquiry which sensitively render visible the (im)moral dimensions of such suffering, anti-anorexic practitioners, loved ones, and other concerned citizens can awaken those suffering at the hands of a/b to their own pain – a pain a/b does its best to inure them to. This then enables a vital step in the process of reclaiming one's life from a/b to occur, that is, to recognise one's own suffering and then, even more crucially, to come to understand such suffering as unjust. It is then that sufferers may have the moral outrage and concomitant courage of their convictions necessary to take on a/b and diminish its stranglehold over their lives.

(Abby Higgisson, personal email correspondence, October 11, 2007)

Conclusions

In this chapter we have proposed that the delineation of an alternative, anti-a/b moral framework (coupled with a conceptual view of a/b as 'external') allows the sufferer to momentarily step outside of the (im)moral framework of a/b and perceive its effects free from distortions of its rhetoric. From the vantage point of this rival moral viewpoint, it becomes possible to perceive their suffering, which a/b has heretofore been so successful at minimizing, justifying or endowing with virtue, as, in fact, unjust and 'evil'. This 'defrocking' of a/b lays the foundation for the insider to repudiate the nightmare of the anorexic 'dream' and, instead, to dedicate themselves to the reclaiming of their own moral vision and sense of moral agency.

Acknowledgements

The authors wish to express their thanks to the insiders, Julie King and Abby Higgisson, whose commentaries, suffering and wisdom have deeply informed this chapter.

References

Epston, D. (1998) *Catching up with David Epston: A Collection of Narrative Practice-based Papers, 1991–1996*, Adelaide: Dulwich Centre Publications.

Epston, D. (2008) *David Epston: Down Under and Up Over. Travels with Narrative Therapy*, London: Association of Family Therapy.

Epston, D. and White, M. (1992) *Experience, Contradiction, Narrative and Imagination*, Adelaide: Dulwich Centre Publications.

Foucault, M. (1980) *Power/Knowledge: Selected Interviews and Other Writings*, New York: Pantheon Books.

Frank, A. (2004) Moral non-fiction: life writing and children's disability, in P.J. Eakin (ed.), *The Ethics of Life Writing*, Ithaca, NY: Cornell University Press, pp. 174–194.

Freeman, J., Epston, D. and Lobovits, D. (1997) *Playful Approaches to Serious Problems: Narrative Therapy with Children and their Families*, New York: Norton.

Kleinman, A. (1995) Suffering and its professional transformation, in *Writing at the Margin: Discourse Between Anthropology and Medicine*, Berkeley: University of California Press, pp. 98–119.

Lindemann Nelson, H. (2001) *Damaged Identies: Narrative Repair*, Ithaca, NY: Cornell University Press.

Lock, A., Epston, D. and Maisel, R. (2004) Countering that which is called anorexia, *Narrative Inquiry*, 14(2): 275–302.

Lock, A., Epston, D., Maisel, R. and de Faria, N. (2005) Resisting anorexia/bulimia: Foucauldian perspectives in narrative therapy, *British Journal of Guidance and Counselling*, 33(3): 315–332.

Maisel, R., Epston, D. and Borden, A. (2004) *Biting the Hand That Starves You: Inspiring Resistance to Anorexia/Bulimia*, New York: Norton.

Monk, G., Winslade, J., Crocket, K. and Epston, D. (eds) (1997) *Narrative Therapy in Action: The Archaeology of Hope*, San Francisco, CA: Jossey Bass.

Pia Lara, M. (2007) *Narrating Evil: A Postmetaphysical Theory of Reflective Judgement*, New York: Columbia University Press.

Scheper-Hughes, N. (1995) The primacy of the ethical: propositions for a militant anthropology, *Current Anthropology*, 36(3): 409–440.

White, M. (1995) *Re-authoring Lives: Interviews and Essays*, Adelaide: Dulwich Centre Publications.

White, M. (1997) *Narratives of Therapists' Lives*, Adelaide: Dulwich Centre Publications.

White, M. (2000) *Reflections on Narrative Practice*, Adelaide: Dulwich Centre Publications.

White, M. (2004) *Narrative Practice and Exotic Lives*, Adelaide: Dulwich Centre Publications.

White, M. (2007) *Maps of Narrative Practice*, New York: Norton.

White, M. and Epston, D. (1990) *Narrative Means to Therapeutic Ends*, New York: Norton.

White, M. and Morgan, A. (2006) *Narrative Therapy with Children and their Families*, Adelaide: Dulwich Centre Publications.

19   Feminisms in practice

Challenges and opportunities for an eating issues community agency

Maree Burns, Jane Tyrer and the Eating Difficulties Education Network (EDEN)

Late in the afternoon in 2000 at a secondary school in Aotearoa[1] New Zealand 30 young women are seated at desks awaiting a one-hour presentation on eating issues. Two presenters from EDEN (a local, community eating difficulties agency) have been recruited to deliver the requisite 'talk' about eating disorders. Teachers are busy with year-end commitments and there is a sense that students are filling in time until the long summer holidays. EDEN's session visits topics such as the continuum of eating issues, the influence of socio-cultural factors, and ways for individuals to build resilience against toxic messages. There is a general feeling of reluctance and disengagement and one young woman shouts to a bigger classmate across the room 'you don't need to listen to this, it doesn't apply to you!' The session limps to its conclusion and as the students are filing out one approaches a facilitator in tears with concerns about her own eating issue. In the discussion that follows she discloses her experiences within the school and at home. These include breaches of confidentiality with school counselling staff, teachers role-modelling dieting, a school environment where weight teasing is prevalent and unchallenged, and a family context in which appearance and body shape are prioritised.

Introduction

The above encounter reflects common ways of working in schools in westernised cultures, where 'education' about disordered eating is delivered in de-contextualised and potentially individualising ways. Such interventions (no longer practised in this way by the Eating Difficulties Education Network (EDEN)) are informed by well-intentioned notions that delivering health education will generate greater awareness resulting in an eventual shift in individual (health-related, and in this case, eating dis/ordered) behaviour. But EDEN's experience in this and other schools – combined with a developing appreciation of critical feminist and socio-cultural models

---

1 Aotearoa is a Maori term for New Zealand. Maori are the indigenous people of Aotearoa.

of eating issues – has highlighted the necessity of moving beyond this didactic approach. As this vignette exemplifies, there is an overriding tension between postmodern, feminist conceptualisations of eating dis/orders, as socio-culturally contextualised, gendered and discursively constituted phenomena and a focus on imparting information to students in the hope of generating individual change, as if this were something distinct from the contexts in which those phenomena are constituted and in which young women are immersed. This chapter will therefore highlight some of the ways in which EDEN's work engages with a conceptualisation of disordered eating not as individual psychopathology but as 'culturally embedded, complex and heterogeneous collectivities of discursively constituted subjectivities, experiences and body management practices' (Nasser and Malson, this volume: 74).

We will begin by tracing the history of EDEN's development and its philosophies. Following a consideration of the so-called obesity epidemic and its impact upon socio-cultural norms and values regarding weight and shape, the chapter will focus upon some examples from EDEN's work that illustrate how the agency is attempting to operationalise critical, feminist conceptualisations of dis/ordered eating. Finally, given the not insignificant challenges posed by this approach, we will conclude with a discussion of some of the tensions and dilemmas that this raises. It is important to situate our discussion and highlight that this chapter is unavoidably shaped by our own positionings as (among others) middle-class, Pakeha,[2] feminist women. Jane has a 15-year history of working in the community providing services to women with eating difficulties and has recently completed a graduate diploma in counselling alongside a part-time role at EDEN. Maree has a PhD in psychology and publishes critical, feminist analyses of disordered eating alongside a full-time coordination position at EDEN and has recently completed a graduate diploma in counselling.

EDEN's history

EDEN is a small, not for profit, feminist, community agency in Auckland, Aotearoa New Zealand, providing services to individuals with eating issues, and working in communities in health promoting ways (see www.eden. org.nz). The service offers individuals face-to-face appointments, information, counselling, support groups, referral and library use, as well as providing to the community a school health promotion programme, and education and training for health professionals. EDEN's genesis in the early 1990s took place, in part, as a response to existing clinical services for eating disorders operating within the dominant biomedical paradigm that located psychopathology within individual women and which paid little

2 Pakeha is a Maori term for non-Maori New Zealanders of Western European descent.

attention to the gendered and socio-cultural nature of these problems. From its inception as a small, grass roots, community-based, feminist collective (funded by philanthropic trusts and donations), EDEN has struggled for legitimacy in the eyes of those who adhere to the dominant, biomedical and psychological model of disordered eating, including those responsible for government funding, and other clinical service providers in Aotearoa New Zealand.

At the outset, the feminist-identified founders of EDEN sought to provide another option for those diagnosed with an eating disorder and those with eating and body image difficulties who did not meet diagnostic criteria. Founding principles included a commitment to increasing choice of support options, recognising the central role of socio-cultural contexts, prioritising gender as a key consideration, locating support within the community, lobbying for social change with regard to gendered expectations, working in ways that empower women and incorporating a view of disordered eating as existing on a continuum with, for example, dieting and body dissatisfaction. Although EDEN's approach recognised the particular (oppressive) pressures on women in westernised and patriarchal cultures and the hegemonic nature of the slender ideal (e.g. Chernin, 1981; Orbach, 1978, 1986; Wolf, 1990), there was nevertheless an affinity with the notion that illness would manifest for (some) vulnerable girls and women with risk factors such as perfectionism, low self-esteem, experience of sexual abuse and dysfunctional family relationships.

In this regard, EDEN's philosophies at its inception mirrored the theorising of feminist academics and clinicians whereby women's eating distress was conceptualised as resulting from a combination of societal prescriptions of thinness, struggles with contradictory expectations of femininity and experiences of victimisation (e.g. Bloom et al., 1994; Brown and Jasper, 1993; Fallon et al., 1994). Over the last ten years, alongside shifts in academic feminism's theorising about disordered eating and the rise of postmodern understandings (e.g. Bordo, 1993; Burns, 2004; Burns and Gavey, 2004; Malson, 1998; Robertson, 1992), EDEN's theoretical commitments also began to evolve and today EDEN finds its philosophies reflected in a growing body of critical, feminist academic work. Rather than conceptualising eating issues as pathological responses to patriarchal pressures or as internalisations of the thin ideal, EDEN increasingly sees disordered eating as a discursively constituted range of practices, subjectivities and experiences that are expressive of a multiplicity of gender-specific cultural norms and values (see, e.g., Eckermann, Guilfoyle, both this volume).

This reconfiguring of eating issues necessitated EDEN's reconsideration of its primary focus on supporting and educating *individuals*. In practice, this meant developing two overlapping areas of service provision – working to support individuals with eating and body image difficulties *and* working with/in communities to promote social change. Rather than seeing these two areas as distinct, the key shift has been to recognise that individuals (their subjectivities, practices, experiences and embodiment) are not so much 'influenced' by their socio-cultural environments as they are actually (multiply) constituted within and by the particular discursive contexts within which they are embedded (Bordo, 1993; McNay, 1992; Weedon, 1987). Ethically, therefore, EDEN felt compelled to develop some congruence between working with people to support change in terms of their problematised or disordered eating and, at the socio-cultural level, to promote (arguably) more health-enhancing discourses within the contexts of, for example, families, schools and workplaces.

The implications of this theoretical shift are many and varied, and we will touch upon only a few examples that exemplify EDEN's commitment to working with individuals and communities in ways which take into account the meaning systems or discursive matrices operating at these levels. Before discussing these examples, however, it is important to consider what has become an almost ubiquitous backdrop to current discussions about weight, size, body management and eating/not eating in westernised cultures: the so-called obesity epidemic. We have selected obesity discourse as one particular (and itself multiple) instantiation from a whole variety of cultural 'imperatives' of gendered body management not because it is somehow *more* influential but because it is a current and potent example of the contradictory, gendered, culturally specific discourses that are imbricated in the shaping of eating dis/ordered (including fat, thin, dieting, 'anorexic', 'bulimic') bodies, identities, experiences and practices in the twenty-first century (see Riley et al., 2008).

The 'obesity epidemic' and the context of feminist interventions for dis/ordered eating

There can be little doubt that the current global trend in medical research, public health and lay discourse is to construct 'obesity',[3] weight gain and fatness more generally, as a health problem of epidemic proportions (see also Gard, Rice, Probyn, Throsby, LeBesco, all this volume). Over the last decade and hand in hand with this medicalisation of non-slender bodies has been an intensification of the western cultural aesthetic preference for slender (female) bodies. Within this climate, representations of health increasingly depend upon the embodiment of muscularly toned slenderness. This *image* of health (as slenderness) is meaningful beyond its signification of health: regardless of any *actual experience* of wellbeing, it indicates that care has been taken and effort expended. Conversely, fatness (in most westernised cultures) signifies laziness, weakness, unrestrained desire and deviance. The

---

3 EDEN uses scare quotes around the word 'obesity' to problematise the pejorative implications and the pathologisation of large bodies that this medical term achieves.

biomedical construction of fatness as unhealthy therefore feeds into cultural values about personal, moral responsibilities to maintain health and avoid illness (Lupton, 1995). These values are also profoundly gendered, with a standard of slimness for women already strongly entrenched in the western cultural requirements of femininity and heterosexual attractiveness (Bartky, 1988; Bordo, 1993).

Crucially for EDEN's work, within this gendered standard, the conception of what *is* an overweight body, and therefore of who 'needs' to contemplate 'slimming', is so broad that it includes the majority of female bodies. Obesity rhetoric and fat 'phobia' show up in EDEN's work in numerous ways, presenting challenges across all levels of service provision, including support work with women who express body dissatisfaction, who starve, binge eat, purge, diet and over-exercise. Commensurate with current ideas about 'healthy' body management, clients who contact EDEN often understand their weight to be under voluntary control and report something of a moral imperative to exercise this control (see also Throsby, this volume). Furthermore, combined with the cultural abhorrence of fat, this imperative positions big women in particular as health 'pariahs' and mandates weight loss practices for their 'wellbeing', thus potentially legitimising harmful dieting behaviours and contributing to dissatisfaction with a body that sits outside of 'healthy weight' norms. And, as argued elsewhere (Burns and Gavey, 2004), notions of 'healthy weight' may also shape the experiences, practices and identities of women who could be described as 'bulimic' and not 'overweight' by medicalised standards. Critical feminist analyses of obesity rhetoric and 'healthy weight' discourses thus support EDEN's work with women of *all* sizes, facilitating recognition of these incredibly potent gendered discourses of body size and body management.

Given EDEN's commitment to work in ways that recognise that individuals are located and configured within socio-cultural discursive contexts, how do we wrestle with 'healthy weight' discourses that infuse the experiences, practices and identities of EDEN clients and how do we offer alternative discourses at a community level? One way that EDEN is supported in this task is by working within a Health at Every Size Approach (www.jonrobison.net/FDNH/INDEX.HTM). The main tenets of this somewhat marginalised paradigm (see also LeBesco, this volume) are to promote body satisfaction and celebrate diversity in body size, to endorse eating a wide range of foods in response to hunger/fullness and to encourage enjoyable, sustainable physical activity. The approach also considers that countering the reductionist focus on weight as the primary determinant of health is (more) likely to promote health and wellbeing for people across the so-called weight/dis/ordered eating continuum. As such, it is an approach that can also be utilised in educational and health promotion initiatives at both the community/public health levels *and* with individuals. With regard to the latter, acknowledging the potentially negative and wellbeing-compromising ways in which discourses of 'healthy weight' construct differently sized bodies, inform subjectivity and mobilise harmful weight management practices, is vital. It provides the impetus to deconstruct notions of and practices associated with 'healthy weight' and to work with clients to consider alternative subject positions and discourses of size and embodiment that may indeed be more wellbeing-enhancing (see also Guilfoyle, Epston and Maisel, both this volume).

Commensurate with EDEN's commitment to environmental social change and to proffering alternative discourses at a more public level, the agency has also been involved with lobbying government and seeking consultation with various powerful health promotion agencies to promote less reductionist understandings of health that are not linked to weight. Once again, this commitment acknowledges the limitations of working with individuals around 'size acceptance' and eating disorder 'recovery' given dominant societal meaning systems that tend to pathologise fat and weight-gaining bodies and which promote weight loss practices.

The politics of self-referral

Correspondent with its aim of being accountable and accessible to the community in which it is located and to the women it serves, EDEN has always had a self-referral policy whereby individuals are welcomed into the service if *they* have identified an eating or body image issue for themselves. This policy also extends to carers, partners or family members who are concerned about a loved one with an eating difficulty and who are seeking support and information. Rather than gate-keeping access to EDEN's individual services or demanding compliance to a particular 'treatment regime', EDEN encourages individuals to identify and name their own 'troubled' eating experiences and seek support/information when they are ready to do so. This policy also provides space and access for those whose issues would not meet a diagnosis of, for example, anorexia or bulimia and who would therefore be unlikely to be eligible for publicly funded (and clinically orientated) eating disorder services. And, whilst the diagnostic categories of Eating Disorder Not Otherwise Specified and, imminently, of Binge Eating Disorder in the *Diagnostic and Statistical Manual of Mental Illness*, entail inherently problematic assumptions, it is pertinent that these 'problems' suggest levels of distress associated with what has been labelled 'subclinical' disordered eating similar to those diagnosed with anorexia or bulimia (Turner and Bryant-Waugh, 2004). This supports EDEN's self-referral policy and brings into question the application of strict entry criteria to services based upon clinical diagnosis. It troubles the distinction between pathologised and more 'normative' forms of 'disordered' eating: a disruption that is achieved by EDEN's open-door policy and is communicated in community statements issued via EDEN's website, brochures and other public relations communications.

Therapeutic modality

As other chapters (Guilfoyle, Epston and Maisel, Treadgold et al., Gremillion) in this volume discuss, narrative and collaborative therapy approaches are usefully deployed in relation to disordered eating problems and EDEN has recently been using these approaches with clients. With its ability to incorporate issues of gender, power and the central role of language as meaning-making and action-orientated, narrative therapy is able to explore dis/ordered eating problems within the socio-cultural contexts within which they arise. Thus, eating difficulties are reframed not as illnesses but as collections of practices and identities that are mobilised by the gendered, racialised, and classed relations of power within clients' milieu. Within westernised cultures, for example, narrative therapy can consider dis/ordered eating practices and identities (potentially) as distillations of many of the culturally normative gendered values of capitalism, including competition, perfectionism, individualism, idealised feminine beauty, self-control and discipline, among others. Feminist narrative therapy approaches, with their emphasis on externalising problems (Epston and Maisel, this volume), are also radically non-pathologising, which is important when working with people (especially women) with eating issues, who often feel ashamed, blamed, isolated and defective (see Guilfoyle, this volume). Within these approaches the post-structuralist ideas underpinning notions of the self as located and multiply constituted in discourse provide a non-blaming way of understanding identities associated with, and practices of, for example, restriction, self-starving, binge eating (Surgenor et al., 2003). Furthermore, and overlapping with feminist goals (Gremillion, 2004), narrative therapy views the person with the problem (rather than the therapist) as the expert in their own life and therefore works with clients' knowledges, resources, hopes and preferred realities rather than prescribing and imposing these as traditional psychological interventions can do (see also Saukko, Epston and Maisel, Moulding, Treadgold et al., all this volume).

Holistic approaches to working in schools

As illustrated at the start of this chapter and according to research evidence focusing on eating disorder prevention (see Levine and Smolak, 2006), an individually-based focus (or classroom-based focus) to eating and body image difficulties can be limited (and may even be iatrogenic) where it fails to address dominant meanings, discourses and practices within the school environment (Piran, 2005). As we have argued from a critical, feminist perspective, 'requesting' individual change is potentially unrealistic when tackling body and eating issues, given these are constituted by the meanings circulating within socio-cultural environments. This belief informs EDEN's Bodyimage Wellbeing In Schools Education (BWISE) whole-school approach, which was developed in response to experiences such as that outlined in the opening vignette. It acknowledges that schools are communities where gendered norms and values about body size are (re)produced and embodied at all levels (e.g. peer group norms, curricula, teacher role-modelling, school policy, etc.) shaping subjectivity, dietary and body management practices for their members (see also Piran, 1999; Rich and Evans, 2008).

In the opening vignette there is an incident of weight teasing where a student loudly comments on the body size of a classmate; there are teachers inadvertently role-modelling weight loss practices and there is very little (if any) sense in which norms and values about bodies/selves is a school-wide concern impacting the embodied subjectivity of every constituent. EDEN's programme targets the school culture as a whole, focusing on peer leadership, staff training, parent education, curriculum input, policy development and strengthening community and referral pathways. To provide a taste of how BWISE acknowledges the centrality of context, consider the peer leadership stream. This component provides training and support for groups of students interested in becoming Body Image Leaders, who are encouraged to act as peer mentors who role-model critical thinking to their peers regarding the conflicting messages received about bodies and appetites, the unacceptability of bullying and weight teasing, the dangers of dieting and the importance of diversity and critical thinking. Body Image Leaders have opportunities to provide education to other students, producing information resources and giving presentations and workshops in class and assemblies. They act as critical observers of their environments and provide feedback to EDEN staff and to the school community about changes that they would like to see within their school that would promote body satisfaction. As such, they are agents of social change within their school, embodying and role-modelling alternatives to their peers. The combined six streams of the whole-school approach thus supports the development of school environments where discourses of embodiment, weight and body management do not reproduce the particularly toxic and pervasive meanings of slenderness exemplified via, for example, discourses of feminine restraint, perfectionism, obesity prevention or 'healthy weight'.

Tensions

As a feminist community agency, EDEN's self-referral policy is a freedom from inflexible clinical pathways and assessment and diagnostic procedures, which brings with it some dilemmas. These include difficulties with demonstrating the effectiveness of EDEN's work with individuals in a context where dominant biomedical/clinical perspectives generally measure effectiveness using statistics on, for example, BMI, diagnosis, duration of illness, 'comorbidities' and 'psychological outcomes'. Given that these measures usually form the basis upon which service efficacy is demonstrated and funding is allocated, EDEN's position outside of the accepted framework has consequences for legitimacy, funding and professional networking – despite overwhelmingly positive feedback from EDEN clients about their involvement with the agency. Relatedly, while narrative and postmodern approaches appear promising (see Weber, 2007; Weber et al., 2006; see also Treadgold et al., Epston and Maisel, Gremillion, all this volume) and are generating interest within the clinical literatures (e.g. Surgenor et al., 2003), they have not (yet) been systematically evaluated and therefore do not enjoy the legitimacy of mainstream approaches such as cognitive behavioural therapy. Hence, EDEN technically does not have an 'evidence base' from which to work using narrative approaches.

A further tension for our small, alternative and under-resourced agency, and one that further undermines service recognition, funding and development opportunities, is a misunderstanding of EDEN's critique of 'obesity epidemic' rhetoric and of fat 'phobia' more broadly. This is a viewpoint considered by some as almost heretical. When huge social marketing campaigns, health budgets and commercial interests are directed at encouraging people to control or lose weight, EDEN's message is often misconstrued as one that promotes overeating or 'unhealthy' lifestyles. This has never been EDEN's aim. Rather, we are concerned by the 'fat kills' message and the ways that this intersects with other salient (and gendered) weight norms to shape subjectivity and support body management and weight loss imperatives. EDEN seeks, instead, to provide a range of ideas about embodiment, including possibilities about *how* to eat and live actively (according to alternative body trust principles) rather than *what* to eat (according to mechanistic instructions about good and bad food and 'standardised' levels of cardiovascular exercise). This misrepresentation of EDEN and its work impacts on the agency's ability to build useful partnerships with other public health agencies whose work focuses on nutrition, exercise and weight (obesity) management.

Finally, working within EDEN's whole-school approach on an issue that has traditionally been regarded as a problem for particular individuals/ students rather than the whole-school community, brings with it a host of challenges. Indeed, when dis/ordered eating is reconfigured as practices/ identities that are (re)produced within communities, there is a commensurate pressure for that community to examine itself and to be accountable for the norms operating there. With its school programme, EDEN is asking schools to find ways to promote alternative meanings around body size, shape and health across all levels of practice and interaction. Of course, there are considerable pressures on schools to maintain a particular reputation – to 'look good' – and this may be at odds with schools taking responsibility for their role in the (re)production of messages/discourses that may (unintentionally) be supportive of dis/ordered eating. For these schools, identifying and intervening with individual 'vulnerable' students can therefore remain the preferred *modus operandi*.

A further dilemma in schools is that EDEN may inadvertently contribute to confusion for young people by promoting ideas that may be at odds with family, peer, sport and health ideals around body size and weight. Indeed, the 'reality' for some young people (girls and women in particular) is that it may be 'easier' in some ways to maintain a smaller body through disordered eating practices than to have a bigger body which attracts appearance commentaries, weight teasing and harassment (see Rice, this volume). Hence, it is important to work with students and staff to promote understanding of their own roles in potentially transmitting culturally salient values around body size and body management. What EDEN encourages is an awareness of the possibilities that exist for each person as a part of a larger community for embodying and promoting alternative ideas about weight, appearance and personhood.

Conclusions

Although there are many other aspects of EDEN's work that could have usefully been incorporated into this chapter, we hope that the above examples provide a thought-provoking introduction to EDEN's approach to critical interventions in this field. Our intention has been to illustrate the usefulness – and some of the challenges – of critical feminist approaches for working with dis/ordered eating at individual and social change levels. One of the main messages we have sought to emphasise here is that understanding people (their identities and practices) as constituted within and by the socio-cultural (discursive) contexts in which they are embedded requires a commitment *at the same time* to work towards 'mainstreaming' alternative and subjugated knowledges about embodiment, weight and gender. Indeed, it is impossible to work effectively with people or at a social change level without a paradigm that disrupts the dominant gendered power relations that circulate within westernised cultures. Above all, this is a hopeful and compassionate approach to dis/ordered eating that acknowledges that other options are possible. It depathologises and deindividualises what have become 'normative' but simultaneously 'problematised' body management practices for large numbers of women and girls. Importantly, it seeks to promote alternative discourses of gender which are less infused with restrictive ideals for selves and bodies, and are more open to the myriad possibilities that exist for identity, selfhood, embodiment and behaviour.

References

Bartky, S.L. (1988) Foucault, femininity and the modernisation of patriarchal power, in I. Diamond and L. Quinby (eds), *Feminism and Foucault: Reflections on Resistance*, Boston, MA: Northeastern University Press, pp. 61–86.

Bloom, C., Gitter, A., Guttwill, S., Kogel, L. and Zaphiropoulos, L. (1994) *Eating Problems: A Feminist Psychoanalytic Treatment Model*, New York: Basic Books.

Bordo, S. (1993) *Unbearable Weight: Feminism, Western Culture and the Body*, Berkeley: University of California Press.

Brown, C. and Jasper, K. (1993) *Consuming Passions: Feminist Approaches to Weight Preoccupation and Eating Disorders*, Toronto, Canada: Second Story Press.

Burns, M. (2004) Eating like an ox: femininity and dualistic constructions of bulimia and anorexia, *Feminism and Psychology*, 14(2): 269–296.

Burns, M. and Gavey, N. (2004) Healthy weight at what cost? Bulimia and a discourse of weight control, *Journal of Health Psychology*, 9(4): 549–565.

Chernin, K. (1981) *The Obsession: Reflections of the Tyranny of Slenderness*, New York: Harper and Row.

Fallon, P., Katzman M.A. and Wooley, S.C. (eds.) (1994) *Feminist Perspectives on Eating Disorders*, New York: Guilford Press.

Gremillion, H. (2004) Unpacking essentialisms in therapy: lessons for feminist approaches from narrative work, *Journal of Constructivist Psychology*, 17: 173–200.

Levine, M.P. and Smolak, L. (2006) *The Prevention of Eating Problems and Eating Disorders: Theory, Research and Practice*, London: Lawrence Erlbaum.

Lupton, D. (1995) *The Imperative of Health: Public Health and the Regulated Body*, London: Sage.

Malson, H. (1998) *The Thin Woman: Feminism, Poststructuralism and the Social Psychology of Anorexia Nervosa*, London: Routledge.

McNay, L. (1992) *Foucault and Feminism: Power, Gender and the Self*, Oxford: Blackwell.

Orbach, S. (1978) *Fat is a Feminist Issue*, New York: Paddington Books.

Orbach, S. (1986) *Hunger Strike: The Anorectic Struggle as a Metaphor for Our Age*, New York: Norton.

Piran, N. (1999) The reduction of preoccupation with body weight and shape in schools: a feminist approach, in N. Piran, M.P. Levine and C. Steiner-Adair (eds), *Preventing Eating Disorders: A Handbook of Interventions and Special Challenges*, Philadelphia, PA: Brunner/Mazel, pp. 148–150.

Piran, N. (2005) Prevention of eating disorders: a review of research, *Israeli Journal of Psychiatry*, 42(3): 172–178.

Rich, E. and Evans, J. (2008) Learning to be healthy, dying to be thin: the representation of weight via body perfection codes in schools, in S. Riley, M. Burns, H. Frith, S. Wiggins and P. Markula (eds), *Critical Bodies: Representations, Identities and Practices of Weight and Body Management*, Basingstoke: Palgrave Macmillan, pp. 60–76.

Riley, S., Burns, M., Frith, H., Wiggins, S. and Markula, P. (2008) *Critical Bodies: Representations, Identities and Practices of Weight and Body Management*, Basingstoke: Palgrave Macmillan.

Robertson, M. (1992) *Starving in the Silences: An Exploration of Anorexia Nervosa*, New York: New York University Press.

Surgenor, L.J., Plumridge, E.W. and Horn, J. (2003) Knowing one's self anorexic: implications for therapeutic practice, *International Journal of Eating Disorders*, 33: 22–32.

Turner, H. and Bryant-Waugh, R. (2004) Eating Disorder Not Otherwise Specified (EDNOS): profiles of clients presenting at a community eating disorder service, *European Eating Disorders Review*, 12: 18–26.

Weber, M. (2007) Narrative therapy, 'eating disorders', and assessment: exploring the constraints, dilemmas and opportunities, *International Journal of Narrative Therapy and Community Work*, 2: 63–70.

Weber, M., Davis, K. and McPhie, L. (2006) Narrative therapy, eating disorders and groups: enhancing outcomes in rural NSW, *Australian Social Work*, 59(4): 391–405.

Weedon, C. (1987) *Feminist Practice and Poststructuralist Theory*, Oxford: Blackwell.

Wolf, N. (1990) *The Beauty Myth*, New York: Vintage Books.

20 Rediscovering a daughter

*Richard Treadgold, Ann Treadgold and
Diana Treadgold*

When our daughter fell ill with anorexia, it triggered about three years of a
rollercoaster ride of horrific counselling, worsening physical frailty, deep
soul-searching and the life-saving discovery of an amazing counsellor
before she came free. Starting with 'conventional' psychiatric counselling
that was painful to endure, we found an alternative therapy that was almost
as strange as the conventional had been painful, teaching us a new way of
thinking about Diana and anorexia.

We tell our story to support the search for what opposes anorexia and
what liberates its victims.

In early 1994, Diana, 13, our third child, became vaguely ill and lost her
appetite. Our doctor and a gastro-enterologist found nothing wrong. The
next move was to be counselling, but Diana swallowed a mixture of pills
from the medicine cupboard, luckily none dangerous, then stayed awake all
night drinking coffee, fearing she might die. We took her to the Child and
Family Unit at the children's hospital. Her weight-loss seemed magnified by
her feral mood. She was all sinews and strain, bones and tendons. Her level-
headed, hearty attitude was replaced with fret and worry. During an
interview with a psychiatrist we heard that she was feeling 'unsafe' and
hearing negative voices. How could this have happened?

She was diagnosed with depression and prescribed anti-depressants. She
went to the hospital every day for weeks of counselling and schooling. But
her depression deepened and her lovely smile vanished into a gaunt, wasted
face. A darkness came down on us. There's no other way of saying it.

The doctors wanted to give her ECT (electro-convulsive therapy).
If depression was the problem, ECT could be successful. However, if it
was anorexia, ECT would achieve nothing. Concerned that our daughter's
brain might be 'fried' with no assurance of getting better, we sent her on
holiday with family. Her mood lifted, but she ate little and lost more
weight.

Her return to the hospital after two weeks marked a further slide into
darkness. The head of psychiatry was furious with Ann for 'letting' her lose
more weight. Diana was now too frail, so he had missed 'his' chance for
ECT. How dare he get angry with us, who were trying to help her! Their

diagnosis now was anorexia nervosa. But what did this mean? What should we do? We were referred to the Eating Disorders Unit (EDU).

> Attending the Child and Family Unit during the day, for the first couple of weeks after I was 'TOLD' that I had anorexia, they pretty much left me to my own devices. In the lunchroom, I became 'one of the girls with anorexia' who's not eating. Some of the other anorexic patients taught me how to hide food and throw up (although vomiting never appealed to me) when we went for walks in the hospital grounds. The psychiatrists became more patronising. I felt I had become smaller and less important. No one seemed to understand what I was trying to say. It just got so frustrating, so why waste my breath? I stopped talking to them.
>
> (Diana)

A family meeting with the psychiatrist, Henry, and his female associate at the EDU did not go well. We left feeling confused and intimidated and Diana refused any more counselling. As her parents, we were apparently responsible for her plight, so we agreed to be counselled in her place.

> I was so angry – it seemed so stupid to be talking to Mum and Dad when I was the one who was apparently sick. Although I didn't want to talk to the psychiatrists, I was confused because the lack of attention made me feel completely unimportant.
>
> The only attention I received from the psychiatric team was to be weighed before Mum and Dad's counselling sessions. 'You're getting thinner; I don't know how much longer you've got to live,' they would pronounce. 'We don't know what weight your body will stop at. I mean, you could die at any point.' It wasn't convincing. In my opinion, if he didn't know and I felt fine, there was nothing to worry about.
>
> However, the constant upsets after the counselling session made me feel terrible. The only reason Mum and Dad were there was because of me and it just seemed completely and utterly pointless to make them so upset.
>
> (Diana)

We attended counselling twice a week and felt increasingly uncomfortable. We had assumed that whatever Henry said was right. Yet he started to say and suggest disturbing things. Diana would always be weighed when we went to the EDU. Sometimes we were told we could not discuss her eating because 'anorexia is not about food'. Yet at other times they said: 'What are you doing? You're not feeding her enough; you're killing her.'

How much more abusive could a counsellor get than to accuse clients of killing one of their children? But since we were there to help her, we were opening ourselves to these people and we believed them. It was awful to believe that we were killing her. Shocking. He asked were we prepared to do whatever was necessary to save Diana, intimating that we should force food into her. That evening we restrained her as she kicked, punched, bit and swore. We mashed her boiled vegetables all together through a sieve, jammed her teeth apart with a rubber wedge and poured some of it in. We violated our daughter and we seemed to butcher our ideals and beliefs about caring for our children. We never did it again. Diana now agreed to eat, but refused to feed herself, so Ann had to do it.

> Henry astonishingly claimed to be 'parenting' us, while making demeaning comments like 'mothers are highly overrated'. It was intimated that I had been overprotective, suffered from unrealistic expectations and had demonstrated to my daughters that a woman's life was to first and foremost care for everyone else's needs and that was a bad thing.

> Months of counselling went by. Diana's distress increased as she saw me leave the sessions in tears and heard Richard and me arguing. Almost every day one of us threatened angrily to leave or indeed left the house in a flap because the counselling was a hostile interrogation that drove us apart. Henry uncovered problems in our relationship and practically taunted us with them. Far from helping us, it divided us and made us despair of ever helping Diana.

> Henry claimed that I wasn't being strict enough on Diana. He turned to Richard, challenging him to get more food into her. He added that if Richard couldn't accomplish this task, 'he might as well resign as a parent'. The pressure increased and fights over food reached a new intensity. Diana often ran from the dining room, shutting herself in a room or escaping the house. Richard tried to stop her leaving or carried her home kicking, screaming and biting. Sometimes he had to restrain her from scratching and biting herself.
>
> (Ann)

Forcing her home in full public view, I felt self-conscious and ashamed, but I wasn't going to leave her alone after hearing her express disturbed and suicidal thoughts. Escaping meals meant, to Ann and me, no escape at all, just the closer approach of death. It seemed the exact opposite for Diana: anorexia's spell made the eating seem like death.

The physical exertion of restraining her was nothing compared with the emotional strain. I was dead scared she was going to die from this thing. I was angry at her and anorexia, angry at the abuse she shouted, angry at being in a situation that I so desperately lacked the skills to handle.

After one exhausting incident, I slumped on the sofa. Nothing was working. What on earth could I do? I wept openly. I wanted to be a strong man and I thought the weeping came from weakness. But it came from deep in my heart. I had the obscure feeling something had dissolved that hadn't let me cry until then.

(Richard)

Henry made it clear that sorting out our problems and helping Diana recover was of no particular concern to him. He said: 'This is only a job to me. It's just a way of earning money.' We had to find a more compassionate counsellor. Diana's college guidance counsellor referred us to a therapist she knew called David Epston.

During our first meeting David greeted us warmly and listened to our story. Diana sat quietly staring at the floor, not speaking. He read us stories of victims of anorexia and their parents taken from the archives of the Anti-Anorexia Anti-Bulimia League. We saw we were not alone; that arguments over food, excessive exercise and trickery around eating were everywhere. We learnt that the battle could rage for years, many died and the misery was widespread. To examine and reveal the intrusive nature of the anorexic spell and find ways of breaking free of it, David explained that 'narrative therapy' (see also Epston and Maisel, this volume) aimed to 'externalise' the problem – to separate it from the person. Narrative therapy says that the person is not the problem – the problem is the problem.

When he talked about anorexia, strangely, David would refer to it in the third person. He might ask: 'How does anorexia make you feel unworthy to eat when you want to eat?' He endowed it with motives: 'Do you think anorexia seeks your corpse rather than your well-being?' He compared the rule of anorexia to a concentration camp, with guards, punishments, torture and harsh privations.

This irritated me and I worried about being recruited into a strange ideology. Was this a scientific approach? I wanted my medical professionals in white coats, detached, not friends, but faultless; this cheerful chap in bright cycling shorts did not fit that image.

Yet I came to see that the emotional weight of his descriptions, steeped in the agony of the death camps, actually matched the weight we felt every day, because it mirrored the life-and-death stakes of Diana's struggle with anorexia.

(Richard)

Since Diana didn't want to speak to anybody about anorexia, we agreed that David should teach us narrative therapy. We would then learn how to practise it on Diana. Nobody knew if that would work.

He was completely different from the hospital counsellors. It was like he knew my secret, knew what was going on, but if he knew that, then he could possibly change things and that was a threat. I trusted no one except anorexia.

(Diana)

David encouraged us: 'You formed your own opinion about what was good for you in a situation of desperation. You decided to stop attending the hospital counselling although they told you Diana would deteriorate quickly if you did. It takes strength for anyone to stand up against professional power and knowledge, which is highly sanctioned in our society. But you did it in a respectful way. I remember you telling me that "the hospital counsellors probably meant well, but they didn't realise what a negative effect they were having on us". To some extent you had to really believe in yourself and what you know, to speak against that incredibly powerful institution. You must have been pretty grounded with your own knowing, your own wisdom to do so, and that told me something about you. That you are no pushovers.'

David called his approach 'anti-anorexia'. The anti-anorexic language of narrative therapy let us address anorexia separately from Diana and there was a complete turn-around in our relationship with her.

(Richard)

He asked us questions we had never heard at the EDU. They all implied that we either knew something of value or might soon do so. His inquiries began with phrases like: 'Can you help me understand . . .', 'Can you teach me how . . .', 'Would you be so kind as to assist me with . . .'. David considered us collaborators on a life-or-death project – Diana's anti-anorexia – calling himself a 'co-consultant' with us. We were amazed he honoured us in this way. We felt more powerful. He read to us many pieces of writing from New Zealand and around the world by people either captured by anorexia or helping loved ones who were themselves captured.

Heather-Ann's *Anti-Anorexic Diary*, faxed to us by David, set down the ten 'Rules of the Anorexia Concentration Camp', including:

1 You are not a person, you are only a bodily object which we can weigh, measure or assess at will.
2 You no longer have a mind of your own. We will tell you what to think and how to act.
3 Any protest you make, such as robbing us of your person, we will severely punish. Your punishment will be back-lashings of guilt and self-starvation.
4 We will work you to death and the only time you will be allowed to rest is in your sleep.

8   Your job in life is to die with an anorexic smile on your face.
9   You are never to speak for yourself – you are only to ask questions.

Anorexia demands that its victims prepare food for others, while they themselves must resist eating. Diana baked us a cake. She approached the table and offered Richard a piece. He asked her: 'Are you going to have a piece?' Diana shook her head sadly and said she wouldn't. In an apologetic voice, Richard explained: 'Well, if anorexia is not going to let you eat any cake, then I'm not going to eat it either', and he walked into the kitchen and tipped it into the bin.

Diana looked horrified. 'What are you doing?' she protested angrily. Richard spoke firmly but kindly: 'I can't enjoy eating the cake, when anorexia is not allowing you to enjoy it.' 'What are you going on about, this is nothing to do with anorexia. After all I've done, making a cake for you. I don't know why I bother. You hate me!' she screamed. 'I can't believe you, you're mad. Look, it's me making the cake, ME, not anorexia!' Overwhelmed with frustration and anger, Diana fled sobbing to her bedroom.

> At first I found this anti-anorexic approach upsetting. I was so afraid that Diana believed that we were rejecting her rather than uncovering and confronting anorexia's mistreatment of her. I had understood the principle of addressing anorexia as a separate entity, but to hear such challenging words coming out of my husband's mouth was frightening.
>
> (Ann)

Despite our best intentions we were still expecting certain behaviours of Diana, much as anorexia was doing. We often demanded (unsuccessfully!) that she eat certain types and amounts of food. We also expected her to show some independence and exert some self-control over her anger. Wherever she turned, she faced demands to do certain things or be a certain kind of person. If Diana was to get her life back, she needed to distinguish her own tastes.

We practised conversations that externalised anorexia until they became natural and Diana became accustomed to hearing anorexia described as a destructive influence in her life. For example: 'No, Diana, you haven't put on weight, although I'm not going to pretend I'm not worried. I think if anorexia had its way you would completely disappear. Your body is still dangerously underweight, but I understand your concern about gaining even the tiniest amount. Anorexia just won't let up, will it? You know, to be honest, I'm much more interested in talking about what you want for yourself, what you are interested in and what you enjoy.'

Learning to tell the difference between what was Diana speaking and what was anorexia speaking was vital. We then understood her, she felt she was being heard and anorexia, simply by being identified, had much less power to direct her life. This separation became a revelation. Diana was blameless; anorexia was impersonating her, using her voice for its own purposes. We could oppose anorexia and champion our daughter. Diana could fly into a fit of fury if she gained weight. 'I've gained 100 grams in three days, how the bloody hell could you let this happen to me? You promised you wouldn't! You want to make me fat again! I hate you!'

The challenge for us was to try to surrender our own angry response, to remember it was not Diana's intention to blame us but anorexia's and then find something helpful to say. She was full of fear and anorexia told her that we were sabotaging her efforts. It took a lot of patience to keep reassuring her.

> What you want is important to us. We will support you in anything you want to do. But we will not support anorexia's wishes for you. We trust your ability to make good decisions and care for yourself.

Although we were tempted to keep things nice and sweet, because we were so fearful of provoking an anorexic rage, sometimes expressing anger was unavoidable. Seeing anorexia as separate was a blessing, since we could shout and curse at anorexia freely without blaming Diana.

> I'M SO BLOODY ANGRY AT ANOREXIA!! IT MAKES YOU LASH OUT AT EVERYONE, IT WON'T LET YOU EAT OR FEED YOURSELF, IT MAKES YOU LIE THERE ON THE BED CURLED UP, IT WON'T EVEN LET YOU SPEAK TO US!

Externalising problems also gave us the confidence to confront our own differences. We were more honest with each other. If we were feeling bad, we didn't hide it. Sometimes we even swore. But walking off angrily without resolving grievances became a thing of the past.

David showed us things that we could praise Diana for. Simple, honest statements of praise and admiration changed the atmosphere tangibly. Anorexia's daily drudgery and carping criticism could weigh like a grey burden upon yesterday's moments of freedom, so when we started acknowledging Diana's small victories and moments of resistance, it was like lighting a torch in the great darkness of anorexia.

> Slowly I began to see that anorexia was standing in the way of me achieving some independence in my life. I began to ask questions:
> What do other people do when they realise they have anorexia?
> How do they behave?
> What do they do about food and eating, do they go on a special diet? Do they go into hospital?
> How can I suddenly change something that has ruled my life for a long time?
>
> (Diana)

As our confidence grew to talk to Diana about anorexia's evil intentions for her, anorexia stepped up its campaign to take her life. Suppressing our rising panic, we reminded her constantly that we supported her right to a life of freedom and happiness. We no longer regarded Diana as badly behaved, vain, attention-seeking or controlling. Anorexia was attempting to murder our daughter before our eyes. It no longer seemed like exaggeration to describe anorexia as a murderer or the devil himself. In fact, these terms accurately described what we were facing. We no longer insisted Diana eat, although we did everything we could to encourage her. But Diana was losing the battle against the insistent demands from anorexia.

> Many times I tried to prepare myself a meal and eat it, but the more I longed to break free and do something normal, the louder anorexia became, until all I could hear was it screaming orders and abuse at me day and night.
>
> (Diana)

On the morning of 2 July 1996, Ann rang David in complete despair. Diana was refusing food and even water and our GP was wanting to admit Diana to hospital. For a month or more her attempts had been blocked by the EDU, who, astonishingly, refused to admit her because we had previously declined their services. Our GP managed to circumvent normal procedure and Diana was finally admitted to the children's hospital. Overwhelmed by anorexia and devoid of energy, Diana simply refused any food. We were asked to allow her to be treated under the Mental Health Act, letting the doctors force-feed her through a tube. They said it was the only way to safeguard her life. Our previous experience with the hospital made us sceptical, but we agreed, with the proviso that David continue as her counsellor. The hospital went along with this, which was highly unusual.

But it was a great relief. We knew Diana would not survive unless she got some nutrition, yet the door was still open to continue an anti-anorexic dialogue with her. We believed that, more than the food and medicine, that would be how she would recover her freedom.

Fax from David Epston to Diana 10 July 1996

Dear Diana,

I really admire you for having the courage to do what the doctors are asking of you to secure your life. I bet Anorexia is screaming its head off trying to terrify you. Your mum certainly gave me the impression that you were really acting for Diana on so many occasions. At times, you have had to stand up for what you know and what you believe is right and more often than not you have been right. Do you think

Anorexia is starting to think differently about you? That it just can't kill you off like so many others it has murdered?

. . .

Yours anti-anorexically,
David

Her diary explains some of her struggle to reclaim her life:

Diana's diary: Friday 12 July

8.00am: You know this is a very confusing illness, sometimes it's harder than others. If I have some food and find it easier, I get tormented later for not being more upset. I need help to push all of these thoughts away, but the environment I'm in now with all these different people with aggressive behaviour and natures is not helping.

Some of the hospital restrictions echoed the restrictions of anorexia:

Eating required amount earns toilet privileges and use of bathroom. This is earned from meal to meal.
Four meals a day earns one 10-minute shower.
Eating all meals, i.e. all of food, earns:

-   Outings, i.e. family over the weekend (only sitting in van – no activity or walking around).
-   Make phone calls from nurses' station.
-   Visiting grandmother in hospital, but must be taken in a wheel-chair.

Her diary records her efforts against anorexia:

Diana's diary: Sunday 14 July

I have decided to fight back! I will do anything to get this tube out, but I also need other people to know that I am going to need a lot of help. I am sick and tired of being treated like this by ANOREXIA (but that doesn't mean that it's gone). I just want to go home and be with everyone I love and get my job back!

Diana and I had made a firm decision after she entered hospital that we would never again return to the practice of my feeding her. Anorexia had trapped us in an intolerable routine, and we needed to break free of it. Although I was sometimes present during lunch, I didn't help with the actual feeding. My support lay more, as did Richard's, in derailing anorexia's criticism of Diana. We reassured her that anorexia's threats that 'she would suddenly gain kilos just by eating one meal' or that 'she was a pig just because she was eating' were untrue.

(Ann)

Diana needed us to put an anti-anorexic interpretation on events. One day, Ann found Diana distraught when one of the nurses tried to force her to eat. Ann said:

I'm sorry you're having a difficult day. It must be hard for you when the nurse doesn't understand how upset anorexia makes you when you eat or gain weight. Do you think she understands how loudly anorexia screams at you?

In response, Diana said:

No, I guess she doesn't understand or she wouldn't be so impatient with me. I don't feel that good about throwing food over her, although part of me feels like she deserved it.

'The nurse is probably doing the best she can under the circumstances,' Ann said. 'It's actually anorexia that confuses the situation and stops you having the freedom to feed yourself and eat when you need to. Anorexia is good at making people angry.' One of Diana's greatest allies was Laurel, herself a survivor of anorexia. David Epston had met her in the course of his work and introduced them. Diana sought her advice about how she had dealt with hospitalisation; Laurel responded:

1   To try not to fall into the idea that I had a certain period of time in which I *had* to recover.
2   To realise that anorexia was not a dark part of me, a bad part of myself, but rather something that was affecting me.
3   To take small steps towards health and to realise that each small step was a big step away from anorexia.
4   To be easy on myself.
5   Finding distractions like writing or drawing or other projects that occupied my hands and my mind. To be anti-perfectionistic about these projects.
6   To start to rediscover some of the ideas, talents, interests that had been abandoned while anorexia took over.
7   To realise that recovery is a process that can, and often does, take a long time. To trust that it is worth it. To realise that each person recovers at their own pace.

8 To ask myself: 'What kind of lifestyle do I want? One that is anorexia filled or one that is self-fulfilled?'
9 To recognise that each step I take away from a/b (anorexia/bulimia) is going to make it panic and try harder to draw me back.

Diana read and re-read Laurel's words.

> I felt as though Laurel was speaking directly to me and for the first time in a long time I felt I understood the way forward. Staring out of the hospital window I watched a jogger running in the evening light and longed to be free, to go where I wanted and do what I wanted.
>
> (Diana)

> On Sunday 27 July 1996, Diana rang me: 'Mum, I want to do something anti-anorexic, what shall I do?' Realising that if I told Diana what to do, I would be no different from anorexia, I turned it back to her: 'That's great, what would you like to do?' 'Well, there's some banana cake in the dining room, I might eat a few crumbs.' And she did.

> I visited Diana the next day. Her face looked more relaxed and her eyes had a twinkle that I had not seen for a long time. She asked for some money to buy a packet of potato chips from a vending machine. Normally, a matter of no consequence, but in fact it was a miracle – the spell had been broken. Diana began to eat again and reclaim her life.
>
> (Ann)

Much later, Diana told us that when she left the hospital anorexia made her an offer: 'If things get too tough for you, I'll still be here. You can always return to me.' It promised: 'If you start to put on too much weight, you can just stop eating. It's not a problem. You've done it before, you can do it again.' She explained:

> That's how anorexia convinces you that starving yourself is the most normal thing in the world. Sometimes that offer was tempting. But every time it returned, I would reassess my life and decide to appreciate the good things. I rejected the dark agonies that I now knew were the only things anorexia could deliver. Now there was hope of a better life.

> I am now the mother of three lovely sons, the most recent of whom was born in November 2007. Since I reclaimed my life from anorexia, challenges have been numerous. Re-educating myself, entering the workforce, getting married and the breakdown of the marriage have

tested me. A newer and richer partnership and best of all the joy of motherhood have been my reward.

At eight years old, my sister Emma said: 'Anorexia is the best thing that ever happened to our family. We wouldn't understand as much as we do now if we hadn't gone through this.'

Anorexia is not something I would wish on anyone, but I think that in finding the strength to oppose it, I found a strength of character and a vision of life that I might not otherwise have gained.

(Diana)

Learning to externalise problems has been life-changing. It remains a challenge, as over time it is forgotten and then again rekindled. In practising this, we have found new respect for ourselves and others and courage to persevere against injustice. We want to express our deep admiration for David Epston, who actively practises moral principles most people simply discuss and thus challenges and enriches our vision of life.

We had started with little more than a steely conviction to do whatever it took to save Diana – the rest was unknown to us. Now the worst is over, the future is still unknown, but our life has returned. It's the same as before, yet it's different.

This light, that spreadeth everywhere, such light! Such joy! It changes everything.
This is the Pit! Yet gone
Is fear and ugliness and
Pain.

21 Complexities of power and meaning

A reflection on Parts IV and V

Helen Gremillion

It is a pleasure to write a reflection on these chapters examining 'therapies' as well as community-based interventions for eating dis/orders, understood from constructionist and feminist perspectives. Before I begin, let me situate myself and my work in relation to the topics at hand. I am a middle-class, heterosexual, Euro-American woman whose academic work – informed by gender studies, anthropology, post-structuralist approaches to counseling, and cultural studies – is both a reflection of and a critical response to my location within powerful discourses of identity and belonging that are marked by an ethics of individual achievement, both scholarly and bodily (the latter in terms of health and 'fitness'). To date, an important part of my life's work has been a constructionist and ethnographic analysis of main-stream, hospital-based, 'multidimensional' treatments for anorexia (Gremillion, 2003). I have argued that dominant therapies for and analyses of eating dis/orders in the US (but with relevance elsewhere) participate in socioculturally normalized and historically specific conditions of possibility for these problems (cf. Gremillion, 2008). I have also argued that narrative therapy, which is discussed in three of the chapters included in my reflection here, is a very promising 'alternative' intervention. I am not a therapist, but for some time now I have been developing numerous research and practice collaborations within narrative and collaborative therapy communities, and I have been a participant in many narrative therapy training workshops.

What is most striking to me about these chapters is their similar approach to a critical analysis of power relations and of culturally domin-ant meanings. Each of these chapters describes the sociocultural production of eating dis/orders in terms that problematize familiar dichotomies of power/resistance, culture/individual, and normal/abnormal. None of these authors assume that 'culture' or 'power' writ large (e.g. norms of slender femininity) are reproduced or reflected wholesale at the level of individual experience. As Burns et al. point out, such a conceptualization requires a construct of at least implicitly pathologized, 'vulnerable' individuals (as opposed to those who remain 'healthy' and presumably unaffected by eating difficulties). Instead of subscribing to a top-down understanding of how eating problems are produced and reproduced, these authors identify a range of culturally and institutionally powerful discourses and practices that constitute people's experiences in both hierarchical and contradictory ways. For example, Surtees notes that, as a nurse within an eating disorder hospital unit, she is constantly under pressure to perform a 'healthy' embodiment, in spite of the porous boundaries that separate professionalized and pathologized bodies in her work context. Similarly, Moulding identifies the achieved character of normative psychiatric discourse that positions 'eating disordered patients' as heteronormative 'daughters' in relation to 'fatherly' healthcare practitioners. These examples show that status quo representations of health are fractured and unstable, because they are suffused with, and also themselves create, disavowed relations of power. There are important implications here for how to theorize resistance and change.

As Guilfoyle insists, no one can escape power relations. Constructionist accounts of culture and power have thoroughly problematized utopian claims to positions of exteriority with respect to existing sociocultural conditions (Butler, 1990; Foucault, 1978). As all of these chapters suggest, effective forms of resistance and intervention will therefore not emerge from or occupy a space 'outside' of the status quo (see also Katzman, Foreword to this volume); rather, alternative ways of being must be crafted in an active relationship to normative constructs. Note that these constructs are still seen to be quite powerful and constraining, in spite of their malleability (cf. Gremillion, 2004).

These chapters contain intriguing overlaps and discontinuities when we consider the question of how best to go about reconfiguring the discursive practices that support dis/ordered eating. Epston and Maisel state that their articulation of 'anti-anorexic/bulimic' narrative therapy is a 'radical' form of externalization. At first blush, this approach might appear to recapitulate modernist (non-constructionist) dichotomies of power/resistance and culture/individual. In this form of therapeutic work, anorexia and anti-anorexia are in a polemical struggle of life and death. However, this dichotomized representation is not naturalized as 'truth'; rather, anorexia/bulimia (a/b) is quite deliberately portrayed as 'being' the totalizing and devastating force/voice that is often the manifest *effect* of a/b discursive practice. The point of such polemics is to allow space for a re-authoring of identity in the very midst of deconstructing a/b's often deadly 'tactics'. Several authors – Burns et al.; Epston and Maisel; and Treadgold et al. – identify the moral dimensions of this work, which requires accountable self-positioning on the part of practitioners, as well as ongoing efforts to identify and name the institutional reproduction (and reification) of eating problems in settings such as treatment facilities and schools. In a different vein, but one that similarly acknowledges the discursive reach of eating dis/orders, Guilfoyle and Throsby address the ever-present risk that 'alternative' (or seemingly alternative) experiences and interventions will be folded into or co-opted by status quo representations. Throsby points out that, when people invoke biological arguments in favor of receiving weight loss surgery, they are participating in problematic medicalized claims about the inherent unhealthiness of fat even as they are working to disarm moral judgments about their weight. Guilfoyle writes about the potential for clients in therapy – particularly when they are interacting with others outside the therapy room – to interpret feminist/narrative interventions in ways that can reinforce rather than challenge the problems they face.

It is interesting to compare Epston and Maisel's description of therapy for eating dis/orders with that of Guilfoyle. Both are committed to a feminist and narrative process of helping to re-author identities that are caught up in complex, contradictory and gendered power relations; both argue that the therapist is unavoidably located within the webs of power that constitute a key subject of critical analysis and practice in this kind of work. However, while Epston and Maisel advocate an anti-anorexic thera-peutic stance that they call 'moral witnessing', Guilfoyle suggests that because the therapist cannot avoid his or her own location in shifting 'social antagonisms' (cf. Laclau and Mouffe, 2001), s/he should be wary of trying to occupy or promote any stable 'political' position. These different per-spectives raise some important questions about the particulars of the therapist's agency in people's lives and about her/his (co-)authorship of meaning. Under what conditions might it be appropriate – or vital – for a practitioner to 'take a stand' against problems and/or 'in favor' of alterna-tive identities? How does one conceptualize and situate therapeutic action and intention when the politics of therapeutic intervention – broadly construed as the power-laden contexts for experiencing and interpreting problems and for the re-authorship of identities – are understood to be multi-layered and contradictory?

In spite of a range of possible answers to these questions, the authors of these chapters seem to share the view that constructionist transformations of dis/ordered eating entail purposeful reconfigurations of power relations and cultural meanings. Interventions are never seen as neutral, arbitrary, or unconstrained. Also, importantly, the therapist and client(s) are by no means the only co-authors of reconfigured personhood in this work. Several writers here, including Epston and Maisel (cf. Maisel et al., 2004) and Guilfoyle, agree that the formation of 'alternative' communities of support is necessary for an ongoing deconstruction of problems, as well as an ongoing reconstruction of preferred identities and ways of being. Regarding struggles against anorexia, Treadgold et al. attest to the crucial importance of access to the anti-anorexic stories of other 'insiders'. Burns et al. work directly at a public level (e.g. in schools and with health promotion agen-cies) to 'mainstream' and circulate feminist constructionist understandings of eating problems. Finally, Surtees, Moulding, and Throsby all point to the need for systematic sociocultural changes, given the entrenchment of problematic discourses and practices within (mainstream) healthcare institutions.

One current and problematic discourse/practice within mainstream approaches to treating eating disorders is cognitive-behavioral therapy (CBT), which is not analyzed in these chapters but is important to scrutinize from a feminist constructionist perspective. I here devote a bit of space to this task. CBT is practiced widely, and many professionals consider it to be the 'gold standard' for treating bulimia (Costin, 2007); and yet, CBT routinely occludes the sociocultural and gendered conditions of possibility for eating disorders.

A basic premise of CBT is that symptoms result from

> cognitive distortions . . . such as all-or-nothing thinking, overgeneralizing, assuming, magnifying or minimizing, magical thinking, and personalizing. Such distortions are well recognized in eating disorder clients and influence their behavior. A disturbed and distorted body image, paranoia about all food being fattening, and binges based on the belief that one cookie has already destroyed a perfect day of dieting are common unrealistic assumptions and distortions.
>
> (Costin, 2007: 115)

The goal of treatment is symptom reduction or cessation through cognitive 'restructuring'.

The most striking problem with CBT is that it locates within the thought processes of individuals – deemed 'pathological' – sociocultural discourses that constitute eating problems. In her critique of CBT for anorexia, Burns (2008) writes:

> Given that within Western socio-cultural contexts discourses and representations of the super thin female body and dieting/weight control, are deployed to account for health, beauty, success, femininity, control, achievement and normality, it is possible to understand 'anorexic' cognitions not as distortions or erroneously 'overvalued ideas' but as a seamless continuation of the toxic (but 'real') messages that saturate the lives of young women.

In their reading of such problems as 'cognitive distortions', cognitive-behavioral therapists can be seen to participate (unwittingly) in a profoundly gendered cultural logic of individualism and rational self-control that is arguably constitutive of eating difficulties (Gremillion, 2003), and of problematic constructs within psychology more generally – constructs that have a long history (Gergen, 1995).

A number of studies purport to show that CBT is effective in treatments for bulimia, but these results are contested: 'There are . . . studies surfacing showing that other forms of therapy are as useful as CBT. In fact, the majority of clients with bulimia do not recover with the cognitive behavioral approach' (Costin, 2007: 117). But even if CBT 'works', it is important to consider carefully the meanings and experiences that constitute 'cure'. As Burns points out, 'the cessation of purging activities as a measure of wellness for women with bulimia is based on notions of normativity and functionality, that potentially have little to do with a woman's experience of well-being or her (possibly ongoing) negotiation with cultural messages concerning women's bodies' (Burns, 2004).

CBT is a clear example of a therapeutic practice encoding complex layers of power and meaning which require unpacking. Interestingly, a narrative approach to eating problems might engage in a critical-discursive reading of a client's thoughts that a cognitive-behavioral therapist would see as 'distorted'. But the thoughts in question are not thereby the 'same thoughts'. The issue here is not simply one's perspective. As all the chapters in Parts IV and V of this book show, the particularities of readings and interpretations in therapy (and analyses of therapy) are significantly *constitutive* of clients' – and therapists' – realities (see Zimmerman and Dickerson, 1996). In my view, there is no 'combining' of a narrative and CBT approach; their divergent epistemologies produce quite different lived 'truths'.

On the other hand, there are strong lines of feminist and constructionist thinking that have a shared epistemological basis. I close my reflection with some thoughts about the conditions of possibility for feminist constructionist interventions surrounding eating dis/orders. As someone with a background in feminist and post-structuralist anthropology, I have been tracking for some time the shifting constructs of gender accompanying the 'constructionist turn' that has profoundly shaped a number of fields since the 1980s. Rather than signaling a 'type' of identity or a 'social role', gender is increasingly represented in a range of disciplines as a symbolic and cultural construct that is constitutive of social relationships and hierarchies (cf. Butler, 1990; Elliott, 1998; Flax, 1990; Haraway, 1990; Hare-Mustin and Maracek, 1994; Malson, 1998; Sawicki, 1991; Scott, 1988; Unger, 1990; Yanagisako and Delaney, 1995). In keeping with this shift, Surtees and Moulding show how gender is invoked and performed in the making of both professionalized and pathologized identities. Moulding also addresses the imbrication of gender and heteronormativity; and Burns et al. describe the simultaneously 'gendered, racialized, and classed relations of power' that shape capitalist constructs informing dis/ordered eating. In sum, as a number of these chapters reflect, gender has long been analyzed in constructionist terms that articulate with a range of hierarchizing discursive practices. It is my belief that constructionist feminist approaches to dis/ordered eating are most fruitfully understood as a part of this legacy.

In recent conversations with some therapists who are interested in developing a feminist constructionist practice, I have noticed a tendency to dichotomize (and a stated desire to 'combine') extant 'feminist' and 'constructionist' therapies. As Moulding suggests, some post-structuralist thinkers (e.g. Michel Foucault) have rightfully been taken to task for failing to theorize gender; also, as Guilfoyle (p. 198) points out, there is 'no singular "feminist therapy" for eating disorders' (certainly not all contemporary feminist therapies are constructionist or consider multiple axes of identity). However, in my view, it is problematic to describe 'feminist' and 'constructionist'/post-structuralist/narrative/discursive approaches to therapy as necessarily following different trajectories. Such a representation runs the risk of generalizing and simplifying both sides. The chapters I have discussed in this book reveal an already-established history of feminist constructionism that holds great promise for unraveling and reconstructing the sociocultural conditions of eating dis/orders in all their complexity.

References

Burns, M. (2004) Constructing bulimia: implications for subjectivity and practice, unpublished doctoral thesis, University of Auckland, New Zealand.

Burns, M. (2008) Constructing anorexia and its causes, unpublished manuscript.

Butler, J. (1990) *Gender Trouble: Feminism and the Subversion of Identity*, New York: Routledge.

Costin, C. (2007) *The Eating Disorder Sourcebook: A Comprehensive Guide to the Causes, Treatments, and Prevention of Eating Disorders*, 3rd edition, New York: McGraw-Hill.

Elliott, H. (1998) En-gendering distinctions, in S. Madigan and I. Law (eds), *Praxis: Situating Discourse, Feminism and Politics in Narrative Therapies*, Vancouver: Yaletown Family Therapy.

Flax, J. (1990) *Thinking Fragments: Psychoanalysis, Feminism, and Postmodernism in the Contemporary West*, Berkeley: University of California Press.

Foucault, M. (1978) *The History of Sexuality, Volume 1: An Introduction*, New York: Vintage Books.

Gergen, M. (1995) Postmodern, post-Cartesian positionings on the subject of psychology, *Theory and Psychology*, 5(3): 361–368.

Gremillion, H. (2003) *Feeding Anorexia: Gender and Power at a Treatment Center*, Durham, NC: Duke University Press.

Gremillion, H. (2004) Unpacking essentialisms in therapy: lessons for feminist approaches from narrative work, *Journal of Constructivist Psychology*, 17: 173–200.

Gremillion, H. (2008) The race and class politics of anorexia nervosa: unravelling white, middle-class standards in representations of eating problems, in P. Moss and K. Teghtsoonian (eds), *Contesting Illness: Processes and Practices*, Toronto: University of Toronto Press, pp. 218–238.

Haraway, D. (1990) *Simians, Cyborgs, and Women: The Reinvention of Nature*, New York: Routledge.

Hare-Mustin, R. and Marecek, J. (1994) Gender and the meaning of difference: postmodernism and psychology, in A.C. Hermann and A.J. Stewart (eds), *Theorizing Feminism: Parallel Trends in the Humanities and Social Sciences*, Boulder, CO: Westview Press.

Laclau, E. and Mouffe, C. (2001) *Hegemony and Socialist Strategy: Towards a Radical Democratic Politics*, 2nd edition, New York: Verso.

Maisel, R., Epston, D. and Borden, A. (2004) *Biting the Hand that Starves You: Inspiring Resistance to Anorexia/bulimia*, New York: Norton.

Malson, H. (1998) *The Thin Woman: Feminism, Post-structuralism and the Social Psychology of Anorexia Nervosa*, New York: Routledge.

Sawicki, J. (1991) *Disciplining Foucault: Feminism, Power and the Body*, New York: Routledge.

Scott, J. (1988) *Gender and the Politics of History*, New York: Columbia University Press.

Unger, R.K. (1990) Imperfect reflections of reality: psychology constructs gender, in R. Hare-Mustin and J. Marecek (eds), *Making a Difference: Psychology and the Construction of Gender*, New Haven, CT: Yale University Press.

Yanagisako, S. and Delaney, C. (eds) (1995) *Naturalizing Power: Essays in Feminist Cultural Analysis*, New York: Routledge.

Zimmerman, J. and Dickerson, V. (1996) *If Problems Talked: Narrative Therapy in Action*, New York: Guilford Press.

Index

Aboriginal Australians 119
acculturation 79, 82
advertising 18, 39, 55, 115, 185, 186
AIDS 16, 52
Alexander, Stephanie 121
anorexia (nervosa) 1, 3, 10, 11–12, 14,
   16–17, 27, 29–31, 47, 63, 65–71, 92,
   114, 125, 131–2, 146–9, 152, 162, 173,
   175–81, 199, 201, 210, 213–19, 224,
   226, 233–44, 245–6; benefits of 87;
   counter-morality of 210, 211–12,
   215–17; diagnostic criteria for 186;
   and ethnicity 47, 54, 81–2; and
   genetics 54, 135; 'holy' 91; and
   language 12–13, 213–15; as lifestyle
   choice 88; morality of 210–11,
   217–19; panics over 122, 185;
   personification of 215–18, 236–43;
   and social class 31, 54; theories of 64,
   66, 74–5, 78, 114, 126, 136–42, 176,
   185
anorexic *femme fatale* 177–80
anorexic *fille d'Eve* 178–80
anorexic *ingénue* 175–7, 180
'anorexic paradigm' 48, 50
anthropology 218, 245, 249
'anti-anorexia' 237, 247
Anti-Anorexia Anti-Bulimia League
   236
Aotearoa *see* New Zealand
Attwood, Margaret 29
Australia 51, 113–14, 119, 121, 173,
   212

Bakhtin, Mikhail 69–71
Bangladesh 25
Barbie 54
Beckham, Victoria 135
behaviourism 160

Benincasa, Catherine (St Catherine of
   Siena) 27
Berry, Halle 55
'Big Food' 41
binge eating disorder 226
binge-purging 15, 16, 18, 28, 31, 46, 48,
   90, 92, 94, 131, 133, 146, 225, 249
biomedicalization 17, 39, 150–1, 153,
   160, 222–3, 225, 228
blogs 10, 117
Blue Dragonfly 87
body (as) image 114, 133, 136, 140, 143,
   164, 167; in Africa 52–3; of black
   women 48–9; disorders of 57;
   problems with 28, 46–54, 75, 88,
   140
body as inscribed surface 5, 124–5, 129,
   133, 138–41, 143
'body image distortion syndrome' 46,
   48
Bodyimage Wellbeing In Schools
   Education (BWISE) 227
body management 1–2, 74, 79, 90,
   124–5, 129–30, 132–3, 136–8, 146,
   166, 187, 222, 224–5, 228–30;
   pathologised 74, 127, 180
Bruch, Hilde 11, 28, 29, 63–7, 69, 151–2
Buddhism 80
bulimia (nervosa) 1, 3, 11–12, 16, 27, 28,
   30–1, 48, 74–5, 78, 82, 92, 124, 127–8,
   131–2, 136–9, 146–9, 162, 173,
   179–80, 210, 213–19, 224, 226, 246,
   248; benefits of 87; counter-morality
   of 210, 211–12, 215–17; and language
   12–13, 213–15; morality of 210–11,
   217–19; personification of 215; and
   social class 31
Burkina Faso 24
Bush Administration 115

'Campaign for Real Beauty' 55
Canada 13, 98–100, 102, 104, 105, 203, 242
capitalism 39, 150, 227, 249; consumer 5, 41; transnational 5
'carbon footprint minimisers' 10, 17
Carpenter, Karen 66
Cartesian dualism 12, 31, 125–6, 130, 199
celebrities 89, 136
Cheyne, George 26, 31
China 51, 116
Cinderella (Disney) 55
cognitive(-behavioural) therapy 159, 198, 248–9
communism 63, 66, 69, 78
Confucianism 81
consumerism 13, 51, 65, 67–70, 137–40, 142–3, 150, 167
Cornaro, Luigi 26
cosmetic surgery 18, 53, 57, 167
Costin, Carolyn 56
counselling 222, 233–5, 245
cultural imagery 51, 124, 126
cultural studies 4, 114, 118, 245; feminist 114, 118–19, 121, 146
culture(s) 14, 16, 31–2, 37, 48, 53–4, 57, 75–9, 97, 135–6, 149, 153, 202–4, 212, 245–6; African 52–3, 105; Asian 51; beauty 64; Canadian 105; consumer 51, 65, 67–70, 137–40, 142–3; dominant 48, 52; Fijian 51; and food 22, 120; Gambian 115, 120, 121; globalised 79; immigrant 64–5; and the individual 245–6; 'low' 66; mainstream 75, 82, 89; mass 63, 66–9, 72, 138; meaning of 54–6, 76, 135; minority 76–7; 'national' 76; and nature 18–19; non-western 77–8; nursing 161; oppressive 4; 'partial', 76; patriarchal 1–2, 13, 94, 223; popular 47, 64; school 228; supermarket 120; traditional 52; western 4, 38, 74–8, 82, 89, 97, 124–5, 130, 137–8, 146, 215, 221, 223–4, 227, 230; youth 113, 122
culture-clash 75–8, 82

Daly, Mary 13, 14, 15
Darego, Agbani 52, 53
'dead angels' 17
depression 48, 54, 56, 192, 233
Descartes, René 31
diabetes 114, 188–9

dialogics 4, 68, 69
dietary deficiency 23
dieting 26, 51–2, 55–6, 79, 88, 90, 105, 106, 135, 151
different ability 3
discourse analysis 173, 188
'discursive environment' 40–1

Eating Difficulties Education Network (EDEN) 221–30
eating disorder not otherwise specified (EDNOS) 1, 226
'eating disorders' (or 'dis/orders') 1–3, 5, 29, 46, 63, 71–2, 74–7, 82–3, 87, 122, 124–7, 130, 135, 138, 147, 159–62, 172, 178–9, 185, 198, 221, 226, 246–9; in Asia 51; and black women 47–50; conceptualisation of 3–4, 74, 124–5, 131, 164, 182, 222–3, 226; as cultural problem 53, 136; 'culture-bound' 74, 135; discourses on 63, 181; and ethnicity 31, 46, 79, 82–3; in Fiji 51; formulations of 198–9; meanings of 130–1; prevalence of 31, 75, 76; prevention of 227; as psychopathology 74, 76, 152, 172, 222; and social class 31–2, 46; in non-western societies 75
eating disorders nursing 159–68, 246
eating distress 129–33
Egypt 77
electro-convulsive therapy (ECT) 233
embodiment 5, 9, 12, 42, 119, 124, 160–1, 230, 246; of 'anorexia' 81; fat 3; gender and 114; hyper- 81; language of 116; pathologised 3–4; problems with 99; theories of 13, 124–6
'emo gaunt' 10, 17
'emo' websites 10
Enlightenment 13–14, 18
EPODE 120
ethnicity 5, 19, 40, 75, 78–9, 99, 114, 120
ethnography 81, 121, 122, 159–61, 168, 245
Eve 177; archetype of 179
exercise 26, 31, 42, 153, 187, 191n4; addiction to 48, 53, 55, 57, 225
existentialism 10

'false consciousness' 18, 63, 67, 71
fantasy 29–30
fascism 63, 66, 69
fashion designers 135

fashion industry 18, 54, 55, 135
fasting 25–8, 30
fat acceptance 117–18, 121
fat activists 36, 152
'fat phobia' 81, 147, 225, 229
Fat Teens Can't Hunt 119
fatness 3, 30, 36, 56–7, 97–107, 127, 146–52, 197, 211, 224; depictions of 97; hatred of 42, 187; pathologised 3, 5, 146, 149, 151n2, 153; and technology use 36–7
feminism 22, 30–2, 72, 77, 94, 118, 127, 132, 146–50, 152–3, 200; critical 18, 74, 124, 128, 130, 138–9, 146–7, 200, 223; Egyptian 77; liberal 70, 167; 'new' 13; postmodern 13, 17, 124, 168; traditional 13
feminist approaches 1–2, 12, 18, 74, 93, 97, 99, 102, 122, 196, 245, 247–50; critical 1–5, 12, 18, 74–5, 79, 125, 146, 162, 168, 198–9, 221, 227, 230
feminist theory 5, 9–10, 12, 14, 15, 17, 30–2, 37, 40, 64, 67, 75, 89, 97, 99, 124, 126, 129; critical 10, 15, 19, 75, 82, 125, 130, 132, 136–8, 141, 199, 221–3, 225
feminist therapies 198, 200–3, 249–50
femininity 66, 81, 88, 104, 106, 127n1, n2, 142, 162; constructions of 91–2; discourses of 104, 199, 228, 245; 'failing at' 103–4; 'good' 91; heteronormative 172, 180, 182; 'hyper-' 173, 175, 177, 180; 'ideal' 80, 91; 'misguided' 140; 'slender' 127, 131, 225; 'traditional' 77, 81
femmes fatales 177–82; in literature 177n2
Fiji 51
fitness 37, 49, 98, 101–3, 107, 129
Flockhart, Calista 54
Fonda, Jane 49
food abundance 22, 25–7
food scarcity 22–4
Foucauldian theory, 4, 25, 114, 129, 138 9, 190
Foucault, Michel, 11, 12–13, 15, 57, 93, 105, 118, 124, 129–30, 132, 138–9, 143, 153n4, 188, 196–9, 212, 249
France 13, 25, 28, 32, 77, 120–2, 179
Frankfurt School 66
Freud, Sigmund 14, 28, 29, 175
Fromm, Erich 66
Fromm-Reichmann, Frieda 65, 66
fundamentalism 78

Gambia 115, 120, 121
Garber, Victor 55
gastric band 191
Gaultier, Jean Paul 135
gender: ideologies 1, 131, 142; politics 5, 77–8, 81, 143; roles 67–71, 77
Genesis 177
'girl problem' 37
global urbanisation 116, 121
globalisation 5, 9–10, 15, 75, 79, 116, 121
gluttony 25, 26, 151
Goldberg, Whoopi 55
'good anorectic, the' 90–1
governmentality 12, 150–1
Gull, William 27–9
'gym junkies' 10

Hamm, Mia 48
Health at Every Size 153, 225
healthism 3, 5, 17, 167, 197
'healthism saints' 10
'heroin chic' 10, 17
heteronormativity 3, 135n1, 172, 176, 179, 180, 182, 249
heterosexism 197, 199
Hong Kong 81, 113, 116, 120, 122
hysteria 27, 81, 180, 181

identity politics 114, 118, 197
immigration 65, 69
India 24, 78
industrialisation 5
infant malnutrition 25
internet 10–11, 87–94, 152
Ireland 23
Islam 80
Islamic societies 77–8, 81

Japan 46, 51, 80–1
Jones, Marion 48, 55

Kelley, Christina 56
Kitchen Garden 121
Klein, Melanie 29
Knowles, Beyoncé 48, 49, 55

Lacan, Jacques 13
Lasègue, Charles 28–9
Lebanon 77
Li'l Kim 49
Little X 48
Lopez, Jennifer 48

'Madonna' archetype 179
marketing 39
masculinities 3
media 4, 10–11, 18, 51–4, 66, 69, 74, 79,
    89–90, 113–4, 118, 126–7, 135–6,
    140, 143, 149
medicalisation 12, 98, 167, 214, 224,
    247
Merleau-Ponty, Maurice 14
models 53; catwalk/runway 10–11, 118,
    185; fashion 50, 135; full-size 55–6;
    'heroin chic' 10; magazine 89, 92, 94;
    pubescent 10; skinny 46, 48, 66, 89,
    118, 185
Monroe, Marilyn 53
'moral witnessing' 247
morality 40–1, 91, 105, 150, 210–12,
    215–17; counter- 211–12, 216–17
Morocco 77
Moss, Kate 53, 54, 135
'multiple gazes' 13
music 66

narrative analysis 99
narrative therapy 68, 198, 199, 201, 209,
    212–13, 227, 229, 236, 245, 250
neoconservatism 66, 69
Nepal 24
New Zealand 118, 159–68, 212, 221–30,
    237
Nigeria 52–3
'normalising gaze' 11, 15–17
normativity 67, 71, 92, 120, 137, 138n2,
    144, 180, 227, 246, 249
novel, the 70

obesity 1, 3, 35–6, 42, 63–5, 97–8,
    114–16, 119, 121, 148, 151n2, 185,
    224; causation of 186–7, 190, 192;
    childhood 36–7, 40, 63–4, 113n1, 120,
    146, 149; 'diagnosis' of, 186; as
    disease 39, 98, 107, 188; and fast-
    food/junk-food advertising/outlets 37,
    41, 115, 186; and gender 37; and
    genetics 190–1; and income 114; and
    malnutrition 115–16; and physical
    education 37; research on 36–41, 98,
    186; and surgery 186–93; and
    technology use 36–7; theories of 64;
    'war on' 42, 185–8, 190; youth 113n1,
    115
'obesity epidemic' 5, 36, 41–2, 98–9,
    107, 115, 151, 185, 189, 191, 222, 224,
    229

'obesity myth' 98
obesity science 36–9, 98
object relations 198
objectification of bodies 11, 12, 132,
    203
Orbach, Susie 1, 13, 30–1, 117
Overeaters Anonymous 148
overeating 28, 98, 117, 148–9, 163, 229;
    compulsive 148

Pakistan 24
pathologisation: of bodies 4, 190, 192,
    224n3, 226; of disordered eating 88,
    136; of eating 3–4; of fatness 3, 5, 151,
    224n3, 226; of girls and women 74,
    192
patriarchy 1–2, 13, 81, 93, 94, 135n1,
    136, 142, 147, 199, 223
peer mentoring 228
'perceived parental control' 77
personality disorders 198, 200, 203
Peters, Bernadette 55
phallocentricism 14
phenomenology 4, 13, 17, 18–19
Plato 31
political protest 31
post/colonialism 5
post-Freudians 29
postmodern feminisms 13, 17, 124, 168
postmodern theory 2, 9, 10, 13, 15, 17,
    40, 124–5, 137, 139–41, 144, 160, 168,
    222, 229
post-structuralist perspectives 2, 9, 10,
    13, 15, 17, 40, 89, 97, 99, 160, 162,
    167, 173, 249–50
power-relations 196–204, 245; gender 1,
    31, 101, 137, 141, 172, 173, 200, 227,
    230, 246–7
'pro-Ana' websites 10, 17, 87–8, 90–4,
    94, 152
'pro-eating disorder' websites 87–94,
    152n3, 201
'pro-Mia' websites 10, 90–4
Protestant work ethic 150
psychiatrist–patient relationship 172–82
psychiatry 160, 162, 166, 172–82, 233–4,
    246
psychoanalysis 4, 14, 18, 28, 81, 175;
    relational 198
psychology 3, 162, 248
'psychosomatic families' 11

race 46–9, 78, 82–3, 99, 102, 103, 104,
    119, 149n1

racism 63, 70, 100n1, 104, 119, 192
reflexivity 5

Sasaki, Jun 46
Schalk, Sami 46
science 35
self-sacrifice 42, 91, 147, 215
self-starvation 9, 12–13, 14, 17–19,
    79–81, 94, 140, 225, 227, 237;
    explanations for 11–12, 18, 114; as
    lifestyle choice 91
self-surveillance 12, 93, 167, 199
sexism 63, 66, 68, 70–2, 98, 117
sexual abuse 28, 53, 177, 198
sexual orientation 3
Simone, Raven 55
Simpson, Wallis 16, 113
size acceptance 153, 226
'Size Zero' 185
slenderness *see* thinness
slimness *see* thinness
social antagonism 196–8, 200, 202–4,
    207
social class 5, 19, 22–3, 26–7, 40, 48–50,
    74, 114, 119, 120, 149n1
social constructionism 4, 245–50
socialisation 16, 203
socialism 77–8
sociology 9, 18
Sontag, Susan 16, 17
South Korea 51
spirituality 191n2
Starving for Perfection 87
sub-cultures 11
suffragettes 30, 77
supported eating 159, 163, 165
surveillance medicine 167
Survivor 119

Swan, The 118
Syria 77
systemic therapy 198

'taste education' 121
technologies of the self 129–30, 132,
    163–4, 167
terroir 121
therapeutic intervention 3
thinness 3, 5, 69, 74, 79–80, 140, 146,
    197, 225, 245; aesthetics of 82; cults of
    10–11; as ideal 89–90, 125, 135–7,
    147, 151, 223; images of 10, 89, 124,
    126–7, 131–2, 136, 248; pursuit of 11,
    116, 126, 185, 211
transference 175
transnational consumer capitalism 5
Tunisia 77
Turkey 77

'unfitness' 100, 107

veiling 77–8, 80–1
Versace, Gianni 135
virgin/whore discourse 179–80
vitamins 23–4, 87
Volosinov, Valentin 69–71
vomiting, self-induced 9, 26, 31, 51, 128,
    131, 234

Walden, Sarah 48
weight loss surgery (WLS) 186–93
weightism 98
Weil, Simone 32
Weimar Republic 66
Wesley, John 26
Williams, Serena 48
Williamson, Tenisha 46